Edited by David Fogel & Joe Hudson

JUSTICE AS FAIRNESS

Perspectives on the Justice Model

CJ Criminal Justice Studies
Anderson Publishing Co.

JUSTICE AS FAIRNESS: Perspectives On The Justice Model

Library of Congress Catalog Card Number: 79-55197
ISBN: 0-87084-287-0
The project editor for this book was Candice Piaget.
Cover design by William A. Burden

Contents

Contributors

Anderson, Stanley	Professor, Department of Political Science, University of California, Santa Barbara
Baunach, Phyllis Jo	Visiting Faculty Research Associate, University of Maryland; on leave from the National Institute of Justice, Washington, D.C.
Blalock, Ira	Chairman of the Oregon Parole Board
Bronstein, Alvin J.	Executive Director, National Prison Project of the American Civil Liberties Union, Washington, D.C.
Chein, David B.	Minnesota Crime Control Planning Board, St. Paul, Minnesota
Conrad, John P.	American Justice Institute, Sacramento, California
Fogel, David	Professor and Director of Graduate Studies, Department of Criminal Justice, University of Illinois at Chicago Circle
Galaway, Burt	School of Social Development, University of Minnesota at Duluth, Duluth, Minnesota
Hudson, Joe	Office of the Auditor General of Canada, Ottawa, Canada
Maghan, Jess	Director, Correctional Law Project, American Correctional Association, College Park, Maryland
McAnany, Patrick D.	Associate Professor, Department of Criminal Justice, University of Illinois at Chicago Circle
Prettyman, E. Barrett, Jr.	Private attorney with the firm of Hogan and Hartson in Washington, D.C.
Schaller, Jack	President, The American Institute of Criminal Justice, Philadelphia, Pennsylvania
Shireman, Charles	School of Social Service Administration, University of Chicago

Preface

There is only one thing worse than operating an enterprise as complex as a State Department of Corrections without a mission and that is inventing a rhetoric for legislative and public consumption while implementing quite different practices. There is also a difference between a corrections agency that develops a mission with the full participation of staff and one that proclaims one mission and in practice makes no effort to reach it. In military terms the former may lose some battles but understands the reason for the war while the latter might be seen as mercenaries leaping from tactic to tactic engaged in a mindless series of battles.

The deliberate masking of brutal practice with the rhetoric of rehabilitation is cruel and inhumane. While we have made progress in this decade with realistic mission-setting, brutal practices continue. Having participated in some three dozen federal and state civil rights cases in the last few years, I find it embarrassing that as we approach the end of the century we still find top correctional executives in court standing behind both their otherwise impeccable credentials and lofty departmental mission statements defending incredibly questionable practices within their prisons.

For example, in the last two years I found in the northeast that after an elaborate classification process approximately one half of the prison population was intensively tested, screened, and subsequently classified into an "idle crew." A western state, which boasts an automated classification process, has some fifty percent of its prison population similarly unemployed. There the idle are called "transitional workers." At this same prison officials use a tactic called "confidential information" to punish inmates without benefit of sharing the source or subjecting the "confidential information" to the possibility of denial, rebuttal, or other forms of public verification. One of the largest states in the midwest, its modern rhetoric about law and order notwithstanding, does not provide women with programs anywhere approximating those available for male inmates, claiming that to do so would not be "cost beneficial." The judge in the case found that the equal protection clause of the Constitution is silent on "cost/benefits."

In another midwestern state a corrections department which uses the word 'Rehabilitation' in its official title appeared in Federal Court in June, 1979 to defend racial segregation in its reception process and the use of four-way restraints without medical supervision.[1] Racial segregation was not denied; it was justified as a "tension-reducing" mechanism.

Furthermore, expert testimony in support of such a practice was given by a former director of one of the largest corrections systems in the United States who incorrectly claimed to represent the National Institute of Corrections. The federal district judge enjoined the prison officials from continuing both practices. Incredibly, the state has decided to appeal.

In still another historically "progressive" state in the east, in face of a state law requiring two hours' out-of-cell exercise daily, the corrections agency had to be brought to court because it decided that inmates placed on "Restrictive Housing" status could handle less than thirty minutes of exercise per day. In that state, corrections officials are blazing a new path to national embarrassment by not allowing the plaintiff's expert witness into the prison because the warden "doesn't like him."[2]

I would like to report that since the publication of *We Are the Living Proof . . .* (Fogel, 1975), there has been a new breed of correctional leadership emerging which is unafraid of criticism, interested in correctional progress beyond their own bailiwicks, and marching to the drum beat of the U.S. Constitution. I would *like* to but I can't. I can point to some, but their number is not impressive — not impressive or significant enough to threaten the many mindless correctional practices that continue to persist in our prisons.

Emerging Trends

The future of the field is not totally dismal, however. One force that bears watching is made up of mid-level corrections executives, the largest number of whom were hired in the 1970's and have been better educated than their colleagues. They have yet to be heard from. They are a new force in the sense of having been socialized into the field since the explosive growth of training and education programs in criminal justice in the last ten years, that is, since the inception of the Law Enforcement Assistance Administration (LEAA) and the National Institute of Corrections (N.I.C.). We'll have to wait and see what happens to them as they begin to take the reins of leadership in the next decade.

There is also a growing realism in the purpose-of-prison debate in both public and professional circles. Simply put, we are beginning to talk less about the prison as a crime reduction agency. The prison has enough of a burden to operate lawfully. This growing realism, I think, is a healthy trend. It will help us to realize that the way to make inroads into reducing crime will not be, in Illinois for example, to rebuild Stateville prison but to rebuild the impoverished West Side of Chicago. Right now the rhetoric of prisoner rehabilitation diverts us from other more productive socio-economic programs which must be undertaken if crime reduction is the goal.

I do see a growing reduction in rhetoric, a narrowing of claims about what prison can do. If we can't cure we can at least care far more humanely and constitutionally. In the immediate future I think we will stop making war on crime and in the process stop criminalizing greater proportions of our population. We will seek speedier, more certain measures to improve the quality of our system of justice. Finally, we will soon stop chasing recidivists as if they were microbiotic mutants, blaming ourselves as professionals for their increasing number or praising ourselves when their numbers temporarily diminish.

Still another development which is promising emerges from rather unlikely historical sources. The state of Mississippi, following *Gates* v. *Collier*, decided that rather than embroil itself in a decade of appeals they would use the timetable set up by the court to modernize.[3] At this writing Mississippi's entire old prison system has been scrapped. Mississippi will soon be the state with the greatest percentage of prisoners under modern housing. Perhaps even more interesting is the pragmatic approach taken by the state of Oklahoma which has (also partly as a result of a federal court order) decided to adopt as its mission the full implementation of the standards of the American Public Health Association and the American Correctional Association. This is both highly inspirational and aspirational, and gives us a directed focus for the correctional mission. The entire field could easily emulate Oklahoma and have few concerns about keeping busy until the end of the century.

Justice As Fairness

This collection of commissioned essays is intended as a companion work to my earlier book, *We Are the Living Proof — The Justice Model for Corrections* (Second Edition, 1978). In that volume I tried to develop a largely rhetoric free and pragmatic mission for corrections which would lend itself to more precision. While the correctional mission is inextricably linked to the purpose of the criminal law and a conception of the nature of human behavior, we need not await scientific validation before insisting that correctional administrators explicate their missions with greater precision than heretofore available.

The justice-as-fairness perspective seeks to bring a commonsense working definition to the prison mission. Employing a perspective suggested by Stephen Schafer in his book, *The Political Criminal — The Problem of Morality and Crime* (1974), I have used the following group of postulates to guide me in the search for the proper role of treatment in a prison setting and thus a foundation for a mission for corrections.[4]

The criminal law is the "command of the sovereign."

The threat of punishment is necessary to implement the law.

The powerful manipulate the chief motivators of human behavior — fear and hope — through rewards and punishments to retain power.

Socialization (the manipulation of fear and hope through rewards and punishments) of individuals, however imperfect, occurs in response to the commands and expectations of the ruling social-political power.

The criminal law protects the dominant prescribed morality (a system of rules said to be in the common and best interest of all), reflecting the enforcement aspect of the failure of socialization.

In an absence of any absolute system of justice or "natural law," no accurate etiologic theory of crime is possible, nor is the definition of crime itself historically stable.

Although free will may not exist perfectly, the criminal law is largely based upon its presumed vitality and forms the only foundation for penal sanctions.

A prison sentence represents a punishment sanctioned by a legislative body and meted out through the official legal system against a person adjudged responsible for his behavior. Although a purpose of such punishment may be deterrence or rehabilitation, more specifically such punishment is the deprivation of liberty for a fixed period of time.

When corrections becomes mired in the dismal swamp of preaching, exhorting, and treating it becomes dysfunctional as an agency of justice. Correctional agencies should engage prisoners as the law otherwise dictates; as responsible, volitional, and aspiring human beings, and not conceive of them as patients.

This set of propositions is what I have called the *justice perspective* to distinguish these principles from the *rehabilitative perspective*. The implication of my argument is not that rehabilitation should be abandoned in prisons, but rather that it should be made voluntary. With characteristic parsimony and clarity, Norval Morris long ago suggested a path out of our moral thicket: "Power over a criminal's life should not be taken in excess of that which would be taken were his reform not considered as one of our purposes."[5] In a democracy we should not restrict freedom except on clearly established and promulgated bases. The lengthening or shortening of sentences, for example, based on unreliable professional claims, does not meet this test.

Finally, if we cannot coercively treat with reliability, we can at least be fair, reasonable, humane, and constitutional in practice. As Mattick stated: "It is, perhaps, gratuitous to assert that those who have been convicted of breaking the law are most in need of having respect for the law demonstrated to them."[6] Although no such claim is made here, there is a certain plausibility in the notion that a lawfully guided term of imprisonment might have the carryover effect of persuading the frequently unlawful into more frequent lawful ways of dealing with problems. Maybe this is the most we can hope to accomplish in our prison influence attempts: to get non-law abiders to be more law-abiding, by lawful treatment.

The period from the 1960's until the end of this century will be known historically as a significant and conscious departure from the barbaric conditions and practices of confinement in the past. But of great importance for the future of humane care is the architecture, and here we are obviously in a mess. We still have archaic Stateville and a progressive Vienna coexisting in Illinois. The facilities we build today will largely determine the future quality of prison life and work. Renaming guards "correctional officers" or "counselors" won't be enough. Renaming cons "clients," "inmates," or "residents" will also not suffice. We will have to stop embedding zoo-life steel cages into concrete several tiers high.

America has crowded what Zimring calls a "stand-in" population into its prisons. This symbolic convict group imperfectly reflects the general offender population. A great myth has arisen wherein correctional officials have attempted to convince the public and legislatures that coercive rehabilitation is an adequate response to both crime and constitutionally infirm prisons. The pursuit of rehabilitation as a superordinate goal by the correctional establishment (with notable exceptions) has lulled legislators, who have primary responsibility for modernizing the prison system, into believing that small increments in clinical staff allocations could both "cure" criminals and prevent prisoner uprisings. Thus, a misplaced emphasis on rehabilitation has served to psychologize a political question and produce self-limiting parameters to the responses.

Functional management in even modified fortress prisons can help. And an intensively and sensitively trained custody staff that can relate to the small groups of prisoners assigned to them based upon a matching of prisoner needs and staff talents will also help bring peace and rationality in programming. This means that correctional planning will have to pay far more attention to the simple but most significant question of the dignity of the work and living prison environment. Rather than worry about curing criminality I believe our immediate task is to reduce our rhetoric to develop a mission which calls upon us to first cause no greater harm during the prison stay than necessary.

In a sense our problem has been the availability of too much fancy rhetoric, and thus the unavailability of precision in pinning us all down to a clear-cut, explicated, and manageable mission. I don't mean by this that a mission statement should be viewed as a director's memo. Pushing buttons doesn't work with any more precision, absent a line level commitment to a common goal, than having a series of unexplicated and even conflicting missions. We simply need to talk straight to staff, convicts, and the public about what we can reasonably hope to be accomplished during a prison term, particularly in an era of diminishing resources. But above all we should not over-promise on the rehabilitation side nor underproduce in the area of constitutional practice.

Any mission statement for corrections that is silent or soft on the place of coercion is simply misleading at best and dishonest at worst. The difference between maximum custody and minimum security is the degree of coercion absent in the latter but which is dependent for its very existence upon the presence of the former. In other words, you can't have minimum custody without the threat of maximum custody. Even in sessions between probationers and/or parolees and their officers the invisible coercive shadow of maximum custody is cast over the participants. Deep down both know it.

From my limited view some criteria for mission building should be:

To pursue justice-as-fairness rather than rehabilitation.

To provide expanded opportunities for prisoner self-improvement rather than maintaining the coercive practice of herding prisoners into available program slots, dangling the reward of possible early release in exchange for attendance.

To develop "common-sense advocacy" services (e.g., classification, educational and vocational counseling, legal services, conjugal visiting, health and sanitation services).

To provide state level corrections to care for only the residual, dangerous offender. The others might be contracted with the growing private sector field.

To abandon the fortress prison structure.

To make an enormous commitment to line staff recruitment, training, safety, involvement, upgrading and a salary to match their heroic effort.

No prisoner should reasonably expect more from his or her stay, but in a nation with democratic aspirations no correctional system should be permitted to deliver less.

Prisons will better serve a democratic society by operating under lawful constitutional standards of humaneness and prisoner involvement than by seeking their guidance from the latest psychological, medical and/or religious fad. After all, much of the progress of our planet can be laid to the unregenerated convict whom we couldn't rehabilitate (Christ, Gandhi, Thoreau, Mrs. Pankhurst, Voltaire, Kenyatta, Joan of Arc and Malcolm X are among examples).

Since the justice model debate began, a number of scholars and administrators have understood, misunderstood, applied, modified, criticized and disagreed with it or some of its elements. This volume is not intended to defend, rather, to elaborate. Since my earlier book received much attention for its determinate sentencing recommendations, this book purposely spends more time on other in-prison applications of the justice model.

Within the covers of this volume the reader will find the authors in some cases critical of earlier justice perspective ideas or in some cases taking the ideas beyond the original parameters to practice applications in a variety of correctional settings: treatment, prison industries, guard training, parole decision-making, case law, convict self-governance, the ombudsman, juvenile justice and alternatives to imprisonment.

The unabashed mission of this book is to put forth a justice perspective, common sense advocacy position for the field of corrections. We focus on three audiences: correctional practitioners who are largely responsible for creating the prison's moral environment, legislators who seek a common sense understanding in reaching their decisions which so vitally affect resource allocation for corrections and finally to the next generation of criminal justice practitioners who are now in American institutions of higher learning trying to unravel the field's tortuous history in preparation for taking leadership and forging new, future directions. It is to these groups we direct this volume in the hope of further advancing the debate about the mission and future of corrections.

David Fogel
University of Illinois
at Chicago Circle

Notes

[1]A prisoner in four-way restraint is laid on his back with leg irons binding his ankles to the bed frame; his arms are extended beyond his head so that his wrists extend through the cell bars and are manacled. The "usual" length of time of such restraint is three to four days. This author was expert witness in the case and was told by the duty officer (in the presence of representatives of the state Attorney General, the U.S. Department of Justice and the F.B.I.) that the longest period a prisoner was kept in such restraint was fifteen days! *Stewart v. Rhodes*, 473 F. Supp. 1185 (S.D. Ohio, 1979).

[2]*Rice v. Howard*, Court of Common Pleas, Allegheny County, Pennsylvania (Docket No. 79-15932).

[3]*Gates v. Collier*, 349 F. Supp. 881 (N.D. Miss. 1972).

[4]See Fogel's *We Are the Living Proof – The Justice Model for Corrections*, (Anderson Publishing Co., 1978). Chapter IV for an elaboration of this discussion.

[5]Norval Morris and Colin Howard, "Studies in Criminal Law," (Oxford, 1964), pg. 175.

[6]Hans W. Mattick, "The Prosaic Sources of Prison Violence," (Chicago, 1972), pg. 1

PART 1

Justice as Fairness: An Overview

Introduction

The three papers contained in this section provide a conceptual framework for the justice-as-fairness approach dealt with in this book. What is the appropriate goal of the justice system and what are the practice implications of holding to such a goal, especially in terms of the exercise of official discretion? These are two of the central questions addressed in the three papers in this section as well as in later sections of the book.

Running through many of the arguments raised here is the distinction between system goals of rehabilitation and retribution. Based on notions of defects of the criminal offender, the rehabilitation approach suggests that the appropriate role of corrections agencies is to identify and correct the presumed causative agent. So as to most effectively carry out the rehabilitative mandate assumed by them, corrections officials require great latitude to make decisions about the offender. Such decisions are frequently held to be best made if not open to the examination of non-expert others.

The retributive position, in contrast, is essentially non-utilitarian, holding that punitive sanctions should be imposed on the offender simply for the sake of justice. Punishment is deserved; the form and severity of the punishment must, however, be proportionate to the criminal act. The right of the state to impose treatments of one sort or another on the offender holds no place in this approach.

The justice-as-fairness approach is clearly based on principles of retribution. This theme is dealt with in Chapter 1 by John Conrad. The historical evolution of the so-called medical model of offender rehabilitation is traced and comparisons are made to the justice model.

John Conrad has had a distinguished career as an administrator and researcher in state corrections agencies, federal criminal justice planning agencies, universities, and most recently in a private corporation. Some of his experiences as a young social worker in San Quentin are recounted here to illustrate differences between the idea of rehabilitation and its practice in the prison setting. The contrast between the grand promise of rehabilitation and the hard facts of reality is continued in E. Barrett Prettyman's paper on the Patuxent Institution in Part 2.

Conrad considers the operating assumptions and major ingredients of the rehabilitative and retribution approaches and draws implications for justice-as-fairness. He concludes with a set of specific proposals for restructuring the prison into a "school for citizenship."

Patrick McAnany, a professor of criminology, is the author of the second paper in this section. The issue of system goals provides a backdrop to McAnany's discussion of discretionary decision making by criminal justice officials. Several recent critiques of discretion are reviewed and some of the more prominent reform measures assessed before the author turns to a consideration of problems likely to be encountered in structuring the discretion of officials. McAnany's key point is that focusing the debate on the means to be used for structuring discretion rather than on goals or ends is likely to result in compromising the degree of fairness built into the system. No doubt, McAnany is right; the trouble is that agreement on system goals is likely to take a long time. Meanwhile, piecemeal reforms at structuring discretion are probably going to move the system closer to justice-as-fairness. Illustrations of this point are given in the papers by Ira Blalock in Part 2 and by David Chein and Joe Hudson in Part 3.

Justice-as-fairness demands consideration of the plight of the crime victim as well as the criminal offender. Probably the only criminal sanction that directly involves both parties is restitution. The idea that criminals should make up, to some degree at least, for the harm arising from the offense has been supported by both proponents of rehabilitation and retribution, although the rationale for their support differs markedly. The perspective taken in the final paper in this section is based on a retributionist approach; restitution is seen as a punitive sanction, not as a rehabilitative treatment. Offenders are held to be responsible for their acts and justice requires that they repair in some way the harm done.

Joe Hudson and Burt Galaway have had experience in developing and operating restitution programs and are currently involved in conducting research on restitution projects around the country. They first review the historical evolution of restitution and consider more recent policy, legal, and program developments before turning to an examination of the extent to which restitutive sanctions are conceptually and practically consistent with justice-as-fairness. Like John Conrad and E. Barrett Prettyman, these authors point to the difference between promise and reality. Conceptually, the idea of restitution seems compatible with the notion of justice-as-fairness. In practice, however, restitution is all too frequently used as a sanctioning supplement rather than as an alternative to imprisonment, and victims are largely denied opportunities that the concept affords for involvement in the operations of the justice system.

1. Where There's Hope There's Life

John P. Conrad

I

My career as a penologist began at San Quentin in the late forties under the auspices of an enthusiastic psychiatrist who hired me to be a "neuro-psychiatric social worker." I had always thought that it was quite enough to be a psychiatric social worker, but my mentor explained that in the prison environment it was important to have an impressive title, the more polysyllabic the better. During my orientation he went on to say that prisons were changing and I was getting in on the ground floor of an upward sweep of professionalism in corrections. Enlightened people were beginning to understand that the poor devils serving time were sick and handicapped men who needed neuro-psychiatric treatment. The day was not far off when wardens would be psychiatrists. Obviously a neuro-psychiatric social worker would have an important role to play in this new kind of prison, designed for treatment rather than punishment.

Recently released from the army and in possession of authentic if modest credentials as a psychiatric social worker, I decided to see what I could do in this new world. I was not alone. There were many adventurous people of my generation who saw the prison as a frontier in human relations, and some of them were working at San Quentin. We thought the prison was a social institution that was so backward, so brutal, and so corrupt that it had to be improved to be tolerable in a civilized society. Surely, we thought, it would respond to the introduction of talented young social scientists like ourselves. This view did not endear us to San Quentin veterans, but change had powerful support in Sacramento, and they had to put up with us. The scepticism of the convicts was also evident, but we were confident that they would come around as time went by and our helpfulness moderated the repression that permeated the prison community.

I have never wavered in my belief that prisons must be improved, but I have had to change my opinion about the means to achieve that end. In those days, we were all under the sway of what has since been called the "medical model," a term that has been overworked in the criticism of social institutions. I am sure that it was wrongly applied to what my psychiatric colleagues and I were doing.

There was little resemblance between our activities and what goes on in the medical care of ordinary people. If our practice conformed to a model, its most prominent feature was coerced change. The logic was inexorable. Criminals came to prison because of some character defect that caused them to commit crimes. Unless that defect were remedied by individualized psychiatric treatment, coordinated with educational and training programs, there was every reason to believe that these criminals would go out to commit more crimes. The crimes were the symptoms of deep-seated psychiatric disorders for which remedies had to be found. In principle, a man had to change if he was to be released from prison.

This model is eroding. Much of the credit for its dissolution must go to David Fogel, who saw the chicanery and unfairness of what passed for correctional treatment and proposed an honest alternative, the "justice model." In this essay, I shall account for the efflorescence of the so-called medical model, and describe it as it was in its heyday, showing that what happened in reality did not conform to the suppositions of the model. I shall argue that the rehabilitative goals that we thought to be paramount in the medical model are much more likely to be achieved in the justice model. At the same time, I think we can go beyond the justice model to an emphasis on citizenship, and I shall conclude my essay with some reflections on how a just prison society might be an environment in which convicts can become citizens.

II

In the history of society's treatment of criminals there has always been agreement that they must be punished but much difference of opinion as to what is to be gained thereby. The oldest view is that the wrongdoer must be punished, but that justice requires that the right to punish must be taken from the victim or his kin and assumed by the state. This is the retributivist position. It is a position that moralists are uneasy in accepting, and it is a position that is flatly rejected by many. Those who accept it argue that it is simple logic: if a man is guilty, he is to be punished, but only a guilty man can be punished because punishment can only be the consequence of guilt. When suffering is inflicted on an innocent man, it cannot be punishment. For Immanuel Kant, justice required punishment when guilt was determined:

> The law concerning punishment is a categorical imperative, and woe to him who rummages around in the winding paths of a theory of happiness looking for some advantage to be gained by releasing the criminal from punishment or by reducing the amount of it . . . If legal justice perishes, then it is no longer worthwhile for men to remain alive on this earth.[1]

It is one thing to lay down a bloodless principle; it is another thing to contemplate the sanguinary quality of punishment as it has been administered throughout the history of Western civilization. The numerous crimes for which capital punishment was administered and the gruesome tortures that often preceded the execution itself long troubled the stoutest apologists for severity. The hideous practice of drawing and quartering the condemned man in a public place persisted for centuries in Western Europe and only came to an end in the eighteenth century as a consequence of the Enlightenment and the French Revolution. Retributivists continued to insist on the need for the death penalty, but also argued that it was necessary to deter the criminally minded from the commission of offenses against their neighbors.

The idea of punishment for the purpose of preventing crime goes back to Plato, who held that:

> In punishing wrongdoers, no one concentrates on the fact that a man has done wrong in the past, or punishes him on that account, unless taking blind vengeance like a beast. No, punishment is not inflicted by a rational man for the sake of the crime that has been committed — after all, one cannot undo what is past — but for the sake of the future, to prevent the same man or, by the spectacle of his punishment, someone else from doing wrong again . . . .[2]

In a later dialogue, Plato was even more specific, saying through Socrates that "a just penalty disciplines us and makes us more just and cures us of evil."[3] Finally, in his last writing, as an old man deeply concerned about the deteriorating quality of life in Athens, he declaimed against crime with much more severity but still held consistent with his earlier views:

> Whosoever shall be taken in sacrilege shall, if slave or alien, have his misfortune branded on hands and forehead, be scourged with such number of stripes as the court may think proper, and be cast forth naked beyond the borders. For if he suffer that judgement, he may perchance be made a better man by his correction. For truly judgement by sentence of law is never inflicted for harm's sake. Its normal effect is one of two; it makes him that suffers it a better man, or failing that, less of a wretch . . . .[4]

Note that even in the pessimism of old age Plato explicitly disavowed retribution as a legitimate aim of punishment, and insisted that the purpose must be the prevention of crime. His views cannot be said to have had much effect on the administration of criminal justice throughout the millennia that have passed since he pronounced them, despite the immense authority that Plato has wielded over philosophers ever since his time.

The horrors and the squalor of criminal justice as administered in even the most enlightened countries induced philosophers to reconsider the retributivist position which, in the actuality of the court room and the gallows, was the universally prevailing justification of punishment. To the extent that apologists felt it necessary to justify the blood, filth, and callousness that passed for justice, they argued for the necessity of general deterrence. One now forgotten moralist wrote that "prevention is the great end of all legal severity; nay the exerting that severity by making examples of the guilty, has no other intention but to deter others." He concluded that since the value of punishment depended on the fear inspired in potential wrongdoers, then capital punishment must be superior to any other penal measure. "The terror of the example is the only thing proposed, and one man is sacrificed to the preservation of thousands."[5]

An alternate line of reasoning began with Francis Bacon and culminated two centuries later in the essays of Montesquieu and Beccaria, who deplored the ferocity of the written law and the caprice of its execution. This strain of generous thought led to the contributions of that extraordinary social inventor, Jeremy Bentham (1748-1832). It is far beyond my charge to freshen up the memory of this astonishing man or to do his name the justice it deserves. But an understanding of the history of punishment during the last two centuries requires us to begin with a consideration of his achievement.

Bentham thought of himself as a *censor* of the law, committed to its restatement as it ought to be. As a student he had observed the senseless jumble of the London courts, the morass of antiquated legislation and procedures, and the indifference of the bench and bar to the need for reform. He also was aware of the eloquent arguments of the moral philosophers who appealed for change. It was his conviction that eloquence could indicate good intentions but never would change the system. Nothing that the law touched failed to interest him, but one of his most enduring preoccupations was the punishment of criminals. Like all seriously concerned people of his time, he had read the exposure of prison conditions that John Howard had forced on a shocked world.[6] He determined to put a remedy into effect — the famous Panopticon in which prisoners would be educated, put to constructive work, and subjected to other reformative processes in a strange architectural innovation that provided for their being under constant observation by custodians they could not see. He spent much of his private fortune and twenty years of effort in a vain effort to induce the ministers of George III to allow him to build a pilot model.[7] Preoccupied with the expense and the dangers of the Napoleonic Wars, they never allowed Bentham to proceed. It remained for the state of Illinois to build the most famous models of the Panopticon at Stateville, where they still stand today, inefficient and generally condemned as impractical.

Insofar as Bentham is remembered nowadays, it is customary to think of him as a quixotic and unreadable legal philosopher whose voluminous works are too much trouble to explore. Certainly the contemporary student of penology can find more profitable uses for his time than to immerse himself in the complex thought of the founding father of Utilitarianism. But Bentham's contemporaries took him very seriously indeed, and so did a succession of followers who subscribed to the general themes of his thought and refined them further. It is easy to smile at the foolishness of the Panopticon — though it was certainly no more foolish than its architectural rivals, the Pennsylvania and the Auburn prisons, and much more generous in concept and intent. But the idea behind the Panopticon was truly unique in Bentham's time, and it has survived to this day in the rhetorical commitment of penology to the goal of rehabilitation.

He began with an analysis of the purposes of punishment that sounds almost conventionally modern:

> With respect to any particular delinquent, we have seen that punishment has three objectives: incapacitation, reformation, and intimidation. If the crime he has committed is of a kind calculated to inspire great alarm, as manifesting a very mischievous disposition, it becomes necessary to take from him the power of committing it again. But if the crime, being less dangerous, only justifies a transient punishment, and it is possible for the delinquent to return to society, it is proper that the punishment should possess qualities calculated to reform or intimidate him.[8]

Bentham's fertile mind did not stop at the Panopticon, where prisoners would be reformed; he also thought he saw a need for a terrifying prison that would contain the most "mischievous" criminals. It would be painted black, and everything possible would be done to its exterior to impress the public with the terrible fate awaiting the recalcitrant and dangerous offender, although the activities taking place inside would not be comparably punitive.

For the social philosopher Michel Foucault, the Panopticon was a machine for amplifying power, and its legacy was not to penology alone but to an industrial civilization which had come to realize that increased power was necessary to its perpetuation and that information was the essence of power.[9] It is doubtful that Bentham saw this point; he did not have the advantage of Foucault's hindsight. For him, the Panopticon was an experiment out of which the solution to the problem of crime might be found — and certainly the problem of the criminal would be solved. In an almost rhapsodic vein he extolled the benefits of his innovation:

> Morals reformed — health preserved — industry invigorated — instruction diffused — public burthens lightened — economy seated, as it were, on a rock — all by a simple idea in architecture![10]

It is clear that Bentham's chief gift to penology was to be the notion that if punishment is to serve the purpose of prevention, it has to be planned accordingly. Criminals were not to be indiscriminately sent to the gallows, often for crimes which would hardly qualify as felonies by twentieth century standards, nor were they to be consigned to the hulks lying in the estuaries of the Thames, to freeze and starve in horrifyingly overcrowded conditions. The state had a duty to criminals when it took them into custody, and that was nothing less than to reform them so that they could return to society as citizens. The novelty of this idea, when compared with the prevailing approach to punishment, was nothing less than revolutionary. None of his predecessors, not even the redoubtable John Howard, had taken it on themselves to prescribe an alternative to the existing penology.

That was the beginning of the rehabilitative ideal. It is notable that Bentham was indifferent on the topic of the rights of prisoners — or the "rights of man," a catch phrase of the time given currency by the apostles of the French Revolution. For him, the term was "nonsense on stilts," a meaningless interference with the state's duty to provide for the happiness of its subjects. There is no escaping the authoritarian quality of Bentham's Utilitarianism. The Panopticon depended on a means for amplifying power over the individual, as Foucault has pointed out. That power was to be used to constrain prisoners to conform with the standards of the society that held them in custody. Bentham did not question society's right to demand that prisoners conform, regardless of the poverty that might have caused their criminality in the first place. The cure of poverty was an entirely different problem, but Bentham also had some ideas about how that was to be accomplished. Until the fruition of his plans for a new and happier society, the poor would have to be patient and endure their privations without recourse to predation against their more affluent neighbors.

I think it is incontestable that Bentham was the first to design a system of punishment that provided for incapacitation and rehabilitation as proper goals of criminal justice. He also allowed for intimidation, as we have seen, and practical penologists of the centuries that followed have found this goal much easier to pursue. It is likely that the progenitors of the American prison system found his ideas useful, even though they preferred their own architectural innovations to the Panopticon. They, too, thought that punishment had to serve the goals of incapacitation, reform, and intimidation, but none of them persevered in administration once their reforms had been achieved. They were succeeded by embarrassing monsters of callousness like the once-notorious Elam Lynds of Auburn and Sing Sing, who thought that reform and intimidation were the same thing; the great objective of penology was the breaking of the criminal's will.[11]

It was not until after the great climacteric of American history, the Civil War, that serious efforts were made to make the objective of rehabilitation a significant objective of criminal justice. In 1870, five years after Appomattox, the first meeting of the National Prison Association took place. It was the occasion for formulating 37 paragraphs of a Declaration of Principles, beginning with a first Principle that "Reformation, not vindictive suffering, should be the purpose of penal treatment of prisoners."[12] The Principles receive respectful praise from many quarters, but commentators invariably note that American penology still has a long way to go before the more significant of the Principles are realized. The verbal commitment to rehabilitation has been impressive and unqualified, but its execution is far from matching the lofty aspirations of 1870.

III

The route from Jeremy Bentham's Panopticon to the San Quentin Psychiatric Department, where this essay began, is long and tortuous. There are many who have joined the procession: clergymen, educators, psychiatrists, social workers, public administrators, and social scientists of every disciplinary allegiance. The intellectual commitment to the goal of rehabilitation is beyond dispute. With the advent of empiricism to the methods of administration, penologists like myself have been engaged in a Sisyphean effort to prove that rehabilitation succeeds when measured by the numbers of released prisoners returning to crime. Yet the famous work of Robert Martinson summarized the almost uniform defeat of those who have tried to prove the effectiveness of penal treatment.[13] This is the appropriate point to return to the San Quentin Psychiatric Department to find out the reason for the dismal truth that rehabilitation does not seem to "work."

Our Chief Psychiatrist was a positivist who thought that the facts about crime and criminals were either available or readily ascertained. As professionals, our problem was to act on these facts within the context of modern psychiatry. The Chief estimated that about 10% of the San Quentin prisoners were psychotic, about 30% were psychoneurotic, and the rest were psychopathic. He did not concede the possibility that any of them were within the boundaries of psychologial normality. All were in need of psychiatric care, but ten professionals could hardly provide treatment services for 5,000 prisoners. We had to sort out this mass of human frailty and malignity to decide who needed us most. The Chief was certain that as the value of our services was demonstrated by the law-abiding performance of prisoners paroled to the community, the ranks of professional workers would be extended so that more convicts could be cured. As the Chief liked to say, we were on the ground floor.

The psychotics, the murderers, and the sex offenders were our first priority. Other prisoners who asked for the treatment that we knew they needed received what was left of our attention. Surprisingly, a fair number of them decided that it might be to their advantage at parole board hearings to possess a smattering of the psychiatric vernacular. Along with the rest of the non-psychotic caseload, these volunteers got group therapy.

The Chief's version of this treatment modality was indistinguishable from a lecture on mental health and how to achieve it, delivered to as large a group as could be accommodated in one of the San Quentin schoolrooms. Because of scheduling problems, many prisoners heard the same lecture a great many times, but this did not disconcert the Chief, who thought that repetition was the foundation of the learning process. That may have been true, but I decided that I could not match the Chief's eloquent exposition of the ingredients of mental health. I obtained his permission to experiment with non-directive therapy. It turned out to be an experiment in which the outcome could not be determined. I never found a way to discover how many prisoners were helped by my efforts, although many took pains to tell me how important a part my treatment had played in turning their lives around. Such blandishments were to be expected in view of the possibility that I might have a chance to say something favorable to the parole board about those who offered them. I think the prisoners' positive attitudes also tended to bolster our faith in what we were doing; we operated on faith rather than empiricism, but I doubt that our version of group therapy did anyone any harm.

The psychotics had a different way to go. A few were in the late stages of syphilis and were shipped off to a hospital for the criminally insane, a fate even more dismal than a protracted term at San Quentin. The rest got shock therapy, a procedure whose benefits were hard to discern, but which certainly deterred a lot of convicts from seeking psychiatric care. The death of one patient in insulin shock treatment caused the county pathologist to ask if we had a rationale for administering this drastic treatment. It seemed to him that this dangerous intervention was a way of giving psychiatrists something impressive to do with very sick patients, but without results that justified the risk. The Chief was naturally infuriated by this comment, but it has stayed with me. It epitomized everything we were doing in the name of the medical model. We did not have a reasoned basis for the intervention and we had no way of testing our effectiveness by observing the results. Whether it was group therapy, individual counseling, or electric shock (we quietly gave up insulin shock after that fatality) we did what we could with the authority of modern medicine reassuring us that it was right, and we hoped for the best.

So much for the medical part of the medical model. My duties did not end with the administration of group therapy. Much, if not most of my time was devoted to preparing psychiatric assessments for the parole board. The task of the Psychiatric Department was to provide the board with an evaluation on a "special calendar" of the mental and emotional condition of all prisoners appearing before it; these prisoners consisted of all murderers and sex offenders, all psychotics, and anyone else whose odd behavior caused the board members to request a professional opinion. The evaluation reports were based on a review of each man's medical and psychiatric record and an interview from which we hoped to get a perspective on his prospects for post-release adjustment. Our report would conclude with an estimate of his chances for survival on parole.

My discomforts about my role in this process were numerous. In principle, the Chief reviewed my reports and by signing off, gave them the color of psychiatric authenticity. He never changed them, and that might be taken as flattering confidence in my discernment, but I was uneasy anyway. I had no way of verifying my predictions, especially with respect to those whom I rated as unfavorable prospects for parole success. I soon found out that whereas those whom I rated as favorable prospects might or might not get a favorable decision from the board, those who were rated unfavorably were invariably denied parole. As in our efforts at psychiatric treatment, we were engaged in a process the validity of which we could not verify.

Years later, long after I had left the Psychiatric Department, social scientists began to refer to what we were doing as the "medical model" of corrections. I have already indicated that I think this is a wholly erroneous designation, and I want to underscore the error. First, we were providing treatment without benefit of two essential criteria of medical practice: a theoretical rationale for intervention and a procedure for determining the effectiveness of what we were doing. Second, volition, so essential to the physician-patient relationship, was absent. Our patients had no choice. They could not elude the Cerletti apparatus, as the Chief coyly referred to the electric shock device, nor could they escape the psychiatric evaluation that we submitted whether they cooperated or not — and some did not. They had to accept what we offered them, whether they believed in it or not, and I doubt that many of them did. Third, the confidentiality of the relationship was routinely breached in our reports to the board, all with the knowledge of our patients but never with their consent sought or given. These deviations from the medical model as it is known in conventional practice are so gross as to make the use of the term an inexcusable euphemism for what we were doing and for a great deal that is still being done under the rubric of correctional psychiatry.

IV

It is often argued that the model described above — which I will no longer dignify by calling it "medical" — extends to the entire correctional process as it was and still is practiced wherever the indeterminate sentence is in force. The belief system was and remains simple and plausible. The prison staff administers treatment, preferably individualized, to meet the specific needs identified in diagnostic procedures at the time the prisoner was received. The parole board monitors the process and, when satisfied that rehabilitation had gone far enough, authorizes the parole of the treated prisoner — whose treatment will continue in the community. The critical factor in deciding the appropriate time of release is thought to be progress toward the previously identified rehabilitative goal, as reported by the staff and verified by the board.

As a veteran observer of the conduct of parole board hearings in a number of states, I have concluded that with few exceptions, rehabilitation has never been more than a vehicle for dialogue between the board and the prisoner. The ritual references to progress in treatment, which constitute so much of the exchange between parole board members and convicts, have been derided by caustic observers for many years and with good reason. If parole boards really made judgments based on their assessment of clinical progress, their decision making could be condemned as basically dishonest. It is not possible to measure the extent and significance of personality change, nor is it feasible to predict anyone's future behavior when faced with the enormous variety of unforeseen situations that may confront anyone in contemporary society. If parole boards did as they have often claimed to do, they would be attempting the manifestly impossible — always a corrupting process. To attempt what one knows cannot be done and then to claim that one has done it, forces the claimant to rationalize. Parole board members of the time when I wrote those reports found many ways of rationalizing their conduct. Some of them supposed that the hearings were therapeutic experiences for the convicts who appeared before them, and there was a great deal of heavily didactic counseling done on those occasions. Others supposed that somehow they were protecting the community from the dangers these convicts presented. Still others thought that they were motivating convicts to do something to better themselves.

But in reality, the parole board for which I worked and those that I have since observed pay little attention to claims made for a convict's progress toward rehabilitation. Decisions define the true policy under which any public body functions. A convict appearing before the board with a record of substantial effort in school and at work may be denied parole, not because the board doubts the veracity of his claims, but rather because his was a serious crime and he had not served enough time. Conversely, minor offenders may be turned loose without any evidence of change simply because enough time had been done. What has always counted most in decision making is the severity of the convict's crime and previous record, and the decision maker's opinion about the risk of the offender returning to a life of crime. The exhaustive work of Gottfredson, Wilkins, and Hoffman in developing guidelines for the United States Parole Commission's sentencing practice confirms the irrelevance of treatment for penal decision making.[14] Charged with developing a system of guidelines for parole decisions, these investigators made a statistical study of the actions of the parole board and discovered that severity of the offense and risk were the two most important variables in determining release decisions.

I think that this has always been the case. There is a great deal of coercion in prison, but little of the coercion is applied to whatever rehabilitative processes may be offered. What has appeared to be "coerced rehabilitation" is the rationale for the indeterminate sentence, a powerful implement for the control and intimidation of the prisoner. The charade before the parole board is a dialogue about rehabilitation. The apparatus is used to impress the prisoner that the state is powerful and the next time he offends the experience will be even more unpleasant. The parole board can fix a term in most states for most crimes within a very long range of years — for a whole lifetime under the former California law. The deterrent effect on the individual prisoner is impressive; about 50% of California parolees do not recidivate. But no one claims that that performance is substantially due to the effectiveness of treatment programs.

The "justice model" puts an end to charades of coerced rehabilitation enacted before parole boards and to the parole board itself. The indeterminate sentence is to be replaced by the flat term, to be settled in court within statutory limits. I will leave it to others to review the variants of Dr. Fogel's justice model as enacted in the states that have adopted it. The flat term, which is integral to the model, is a principle whose time has come, even though formidable conceptual and administrative problems remain to be solved if the transition is not to be a painful and costly process.

It is the emphasis on justice that deserves our applause. Whatever else is done in prison, fair play and the due process of law will have primacy.

We will abandon pretenses about rehabilitation that serve no other purpose than to inspire fraudulent conduct on both sides of the decision maker's desk. We will recognize that prisoners must have a voice in the community in which they live and that they should have the means to obtain redress of their grievances against a system that may make mistakes because it is ruled by fallible human beings. Their terms will be fixed according to the gravity of their crimes and records and without the introduction of procedural ambiguities.

Justice is therapy. Injustice has no place in American society, even in the prison, a social institution for the control of our unworthiest fellows. In a prison in which justice is ascendant, the prisoner may choose to become a citizen. It is at this point that I want to go beyond the "justice model."

V

Obviously my position is basically retributivist. In spite of Plato, in spite of the Utilitarians, the evidence is that the criminal justice system cannot prevent crime by the processes of intimidation, reform, or incapacitation. The impact of the criminal justice system on offenders does not and cannot significantly reduce the volume of crime.

This is the point at which we must clear our minds of wishful thinking and the attractive suppositions of the theorists who have roamed over the system without benefit of empirical test. Once the data of criminal justice are seen for what they are, we discover an inconvenient truth: our penal system depends on a principle of symbolic punishment. Yet it cannot intimidate, reform, or incapacitate enough criminals to make more than a modest dent in the crime rates. In a contentious essay on the effect of the determinate sentence in California, Caleb Foote demonstrated the symbolic nature of the system. Proceeding from the ominous but little noticed statistic that in California only 10 to 15% of the felons convicted in Superior Court are sent to prison, he arrived at the following formulation:

> If the masks of individualization and rehabilitation are stripped away, the basic function of discretion in paroling and sentencing is revealed: to adjust an impossible penal code to the reality of severe limitations on punishment resources. By an impossible code I refer to the fact that given economic restraints, full or equal enforcement is out of the question . . . . From the masses of convicted persons legislatively declared to be eligible for imprisonment, most must be diverted and only a small proportion winnowed out for actual imprisonment. What we have is a system of symbolic punishment in which each San Quentin inmate stands for half a dozen or a dozen other convicted felons

> who are by any standards equally eligible to be there but for whom there are no beds . . .[15]

Professor Foote thinks this system is profoundly unjust and immoral, and it is certain that a retributivist who followed Kant's categorical imperative would agree. It is, however, a reality and its consequences for the incidence of crime must be seen for what they are. A strictly symbolic administration of punishment cannot have more than a symbolic effect on crime. In the eighteenth century reliance was placed on capital punishment as the primary instrument of control by criminal justice. The result was that too many criminals were sentenced to be hanged and the king had to pardon a substantial number of guilty men. We are in a comparable situation now; too many criminals are eligible for prison and the courts must limit sentences to a few who are either unluckier than their fellows or who may, we hope, deserve punishment more. To intimidate those who finally make their ways to prison may be of some use in preventing those particular individuals from repeating their crimes, but it is not to be expected that the successful intimidation — or rehabilitation — of all prisoners will be noticeably reflected in diminished crime rates.

During recent years various commentators, policy analysts, statisticians, and economic model builders have concentrated their attention on the possibility of reducing crime rates by incapacitating chronic recidivists, persons who are so unresponsive to intimidation that they return to crime as soon as the restraining arm of the law is lifted.[16] Research in which I have been engaged shows that even a sentencing policy calling for an absurd level of severity — a five-year sentence on the conviction of *any* felony — would succeed in reducing violent crime by no more than one-third. At the same time, such a policy would increase prison populations by 400 to 500%. Any less severe sentencing policy would result in a much smaller reduction of crime.[17] Our studies correspond with similar findings by other research groups. Any law designed to establish a group of offenders with common characteristics could not succeed in reducing crime. This is not to say that the legislatures and the courts should ignore the state's duty to protect its citizens from selected offenders who are judged to be dangerous. Collective incapacitation is a hopeless strategy, but the selective restraint of criminals whose records inspire public apprehension is necessary to confidence in the judgment of the courts and other officials charged with making decisions with respect to the disposition of criminals.

Despite the symbolic character of punishment as it is now administered, and probably always has been administered in most countries, and despite the strictures of Caleb Foote on the immorality of such an impossible system, the prison system is a reality and will continue to be so. It is a retributivist system, the purposes of which may be thought to be preventive, even though it cannot succeed in that aim. It administers the consequences of crime for a few offenders who were unlucky enough to be caught and convicted.

The father of modern sociology, Emile Durkheim, held that we punish offenders so that social cohesion may be maintained; it is not conceivable that a community could tolerate a situation in which criminals are not punished. Obviously we are in a situation in which many criminals are not apprehended and many who are caught are punished only nominally if at all. But the fact that some criminals are punished is pragmatically better than if no criminals at all were punished. Therefore the prison exists to demonstrate to society that the wicked and foolish may on occasion suffer serious consequences. I will argue that it might also become a place in which justice and citizenship can be experienced, sometimes with lasting good effects.

VI

The idea of citizenship is one of the many contributions of the ancient Greeks to the development of civilization. We forget, however, that the Greeks in their day, and all their democratic successors up to the late nineteenth century, restricted citizenship to members of a privileged social class. For the free Athenian to exercise his rights and perform his civic duties, it was necessary that there should be helot slaves to do the hewing and drawing. The rights of the Athenian slave were real but limited; their enjoyment of the democracy of the agora was distant and non-participatory. So it was, until the nineteenth century, even in this land of the free, where it took a major convulsion to rid the society of the institution of slavery. And universal citizenship has now been accepted in most Western democracies in the course of the present century.

Except for convicts. American citizenship rests on a tripod of rights, civil, political, and social, most of which we strip from the citizen when he goes to prison. Citizenship also imposes obligations and responsibilities from which we exempt prisoners when we deprive them of choices in the exercise of their rights. We used to call this deprivation "civil death" and although the term is out of favor, it describes the predicament of the convict in most American prisons today. The situation is changing, partly because of practical reformers, partly because of the courts, the ombudsmen, and the vigilant civil libertarians. There is no longer a question of maintaining prisons as enclaves of unrestricted autocracy such as we used to tolerate. The time has come when we must exercise our political ingenuity to create prison communities that are based on limited but inalienable civil, political, and social rights.

In the process we may discover a new purpose for the prison. It can and should become a school for citizenship. For what is a criminal but a man or woman who has failed to observe his or her responsibility to respect the rights of others to safety of person or property? Prisons are mostly filled with street criminals, and one way to look at the street criminal is to recognize that most of them are losers in American society. I define these losers as that minority of our population which exists outside the security system in which careers, employment, income, and pensions are to be expected with reasonable certainty. Losers manage on the margins of society — on day labor, public welfare, and various other kinds of irregular living, including crime. It is a small minority in the total American population, but more than enough to fill our prisons many times over.

The loser is technically a citizen, but his rights receive limited respect. His ability to meet his responsibilities is so impaired that he seldom knows from experience what it is to be a citizen. Most losers only know that citizenship is one of the many goods of which they have been deprived. When the loser arrives in prison he finds himself in a mass of humanity, with no experience of citizenship, its rights and its responsibilities. This did not matter in the days of the "civilly dead" convict who had no hope of being restored to a social role allowing for more than the right to survival. It matters a lot in these days when prisoners *are* accorded rights, but little or no opportunity to exercise them and little experience in their exercise before their arrival in prison. To the extent that we expect prisoners to eventually return to society as self-supporting and self-respecting citizens, it is essential that they should learn the meaning of citizenship, as people in the secure classes learn it in childhood.

How are prisoners to learn? Let us begin by defining the rights that prisoners should and can be allowed to enjoy, along with the responsibilities that accompany those rights. The prison of the future should be a place of restraint where convicts who function as citizens discover the advantages of doing so, whereas convicts who do not will suffer the consequences. The latter category, so dangerous in contemporary prisons, will attenuate as the convict's rights and responsibilities achieve recognition. The prison cannot become a community like a Greek city-state, but to the extent that a sense of community grows it will be because the individuals in it live like citizens instead of caged criminals.

A right is a claim which some other person or entity is bound to honor, either by custom or by law. Enforcement of rights can be assured by litigation, but this course is unsatisfactory because it casts a pall of formality and negativism in ordinary human relations. Rights which are enforced by custom and accepted as the requirement of propriety will be better observed and less resented. In what follows, I will propose seven general rights that prisoners should enjoy. Rights are limited by the individual's observance of his responsibilities; failure to meet responsibilities will have an adverse effect on the enjoyment of rights. The rights and responsibilities I shall enumerate here are essential elements in what I think of as the "citizenship model of corrections."

1. *The right to personal safety.* The dangers of the modern megaprison are well known and they are not exaggerated. A man in custody is helpless to protect himself in the human morass in which we usually hold him in this country. The guards cannot assure his protection and sometimes cannot even protect themselves. The obligation of the state to provide safe custody is imperative. We do a bad job now by using antiquated prison plants and by providing insufficient staff to make life safe. Corresponding to the right to safety is the prisoner's responsibility not to increase the hazards of the community. When he does so by assaults or threats, the consequences should be real and severe.

2. *The right to care.* Decent clean housing, adequate diet, enough clothing, and medical care when required are axiomatic basic needs for all citizens. Prisons which are crowded like pigsties will never generate a reconciliation between convict and society, nor is the demeanor of a citizen likely to be found within them. Prisoners must be responsible for living as decently as they can in decent surroundings provided by the state.

3. *The right to personal dignity.* Self-respect is hard to come by in the poor and disorderly parts of town where most prisoners formerly lived. Regardless of his origin, the prisoner's sense of worth has been further damaged by the humiliations of confinement. The staff must do what it can to restore it, not to damage it further. That responsibility must be shared by all prisoners; the indignities and verbal abuse so commonly visited by prisoners on each other should be discouraged.

4. *The right to work.* No country does as badly as ours in providing occupations for prisoners. Indeed, like the poor in America, their redundancy is painfully evident — society has no use for them, and their response is to be seen in the disorder of the prison yards and cell-blocks. The right to work and the right to a wage constitute a pair of rights without which the other rights of a citizen lose their meaning. A prisoner should work if he wants to, and he should be paid on the same basis as he would be paid in the free labor market. He should meet his responsibilities for his dependents like the rest of us, and he should save for his future if he can. He will need a nest egg more than most citizens ever will.

5. *The right to self-improvement.* Everyone agrees that convicts should not be forced into educational programs or other activities provided for their own good. Although the idea of coerced rehabilitation has been

discredited, there is no reason to close down opportunities for self-improvement which the prisoner can elect. To do so is to foreclose hope — as cruel a punishment as we can devise.

6. *The right to vote.* The electoral disabilities imposed on convicts protect no one and serve only to add a pointless humiliation to the prisoner's burdens. His participation in the democratic process should be encouraged in the interest of making citizenship a real and vital feature of his life.

7. *The right to a future.* Under this right, I include the right to contact with families and friends and the general outside community so far as these encounters can be made within the necessary restrictions of custody. A man who is isolated from the world can hardly plan for a future, as we see all too often in the cases of men who are returned to the community only to live in the same isolation as they did when locked up. Citizens have to look ahead to meet their responsibilities, but the citizen in prison has nothing to look to if the community is not in sight.

Some of these rights can and should be put into immediate effect. Others will take time. The replacement of our fortress-like monstrocities inherited from the nineteenth century will not be accomplished soon. It will take even longer to close down the recently built prisons that were so improvidently designed as to be obsolete before they were occupied. The nation's economy being what it is, we cannot expect that there will be a thriving prison industry program in every state within an easily foreseeable future. But if we can set our sights on these goals and recognize those rights that can be immediately conferred, we can begin to make sense out of our prisons.

VII

Justice depends on a reciprocity between the state and its citizens and among citizens themselves. A man whose rights are not protected by the state has no rights. A man who has no rights cannot be expected to observe the rights of others. If justice is really therapy, as I believe, it can only be administered to a citizen, not to a civilly dead convict.

Americans take pride in learning from experience. In hardly any other domain of human services are the lessons so hard to learn and so contradictory as in corrections. We have learned that the prison is not a place where rehabilitation can be routinely administered. We have learned that the really important differences between citizens and convicts are artifacts of law and custom, not inherent in the nature of the offender. The prison where a man can choose, act, and see the consequences of his choices will not necessarily produce a man who will be a successful citizen when he is released. We must continue to expect that many ex-convicts will get into more trouble, even if we standardize the citizenship model for general adoption. But at least we can make constructive use of the convict-years that are now so weary and so wasted.

The prison is not a significant solution to the crime problem. We have prisons because we do not know what else to do with some offenders. But the prison in which duties, rights, and responsibilities are pitched at a higher level than the sullen and demeaning prison practices we now maintain will turn out some men and women who will be better for the experience. A man prepared for citizenship is better than a possible non-recidivist any day.

Enthusiasts for the prison in the years when it was new, freshly minted from the minds of Bentham and his fellow reformers, thought of it as the sovereign cure for the ills of the human spirit. Indeed, Bentham thought the prison might well be adapted for the care of paupers, orphans, and the mentally ill — anyone whose circumstances had been or might be contaminated by the wicked influences of the city. That belief has ebbed and flowed during the last two centuries. The Chief Psychiatrist at San Quentin thought that the magic of modern psychiatry could convert the old prison — of which he disapproved as much as the most zealous reformer — into a sort of hospital. Experience has discredited his optimism, and the magic has been demystified. The enthusiasm is gone, penology is drifting, and prisons are much more dangerous for everyone than they used to be. It is time for a new model; the citizenship model which I advocate will not infallibly cure prisoners, but it might cure the prison of its serious shortcomings.

Ordinary citizens are not welcome visitors to our prisons; if they gain admission at all they are unlikely to see more than the carefully selected show-places: the school, the mess-hall, a kitchen filled with stainless steel cooking vessels. They are unlikely to be allowed to walk through the yard and observe the scores of idle men, waiting and loitering and scheming. They will certainly not walk past the segregation units where recalcitrant young men scream epithets, throw filth at the guards, and yell for attention. And a free conversation with the prisoners will suggest that positive results cannot be expected of the penal process. The system blocks the offender at every turn. If we insist on justice and provide an arena in which a convict can behave like a citizen, because such behavior is expected as a matter of course, at least the system will be compatible with the superior goal of reconciling the convict with society. To paraphrase Kant, wherever justice perishes it is not worthwhile for a man to live. But a free people can make justice live — even in the stark environment of the American prison.

Notes

1. Immanuel Kant, *Philosophy of Law,* quoted by Alf Ross, *On Guilt, Responsibility, and Punishment* (London: Stevens, 1975), pp. 54-55.
2. Plato, *Protagoras,* 324b.
3. Plato, *Gorgias,* 478d.
4. Plato, *Laws,* 854d.
5. Martin Madan, "Thoughts on Executive Justice," *With Respect to Our Criminal Laws, Particularly on the Circuits. Dedicated to All Judges of Assize and Recommended to the Perusal of All Magistrates; and to All Persons Liable to Serve on Grand Juries – By a Sincere Well-Wisher to the Public* (London, 1785), quoted by Leon Radzinowicz, *History of the English Criminal Law.*
6. John Howard, *The State of the Prisons* (New York: E. P. Dutton, 1929).
7. Mary Peter Mack, *A Bentham Reader* (New York: Western Publishing Company, 1969), p. 192.
8. Jeremy Bentham, *Works, vol. I* (New York: Russell and Russell, 1962), p. 396.
9. Michel Foucault, *Discipline and Punish* (New York: Pantheon, 1977), pp. 195-228.
10. Bentham, vol. IV, p. 39.
11. Gustave de Beaumont and Alexis de Tocqueville, *On the Penitentiary System in the United States and Its Application in France* (Carbondale and Edwardsville, Illinois: The Southern Illinois Press, 1964), pp. 161-165.
12. The full text of the Declaration of Principles is contained in the republished *Proceedings of the First National Prison Congress,* and is available from the American Correctional Association, College Park, Maryland.
13. Douglas Lipton, Robert Martinson, and Judith Wilks, *The Effectiveness of Correctional Treatment* (New York: Praeger, 1975).
14. Don Gottfredson, Leslie T. Wilkins, and Peter Hoffman, *Guidelines for Sentencing and Parole* (Lexington, Mass.: Lexington Books, 1977).
15. Caleb Foote, *Deceptive Determinate Sentencing,* (In *Determinate Sentencing, Reform or Regression?,* Proceedings of the Special Conference on Determinate Sentencing, June 2-3, 1977, Boalt Hall School of Law, University of California, Berkeley, pp. 133-140.
16. For an authoritative review of the research, see Alfred Blumstein, Jacqueline Cohen, and Daniel Nagin (eds.), *Deterrence and Incapacitation: Estimating the Effects of Criminal Sanctions in the United States, on Crime Rates* (Washington: National Academy of Sciences, 1978).
17. Stephen Van Dine, Simon Dinitz, and John P. Conrad, *Restraining the Wicked* (Lexington, Mass.: Lexington Books, 1979).

2. Justice in Search of Fairness

Patrick D. McAnany

Mr. Justice Blackman wondered if Delaware had an official policy on random stops [*of automobiles*].

Counsel said that local law offices don't require their officers to make random stops, but that the officers often perform them.

This exchange prompted Mr. Justice Stevens to ask whether the officer here was following orders to make random stops or whether he "just did it."

"He just did it," counsel said.[1]

This brief exchange sums up the problem of discretion: low-level choice unguided by anything more identifiable than past experience and personal preference. There is nothing inherently malevolent in a police officer making a decision to stop a driver to inquire about proper licensing. But there is something wrong when police and other officials in the criminal justice system resort to coercive power without visible standards to guide them. It is the problem of fairness that has powered the critique of discretionary decision making over the past decade and has led to a search for acceptable standards.

What that search has generated is a great deal of heat across the criminal justice system to define general policy guidelines and to create appropriate standards to enact them. The general policy, however, has become snagged over what goals the criminal justice system should pursue. Among a limited number of traditional choices — rehabilitation, deterrence, restraint, or retribution — only rehabilitation has been finally rejected as inappropriate, and then only as a primary goal. The other goals have been discussed without any final resolution of their implicit antinomies. But most critics regard the matter of goals as a subject for philosophical debate; it is the intermediate matter of standards that is now gaining their increased attention.

The argument is cogently made that discretion is so broad today that any limitations will provide some measure of relief from the unfairness of individualistic and disparate judgments. However, as these standards are teased out, old questions arise. For instance, though there has been a general agreement that discretion is best limited under a justice model approach,[2] one of the more creditable efforts at developing standards for controlling discretion has created a combination of offense severity with personal characteristics of offenders, though controlled for consistency of application across large groups of offenders.[3] What this effort does is raise again the issue of whether it is ever fair, even if the practice promotes consistency, to punish a person for personal status, however predictive of future behavior that status might be.

Much has happened over the past decade to foster the interest in fairness in administering criminal sanctions. Yet this interest has not been directed only toward the concept of fairness to individuals; the concept of justice in regard to the community at large has entered and tinctured the debates. If there are no guidelines for official processing, then the power to dispense may be as prevalent a power as the power to bind. Indeed, this dispensing power creates a problem for society by releasing criminals at large, and magnifies the problem of unfairness when individuals are bound by the system and punished out of proportion to their deeds.

The debates over discretion and fairness have raised another issue. Since the criminal process is an interdependent one, if not fully systemic in nature, then unfairness at any point along the line tends to be sustained in later steps, and perhaps even magnified. This sense of being unable to isolate unfairness at a single point in the system makes the debates over only sentencing less critical. We know that however much we right wrongs here, we tend to contaminate later portions of the network by allowing decisions to be made which may ultimately undo the justice made at sentencing. In short, failure to coordinate reform across the system may displace discretion to other parts of the system.

In discussing standards, whatever their nature, a major issue has become where do they derive from and how are they created. For instance, whatever types of standards police may become subject to, it is important for the police, as well as for the rest of us, to determine who will create these standards and under what conditions. Will they be created by police without any legislative or judicial oversight? Will the public — and which segment of the public — have an input? The same questions can be posed for each of the major decision-making agencies along the criminal justice continuum. While there have not been definitive answers to these questions, there have been particular reforms that support one or another answer.

This chapter will attempt to draw these various problems into a critical whole, keeping in mind the element of fairness which has grounded the debates. The first section will be devoted to an overview of the critiques that have led to debunking of expertise and to demands for control of discretion. The second section will be devoted to a discussion of various reform responses to these critiques and to a brief estimate of their current level of implementation. In the final section, I will raise several problems with the current justice model approach which suggest that, unless there is more agreement on goals, we will inevitably fall back into compromises that diminish the value of fairness. For instance, how should a justice system deal with prior offenses? How do we create an adequate severity scale, both for offenses and for penalties? How closely should punishment be scaled to offense using local or regional values? These are questions which have been repressed in debates over more immediate issues, but which are now back on the doorstep of the justice approach to discretion.

The Decline of the "Expert": Discretion Under Attack

Discretion in the 1960's

Professor James Vorenberg describes a system of *appropriate* discretion as one in which "decisions are made at the highest level of authority and with the greatest degree of visibility permitted by the nature of the decision and the context in which it is made."[4] When one projects back upon the current system such a pattern of appropriateness, the margins of difference are frightening. This problem is not a recent one. Indeed, discretion as a concept in law appears coeval with law itself. To start no further back in criminal justice than the Wickersham Commission in the 1930's, one finds a detailed interest in how discretion was abused by officials.[5] It is true that the notion of the criminal justice enterprise as a somehow enclosed system is new, and this conception gives a peculiar potency to the concern for discretion because any unfairness injected at one point in the system reverberates and accentuates as the system narrows upon the few who are punished.[6] The concerns of the last decade, however, may be located in more precise historical antecedents.

The 1960's was the decade when criminal justice became professional news. The President's Crime Commission delineated the dimensions of the crime problem at great length. It noted (and predicted) an increase in crime rates throughout the country; it indicated that racial differences among both victims and suspects were unacceptably high; it supported the principles of due process which the United States Supreme Court had mandated for the handling of suspects; it offered data and recommendations for change; it promised federal support for those systems willing to undertake the arduous work of change; and it pinpointed several problem areas where the narrowing of discretion was called for, in particular among police. The assumption in all of this was that crime could be reduced at the same time that due process was increased.[7] That this assumption was not borne out in fact has a great deal to do with the attack upon discretion in the 1970's.

Without recognizing the implicit contradiction, the Commission recommended increasing the discretion to divert persons from the criminal justice system at the same time as they recommended more careful controls on police processing of other persons.[8] Latitude in the disposition of offenders appeared beneficial to many. Since the system was overloaded and perhaps even crimogenic, the more persons diverted, the better. Standards for such shortcutting were necessarily vague because they depended more on individual characteristics of offenders than on an objective criteria of acts. Professionals acquainted with behavior could derive standards from practice. Court intake workers, probation officers, correctional counselors, and parole board members would qualify as the experts who could choose among clients for early termination of involvement. But police were distrusted because they lacked training and possibly the correct motivation to exercise this same dispensing power. Yet the general problem in *both* correctional and police decisions was that the dispensing of some implied the retention of others. Since there was no control over how choices were made, the very humaneness of the system (decisions made on individual bases) became grounds for its unfairness.

Ultimately, the discrediting of the expert was more a matter of statistics than proof of personal prejudice. It was the fact that the crime rate rose as our society became more affluent that alerted many to the weakness of the assumption that correctional rehabilitation choices could reduce crime. But it was not *only* that. Some persons were aware of the danger to individual rights posed by such a loose fit between power and policy. The late 1960's produced several significant pieces of literature that grounded the later attack on discretion.

The Early Critics of Discretion

The first set of literature located the problem in the debate over goals for criminal justice. Professor H. L. A. Hart imported the debate from England with his book, *Punishment and Responsibility.*[9] In this work he insisted against Lady Wootton that personal responsibility should remain essential in defining and punishing crime despite the fact that criminal law was preventive in purpose and not retributive. The behavioralist approach which Lady Wootton represented so vigorously[10] was based on the notion that criminal justice best fulfilled its preventive mission through rehabilitation or incapacitation, neither of which required personal responsibility, or guilt, for crime. Herbert Packer continued the discussion for an American audience by opting for an act-based, as opposed to an actor-based, system.[11] While he rejected the retributive thesis of desert, he followed Hart in asserting that the preventive goals of criminal law be limited by application of sanctions to those persons who have been convicted of crime based on personal responsibility. In addition, he did not reject out of hand the possible future technology which would allow us to predict accurately who will recidivate. But he limited the reach of present criminal law to those convicted. The concern that each of these authors manifested about discretion is the same: without limiting the sanction to the guilty, the system is open to uncontrolled selection of precriminal types for preventive measures of control.

The second significant piece of literature was Professor Kenneth C. Davis' *Discretionary Justice.*[12] It was a comparative piece in which criminal justice was contrasted unfavorably with other administrative law systems where the fundamentals of rule-making due process had engendered adequate controls on discretion. Looking at police, prosecutors, and parole boards, Davis noted several things. First, the impairment of fundamental liberties which criminal justice activities potentially involved was much graver than those of other administrative processes. Second, there was no tradition among criminal justice agencies of the due process restraints of rule making common to other administrative agencies. Discretion which these officials exercised might by concession be regarded as based on expertise, but each decision made individualistically is also made without being subjected to checks by supervisors, to administrative appeal, or to review by the courts. Davis does not suggest that any criminal justice official uses his position to overbear citizens; only that there is no way to distinguish between those who do wield oppressive power and those who do not. In the end, justice suffers where there is no way to illuminate its quality by rules and review.

These several pieces were a prelude to the real attack on discretion that began in the 1970's. The Quakers opened the debate with their American Friends Service Committee Report, *Struggle for Justice.* Its central thesis is presented thus:

> We submit that many distortions and corruptions of justice — such as the discriminatory use of penal sanctions and the use of the criminal justice system to promote conformity and control of classes of persons — depend upon the existence of wide margins of discretionary power in the hands of police, district attorneys, judges, correctional administrators, parole boards, and parole agents. Therefore, discretion is at the core of the problem.[13]

The report went on to delineate a two-fold attack on the problem. First, law should be as narrow and precise as possible and all unnecessary criminal statutes should be eliminated. Second, where some margins of discretion must remain, they should be governed by rules which are created in a public and open process. But discretion was to be the exception, not the rule, in the system envisioned by the Quakers. As a final guarantee that discretion would no longer be used to dominate along class and race lines, the Report required that poor people, most frequently the subjects of the system, be politically empowered to represent their own interests.[14]

Struggle for Justice rejected the main tenets of the Davis creed. They accused the system of oppression, where Davis only suggested the potential for abuse. Further, they rejected the need for discretion, however well controlled it might appear to be under rules and review. Their answer to the argument that a non-discretionary system would be intolerably rigid was to point out that such systems exist elsewhere in the law. More important for the developing history in the field, the Quakers were the first to suggest that sentencing be returned to a determinate form.[15] Further, their central thesis that discretion was being used by the system to discriminate against the poor to further re-enforce an unjust social milieu gave moral suasion to their argument. One of the conundrums of criminal justice was the riddle of why the poor and racial minorities were so heavily over-represented in the system, especially at the deep end. *Struggle for Justice* laid the blame squarely at the door of a system that encouraged the unexamined use of discretion. Such a system mandated that natural prejudices of the dominant culture determine the outcome.

The central feature that focused this system, under the Quakers' analysis, was the so-called expert.[16] Rehabilitation required sentences which were individuated to the facts of each case, more particularly to the factors personal to each offender. Persons trained in medical and behavioral sciences were authorized to determine the length of time it would take to return the offender to a crime-free status. But there was no evidence that the experts grounded their theory or practice on predictable expectations rather than on chance. In fact there was a great deal of evidence that the expertise argument was a cover for other purposes, such as preventive detention.

The Justice Critique and Sentencing

During the next half-dozen years criticism of the system multiplied at an increasing rate. In an era of rising crime rates and an atmosphere of law and order, concerns at both ends of the political spectrum began to coalesce around the issue of uncontrolled discretion. The initial focus of attention was on the disparity among dispositions of offenders who otherwise were alike.[17] This led to the discovery that the system was based on the premise that experts could differentiate among persons likely to recidivate and thereby provide adequate remedies to forestall a return to crime. But if this were so, then how could one explain the continued rise in crime rates, particularly among "corrected" offenders? It was here that the fears of the Quakers fed those of the political right, creating a formidable base of attack. If one approached the matter from a due process bias, discretion without control of rules resulted in denial of liberty to many candidates appropriate for a community release status. If one were inclined toward community protection, then this same discretion created untoward populations of dangerous offenders in the community.[18] Each side admitted that there were, indeed, examples of discretion working opposite harms — liberals saying that dangerous persons had been released and conservatives saying that nondangerous persons had been locked up. By such an admission both could, in conscience, endorse a common remedy.

To mount the attack, the critics tended to use two common strains of argumentation. The first was to demonstrate that the system experts lacked any ability to rehabilitate offenders. This became easier when Lipton, Martinson, and Wilks published their survey of correctional program evaluations.[19] But prior to that and subsequently, there were indications that we lacked evidence.[20] While these types of exposés were not really demonstrations of the inability of the system to rehabilitate, they did deflate the rhetoric that had surrounded corrections for the previous one hundred years. However well intentioned the effort to rehabilitate had been, and whatever successes it had enjoyed in individual cases, there was yet no body of theory or practice that could allow us to predict outcomes over a period of time. Thus, release based on an assertion of ability to do this was false in promise.

The second argument against the expert followed upon the first. If the system could not diagnose or properly intervene, could it at least predict likelihood of recidivism? Again the critics mounted an attack on past performance.[21] Using violence as a criterion of prediction, there were strong statistical arguments that no one could predict with accuracy those who would return to criminal violence in order to eliminate incarcerating those who would not in unacceptably high numbers. The problem of "false positives" became the way the argument was summarized.[22] It was a matter of what one considered "unacceptably high" as to where one came down on either side. Some persons were willing to tolerate a good deal of overruns among those who had broken the law anyway. Liberals, on the other hand, were appalled at incarcerating anyone who did not absolutely need to be restrained. But there was enough common ground to support the contention that the present system lacked the refinement to allow discretion to be exercised unchecked.

A third attack on the expert was rather muted. It was based on the theory of general deterrence. The argument could be made that although general deterrence was a legitimate goal of criminal law, there was little empirical evidence that supported its usefulness in particular cases. How could the legislatures, courts, or parole boards create a tariff system that did not exceed utilitarian limits? The answer lay in the general authority of the legislature both to create crimes and set the general length of sentence, which turned out to be more a political act than a scientific judgment.[23] Individual sentencing and release by criminal justice officials only followed guidelines set down by the legislature as to severity. While there might be cases of courts or parole boards imposing exemplary sentences or refusal of parole based on general deterrence purposes, they were within the acceptable realm of difference. None of the critics made much of this argument. Most adopted the notion that general deterrence was political in nature and not subject to the critique of a narrower behavioralism.[24]

Law Enforcement Discretion

The attack upon discretion began from a broad base in debates over general goals for criminal law and the noting of an almost total lack of rules and rule making among criminal justice agencies. It narrowed with the American Friends' Report where the true villain was a correctional bureaucracy touting a system without a definable theory to ground it. Criticisms finally focused on the sentencing process where incarceration and release on predictive grounds were judged arbitrary. The narrower and more focused the debate became, the more the central issue of unfairness was transformed into a behavioralist one. That is, the major attack looked at the penocorrectional process and found rehabilitation as a groundless assertion of capacity. Eliminate rehabilitation as a goal and the system would recover its sense of fairness. But this constricted view lost sight of the fact that unfairness was earlier asserted as a systemwide trait, running from police, through prosecutors, to the judges, and ending with parole board members. Police for all their unguided efforts had never acted on unsupported theories of rehabilitation, nor had prosecutors. In the demands for a solution to the incarceration-release issue, many critics had neglected the fact that discretion was flabby at the front end, as well as the middle and back end of the system.

Those who had paid attention to police and prosecutors were more likely to be the conservative block concerned with the dispensing power with which these law enforcement groups operated. For instance, the National Advisory Commission on Criminal Justice Standards and Goals indicated that plea bargaining should be eliminated.[25] While the concern for defendants' rights was dully noted, the thrust of the recommendation was toward elimination of leniency for serious felony offenders — justice to the community became a primary concern. So too there was a concern with the police; because they were not subject to sufficient controls, they lost cases by inappropriate enforcement techniques. The recommendation was for an increased supervision by prosecutors who could advise them on ways to preserve cases against important (dangerous) criminals.[26]

By 1977 the expert in the criminal justice system had been thoroughly repudiated by a series of critiques. What became more and more evident was that there was no definable expertise, to the level at least where we were willing to entrust either the rights of defendants or the protection of the public to it. What was needed was a reduction in the discretion which we accorded the various officials along the system pipeline. How that remedy was to be carried out was a matter of some disagreement among the critics. The following section summarizes the major proposals that have emerged and describes the level of their implementation to date.

The Ascendancy of the Justice Model

While the debate over goals for criminal justice had never been the center of attention in the decade of criticism, it remains resolutely present. Both sides of the political spectrum have roundly condemned rehabilitation on a variety of grounds, but mainly because it did not produce results. This rejection did not stir up much enthusiasm for a debate on the other justifications for the criminal system. Rather, the discussion proceeded almost immediately to remedies of replacement. Without really distinguishing among the other goals of punishment, many critics simply asserted the need for a "justice approach" to discretion.[27] Yet a common definition of "justice" was not agreed upon. More often than not the word was used synonymously with one's preferred remedy.

The Courts and Procedural Reforms

Perhaps the most widely agreed upon solution was one already common to criminal law: procedural protections. The distrust of official discretion was patent in the various guarantees of the Bill of Rights, where an adversary process of testing and challenge had guaranteed an open, public, and evidence-based determination of issues of fact and law. Police had been drawn even more explicitly under the scrutiny of the courts by an application of fourth amendment jurisprudence which allowed review of search and seizure actions.[28] The *exclusionary rule* thus became one mode of review that created standards for police discretion. Further, the Supreme Court had gone on to apply due process requirements to other phases of the criminal justice process outside of adjudication. Prison discipline,[29] probation and parole revocation,[30] and other administrative areas of criminal justice were thereby subjected to restraints of procedural rights.[31] Even sentencing and parole release decision making have been gradually drawn into the ambit of "fundamental fairness" used by the court to describe minimal constraints of procedural due process.[32]

There are critical weaknesses with such a solution, however. For one thing, the Supreme Court and the highest state courts have been slow to extend the full range of procedural protections to areas outside of the adjudicatory process. An example of this hesitant displacement of expertise with full scale adversary review is juvenile law. While *Gault* appeared to draw delinquency law clearly within the orbit of the due process revolution, subsequent cases do not bear this out.[33] In fact the Court continues to parse out, on a case-by-case basis, where full due process applies and where it does not. Further, the Court has always reserved broad scope for executive expertise even in areas where some due process is accorded. For example, in parole revocations the Court has continued to go out of its way to assure parole boards that they need only provide minimal due process rights.[34] Finally, if such abovementioned limits were not sufficient to discourage reformers from using this solution, the Court itself has begun to undo earlier precedents where due process was accorded. For example, the exclusionary rule has been whittled and narrowed, and some predict sentenced to extermination within the life of the present Court personnel.[35] Prisoners' rights cases have been stopped short of achieving any full measure of due process guarantees.[36] This is not attributable only to the Burger Court mentality of reduced judicial activism. Essentially, courts in general have begun to regret their entry into the morass of monitoring prisons, police, and other executive agencies.[37]

Goals and Reform

More to the point than the weaknesses in a procedural solution to the fairness issue is the fact that all the procedural rights in the world cannot overcome a substantive rule by which the expert can decide as he wants — after all the evidence is in, of course. This became clear in the sentencing debates. While more due process could not hurt defendants in sentencing, and might even bring judges more into alignment on dispositions, if no rules exist on *why* we sentenced in the first place, then procedure becomes a false tool of fairness. But this raised the spectre of goals and the sense that reform could not wait upon the resolution of the philosophical issues between rehabilitationist and retributionist, deterrist and incapacitator. Indeed, the pragmatic compromises cast in the Model Penal Code were an indication that not only were Americans little inclined to the more enduring issues, but they feared getting bogged down in them.[38] The short-sightedness of the Code's approach might be tested by the length of time its sentencing provisions received favor among professionals. Today the sophistication of the Code and its indeterminate sentencing pattern appears quaint in its aspiration toward both fairness and rehabilitation.

At the same time, the critics of the past decade have not flocked to seminars on goals. Despite the work of the Committee on Incarceration in laying out the issues, this feature of their recommendations has not found great support.[39] Goals may be legitimate for starting the discussion on fairness, but few practical people seem inclined to follow it up in devising systems based on goal priorities. Witness the uncomfortable sense of pragmaticism when one finds a discussion of the parole guidelines model where severity (retribution) is "balanced" with the salient factor score (incapacitation).[40] Intellectually, these concepts appear to have little in common, yet pragmatically they are the fundamental issues in the debate. It is not, as Henry Hart noted for the Model Penal Code framers, that goals can be reduced to unity, but that goals need to be separated and placed within a framework of priority.[41] To date this has not happened.

But if a full-scale debate over goals has not occurred, a partial debate has taken place. As stated at the beginning of this chapter, the critics have gotten far enough into the issues to identify rehabilitation as an inappropriate basis for release.[42] Whether it is also inappropriate as part of an overall program of correction remains unclear. Likewise, the use of predictive techniques for incapacitory purposes has been criticized, but the problem remains unresolved. Though several of the critics roundly condemn the use of dangerousness as an adequate category of prediction, others show confidence in expectancy tables which predict rates of recidivism generally.[43] Deterrence has been largely lumped with retribution or just deserts as "punishment" and remains undiscussed as a separate, and indeed contrary, explanation of the penal system.

Rejection of Discretion and Piecemeal Reform

Barring the complete answer that a resolution of the goals debate might offer, most reformers have opted for narrower remedies, predominately in the form of radical to moderate changes. Their proposals have ranged from creation of a rule-making process, whereby agencies would be given the power to direct their own future more competently, to the abolition of almost all discretion across the breadth of the system. That the majority of these proposed remedies fell within the middle range of some sort of standards to limit discretion should not surprise us. They represented the views of moderate persons who felt an inch was an ell in a system as massive and unevolved as criminal justice.

The American Friends Report advanced the most absolute model for the elimination of discretion.[45] Their argument was, in essence, that discretion reflected a political conception of criminal justice which was intolerable under a constitutional government. The criminal law should be as narrow and precise as possible; police should be bound by a code of full enforcement; courts should offer full due process to each defendant; and sentences should reflect determinate amounts based on the seriousness of the offense.[46] The rigidity of the system was the only guarantee that individual defendants would be treated equally. But there was another element to the overall plan that suggested that the Friends realized that their plan was idealistic. They insisted that the poor and minorities, most often the victims of selective enforcement and sentencing, be politically empowered to determine their own lives.[47] This suggests that an adversarial element would remain strong in even this narrowly specified sort of system; which further suggests that in whatever system, discretion would still persist in some form and need the antidote of adversarial challenge.

None of the other critics went as far as the American Friends. For one thing, most were willing to recognize the arguments made by Professor Davis in favor of discretion as an essential part of law:[48]

> Discretion is a tool, indispensable for individualization of justice. All governments in history have been governments of laws and of men. Rules alone, untempered by discretion, cannot cope with the complexities of modern government and modern justice. Discretion is our principal source of creativeness in government and law.

As Professor Vorenberg laid out the problem, it was a matter of narrowing discretion, not eliminating it.[49] How one narrowed was a problem that was approached from several different angles.

Apart from *Struggle for Justice,* few reformers took a systemwide perspective. Each chose a single phase of the decisional network, or several closely related phases. This made a good deal of sense since the problem of discretion varied across the system and required careful analysis for each phase. But it also created a problem of piecemeal reform. For example, Illinois created determinate sentences within a newly reformed corrections code which had been grounded on Model Penal Code philosophy.[50] Could such an amalgam be expected to function appropriately according to either philosophy? Like all reforms, it was a contest between old ways and new ways, and perhaps the artful compromise was all that reformers could expect. But reform in one area, such as sentencing, without reform in contiguous areas, also generated problems. It has been suggested, as mentioned previously, that controls in sentencing will simply displace the power to make decisions to less appropriate places, such as the prosecutor's office or the police station.[51] The dilemma of an all-or-nothing reform was a serious one.

Rule-Making as Flexible Reform

Rule-making has emerged as the most flexible general remedy for unnecessary discretion. It has the advantage of being administrative in nature, rather than legislative. It represents a gradual approach to the problem that builds upon the experience of the agency possessing the discretion and allows rules to be created that have firm foundations in fact. The rule-making process provides for input from both sides of the system because it is open to public debate and discussion; it is subject to continual review for change as experience builds and it has the effect of law once formally adopted by the agency.[52]

But the very reasons that make rule-making so attractive also underlie its weakness. First, criminal justice agencies have not had a history of rule-making.[53] Even the courts have adopted rules of self-governance reluctantly, frequently under interdict of constitutional ruling from superior courts.[54] Further, rule-making supposes a spontaneous activity by agencies that have continually shown a great reluctance to change. Except for direct inducement through contempt of court, little has been accomplished by this self-initiating process.[55] And now even the courts show reluctance to take on serious reform efforts for police and prisons.[56] Another set of problems arises from the effect rule-making might have on legal liability of the agency. Both police and prosecutors have been bothered by the spectre of self-imposed rules which lay foundations for civil liability or defeat of prosecution.[57]

More serious problems lie in the nature of the type of rules to be devised. In some areas of the system the practical problems of creating rules for polymorphous, indeterminate situations seem overwhelming. For instance, some argue that police simply cannot respond to a set of rules that prescribe for complex human relationships.[58] Their work is necessarily individualistic, since police perform a multitude of tasks which include, but also go beyond, arrest for prosecution. Rules would be riddled with exceptions the very first day of their inauguration and police would come to disregard their force.

Another problem with rules is the nature of the policy they are intended to embody. In law enforcement, in particular, there are policies that perhaps should not be widely known. For instance, the unsavory but necessary practices surrounding the use of informers or of immunity granted by prosecutors might be misunderstood by the public.[59] The argument goes that while these areas certainly need controls, to subject them to public discussion might have counterproductive results. The short answer to this may well be that these areas, more than most others, need the sunlight of public discussion since they impinge upon other values in the criminal justice system so directly.[60]

A third difficulty with rules in some areas of the system is the fact that we have relatively little or no objective information on which they might be based. The experience of individual officials has never been accurately coded and only commonsense judgments have prevailed. Yet without some objective norm against which to measure such judgments, rules might very well be a legitimation of rank prejudice.[61]

Parole and Sentencing Guidelines

A major reform effort has gathered around this very type of problem. In the parole area, and now in sentencing, Professors Wilkins, Gottfredson and associates have propounded a "guidelines" approach in which, through statistical methods, various groups of parole board members or judges can determine what norms they are actually following in their dispositional practice.[62] The technique is meant to reflect actual practice and to provide the group with the ability and incentives for consistency, as well as a means of assessing the policy implications of their practice. It is intended as a heuristic device whereby the persons most immediately involved can discover what they are actually doing. Yet it builds into the discovery process a framework of policy in which the severity score of offenses is balanced with the factors indicative of recidivism. This raises the question of whether reality has not been preempted by theory. Does this balance occur in practice, or is it imposed by method? In any event, the guidelines approach has attracted a wide audience of advocates. Not only has the Federal Parole Commission adopted the guidelines approach for parole release decisions, but a growing number of state parole boards have taken up the method in both experimental and adoption phases.[63]

The advantages of guidelines are clear. They offer a measurement of reality to groups under public pressure to account for their actions. The guidelines approach purports to do no more than provide a clear pattern of present practice and to locate the power of policy change in the body of those engaged in the practice.[64] While guidelines might provide material for policy change at a higher level, for instance in a state supreme court or in a legislative body created for that purpose, they still require accountability; that is, guidelines necessitate the recording of any decisions made, thereby monitoring the parties making those decisions. Also, guidelines are subject to change over time.[65] As the decision makers clarify their own standards through practice, they might begin to see a need for a shift where certain categories are inappropriate. This they would accomplish through the use of the "special reasons" exception to the guidelines.

But guidelines have not escaped criticism. The first phase of guidelines may become its only phase as they would tend to "chase the mean" toward a central pattern of actual practice. The only policy would be consistency.[66] The guidelines have also been accused of incorporating racially sensitive factors.[67] If unemployment among minority youth is double or triple that of others, then to incorporate this as a salient factor in predicting recidivism on which longer sentences are based seems doubly unjust. Even in terms of offense severity, one wonders whether offenses have not been scored upon hidden racial measures which reflect our concern about "street crime" instead of about types of less racially identified offenses.

Finally, guidelines have been accused of breaching separation of powers. By their very clarity, guidelines demonstrate that the decision group exercising broad discretionary powers in fact determines what the sentence of various individuals will be. By itself, this fact is unexceptionable. But where it crosses with previously asserted power, then the decision maker must justify his authority. Let us take the example of the Federal Parole Commission. In a series of cases, the Federal appellate courts have examined the charge of inmates that the Parole Commission hearing officers have overridden sentences set by courts.[68] The argument is that the court has authority to fix the sentence and within that framework the Parole Commission has authority to apply its guidelines. But where the Commission lengthens the incarceration of the inmate, then it exceeds its power and trenches upon the judicial authority.[69]

Taking this problem a step further back in the sentencing process, it could be asserted that courts themselves should not be free to create norms for sentencing without explicit legislative authority.[70] As long as sentencing authority was indeterminate, few problems arose. But once the ideology of the justice approach is adopted, the tension between courts and legislatures becomes obvious. If the courts, or separate commissions are authorized to determine sentence length according to general standards unspecified in legislation, then in fact a critical policy issue devolves to groups beyond the direct reach of representative government. It will be the judges who in fact are determining penalties, not legislatures. Even though current practice tolerates this very fact, under the more explicit standards of the guidelines, this displacement of power becomes clear and unnerving. This reflects, as well, the concern about police that critics of Professor Davis have raised.[71] If police are given, or found to have, authority to set standards for nonenforcement, does not this create a gap in the logic of separation of powers upon which our general form of government is based?

Legislative Standards and Commissions

One answer to this conundrum lies in legislative standards. The problems with such an approach are considerable. The main objection is that such standards become rigid the moment they are enacted.[72] It is unlikely that the legislature will return to re-examine them on a regular basis. Further, such standards will either be too detailed, and thus immobilizing in practice, or too vague, and without guidance for power. Legislative standards raise, too, the issue of goals. If there has not been agreement on some ultimate grounds of policy choice, then standards will tend to be contradictory and confusing. Unless more clarity is forthcoming on goals, then the legislature will be forced into blind choices.[73] Whether or not sufficient clarity currently exists is a matter of debate. To date, only the determinate sentencing states have opted for such an explicit legislature choice, though just as obviously, even they have not completed their debate on goals.

A halfway approach to legislative standards has been the creation of commissions to accommodate change.[74] These commissions are given authority to review practices and then enact rules or report to the legislature for enactment of rules to govern the practice involved. A combination of legislative standards plus a commission with an oversight function for reform also attempts to compromise the rigidity of legislative action and the nonaccountability of self-imposed standards.[75]

Administrative Decentralization

There is a final reform proposition based on a somewhat different approach to the problem of discretion. This suggests changes in the bureaucracy of the decision-making process for more direct accountability to both the public and the individual offender. While other reformers have probably suggested similar patterns of change, Rosett and Cressey have been forthright in their discussions regarding the practice of plea bargaining.[76] These authors argue that discretion is necessary but in need of greater accountability. The appropriate way to preserve both values is to decentralize decision making and open it up to direct public scrutiny and participation. They would first reduce the range of choices which a prosecutor has by shortening sentences. But they would allow for a creative exchange among all parties to the offense for the determination of sentence. This would mean that patterns of sentences would emerge along sectional lines which would better reflect local choices and, of course, change over time.

This reform suggestion encompasses several items from other proposals. The chief element here is that the public would become more directly involved in the process of norm determination. Professor Davis' rule-making proposal suggests this same thing in his "public comment" process for administrative rule-making.[77] Norval Morris had made much the same suggestion about plea bargaining in his book, *The Future of Imprisonment*.[78] The American Friends suggest a broader, but similar, norm of political self-determination, though without the details of policy input suggested by Rosett and Cressey.[79] One wonders, however, whether any such norm can prevail against an entrenched professionalism which is jealous of its discretionary prerogatives and whether or not the public is capable of a sharp enough focus to prevail against the experience which bureaucracy supposes. Decentralization and participation has its attractions, yet it presumes a great deal of give on the part of the haves, and as well as a great deal of take on the part of the current have-nots.

Implementation of Reform Proposals

The above reform proposals are in various stages of growth and development. For instance, determinate sentencing has been enacted in seven jurisdictions and is under discussion in many more.[80] Sentencing guidelines probably are competing as a solution which offers more flexibility, and yet have not been enacted statewide in as many jurisdictions.[81] Parole release has been abolished in the determinate sentencing states, yet has been undergoing a rapid changeover to guidelines in many other states.[82] Courts continue their efforts to monitor parole-release decisions and have grown move uniform in demanding minimum due process standards for decision making.[83] Probation and parole revocation also continues under court guidance with decisions spelling out implications of earlier precedents.[84] Unfortunately, courts have the basic drawback of retail reform efforts spread over time and across jurisdictions.

While sentencing and parole have been the major theme of reform efforts, other stages of the system have experienced their own kinds of justice revivalism. Police have been preached at by a series of national commissions to develop their own sets of standards.[85] That their response to date has been disappointing does not indicate that police are unaware of the pressure exerted by these specific calls to action. There are jurisdictions that have instituted rule-making.[86] There are detailed models created by academic and professional groups for many of the discretionary areas of law enforcement.[87] Nearly all of the professional authors in the field have made similar suggestions.[38] Whether police can successfully outwait their critics depends largely on the incentive courts and legislatures offer or impose upon them. But if the courts draw back from their monitoring role and legislatures hesitate to undertake direct mandates on police to develop standards, then little can be expected from self-imposed reform.

Prosecutors have been even more immune to direct justice reforms. Asserting the traditional independence of their office, prosecutors have resisted the idea of standards for the selection and prosecution of cases.[89] While plea bargaining as such has had a plethora of suggested standards,[90] other phases of prosecutorial practice have remained obscure. A scattering of offices around the country have undertaken self-imposed standards,[91] but these hardly represent a groundswell of reform. The federal prosecutors have a common manual of practice,[92] but one is left to wonder how far it might reach in scope and what binding power it can or will have. On the other hand, the pressure from sentencing reform brings into focus how much of present sentencing practice depends on the consent of the prosecutor.[93] Without reforms in that office, sentencing guidelines or standards may be nugatory.

Finally, prisons, one of the original sites for justice complaints, have been slow to respond with uniform restraints on their prerogatives. Individual prisons and some statewide systems have been brought to specific articulation of standards by prisoner litigation.[94] But even here the gains tend to be frittered away over time and courts find themselves going back to square one with the same prison at later dates. The Supreme Court and other lower courts have created some general patterns of due process for basic prison decision making, but again enforcement has been sporadic and evasion widespread. In the offing are a set of national standards which the American Bar Association has fashioned.[95] Delay of their final approval has been caused by the desire of the American Correctional Association to either promote their own standards or join the Bar Association in a compromise version of the two.[96] Such standards would have a salutary effect on court response to litigation since a common set of solutions by the protagonists indicates a pragmatic compromise which the courts would be encouraged to adopt. Built into the standards would be a rule-making power which would reflect the wisdom of progressive experience and allow for inmate input.[97] Few prisons have undertaken on their own, or by legislative initiative, rule-making. It appears at this time that the courts, through litigation, are still the best hope of guided discretion.

The Pattern of Justice and Its Implications

Justice and Reform

All of the reforms described in this chapter are based on the fundamental notion, that discretion in criminal justice has been far too broad to render decisions fair to the individuals and public involved. The common element of reform in this discretionary wasteland has been a search for objective standards that could provide control and predictability of official decision making across the system. Although standards at each decision point tend to reflect the immediate purposes of that stage of the system, there has been a common theme which unifies in a general way the logic of all these standards.

The predominant element in the solution has been a rejection of individualization based on a rehabilitative approach. The crime itself, ranked in a taxonomy of seriousness, has been substituted as an objective measure of system response. This logic, while not fully developed into a definitive goal statement, has taken on the coloration of a retributive or "just deserts" system.[98] The problem has been, as mentioned previously, that the policy debate begun by several of the critics has never been concluded. Thus, while the implications of an act-based system are clearly retributive in nature, there is a great deal of hesitation about what such an appellation might mean, and whether other goals, most particularly incapacitation, are to be rejected entirely or somehow reconciled with the overriding goal of just deserts. I want to conclude this survey of justice modeling with some reflections on the logic of what we have proposed as reforms for wayward discretion in light of determining whether we wish to pursue the ideal of a justice-defined system.

Actually, one can identify few retributivists among the legion of critics.[99] Most of the retributive features of the present justice reforms derive from *consequences* of a retributive approach rather than from principles. For instance, proportionality *as a principle* is not so much accepted as its consequences of objectivity, and thus an explicit limit on penalties. When retribution is squarely faced, most of the critics quail at proposing a system of punishment "for its own sake." If moral consensus is enunciated as the basis of retributive condemnation, most would hesitate to say that such consensus is possible, or perhaps even legitimate, in a society politically committed to pluralistic values. My argument is simply this. However attractive a strict justice approach may appear to be, few of the critics have become true believers in this approach and will abandon and modify their positions when the consequences become less attractive, either by way of external constraints or by reason of unwelcome logical extensions of principle. Let us look at some of these external and internal problem areas.

Internal Consequences of Justice

Offense seriousness appears essential to any act-based system of punishment. The problem of creating such a scale is not so much a matter of logic as it is a matter of politics. At present we have an exaggerated bulge at the person-crime end of the scale where minor assaults might reap terrible penalties, while major property offenses merit only fines or small amounts of incarceration. No one denies that this scale reflects some basic value choices common to most societies. Nor can it be denied that the American public harbors a dread of physical assault, especially from strangers. But what is fair to both public and individual offender in this matter? Can we, and do we want to, create a fair scale of seriousness? The politics of offense seriousness have not been widely broached as a problem for justice reforms, but I sense that it is a major roadblock. The sense of fairness which would structure any such rearrangement of felonies most likely would reflect value choices that are identified with subgroups in society. This points to multiple scales across multiple communities of values. How far should we go toward localizing justice as an answer to this problem? Do we not invite a similar anarchy which our present system incorporates?

No one has been willing to confront or discuss the implications of "local justice." It creates formidable problems within the context of a constitutional framework where cruel and unusual punishment is growing more refined. The principle behind "local justice" is simple but illusive: deserved punishment grows out of moral consensus. In simple societies of the past, the unity of community-values-law was an unexceptionable fact. As simplicity gave way to complexity, the fit between law and values became attenuated and was replaced by the external norm of Bentham's utilitarianism. The real issue is whether we have sufficient community to ground a consensus which would bear the weight of punishment. In our pluralistic and mobile world the boundaries are ambiguous and changing, yet the moral consensus that exists in various overlays of organizational groupings seems to demand a notion of subtantive justice. Even if we could resolve this problem, other questions remain.

Seriousness is not a unitary concept, unfortunately. Apart from disagreement among persons on how to scale types of conduct, there remains the problem of gravity of offense based on degree of personal culpability. The Model Penal Code attempted to bring some order to the chaos of common law by propounding a four-level scale of culpability: purpose, knowledge, recklessness, and negligence.[100] Added to this ranking are the complications of age, intoxication, duress, and other states of emotional instability. Whatever an offender may have accomplished by his conduct, we are forced to ask, "With what degree of choice did he act?" An act-based system suggests that we depend entirely on the physical consequences of conduct. This is not the case in a system that makes blame the basis of punishment.[101] This further suggests that we re-enter the world of actor characteristics. But the major difference between such actor-based criteria and those of a rehabilitation system is the narrowness of purpose. When we ask if a person is blameworthy, we have a set of acts which delineate the past, together with testimony about motive, if any. The inferences we draw may be crude as to subjective guilt, but they pale beside the problems of looking at a person and defining why he committed the crime, and then using this as a basis of predicting what he will do in the future. While culpability does argue for continued discrimination among certain persons who have committed the same harmful acts, it need not be seen as essentially destructive of all objective calibration of gravity of offense.

A final factor that complicates the seriousness scale which a just desert system requires is prior offense. It has become another major element of agreement among critics.[102] In order to punish equally for equal crimes, the critics argue, prior offenses must be taken into consideration. The retributive argument is that such prior offenses demonstrate an element of enhanced culpability.[103] The defiant offender surely offends more seriously, for example by his second or third rape. There are problems with exaggerations of scale for prior offenses when we come to the penalty side of the proportion, but for now let us look at other problems. First of all, prior offense suggests that there is a moral continuity between crimes. If we abstain from any element of predictive analysis, it is hard to assert such a basis. Indeed, even should we so suppose, there is the interposition of a penalty which the offender has already suffered. Is it fair to say that the law should count *again* what has been accounted for fairly by the offender in the past? True, repeated violations give us confidence of our moral judgments. But this confidence does not affect the punishment which we impose. However confident we are that a person has indeed intentionally taken the property of another, does the quality of confidence change the norm of intentionality? Can a person be pushed into a moral category of hyper-intentionality? Indeed, repeat offenses might suggest the opposite. In any event, there is a logic to not taking prior offenses into consideration in designating proportion.

Yet such a suggestion seems feckless. Not only is there political unanimity on prior offenses, but the guidelines have clearly demarked it as uniquely predictive of recidivism.[104] While one is grateful for the more objective norm of past convictions as a basis of prediction, still the question is raised as to whether there is any logic to the supposed retributive explanation. Perhaps the logic of retribution breaks down at some point and gives way to the logic of vengeance. If one intends a preventive function for punishment, and prior offense is highly predictive of recidivism, then perhaps two measures instead of one are called for — out of frustration at anticipated failure. To be sure this reaction may well be a retributive one, but it does appear to be at odds with the logic of proportionality.

The problems of constructing a penalty scale appear less arduous. Indeed, they are. But there are concerns here which merit attention. The major problem is one of discontinuities. Between the death penalty (if we suppose it will continue to appear on the books) and imprisonment, and between imprisonment and probation, to name only the major categories, there are telling gaps.[105] Even within categories, such as imprisonment, there are shades of penal severity that have nothing to do with labels, and a great deal to do with public finances. But it is at the lower end of the scale that the logic of retribution suffers most. Even in the states that have adopted determinate sentencing, the option of probation remains a more-or-less free choice of the judge.[106] This means that whether a person serves time or is placed on probation does not directly reflect a difference in crime seriousness. Even supposing we could control for this, there is still a major difference between probation as it currently operates and incarceration. The old rehabilitationist notion of a "continuum of treatment," which meant a continuum of control, was never achieved in practice.[107] Nor is the system likely to be reshaped simply to fulfill the logic of justice.

It is especially when prior offenses are thrown into the equation that proportionality of the penalty scale becomes skewed. In many jurisdictions a second or third felony conviction can bring wildly escalating penalties into play.[108] The problem of proportioning these past convictions is difficult in itself, as mentioned previously. But it becomes a major flaw when set against the background of past and present practice where convictions are only weakly reflective of the crimes committed. This is further exaggerated when the total system of offenses, their scaling, and the inefficiency of law enforcement are added. Can one in conscience make prior offenses that significant a variable in a system that has equality among offenders as a priority value? Is the solution to start counting only when the priors are of face value? I doubt that there is an adequate answer to this problem, unless it would be to treat priors as past cancelled debts and use them only for a type of indication of special caution for counselling, rehabilitation, or the like. And doesn't this begin to look peculiarly familiar as discarded indeterminate sentencing?

The final set of internal problems derives from the fit between the seriousness scale and the penalty scale. A major consideration is the mandatory quality of the application of penalty to offense. The logic of a justice approach appears to demand such an application. Otherwise, choice reverts back to the appliers. On the other hand, nearly every proposal has incorporated a safety clause, allowing for a measure of flexibility.[109] This is grounded on the notion that each case will present unique characteristics which impel slight aggravation or mitigation from the designated penalty. While some slack might be taken up in redrafting substantive offenses to include the major aggravating factors,[110] still there will remain a margin necessary for sound administration. A problem arises when the sum of the margins all along the line simply creates a system where like cases are no longer treated alike. While one can depend on the autonomy of individual parts of the system to make such a possibility unlikely, one wonders how carefully such a problem will be monitored between courts and parole boards, for example, where collusion is always probable.

The penalty scale in the logic of retributive justice has no place for risk of recidivism. The guidelines, as suggested above, are essentially a marriage between a retributive scaled justice and preventive scaled incapacitation. No one has come forward with answers satisfying for this contradictory blend.[111] The suggestion is that prior offenses can be used to predict, but must be scaled to punish. I doubt that that satisfies the meaning of retributive justice. The guidelines do appear to have the merit of delineating actual practice. But within the justice framework this should be a prelude to eliminating the social defense qualities of punishment, even assuming we have the capacity to predict with accuracy who will offend again.

A final problem for the penalty scale lies in the place for "mercy." Unfortunately "mercy" has been exercised so haphazardly all along the line, producing a crazy-quilt justice, that its relationship to unfairness has become uncomfortably close. Nevertheless, once we have accepted the implications of "just deserts," there will be a need for an appropriate clemency power, especially at the deep end of the system where severity is greatest.[112] I doubt that the other actors in the system will be willing to dispense with their brands of "mercy," but logic calls for it to be exercised in an open, political fashion, and only in unusual circumstances. This raises the question of whether the principle of parsimony which is instinct in utilitarian systems operates here. I suggest that it does, but that it is distinctly not mercy. In utilitarian calculus, one apportions only that measure of punishment or incapacitation as will achieve the goal of restraint from crime, no more. The problems have been with our vexing doubt as to how much is needed. *When in doubt, use enough.* This has been justified by a further principle that once we have given the defendant the benefit of doubt as to his guilt and then convicted him, we are justified in erring on the side of the public in restraining him.[113] For retributive justice the calculus is not done in individual cases, but among categories of offenses. The least restrictive alternative would be built into the scale and applied equally to individual cases. Mercy in single cases would be exercised from outside the system at a point of open political process accountable to the public.

External Problem for Justice Reform

The external problems for a justice model are as critical as its internal ones, and perhaps less tractible. I will mention only three. First, the importance, and yet the improbability, of creating a justice model for criminal justice is the moral order it imposes. The logic of such a system suggests a social justice spread broadly in the community. The American Friends' *Struggle for Justice* highlighted the tension between logic and reality when it made its proposals for change. What would a justice system look like set down in a social order where social justice does not prevail? On the other hand, without conscience operating at this end of the total social system, is it likely that we will understand the injustices interwoven in the social fabric? If crime rates among black teenagers are disproportionately high, can we simply apply justice without also asking what this disproportion means? I doubt that we can. I sense that the indeterminate sentence with its patina of rehabilitative gloss spared us the question, whereas retributive justice will not.

The second external problem is the politics of reform. It seems unlikely that the logic of the justice model will change the present monolithic (or is it polylithic?) system. This system has operated on a parochial basis for ages, with professionalism growing steadily to hold it in place. There may be certain changes effected in the language of the laws, but one wonders how far these will penetrate the practice. Then, too, what can even be legislated? The fear is that legislatures will respond to the justice theme by enacting harsh and rigid laws which will guarantee a bloated prison system. The fear is not ungrounded.[114] At best piecemeal legislation is probable, with the dislocations of power such enactments are likely to bring about. To create a single reform, to whatever level of justice one might imagine, and in a uniform fashion, seems impossible. On the other hand, to create a climate of reform within a justice model set before the public in one form or another may be valuable. One senses that the ferment across the system has some unity to it: a growing awareness that we cannot continue to allow discretion to go unexamined and the glaring need for some common philosophy of justice.

The third obstacle to reform appears to be the local community. As already suggested, there appears to be some logic to the focus of attention on smaller groups within society for a sense of justice. The impracticalities of reform appear to re-enforce this sense. Yet can the justice model absorb the realities of tribal justice? The fear of many reformers is that given the opportunity, the local community would exercise a grim retributivism against the unwelcome stranger, the deviant, the rejected in society. This may be so in an unguided system of whim. But there is evidence that community values need to be engaged in order to invest the system with the legitimacy it needs to enforce the morality of the criminal law. I sense this need in our present reforms. Yet we do not have an adequate mechanism to draw upon this source for our standards. How such a future system might look is hard to predict, but the awareness is clearly present and the element of public participation, whether by way of comment on rules, or by direct participation in the resolving of disputes, has been placed on the table for discussion and experimentation.[115] Community participation should not be sold short as a way of forging just standards for the practice of criminal justice.

Notes

1. Oral argument in *Delaware v. Prouse* (No. 77-1571), United States Supreme Court, as reported in *U. S. Law Week* 47 L. W. 3491 (1/17/79).
2. See Chapter 1. By "justice model," I intend to convey a general pattern of control on discretion which emphasizes seriousness of offense as the primary criterion. See McAnany, Merritt and Tromanhouser, "Illinois Reconsiders 'Flat time': An Analysis of the Impact of the Justice Model," 52 *Chicago-Kent L. Rev.*, (1976), pp. 622-26.
3. L. Wilkins, J. Kress, D. Gottfredson, J. Caplan, A. Gelman, *Sentencing Guidelines: Structuring Judicial Discretion* (Washington, D.C.: Law Enforcement Assistance Administration, Feb. 1978).
4. James Vorenberg, "Narrowing the Discretion of Criminal Justice Officials," 1976, *Duke L. J.*, pp. 652-654.
5. National Commission on Law Observance and Enforcement (Washington, D.C., Government Printing Office, 1931). Reprinted Montclair, N.J.: Patterson-Smith, 1968, *Report on Lawlessness in Law Enforcement* (No. 11).
6. For an early and authoritative portrait of the decisional patterns of criminal justice, see F. Remmington, D. Newman, E. Kimball, M. Melli, and H. Goldstein, *Criminal Justice Administration* (Indianapolis: Bobbs-Merrill, 1969).
7. This summary is based upon Vorenberg, supra., note 4, pp. 655-61.
8. *Id.*, p. 660.
9. H. L. A. Hart, *Punishment and Responsibility* (Oxford Press, 1968).
10. Barbara Wootton, *Crime and Criminal Laws* (London: Stevens and Sons, 1963).
11. H. Packer, *The Limits of the Criminal Sanctions* (Stanford: Stanford U. Press, 1968).
12. Kenneth Culp Davis, *Discretionary Justice* (Baton Rouge, La.: Louisiana State University Press, 1969).
13. American Friends Service Committee Report, *Struggle for Justice* (New York: Hill and Wang, 1971), p. 124.
14. *Id.*, pp. 145-53.
15. *Id.*, pp. 147-48.
16. *Id.*, Chapter 6, pp. 83-99.
17. See, e.g., M. Frankel, *Criminal Sentences* (N.Y.: Hill and Wang, 1973).

18. For an example of this school of thought, see James Q. Wilson, *Thinking About Crime* (N.Y.: Basic Books, 1975).
19. D. Lipton, R. Martinson, and J. Wilks, *Effectiveness of Correctional Treatment* (N.Y.: Praeger, 1975).
20. For an earlier survey of treatment programs, see Robinson and Smith, "The Effectiveness of Correctional Programs," 17 *Crime and Delinquency* (1971), p. 67.
21. For an early delineation of the problem, see Morris and Hawkins, *The Honest Politicians Guide to Crime Control* (Chicago: University of Chicago Press, 1969), pp. 185-192. Also, A. Dershowitz, "Preventive Confinement: A Suggested Framework for Constitutional Analysis," 51 *Texas L. Rev.*, (1973), p. 1306.
22. N. Morris, *The Future of Imprisonment* (Chicago: University of Chicago Press, 1974), pp. 62-73.
23. This is illustrated in the Supreme Court's rejection of arguments against the validity of the death penalty statutes for murder where evidence of their deterrent value is clearly lacking. *Gregg v. Georgia,* 428 U.S. 153 (1976).
24. See, e.g., American Friends Service Committee, *Struggle for Justice,* pp. 48-67.
25. National Advisory Commission on Criminal Justice Standards and Goals, *Task Force Report: Courts,* Washington, D.C., 1973. Standard 3.1, pp. 46-49.
26. National Advisory Commission on Criminal Justice Standards and Goals, *Task Force Report: Police,* Washington, D.C., 1973, pp. 283-84. The Task Force recommended that police departments supplement the prosecutor's office with their own legal counsel. Standard 11.2.
27. For a description of some common elements of such an approach, see P. McAnany, "Restitution as Idea and Practice: The Retributive Prospect," in B. Galloway and J. Hudson (eds.), *Offender Restitution in Theory and Action* (Lexington, Mass.: Heath, 1978), pp. 20-24.
28. *Weeks v. United States,* 232 U. S. 383 (1914); *Mapp v. Ohio,* 367 U. S. 643 (1961).
29. *Wolff v. McDonnell,* 418 U. S. 539 (1974).
30. *Mempa v. Rhay,* 389 U. S. 128 (1967); *Morrissey v. Brewer,* 408 U. S. 471 (1972).
31. E.g., the whole juvenile process became subject to a variety of court holdings which are reviewed in various volumes in the Institute for Judicial Administration — American Bar Association, *Juvenile Justice Standards Project,* 23 volumes (Cambridge, Mass.: Ballinger Publishing Co., 1977-78).
32. See, generally, R. Singer and W. Statsky, *Rights of the Imprisoned* (Indianapolis: Bobbs-Merrill Co., 1974) & *Supplement* chapters 11 & 22, 1978. The Supreme Court has under review the issue of how far due process restrains state parole release. *Greenholtz v. Inmates of the Nebraska Penal and Correctional Complex,* No. 78-201; argued 1/17/79, 24 *Criminal Law Reporter,* 4189, Feb. 14, 1979.
33. *In re Gault,* 387 U.S. 1 (1967). For an excellent review of this process of selective application, see L. Schultz and F. Cohen, "Isolationism in Juvenile Court Jurisprudence," in M. Rosenheim (ed.) *Pursuing Justice For the Child* (Chicago: University of Chicago, 1976), pp. 20-42.
34. This was clearly the implication of the right to counsel at such hearings. *Gagnon v. Scarpelli,* 411 U.S. 778 (1973).
35. As Mr. Justice Brennan noted pessimistically in dissent: "In *Mapp,* the Court thought it had 'close[d] the only courtroom door remaining open to evidence

secured by official lawlessness' in violation of Fourth Amendment right . . . The door is again ajar. As a consequence, I am left with the uneasy feeling that today's decision may signal that a majority of my colleagues have positioned themselves to reopen the door still further and abandon altogether the exclusionary rule in search-and-seizure cases." *United States v. Calandra,* 414 U. S. 338 (1974), p. 365.

36. For a recent rebuff, see *Hawkins v. KQED* 98 Sup. Ct. 2588 (1978).
37. See, e.g., interview-article with United States District Court Judge Raymond Pettine, Special Report, "Prison Reform: The Judicial Process," 23 *Criminal Law Reporter,* No. 17 (Aug. 2, 1978); Also, A. Chayes, "Role of the Judge in Public Law Litigation," 89 *Harvard Law Review* 1281 (1976).
38. See, e.g., *Model Penal Code,* Comment, p. 4 (Tent. Draft No. 2, 1954).
39. The Committees Report is contained in A. von Hirsch, *Doing Justice* (N.Y.: Hill and Wang, 1976).
40. The authors of the Parole Commission Guidelines describe their purpose in a recent piece as not attempting "to *change* the policies observed, although it did include the development of mechanisms for increased control of the policies." D. Gottfredson, C. Cosgrove, L. Wilkins, J. Wallerstein, and C. Rank, *Classification for Parole Decision Policy,* National Institute of Law Enforcement and Criminal Justice, Washington, D.C., July, 1978, pp. 2-3.
41. Henry M. Hart, "Aims of the Criminal Law," 23 *Law and Contemporary Problems* (1958), p. 401.
42. E.g., D. Fogel, "*. . . We Are the Living Proof . . .*" (Cincinnati: Anderson Co., 1975).
43. For a general review of prediction problems and sentencing, see J. Coffee, "The Repressed Issues in Sentencing: Accountability, Predictability, and Equality in the Era of the Sentencing Commission," 66 *Georgetown Law Journal* (1978), p. 975.
44. For one account of reconciling these separate rationales, see von Hirsch, pp. 49-55.
45. American Friends Service Committee, *Struggle for Justice.*
46. *Id. passim,* especially pp. 145-53.
47. *Id.,* pp. 158-167.
48. K. Davis, *Discretionary Justice,* p. 25.
49. J. Vorenberg, supra., note 3.
50. P. McAnany, et al., supra., note 2, pp. 659-60.
51. A. Alschuler, "Sentencing Reform and Prosecutorial Power: A Critique of Recent Proposals for 'Fixed' and 'Presumptive' Sentencing," 126 *University of Pennsylvania Law Review* 550 (1978).
52. For the best brief analysis, see K. Davis, supra., note 11, especially pp. 215-33.
53. See, e.g., K. Davis, *Police Discretion* (St. Paul: West Publishing Co., 1975), especially pp. 32-51.
54. For a general assessment, see A. Ashman, "Measuring the Judicial Rule-Making Power," 59 *Judicature* 715 (1975).
55. For example, police have shown almost no initiative in response to repeated calls for rule-making by a variety of national commissions. See, e.g., H. Goldstein, *Policing a Free Society,* Cambridge (Mass.: Ballinger, 1977), pp. 116-117.
56. For example, the Supreme Court recently sidestepped the broader monitoring role of police. *Rizzo v. Goode,* 423 U. S. 362 (1976). For prisons, see, Comment, "Implementation Problems in Institutional Reform Litigation," 91 *Harvard Law Review* 428 (1977).

57. E.g., L. Beck, "The Administrative Law of Criminal Prosecution: The Development of Prosecutorial Policy," 27 *American University Law Review* 310 (1978) at pp. 358-373. But cf. *United States v. Caceres,* 440 U.S. 741 (1979).
58. James Q. Wilson, *Varieties of Police Behavior* (Cambridge: Harvard University Press), 1968 at pp. 278-84.
59. See, e.g., Beck, supra., note 57 at pp. 355-58.
60. For an example of how a public discussion of the issues in a sensitive police area might be structured, see J. Dix, "Undercover Investigations and Police Rule-Making," 53 *Texas Law Review* 203 (1975).
61. For an example, again drawn from policing, see M. Neithercutt and W. Moseley, *Arrest Decisions as Prelude To?* Vol. II (Davis, Calif: National Council on Crime and Delinquency, June, 1974).
62. D. Gottfredson, L. Wilkins, P. Hoffman, S. Singer, *The Utilization of Experience in Parole Decision-Making* (Washington, D.C.: U.S. Government Printing Office, November, 1974); L. Wilkins, J. Kress, D. Gottfredson, J. Caplan, A. Gelman, *Sentencing Guidelines: Structuring Judicial Discretion* (Washington, D.C.: Law Enforcement Assistance Administration, Feb. 1978).
63. Gottfredson, Wilkins and associates report that 31 states wanted to participate in the parole guidelines project and four others showed tentative interest. Gottfredson, et al., supra., note 62, p. 21. A recent article states that at least 15 states have adopted, or soon will adopt, a parole guidelines approach. K. Krajick, "Parole: Discretion is Out, Guidelines Are In," 4 *Corrections Magazine* 39 (Dec. 1978).
64. See, e.g., Wilkins, et al., supra., note 62, pp. 4-6.
65. *Id.*, pp. 29-30.
66. F. Zimring, "Making the Punishment Fit the Crime: A Consumers' Guide to Sentencing Reform," Occasional Papers, University of Chicago Law School. (1977).
67. Coffee, supra., note 43, pp. 1017-28.
68. For a summary of decided cases, see annotations at 18 U. S. C. A. § 4206 (1978).
69. *E.g., Geraghty v. United States Parole Commission,* 579 F. 2d 238 (3rd Cir. 1978).
70. This is a central thesis of the Coffee article, supra., note 43, where the author analyzes the accountability factors of the proposed federal sentencing commission.
71. R. Allen, "Police and Substantive Rule-Making: Reconciling Principle and Expediency," 125 *Univ. Pennsylvania Law Review,* 68 (1977).
72. This point is made generally by Davis, *Discretionary Justice,* supra., note 11. See, also, Zimring, supra., note 66.
73. McAnany, et al., supra., note 2.
74. First recommended by Judge Frankel, supra., note 17, it is now incorporated as a major element of the federal criminal law reform package. See, Coffee, supra., note 43.
75. This is the federal model described in Coffee, supra., note 43. The problem of nondelegation and legislative standards is discussed in Davis, supra., note 11, pp. 27-51.
76. A. Rosett and D. Cressey, *Justice By Consent,* Philadelphia: Lippincott, 1976, especially Ch. 8.
77. Davis, supra., note 11, pp. 97-141.
78. Morris, supra., note 22, pp. 50-57.
79. American Friends Service Committee, *Struggle for Justice,* supra., note 12.

80. Seven jurisdictions have enacted some form of determinate sentencing as of March, 1979. About twenty others are in the process of discussion or enactment.
81. Project staff of the Sentencing Guidelines in Albany, supra., note 62, have indicated that New Jersey has enacted guidelines (1978) and that at least four other states are in the process of developing them (Massachusetts, Michigan, Minnesota and Washington).
82. See materials cited, supra., at notes 62 and 63.
83. Supra., note 32.
84. Singer and Statsky, supra., note 32 at Ch. 26 and *Supplement*.
85. E.g., American Bar Association, *Standards for The Urban Police Functions*, (1973).
86. Goldstein, supra., note 55, p. 117 cites examples of four cities undertaking guideline activity.
87. The American Law Institute, *A Model Code of Pre-Arraignment Procedure* (1975) offers a series of guidelines fashioned along lines of court mandated areas. See, also *Project on Law Enforcement Policy and Rule-Making*, Arizona State College of Law, 1972.
88. See, e.g., Goldstein, supra, note 55, pp. 116-117.
89. A. Abrams, "Internal Policy: Guiding the Exercise of Prosecutorial Discretion," 19 *UCLA Law Review* (1971).
90. H. Uviller, "Pleading Guilty: A Critique of Four Models," 41 *Law and Contemporary Problems* 102 (1977).
91. Vorenberg, supra., note 3, p. 680 cites Harris County, Texas (1974) and King County, Washington (1976) as two examples.
92. United States Department of Justice, United States Attorneys Manual (1976) and Beck, supra., note 57, pp. 314-17.
93. See, e.g., Alschuler, supra., note 51.
94. See, Special Report, supra., note 37.
95. American Bar Association, *Standards Relating to the Legal Status of Prisoners*, published in 14 *American Criminal Law Review* 377 (1977).
96. Special Report, supra., note 37 at 11.
97. ABA, supra., note 95, Standard 8.2.
98. The most developed statements of a philosophy of penal sanctions are found in H. Packer, supra., note 10; N. Morris, supra., note 22; and von Hirsch, supra., note 39.
99. The lone retributivist among recent American professional commentators appears to be Jerome Hall. See his *General Principles of Criminal Law* (Indiana polis: Bobbs-Merrill, 1960, 2d ed.); von Hirsch comes closest to such positions, otherwise. See, e.g., Hanrahan and von Hirsch, *Abolish Parole?*, Washington, D.C.: Law Enforcement Assistance Administration, 1978.
100. American Law Institute, Model Penal Code (P. O. D. 1962), Sec. 2.02 and Commentary, Tentative Draft, No. 4 at 123 (1955).
101. For an analysis of culpability and its impact on a blame-based system, see M. Gardner, "Renaissance of Retribution — An Examination of *Doing Justice*," 1976, *Wisconsin Law Review* 781.
102. See, e.g., van Hirsch, supra, note 39, pp. 84-88; Twentieth Century Fund, *Fair and Certain Punishment* (N.Y.: McGraw-Hill, 1976), pp. 40-42.
103. See, e.g., von Hirsch, supra., note 39, pp. 84-88. But cf. Silving, "Rule of Law in Criminal Justice," in G. Mueller (ed.,) *Essays in Criminal Science* (South Hackensack, N.J.: Rothman), 1961 for contrasting rationales.
104. Coffee, supra., note 43, p. 1022.

105. How these gaps get filled by discretionary choices, see, C. Black, Jr., *Capital Punishment* (N.Y.: Norton, 1974); and F. Zimring, J. Eigen and S. O'Malley, "Punishing Homicide in Philadelphia: Perspectives on the Death Penalty," 43 *University of Chicago Law Review* 227 (1976).
106. See, e.g., Cal. Penal Code, § 1170(a) (1977).
107. The ideal of a scaled system of control is most fully developed in the New York Govern's Special Committee on Criminal Offenses, *Preliminary Report,* State of New York, 1968.
108. For example, Indiana provides for an *additional 30 years.* Indiana Stat. Ann. § 35-50-2-8, (Burns Ann. Supp. 1978).
109. The margins of this flexibility vary. For instance, Norval Morris suggested a ceiling within which individuation could continue, supra., note 22, pp. 13-20; von Hirsch would allow a margin not overlapping with the next higher category of seriousness, supra., note 39, pp. 98-106; and Fogel would allow leeway for mitigation and aggregation up to 50% for minor felonies to 20% for major ones, supra., note 42, pp. 254-55.
110. See, e.g., Twentieth Century Fund, supra., note 102, pp. 37-42.
111. For an attempt that tends to add to the confusion, see Coffee, supra., note 43, pp. 1080-92.
112. For example, Illinois has enacted a natural life sentence for certain type of murderers, Ill. Rev. Stat. C. 38 § 1005-8-1(a) (1) (1979), even though no one expects them to serve natural life. Indeed, the Parole Board's new function might well be absorbed in processing petitions for executive clemency. See, McAnany, et al., supra., note 2.
113. For an analysis of this factor in the system, see Dershowitz, supra., note 21.
114. For the harsh features of the Maine and Indiana laws, see M. Zalman, "The Rise and Fall of the Indeterminate Sentences," 24 *Wayne State University Law Review* 857 (1978), pp. 873-77.
115. For a direct community participation model, The Neighborhood Justice Centers, sponsored by the Law Enforcement Assistance Administration, are perhaps our best examples. See, D. McGillis and J. Muller, *Neighborhood Justice Centers* (Washington, D.C.: Law Enforcement Assistance Administration, October, 1977).

3. Restitution and the Justice Model*

Joe Hudson & Burt Galaway

Conceiving the field of corrections as based on justice seems, at first thought, self evident. In the same way, the notion that rule breakers should be held responsible for undoing the damages done seems sensible. We are concerned here with examining the relationship between these two apparently plausible conceptions. Key ingredients of David Fogel's justice model for corrections will be considered in relation to the use of financial restitution and community service work orders. First, however, we review some of the historical background of restitution and consider more recent policy, legal, and program developments, before assessing the extent to which such sanctions are consistent with the justice model for corrections.

While various writers use the term differently, for our purposes restitution refers to the criminal justice practice of holding offenders responsible for making financial or service payments to either the direct crime victim or a substitute victim.[1] The distinction from victim compensation is in the role of the offender. Victim compensation is a state administered insurance designed to provide reimbursement to a particular class of crime victims, usually victims of violent crimes, for specified losses. In a restitution scheme, in contrast, the offender is held responsible for undoing the damage done, either in the form of cash payments or service to either the direct or indirect crime victim. Most commonly the supervision of restitution payments is conducted by officials within the justice system, such as probation or parole officers, court clerks, or special restitution clerks, counselors, or coordinators.

Renewed Interest in Restitution

The idea that rule breakers should be held responsible for making good the damages done is an ancient settlement procedure. As communities became stabilized around a central form of leadership, legal codes were enacted stipulating the amount of money or goods to be paid by the offender to the victim in accordance with the nature of the harm done.[2] For example, under the system of composition in Anglo-Saxon England, the offender was allowed to "buy back the peace" he had broken by making restitution or "bot" to the victim and a fine or "wite" to the lord or king for overseeing the settlement.[3] The legal codes of Aethelberht (597-616) and Alfred the Great (871-900) contained a comprehensive system of tariffs for injuries done. King Alfred's code provided that damage to an ear was worth a specified amount, a nose another, and different amounts were stipulated for damages done to different parts of the body. An offender who failed to provide restitution to the victim was stigmatized as an outlaw and subject to execution by members of the community.

With the development of the common law during the twelfth and thirteenth centuries, the distinction between civil and criminal law was made and the wite was replaced by a discretionary fine set by the court and the bot transformed into damages assessed by a tribunal. The interest of the state gradually overshadowed and supplanted those of the victim; restitution was incorporated into the civil law of torts and came to play an insignificant role in the administration of criminal law.

While overshadowed by the role of the state in the administration of criminal justice, the idea of restitution did not totally disappear. For example, in 1516 Sir Thomas More urged that thieves be required to make restitution to victims and noted that "the Prince has no more right to stolen goods than the thief."[4] Restitution proposals continued to appear during the eighteenth and nineteenth centuries and writers from both the classical and positive schools of criminology endorsed the use of restitution. Jeremy Bentham[5] argued that restitution should be required as part of the punishment for a crime, particularly in terms of its potential deterrent effect, and Herbert Spencer[6] suggested that restitution be used as an alternative to imprisonment. In the nineteenth century, Raffaele Garofalo[7] and Enrico Ferri[8] incorporated restitution as a component of their social defense proposals, and with the development of probation services during the latter part of the nineteenth century, restitution came to be used as a condition of the probation order.

Over the past decade there has been a resurgence of interest in using a restitution sanction at alternative points in the justice system. In the area of public policy and standards, for example, the use of a restitution sanction has been recently emphasized: restitution is recognized as having precedence over a fine in standards approved by the American Bar Association,[9] has been held to be a useful sanction for both victims and offenders by the Advisory Council on the British Penal System,[10] and was supported as a sanction to be used in the Second Revision of the Model Sentencing Act.[11] The use of restitution as an alternative to imprisonment was specifically recommended by the 1972 Annual Chief Justice Earl Warren Conference on Advocacy,[12] as well as by the United States National Advisory Commission on Criminal Justice Standards and Goals[13] and the Law Reform Commission of Canada.[14]

Legislative interest in restitution has paralleled policy recommendations. Over the past several years, there has been a substantial amount of legislation passed by the various states directly addressing the use of restitution in the justice system. A 1970 Pennsylvania law[15] provides for restitution as part of a sentence and 1974 Iowa legislation[16] made restitution a condition of a deferred sentence for probation. The Maine criminal code that took effect in 1976 provides that one of the explicit purposes to be accomplished in sentencing is "to encourage restitution in all cases in which the victim can be compensated and other purposes of sentencing can be appropriately served."[17] The Tennessee Restitution Centers Act of 1976[18] authorizes the Commissioner of Corrections to establish and promulgate rules and regulations for residential restitution centers. The Centers may be established within or outside of prison; eligible offenders are those convicted for felonies carrying a sentence of five years or less. Virginia legislation of 1977[19] provides that no person convicted of a crime resulting in property damages shall be placed on probation or receive a suspended sentence unless restitution is ordered. Similar to Tennessee statutes, Mississippi legislation[20] that took effect on July 1, 1978, provides for the Department of Corrections to operate restitution centers.

This legislative interest in restitution is likely to generate increased judicial consideration of the legal issues raised by the practice and affect the way restitution is actually used within the justice system. For example, Oregon courts have addressed issues about the appropriate recipients of restitution and have determined that only direct crime victims, as compared to third party insurers, are entitled to receive restitution payments.[21] The Supreme Court in the case of *U.S. v. Durst* ruled that fines and restitution ordered as conditions of suspended sentences for persons sentenced under the provisions of the federal Youthful Offenders Act do not violate the rehabilitative intent of that legislation.[22] With the widespread use of restitution, substantial growth is likely to occur in the volume of case law shaping justice system practices.

The most dramatic evidence of the recent interest in restitution is found in the number and variety of formal program applications. While restitution has been commonly used as either an informal or incidental settlement procedure within the probation services, more formalized restitution projects have been put into operation within the past half dozen years at different points within and outside of the justice system. These projects differ from the more traditional use of restitution by placing explicit emphasis on restitution as a primary focus of project interventions. In addition, these recently developed restitution projects have established procedures for investigating the appropriateness of restitution in particular cases, procedures for the preparation of reports about victims and offenders to assist decision makers, and procedures for monitoring the extent to which offenders comply with the restitution plan.

While the precise number of operational restitution projects in this country is not known, we have some indication of the extent to which they have proliferated on the basis of several surveys conducted during the past three years. A survey of all state planning agencies and state corrections departments in 1976 identified a total of thirteen restitution projects serving adult offenders.[23] Using similar procedures in 1977, forty-six operational restitution projects serving adult offenders were found.[24] In late 1978, a questionnaire was sent to all criminal justice state planning agencies, criminal justice local planning units, and all state departments of corrections in the country.[25] Respondents were asked to identify financial or community service restitution projects operating within the jurisdiction that placed explicit emphasis on the use of financial restitution and/or community service as a primary focus of project interventions for adult misdemeanants or felons, and had established procedures for investigating the appropriateness of restitution in specific cases, for preparing reports about victims and offenders, and for monitoring compliance with restitution plans.

Eighty-seven operational restitution projects serving adults were identified from this survey. Four major categories of projects make up this population of projects: predominantly financial restitution projects in which at least 75% of the clients have only a financial restitution obligation; predominantly community service restitution projects in which at least 75% of the clients have only a community service obligation; projects using both financial and community service restitution for at least 75% of their clientele; projects using either financial or community service restitution for at least 75% of their clientele. This latter category includes projects in which some offenders had only a financial obligation while others had only a community service obligation. In these projects, community service is frequently substituted for financial restitution when it is felt that the imposition of a financial sanction would be a hardship on the offender. The largest proportion of this population of projects involved only a community service obligation (38%), the second largest category involved only a financial restitution obligation (35%), while smaller proportions of the projects involved both financial and community services (12%), or a mixture of financial and community service restitution (15%).

The identified projects are quite new; almost two-thirds of them have operated for less than three years. Approximately three-fourths of them are non-residential. The largest proportion of the projects are administered either by a state corrections agency (28%) or by local city or county corrections agencies (30%). Those projects that involve a community service work sanction tend to be more commonly administered by local corrections agencies or by non-governmental agencies. The projects are located at different points in the justice system, from pre-trial diversion and probation to work release and parole. They concentrate, however, at the probation level with over half dealing with probationers while another one-fifth deal with pretrial cases and another one-tenth with offenders either incarcerated or on work release status. Direct contact between victims and offenders is not a common practice; over three-fourths of the projects do not structure contact between victims and offenders; those projects using victim-offender contacts typically involve a small proportion of total clientele.

Some examples of projects being operated at different points in the justice system can be given. At the pre-trial level, for example, restitution projects have been established as part of a formal diversion program in a number of jurisdictions. Perhaps one of the best known of these is operated by the Pima County Attorney's Office in Tucson. This project serves non-serious felony defendants with formal meetings structured between victims and defendants for the purpose of reaching agreement about the amount and schedule of financial restitution to be made. Staff are involved in structuring victim-defendant meetings as well as in monitoring the completion of the scheduled restitution. Another example of a pre-trial restitution project is the Adult Diversion Program administered by the State Attorney General's Office in Rhode Island. In this project, some of the defendants are involved in only community service work while others make only financial restitution or a combination of the two. Staff help determine the amount of restitution to be made and monitor the defendant's compliance with the order. Victim-defendant contacts are not emphasized in this project.

The state of California has probably made the most extensive use of community service sanctions. Approximately fifty court referral projects have been established around the state to place offenders in tax supported or non-profit agencies for completion of a specified number of service hours. These projects differ in operational settings and funding bases but generally provide for screening defendants for placement and assignment to tasks, training and assistance to staff of user agencies, monitoring client progress, and reporting to courts.

A wide variety of restitution projects involve probationers. The Alternative Community Service Program in Hawaii, for example, is a statewide community service project administered by the judiciary. Project staff are located at various sites in the state and are responsible for implementing community service orders as set by the court. Staff do not get involved in determining the length of the community service order but do have responsibilities for arranging work placements and monitoring the completion of the judicial order. The broad scope of the project is evidenced by the fact that during a recent twelve month period, approximately five hundred offenders were admitted.

The state of Georgia has also made program use of financial restitution and community services with twelve Restitution Shelters established by the state corrections agency. Offenders are on probation and the shelters are seen as an alternative to incarceration in state prisons. All residents are felons, most of whom are engaged in completing community service, although a substantial proportion also have financial obligations. Staff in these facilities do not get involved in making determinations about the amount of the restitution obligation but are responsible for monitoring compliance with the probation order.

While restitution has received attention in the literature,[26] its use within the penal setting is quite rare. One project operating in conjunction with the penal sanction is in the Tennessee State Prison. A private industry has been established in that institution which pays inmate employees a minimum wage from which they are required to make restitution to their crime victims. Probation and parole staff contact victims in order to complete an assessment of the losses sustained and this information is then communicated to prison staff who work with the offender to develop a restitution plan. Approximately fifty inmates a year are admitted to the program and it is anticipated that with the expansion of private industry, the project will involve an increased number of inmates.

A number of restitution projects operate as work release programs. The Restitution Counselors Project in North Carolina is a state-wide work release program operated by the North Carolina Department of Corrections. This financial restitution project has staff located in various state correctional institutions with responsibilities for supervising the restitution obligation of work releasees. The courts are required by state law to set the amount of the restitution obligation and project staff are responsible for monitoring the offender's compliance. During a recent twelve month period, this project involved over five hundred offenders. A similar type of work release project is operated by the Criminal Sheriff in New Orleans out of the Parish Jail. Both financial and community service restitution is required of offenders in this project. Staff make decisions about the amount of restitution to be required and monitor compliance.

One of the few restitution projects operating at the level of parole is the Property Offenders Restitution Program in the Minnesota Department of Corrections. Inmates develop restitution agreements while incarcerated and complete the obligation while on parole to the community. Inmates who meet the project criteria and enter into a restitution agreement are then eligible for early parole release from the institution.

In summary, the last half dozen years have witnessed an exponential growth in the number and variety of financial restitution and community service projects operating around the country. Much of this has undoubtedly occurred because of Law Enforcement Assistance Administration funding, both through state block grants and through three national discretionary funding initiatives — financial restitution projects serving adults, financial or community service projects serving juveniles, and community service projects serving adults. Projects operate at points within and outside of the juvenile and adult justice systems, although the number of projects operating at later points in the system — incarceration, work release, parole — are fewer than those operating at the pre-trial and probation levels.

Restitution and the Justice Model

To what extent are recent developments in restitution policy, legislation, and programming logically consistent with the central ingredients of the justice model for corrections and, if logically consistent, to what extent are practices in line with theory? Among the components of the justice model considered here are justice-as-fairness, offender volition and responsibility, the use of non-custodial sanctions, and consideration for the victim of crime.

Justice as Fairness

The major emphasis of the justice model is on justice-as-fairness. From this perspective, restitution is an inherently fair sanction because of the logical relationship between the penalty and the nature and amount of damages done. The logic that equates causing damages and making good these damages is more straightforward than tortuous equations linking time in prison with damage done. Further, the restitution sanction can be explicitly related to the goal of undoing damages as compared with relatively vague and imprecise goals often characterizing formal rehabilitation programs. The total out-of-pocket expenses incurred by the victim can be fairly easily assessed and ordered in financial terms. Alternatively, damages can be assessed in financial terms and the offender can be held responsible for completing a specified number of community service hours at a given rate of pay.

The logic linking damages to making them good is likely to be perceived by offenders as fair. But, as Margery Fry pointed out several years ago, "to the offender's pocket it makes no difference what he has to pay as a fine, cost for compensation, but to his understanding of the nature of justice it may make a great deal."[27] Through the use of a restitution sanction, offenders may better understand that direct injuries have been done to victims. The responsibility for remedying injuries in terms of completing the restitution order then lies with the offender. In the final analysis, the offender must decide whether or not to complete the restitution and in order to do this, must become actively involved through self discipline.

Research done in Britain and this country on offender attitudes to restitution and community service sanctions generally indicates that they are seen as fair and equitable. For example, research aimed at assessing attitudes held by offenders ordered to perform community service in Britain by Flegg,[28] Pease,[29] and Thorvaldson,[30] found that offenders overwhelmingly defined the sanction as fair. Similar findings were obtained from research completed in this country on financial restitution by Chesney,[31] and Galaway and Marsella.[32] Perhaps even more important for public policy is the research conducted on attitudes about the use of restitution and community service held by important interest groups. Judges, probation and parole officers, victims, attorneys, legislators, and corrections administrators are among the groups that have been surveyed.[33] In each case, restitution and community service were supported as fair and sensible sanctions.

Restitution and community service sanctions also have the potential for fairness by giving offenders opportunities to atone or make amends for the damages done. Gilbert Geis has suggested that making restitution could potentially create within the offender a sense of the true extent of the harm inflicted: "Fiscal atonement could produce in the offender a feeling of having been cleansed, a kind of redemptive purging process, which might inhibit subsequent wrongdoing."[34]

The human need for forgiveness is central to the Judeo-Christian belief system and has been explicitly incorporated as a step in the twelve-step Alcoholics Anonymous program and other programs modeled after it. Furthermore, evidence on the place of restitution in restoring equity in victim-offender relations is available from social psychology. Equity theory suggests that the sense of social equity existing between harmdoer and victim is disrupted as a result of harmdoing.[35] Two types of responses are available to the harmdoer so as to reduce the stress that has been generated. One way is for the offender to use a variety of rationalization strategies or excuses so as to verbally minimize the extent of harm done. These strategies are distortions of reality useful for convincing harmdoers that their actions were essentially equitable. The second way of reducing stress and restoring equity is by making restitution to the victim. A fairly substantial body of research on equity theory propositions has been completed and generally indicates that if harmdoers are given opportunities, they will make efforts to complete restitution and as a result, not use rationalizations in attempts to excuse their behavior. Assuming responsibility for one's actions is likely to be a prerequisite for responsible behavior, especially if the means for acting responsibly are provided. Restitution would seem to be a potentially useful way to demonstrate responsibility.

Community Alternatives to Imprisonment

Imprisonment as a last resort sanction is a key element of the justice model and in principle restitution and community service sanctions lend themselves to use as alternatives to incarceration. Restitution can be used as a supplement to a probation order, as a program ingredient of a residential halfway house, or as a sole probation condition for offenders who otherwise would have been incarcerated in either a local jail or state institution. All of these sanctioning devices currently exist, at least on paper. The crucial issue confronting all diversion-type projects is the extent to which they actually divert from a more severe to a less severe sanction.

Like most of the research done on diversion programming in general, all of the research evidence tends to indicate that restitution and community service projects purportedly operating as alternatives to incarceration in fact serve offenders, who, in the absence of the project, would most likely never have been imprisoned. For example, the community service scheme introduced in Britain in 1972, empowering courts to order offenders to perform unpaid work as a service to the community, had the explicit legislative aim of diverting offenders from prison. Research completed on this program by the Home Office, however, found that only approximately half of those given community service orders would otherwise have received a custodial sentence in the absence of the scheme.[36] Similar findings were obtained from research conducted on the Saturday Work Order scheme introduced in Tasmania in 1972.[37] This community service program was to be offered to offenders only in place of a prison sentence, yet the research shows that overwhelmingly it has been used as an alternative to a bond, probation, or fine. Finally, research conducted on four restitution centers in the state of Georgia[38] showed that these programs only rarely served as an alternative to imprisonment and similar findings have been obtained in province-wide community service and restitution schemes in British Columbia[39] and Alberta, Canada.[40]

While in principle restitution and community service sanctions can be used as alternatives to imprisonment, and while program applications are commonly defended on such a basis, the available evidence presents a consistent picture of programs being used to supplement non-custodial sanctions for offenders who never would have been incarcerated. More than simple honesty is at issue here. What about the case of offenders who would not have been imprisoned if a restitution program was not available, but because of their failure to complete the restitution or community service order, are subsequently imprisoned? This practice tarnishes the concept of fairness — fairness to the offender who ends up being excessively punished, fairness to the public ultimately responsible for financially supporting a program that claims one thing, does another, and may end up increasing the use of custodial sanctions.

Consideration of Crime Victims

The justice model does not neglect consideration of the crime victim and restitution policy statements, legislation, and program applications commonly subscribed to victim oriented goals. But to what extent do victim goals actually reflect program reality and to what extent are they used for public relations or survival purposes?

The obvious benefit of a restitution scheme for crime victims is the receipt of reparations. Potentially, restitution can make the losses sustained from the criminal incident easier to bear. This is not the case when offenders are sanctioned with fines, court costs, probation, or incarceration, and the victim ignored. There are, however, several limitations on using restitution for the purposes of repaying crime victims. First, restitution schemes almost universally apply only to a limited population of crime victims; victims of personal crimes are excluded. Secondly, only victims of property crime in which an offender has been apprehended or convicted are eligible. Most reported crime goes unsolved. Even if eligible, victims of crimes in which the defendant or offender has been placed in a community service scheme will receive no compensation except in the way any citizen might gain by the unpaid work offsetting taxes. Finally, business corporations and insurance companies make up a large proportion of eligible victims and in such cases, restitution is likely to be used to cover potential losses or increased profits for insurance companies by double billing clients — once by receiving payment and then by increasing premiums. For the small proportion of non-corporate victims eligible to receive restitution, however, such payments would seem to have the potential for generating positive attitudes toward the offender and the system of justice and, as a result, help in reducing cries for vengeance. Aware of the potential of receiving restitution, victims may be more likely to report crimes and be more willing to help move the case through the justice system.

Restitution also has the potential for use as a vehicle to involve crime victims in the justice system. Little consideration has traditionally been given to involving the crime victim in the operations of the justice system. After reporting the incident, the victim is usually not provided with any information on the status of the case, is not involved in any of the crucial decisions made about the offender, and is likely to have property retained as evidence for long periods of time. Restitution offers a way in which victims can be meaningfully involved in the justice system. Victims could be involved in decisions about the disposition given the offender, in decisions about the amount and schedule of restitution payments, as well as in maintaining periodic involvement with the offender as the restitution order is completed. Victim involvement was a central ingredient in the Minnesota Restitution Center as well as in the Restitution in Probation Experiment in Iowa. At the Restitution Center, victims were provided with opportunities to engage in face-to-face negotiations with the offender in relation to the amount and schedule of restitution to be made. Program staff were responsible for mediating and facilitating these meetings as well as in monitoring the on-going victim-offender contact made upon the offender's release to the community. Similar program efforts have been attempted in St. Cloud, Minnesota, Kitchener, Ontario, and Calgary, Alberta, Canada, and Elkhart, Indiana. Most of these programs report that victims are willing to have contact with offenders in order to arrive at a restitution agreement.

With few exceptions, however, restitution and community service programs do not bring victims and offenders together to negotiate restitution agreements and victims are not consulted about their views concerning the appropriate disposition to be given the offender. Consequently, the potential use of restitution for victim involvement is not being exploited in existing programs.

Conclusions

Both financial restitution and community service sentencing are potentially consistent with the justice model for corrections. They clearly involve more definite penalties imposed upon the offender and hold potential for reducing the severity of penalties, especially the use of incarceration. In addition, they potentially provide victims with an opportunity for meaningful involvement in the justice system. The unfortunate tendency to add restitution and community service sanctions onto existing sanctions and the reluctance of many corrections officials to pursue

possibilities for the active involvement of victims in the operations of the justice system are deterrents to the realization of the full potential of these sanctions. As interest in the justice model for corrections develops, we would hope to see the increased use of restitution as the sole penalty for the offender and more creative involvement of victims in the sanctioning process.

Notes

*Prepared under Grant Number 78-NI-AX-0110 from the National Institute of Law Enforcement and Criminal Justice, Law Enforcement Assistance Administration, U.S. Department of Justice. Points of view or opinions stated herein are those of the authors and do not necessarily represent the official position or policies of the U. S. Department of Justice.

1. For a discussion of alternative types of definitions for the term "restitution", see Alan Harland "Theoretical and Programmatic Concerns in Restitution: An Integration," in Burt Galaway, Joe Hudson (eds.), *Offender Restitution in Theory and Action* (Lexington, Mass.: D. C. Heath and Company, 1978), pp. 193-202.
2. For a discussion of the historical and cross-cultural uses of restitution, see Laura Nader and Elaine Combs-Schilling, "Restitution in Cross-Cultural Perspective," in Joe Hudson, Burt Galaway (eds.), *Restitution in Criminal Justice: A Critical Assessment of Sanctions* (Lexington, Mass.: D. C. Heath and Company, 1977), pp. 27-44; Bruce Jacobs, "The Concept of Restitution: An Historical Overview," included in Joe Hudson, Burt Galaway (eds.), *Restitution in Criminal Justice*, pp. 45-62.
3. Sir Frederick Pollock and Frederic William Maitland, *The History of English Law*, second edition, volume I (Cambridge University Press, 1968), pp. 449-62.
4. Sir Thomas More, *Utopia*, J. C. Collins edition (London, 1904), pp. 23-24.
5. Jeremy Bentham, *The Works of Jeremy Bentham, Now First Collected Under the Superintendence of His Executor John Bowling*, Part 2 (Edinburgh, Scotland: William Tait Publishers, 1838), pp. 367-388.
6. Herbert Spencer, *Essays: Scientific, Political and Speculative*, Volume 3 (New York: Appleton and Company, 1892), pp. 152-191.
7. N. Raffaele Garofalo, *Criminology* (Boston: Little, Brown and Co., 1914).
8. Enrico Ferri, *Criminal Sociology* (Boston: Little, Brown and Co., 1917).
9. American Bar Association, *Standards Relating to Sentencing Alternatives and Procedures*, New York Office of Criminal Justice Project, Institute of Judicial Administration, 1968, pp. 2.7 (c) (III); American Bar Association, *Standards Relating to Probation*, 1970, pp. 3.2 (c) (VIII).
10. *Non-Custodial and Semi-Custodial Penalties*, Report of the Advisory Council on the Penal System, London, Her Majesty's Stationery Office, 1970.
11. National Council on Crime and Delinquency, Council of Judges, "Model Sentencing Act, Second Edition," *Crime and Delinquency*, 18, October 1972, pp. 356-359.
12. Annual Chief Justice Earl Warren Conference on Advocacy in the United States, *A Program for Prison Reform*, Cambridge, Roscoe Pound — American Trial Lawyers Foundation, 1972, p. 11.
13. United States National Advisory Commission on Criminal Justice Standards and

Goals, *Corrections* (Washington, D.C.: U. S. Government Printing Office, 1973), p. 150.
14. Law Reform Commission of Canada, Working Paper No. 3: *The Principals of Sentencing and Dispositions,* Ottawa, Information Canada, 1974, pp. 7-10; Working Papers No. 5 and 6: *Restitution and Compensation; Fines,* Ottawa, Information Canada, 1974, pp. 5-15.
15. Steve Chesney, Joe Hudson, and John McLagen, "A New Look at Restitution: Recent Legislation, Programs and Research," *Judicature,* Volume 61, No. 8, March 1978, pp. 348-357.
16. *Ibid,* pp. 349-351.
17. Maine Revised Statutes, Section 1151.2 (supp. 1976).
18. Tennessee Pub. Acts 818 (1976).
19. Steve Chesney, Joe Hudson, and John McLagen, *Ibid.,* pp. 349-351.
20. Mississippi Code, Ann, Sections 99-37-19; 99-37-21.
21. *People v. Graco,* 204 N. Y. S. 2d 744 Oneida County Court (1960).
22. *U. S.* v. *Durst,* 98 S. Ct. 849 (1978).
23. Joe Hudson, Burt Galaway, and Steve Chesney, "When Criminals Repay Their Victims: A Survey of Restitution Programs," *Judicature,* Volume 60, No. 7; February 1977, pp. 312-321.
24. Steve Chesney, Joe Hudson, and John McLagen, "A New Look at Restitution: Recent Legislation, Programs and Research," *Judicature,* Volume 61, No. 8, March 1978, pp. 348-357.
25. Joe Hudson and Burt Galaway, "Preliminary Report 1: Overview of Restitution Programming and Project Selection," *National Assessment of Adult Restitution Programs,* School of Social Development, University of Minnesota-Duluth, no date.
26. See, for example: Kathleen J. Smith, *A Cure for Crime*: A Case for the Self-*Determinate Prison Sentence* (London: Gerald Duckworth and Company, Ltd., 1976); Kathleen J. Smith, "Implementing Restitution Within a Penal Setting: The Case for a Self-Determinate Sentence," in Joe Hudson and Burt Galaway (eds.), *Restitution In Criminal Justice*: *A Critical Assessment of Sanctions* (Lexington, Mass.: D. C. Heath and Company, 1977), pp. 131-146.
27. Cited in Steven Schafer, "Restitution To Victims of Crime – An Old Correctional Aim Modernized," *Minnesota Law Review,* 50, 1965, p. 249.
28. Mrs. D. Flegg, et al., *Nottinghamshire Probation and After-Care Service*: *Community Service Consumer Survey – 1973-1976,* unpublished.
29. K. Pease, et al., *Community Service Orders,* Home Office Research Studies, London, Her Majesty's Stationery Office, 1975.
30. S. A. Thorvaldson, "The Effects of Community Service on the Attitudes of Offenders," Doctor of Philosophy dissertation, University of Cambridge, 1978.
31. Steven Chesney, "An Assessment of Restitution in the Minnesota Probation Services," in Joe Hudson and Burt Galaway (eds.), *Restitution In Criminal Justice*: *A Critical Assessment of Sanctions,* pp. 146-186.
32. Burt Galaway and William Marsella, "An Exploratory Study of the Perceived Fairness of Restitution as a Sanction for Juvenile Offenders," paper presented at the Second International Symposium on Victimology, Boston, Massachusetts, September 1976.
33. See, for example: Robin Solomon Bluestein, et al., "Attitudes of the Legal Community Toward Creative Restitution, Victim Compensation and Related Social Work Involvement," unpublished Master's thesis, University of South Carolina, 1977; "The Need for and Acceptance of Community Restitution Centers in Virginia," Virginia Department of Corrections, Richmond, Virginia, September

1978; Joe Hudson, Steven Chesney, John McLagen, "Restitution As Perceived by State Legislators and Correctional Administrators," Minnesota Department of Corrections, St. Paul, Minnesota, September 1977; John T. Gandy, "Community Attitudes Toward Creative Restitution and Punishment," unpublished Doctoral dissertation, University of Denver, 1975; Peter Schneider, et al., "Restitution Requirements for Juvenile Offenders: A Survey of the Practices in American Juvenile Courts, Institute of Policy Analysis, Eugene, Oregon, June 1977.

34. Gilbert Geis, "Restitution By Criminal Offenders: A Summary and Overview," in Joe Hudson and Burt Galaway (eds.), *Restitution In Criminal Justice,* p. 160.
35. Elaine Hatfield and Mary K. Utne, "Equity Theory and Restitution Programming," in Burt Galaway and Joe Hudson (eds.), *Offender Restitution in Theory and Action,* pp. 73-88.
36. K. Pease, S. Billingham, I. Earnshaw, *Community Service Assessed in 1976,* Home Office Research Study No. 39, Her Majesty's Stationery Office, London, 1977.
37. Sheila Barne, "Saturday Work: A Real Alternative?", *Australian and New Zealand Journal of Criminology,* Volume 9, No. 2, June 1976, pp. 95-108.
38. Gerald T. Flowers, *The Georgia Restitution Shelter Program,* Evaluation Report No. 1-150, Georgia Department of Offender Rehabilitation, September 30, 1977.
39. *The Community Service Order Program: The British Columbia Experience, Volume 1*: Ministry of the Attorney General, Province of British Columbia, Victoria, July 1977.
40. Joan Swanton, *Final Report: The Pilot Alberta Restitution Center (September 1, 1975 – October 31, 1977)*, undated.

PART 2

Fairness in Sentencing and Releasing

Introduction

The two chapters in this section deal with justice as fairness in relation to sentencing and release practices. Many of the issues addressed by John Conrad and Patrick McAnany in Part 1 are further explored and illustrated in the papers by E. Barrett Prettyman, Jr. and Ira Blalock.

Chapter IV by E. Barrett Prettyman, Jr., an attorney, is the only previously published work in this volume. It has been included here because it represents an early critique of indeterminate sentencing as well as an argument for the right to treatment. With this article, Prettyman helped pioneer the kind of critical thinking that recently has become more popular in the debate about criminal sentencing. Being ahead of its time, almost a decade ago, this paper did not receive widespread review. Publication here makes it available afresh at the height of the continuing debate.

It is particularly appropriate that the context of Mr. Prettyman's article is the Patuxent Institution for the Defective Delinquent because of the frequently heard defense of indeterminate sentencing and coercive clinical treatment, namely: "We've never had a chance to prove ourselves through proper legislation, funding, and staffing." Maryland's Patuxent had everything going for itself; enabling legislation, adequate funding, the best clinical staff - "patient" ratio in the nation, and a new treatment facility — complete with electronic monitoring, underground movement corridors, and gun towers. It withstood constitutional assaults for almost a quarter of a century. Hailed as a prototype institution by competent clinicians in the mid-1950's, it succumbed to due process restraints just a few years ago. Prettyman's article is a history of the emergence of Patuxent as well as a reasoned critique about the realities of implementing the indeterminate sentence when resources were adequately provided.

Prettyman's paper demonstrates that under an indeterminate sentence the decision to release from custody is as crucial as the decision to incarcerate. Parole authorities have possessed unbridled discretion to make release decisions. The last few years, however, have seen major changes in the structuring of parole board discretion as well as in eliminating their releasing authority. California, Maine, Illinois, and effective in 1980, Minnesota are among several of the states that have acted to abolish the releasing authority of parole boards. The federal Congress is now considering similar legislation.

As the earlier chapter by McAnany pointed out, determinate sentencing can be achieved in several ways, including the use of a sentencing commission, having the legislature set precise prison terms, as well as by parole board reforms so that release dates are set early in the term according to published guidelines. It is this latter approach that is described in Chapter V by Ira Blalock.

By statute and by administrative leadership, Oregon has largely abandoned earlier practices of relying upon experts' reports of the convict's clinical readiness for release. The state's system has explicated its decision-making processes and set them between reasonable, public, and appellate parameters. These changes were not forced on them. The Oregon Parole Board set forth a procedure which was responsive to the critics in the areas of structuring its discretion, setting reasoned limits to prison time, and operating under a just deserts model, rather than a predictive one. Mr. Blalock's chapter details how this came about. It should be noted that he provided the leadership for this sharp break with the past.

4. The Indeterminate Sentence and the Right to Treatment*

E. Barrett Prettyman, Jr.

The indeterminate sentence in its purest form imposes incarceration on a convicted offender for a period that may extend from a minimum of one day to a maximum of life. Such a sentence has been in use for the past eighteen years at Maryland's Patuxent Institution, and its historical and theoretical roots go back to the nineteenth century. The following article is an attempt to evaluate the theory and literature surrounding the indeterminate sentence in terms of the realities of its implementation at Patuxent.

The Patuxent Concept

The young schizophrenic (his description, not mine) sat across from me with a dubious expression.

He had asked why I was interviewing his fellow inmates at Patuxent, the Maryland institution where "defective delinquents" serve out their indeterminate sentences.[1] I had replied that after reading what psychiatrists, psychologists, penologists, and others had to say about the indeterminate sentence, I was interested in the views of those who were actually serving it.

The young man did not believe I could evaluate what I was hearing from the inmates. "Oh, I know they're telling you what they're feeling," he said. "But are they telling you what they're *thinking?*"

It was a good question, and I have pondered it since it was posed. I would like to believe that the inmates were conveying both feelings and thoughts, that I could distinguish and evaluate all I heard, and that I could also recognize the self-serving nature of much that they told me. I have talked at length with prisoners and patients from San Quentin to St. Elizabeths, from penitentiaries in Oregon, Colorado and Georgia to the District of Columbia jail. I have talked with and represented petty thieves as well as men under sentence of death. I can be fooled like anyone else, but experience has also taught me a good deal about what makes and moves the institutionalized man.

What I found at Patuxent was the difference between grand promises and hard facts.[2] If Patuxent had been sold to the Maryland Legislature in the early 1950's as a modest and experimental first step in the direction of therapeutic rehabilitation, and if, since then, its many failures had been recognized and admitted, and corrective action taken, the current controversy that threatens to eliminate the institution entirely might not have developed.[3]

Instead, the "Patuxent concept" was lauded from its earliest beginnings as a breakthrough "accepted by leaders in the correctional field."[4] It was hailed as a model that should be emulated throughout the country[5] and as "an exemplary subject of an essential element in the fair administration of such laws, [namely,] informed and aggressive legislative supervision."[6] Patuxent was said to provide "psycho-therapy, vocational rehabilitation, occupational therapy, and a therapeutically oriented milieu."[7] In addition to group therapy, "considerable individual attention" was said to be "the privilege of many inmate patients."[8] Treatment and rehabilitation were the primary goals,[9] and low recidivism rates were cited to prove that inmates were in fact being rehabilitated.[10]

Having "the key administrator a psychiatrist rather than a penologist" was cited as an "essential ingredient" of the plan's success.[11] The Graded Tier System, by which inmates move from tiers with restricted privileges to tiers allowing more freedom by performing well in the institutional structure, was described as "rewarding behavior which is socially desirable and personally beneficial to the inmate."[12] Psychotherapy, it was said, "carried top priority."[13] The inmates were said to "*clamor* for it" and "demand to know why it is being withheld from them."[14] The attitude of the guards, rather than being authoritarian and primitive, had been deliberately changed to fit more nearly those of the therapists,[15] and the result was that at all personnel levels there was "a more benign, friendlier, and less strained atmosphere than that found in most penal institutions."[16] The inmates had a measure of control over their own discipline;[17] they lost privileges "but were not removed from population," and "[s]evere punishment" was "completely eliminated."[18] The indeterminate sentence itself was described as a "motivating force" that stimulated the patients "to examine their own personal problems, to understand how these problems are related to their criminal behavior, and to do something constructive about them."[19] The goal of Patuxent's overall program was "to create a personality change that will permit the patient to return to society as a productive member."[20] One doctor summed it all up by predicting that "twenty years hence psychiatric historians will regard this statute as one of the major accomplishments of the middle third of the 20th Century."[21]

I do not mean to imply that prior to my visits the enthusiasm for Patuxent was unalloyed. Not only have the institution's recidivist figures been attacked,[22] but numerous constitutional problems have been outlined in law journals.[23] Criticism has ranged from mild questioning,[24]

to strong and emotional attacks. One doctor, who has testified about the institution, found much at Patuxent that "alarmed, appalled, or enraged" him.[25] Two Maryland judges who held hearings on conditions at Patuxent issued a series of orders beginning in November 1971 that required the institution to make changes in virtually all aspects of prison life.[26]

Thus, the conflict between those who regarded Patuxent as an unmixed blessing and those who saw it as a nearly complete failure was beginning to develop even before I began questioning the inmates.

History of Indeterminate Sentencing

The true facts about Patuxent must be viewed against the background of the whole indeterminate sentence movement.[27] The concept of the indeterminate sentence apparently originated with Alexander Maconochie, 1787-1860, who devised a system of progressive classification whereby prisoners earned both good marks and wages, as well as fines. He implemented this system on Norfolk Island from 1840 to 1844.[28] The Archbishop of Dublin, a contemporary of Maconochie, has also been credited as one of the original advocates of the indeterminate sentence — a precept that flowed naturally from his notion of free will and moral responsibility.[29] As others have noted, however, positivists, who rejected the concept of free will in criminal matters, also accepted the idea of the indeterminate sentence on the theory that while dangerousness was preordained, its extent could not be ascertained in advance.[30]

When the Australian and Irish studies emanating from the work of these gentlemen were published in the United States, prominent prison reformers, particularly in New York, became strong advocates of indeterminacy in prison terms.[31] In 1870, completely indeterminate sentences were proposed in a paper delivered to the First American Prison Congress.[32] In 1876, the New York legislature partially complied with these proposals by establishing the indefinite sentence, with imprisonment limited by a maximum sentence.[33]

By 1922, 37 states had adopted some form of the indefinite sentence, although none had yet accepted the completely indeterminate sentence.[34] In the 1940's, the therapeutic community concept was being introduced in England, but in hospitals rather than in prisons,[35] even while a great majority of the federal judges in the United States were voting at a judicial conference against taking the ultimate power of fixing sentences away from judges.[36] Today, indefinite sentencing is so common that a former Attorney General has said: "The day of the indeterminate sentence is coming."[37]

Positive Aspects of the Indetermining Sentence

Over the years, a number of arguments have been advanced in favor of the indeterminate sentence.[38] Among them are these:

(a) It allows the fullest possible implementation of the rehabilitative ideal of correctional reform.[39]

(b) It offers the best means of motivating involuntarily committed inmates to work for rehabilitation, since they hold the key to their release in their hands, and motivation is a prerequisite for many, although not all, forms of rehabilitative treatment.[40]

(c) It offers the maximum protection to society from hardcore recidivist and mentally defective offenders, and public safety is a primary concern of the criminal law.[41]

(d) It helps maintain an orderly environment within the institution.[42]

(e) It prevents unnecessary incarceration of an offender and thus helps to prevent the correctional system from becoming a factory from which first offenders emerge as hardened criminals.[43]

(f) It offers a feasible alternative to capital punishment.[44]

(g) It removes the judgment as to the length of incarceration from the trial court judge and puts it in the hands of a qualified panel of behavioral experts who make their final decision based on considerably more evidence than is available at the post-conviction stage of the trial.[45]

(h) The decision as to length of incarceration reflects the needs of the offender and not the gravity of the crime, in the best interests of both society and the criminal offender.[46]

(i) It prevents correctional authorities from being forced to release from custody an offender who is clearly not ready to rejoin society.[47]

(j) It prevents the problem offender from retreating into a "sick" role during rehabilitation.[48]

(k) It acts as a deterrent to crime.[49]

Despite this rather formidable list, the fact is that the argument for the indeterminate sentence is essentially two-fold — one part seldom referred to or at best mentioned only in passing, and the other strongly relied upon in the name of humanitarian reform. The less seldom articulated argument is that some men are so bent on criminal behavior that they simply cannot be allowed loose in society, now or later.[50] Since society will not accept a life sentence for a series of petty crimes, the indeterminate sentence serves the purpose of achieving long term confinement in selective situations while at the same time holding out the hope of momentary release.[51]

The argument more often articulated is that incarceration without rehabilitation is not only useless but destructive and self-defeating. In the normal prison setting where the inmate knows that he will probably be released after a given period regardless of his condition, his incentive for rehabilitation is minimal. If, on the other hand, the inmate knows that he will be released only when rehabilitated, or that he can be released earlier than the term of his prison sentence if rehabilitated, he will be strongly motivated to work toward that which will precipitate his release. He will take part in and benefit from all of the programs designed to correct his criminal behavior, with the result that he will re-enter society as either a "well" person or at least a person able to function without harm to himself or others. So goes the argument.[52]

Arguments Against Indeterminate Confinement

In the last 20 years, there has been a growing disillusionment with the indetermniate sentence.[53] Among the principal arguments which have developed against it are the following:

(a) Treatment is a myth, and vocational training is a fraud. For various reasons ranging from inadequacy of staffs to the difficulty of therapy in a maximum security atmosphere, inmates are neither treated, trained nor rehabilitated. Claims of therapy simply cloak banishment to institutions devoid of treatment processes. And if there is no treatment, has not the entire case for the indeterminate sentence disappeared?[54]

(b) Even if treatment were honestly attempted by adequate staffs, psychotherapy with involuntarily committed patients is generally considered difficult, and indeterminate sentencing may therefore supply only negative motivation which will be insufficient for achieving long term results.[55]

(c) Even if effective therapy were possible with some offenders, it is neither justified nor proper for all offenders, and there should be a right *not* to receive unwanted therapy.[56]

(d) Since the treatment is token and rehabilitation is almost nonexistent, the indeterminate sentence becomes a device to hide society's dehumanizing treatment of criminals, particularly those who are poor and/or members of minority groups.[57]

(e) Similarly, by taking the criminal off the street while at the same time promising rehabilitation, the indeterminate sentence makes it easy for society to ignore the underlying social causes of crime. To put it another way, indeterminate sentencing allows society to isolate the fruits of its inadequate social policies when they are disruptive but simultaneously to ignore the problem as a whole since the most unpleasant results (crime and criminals) are effectively removed.[58]

(f) In most instances, the indeterminate sentence is used as an instrument of inmate control. The staff and the releasing authority simply play God with the offender, wielding the variable sentence as a weapon.[59] Where a system entails so many discretionary decisions, it is fraught with the potential for abuse.[60]

(g) In practice, the psychiatrist becomes more of a jailer than a healer. While he is supposed to treat the inmate, he also knows that he will have to testify in court at various times about his "patient"[61] and that his recommendation to the releasing authority will virtually determine the inmate's release date. This puts the psychiatrist into an inherently untenable role, brings political pressures to bear on his decisions, and restricts his freedom to work for the best interest of his patients.[62]

(h) The designation of some offenders as mentally ill is extremely arbitrary, as is the identification of those who fall within the statutory definitions of "defective delinquent" or "sexual psychopath."[63] As one commentator has implied in regard to the Maryland definition of a "defective delinquent," it could include virtually every offender except an unhelmeted motorcyclist.[64] Another has broadened the definition only slightly: "Apparently, any potential chronic miscreants could be found to be in sufficient emotional imbalance so as to justify invoking the jurisdiction of the statute."[65] Once the defective delinquents reach the institution, they are such a variable lot that it is virtually impossible to devise a single treatment approach that will meet the needs of the entire group.[66]

(i) There is a great danger that the indeterminate sentence will be used to punish political beliefs and unpopular views, especially those which antagonize the staff. The religious and political nonconformist is the type of inmate who is most likely to fight the therapeutic system and thus to foreclose his own release.[67] Even among offenders, there should be the right to be different.[68] There are arguments for and against involuntary behavioral change, but innumerable authorities have warned against unrestricted use of behavioralistic principles to insure social order.[69]

(j) The indeterminate sentence structure encourages the smart or cunning offender and is more favorable to him than to a less intelligent offender, although the more intelligent offender may be the most dangerous to society. This is because of the ease with which a smart offender can play the game and fool his captors.[70]

(k) Despite the fact that courts are supposed to retain some measure of control, there simply is no adequate protection from life imprisonment in the guise of "the indeterminate sentence."[71] Since release authorities are normally more concerned about protecting the public than with releasing the prisoner at the earliest possible date, the practical result is that the institutionalization may stretch on endlessly.[72] To put it another way, if the psychiatrist recommends against release, and the authorities refuse to release for any reason, no one will know that a mistake has been made. On the other hand, if the inmate is released and becomes a recidivist, the mistake is evident to one and all. Because of this uncertainty and of the difficulty of predicting "dangerousness," the sentence contravenes the individual rights of the inmates.[73] Even where the sentence does not ultimately turn out to be for life, the result is a longer confinement than that which would have occurred had the inmate gone to prison.[74] Moreover, in most persistent offender situations society is as well protected by a maximum sentence of, say, 30 years, since that term removes the offender past the age at which recidivism normally occurs.[75]

It is against the background of these arguments and counter-arguments that I conducted my talks with various inmates at Patuxent. What I found largely supported the critics of the indeterminate sentence.

Inside Patuxent

First, despite claims that Patuxent is either more like a hospital than a prison or has features of both,[76] make no mistake about it being a prison in every sense that counts.[77] It may be one of the "pastel" prisons to which Jessica Mitford has referred — "they look good, shiny, sanitary"[78] — but it is nevertheless a prison. Through double, automatic gates, one enters an area completely surrounded by a barbed wire fence, with armed guards watching from towers. At key points inside the various buildings, guards constantly unlock dividing doors either electronically or with keys. All tiers are closed off by steel doors. As one doctor testified in the *Murel* case, Patuxent has far more locked doors and grill gates than a maximum security prison in the Navy.[79] Each cell is sealed by a metal, solid door with a window. These cells are nine by six feet in size and are furnished with only a bunk having a drawer under it, a commode, a wash basin and a table. Inmates can shower briefly once a week, and recreation is extremely limited.

Strict Rules

"Institutional clothing may not be altered. Any items of clothing in excess of allowable limits will be considered contraband and will be confiscated," says the Patient Handbook.[80] "It is a violation of the rules for any patient to go to, or be found in, any area in which he is not authorized, or for any patient to delay his prompt passage as indicated on his pass."[81] "No patient shall demand, receive, or obtain from, or perform for, any other patient, personal services of any kind."[82] Cell searches, strip searches and physical force by employees are authorized."[83] Although placement in a "segregated confinement treatment facility" is supposed to be limited to 15 days,[84] confinement in "administrative segregation (the M-1 tier) is authorized on "an indeterminate basis."[85] This is true even though confinement in similar physical conditions on the L-1 tier (disciplinary segregation) beyond a period of 15 days was recently held to be cruel and unusual punishment.[86] Prior to the *McCray* decision, inmates sat in single, solitary, filthy, dark, cagelike cells for months without having even reading material to alleviate the boredom. This practice was defended as part of the total treatment concept of the institution, as negative reinforcement.[87]

In view of these facts and of the further fact that confinement at Patuxent is truly indeterminate, surely all judicial dialogue about the commitment hearing being "civil" rather than "criminal"[88] is extraneous, if not downright misleading. There is no avoiding the fact that for the inmate, the result of the hearing, whether it be dubbed "civil," "criminal," "therapeutic," or whatever, is confinement in a prison, possibly for life.

Inmate Attitudes

My last visit to Patuxent was at a time when that institution was plagued with extraordinary tension. I am familiar with prison tensions, but this was something quite beyond the ordinary. Patuxent was the only major penal facility in Maryland that had not experienced a recent uprising of some kind, and rumors were rife that one might come at any time. Class attendance had dropped precipitously. Shakedowns, except for inmates leaving the kitchen, had been eliminated because the guards were fearful of reprisals. There had been recent cases of individual violence (one man cut another from head to foot with a razor), and some incidents that ordinarily would have been broken up and reported immediately, such as forced homosexual acts, were being ignored. I found the Patuxent inmates even more disturbed, frightened and resentful than those offenders confined at more overcrowded and dangerous facilities. Much of what they were feeling, however, was as much directed at the indeterminate sentence as at the external forces at work around them.

One might expect that while inmates with short prison terms would hate the indeterminate sentence, those with long terms would find in it a possible salvation. Not so. Patuxent inmates despise the indeterminate sentence to a man — including those with sentences as long as 25 years who fully expect to be released under the Patuxent system far in advance of that time. They hate it for not knowing.[89] They hate it because in a situation already charged with uncertainties and tensions, there is added the most tense uncertainty of all: their release date.[90] They detest it because while Patuxent officials play down punishment and discipline in their public teachings, the inmates find that the slightest infraction, the smallest offense, even the half-joking insult, may not only result in the loss of privileges but also and far more importantly be inserted into their records and affect their release dates. They despise it because they do not find the "benign" attitude on the part of the guards described by officials. These guards are selected like any other prison guards, and while many are friendly and even helpful, others are all too typically quick-tempered, retributive or sadistic.[91]

The Treatment Game

Inmates hate the indeterminate sentence because it forces them to play a game that for some is demeaning, for others self-destructive, and for still others simply a waste of time. The inmates do indeed "clamor" for therapy, as the institution's Director claims,[92] but that is because therapy provides the only way out of Patuxent short of escape. The Patient Handbook makes this clear. Immediately after stating that "[p]articipation in any program is voluntary," the Handbook goes on to say that "it is expected that you will get involved in those programs that best suit your individual needs. . . . Thus, you hold the key to your own future by participation in the institutional program."[93] And the one "program" that is deemed to fit *everyone's* need is therapy. Not only must an inmate attend therapy (group sessions are from one to two hours a week), but he must, once there, comply with certain well-prescribed modes of behavior.[94] He must talk about himself, his relation to his parents, his past sins. He must recognize that he has been sick and gain insight into what his "problem" has been. Then the offender must begin to recognize that he has been wrong and that it is not in his own interest to cling to past behavioral patterns. Finally, upon ascertaining the nature of his problem, he must evidence a strong intent to overcome it, compensate for it, fight it, or do whatever else is necessary to become a peaceful, useful citizen.

The result? Shamming.[95]

> Look, man, most of us are good at shamming. We grew up in the streets surrounded by confidence games. Literature is available to everyone now — hell, we talk as much about the Oedipus complex as about baseball. We know what these cats want to

> hear. Not the real gory stuff — what you're really thinking — because that scares 'em and makes 'em think you're still dangerous. But you spill your guts in a nice kind of way and act as if you're gaining all these insights. Now that you know yourself and that you killed that girl because you were really killing your mother, you don't have to kill anymore. It doesn't seem to occur to 'em that I might want to kill my mother several times over. Hell, everything I've told 'em is a lie. One big sham.

Listening to this calls to mind two other statements in the indeterminate sentence literature. One was by a Patuxent official:

> Even people who have worked with criminals over a long period of time find themselves getting fooled, for the skill of these men at sincerely appearing to be what the therapist hopes they will be is fantastic.[96]

The other was by a social welfare aide working at Vacaville, California's facility which nearly approximates Patuxent,[97] who found conditions there extraordinarily similar to those I found at Patuxent. She said:

> [The inmate] learns for instance that real involvement in the therapy implies the expression of genuine feelings. Often these are of a highly aggressive nature, however. Revealing these on a verbal level might alert the prison staff, he fears, to the fact that his undesirable impulses may express themselves in action. Furthermore, the mere expression and release of such feelings often makes it more difficult, at least temporarily, for him to conform to the institution's disciplinary demands and restrictions.[98]

> One defensive maneuver adopted by many inmates at Vacaville was learning to play the role of being a good "therapee." Much of the participation in the therapy program seems to consist of a form of role-playing and the inmates quickly learn what is expected of them in therapy, go through the motions, and dupe the therapists quite deliberately and consciously. This is considered to be a highly sophisticated form of "conning."[99]

The shamming, or conning, can develop into elaborate sub-plots. When I asked several inmates how they would advise a new arrival at Patuxent to act in order to obtain his release at the earliest possible moment, they gave very similar prescriptions: At first, be difficult. Don't talk at therapy. Answer all the test questions stupidly. Get into a little trouble, but not much. Then slowly begin to talk. Begin being nice. Do better on the tests. Then really straighten out and talk, talk, talk. Seem to spill your guts. Be repentant.

This certainty that the man who showed improvement had a better chance of early release than the man who, from the very beginning, consistently exhibited the desired configuration was reminiscent of a simliar prescription in another setting:

> In California, one formula — believed to be foolproof by its inmate adherents — prescribed a short period of intense "messing up" on first entering prison followed by a mixture of one-half group therapy and one-half vocational training with a *gradual* reduction in prison misbehavior and a few carefully written letters to close kin.[100]

In the eyes of the inmates, in other words, the indeterminate sentence becomes not the motivating force in improving oneself, as its adherents claim, but the motivation for playing the game necessary for the achievement of the ultimate goal: freedom. Is this "treatment?" The inmates are certain that it is not, even while many concede that in one way or another they may well have benefited from rapping, either at therapy or with other inmates.[101] They draw the distinction between new insights, which many say they have received, and a capacity to reorient both their attitudes and their behavior in the light of these insights. As one young man put it:

> OK, so I've learned that I did a lot of things to get attention because I never got any from my parents. I still need the attention, and I'll still do the same things to get it. That first piece of news hasn't help me a bit.[102]

Psychiatrists might dispute this and say that the "first piece of news" was essential to the next step leading to behavioral control. But the difficulty is that at Patuxent the next steps almost never come. Even assuming that psychiatry were capable of somehow "curing" defective delinquents in a prison atmosphere — an assumption open to a good deal of question[103] — such a cure cannot be accomplished in a two-hour session once a week in the company of from 6 to 11 other inmates. Despite claims to the contrary, individual therapy is virtually non-existent at Patuxent. While there have been statements to the effect that group therapy has certain advantages over individual treatment,[104] the inmates are not fooled. The simple fact is that there are not enough members of the medical staff to treat a population of over 550 men.

Other Sources of Dissatisfaction

The inmates have a myriad of other complaints. Accusations of unfairness and deceit are everywhere.[105] One man, for example, claims that he pleaded guilty as part of a deal with the prosecutor to get him no more than a five-year sentence. "I got the five years, all right, and then I got sent to Patuxent where I can be kept forever."[106] There are constant charges of therapists testifying about men they have not seen, records being lost or destroyed, inmates being unable to move ahead because they have a "bummer" for a doctor instead of one of the good ones, guards selling hack-saws and razors, drugs of all kinds being available, adverse ratings because of an inmate's failure to learn a trade even though the course he was taking has been discontinued, and so forth.

Arbitrary Action

As an example of the kind of arbitrary treatment and unintentional happening that can delay release, several inmates mentioned a recent incident in the yard. One prisoner had escaped through the fence while a number of others with yard privileges were wandering nearby. Because the guards felt that someone must have noticed the escape, every inmate in the yard was penalized regardless of where they were or what they saw. Since the escape was not reported, everyone was presumed at fault. The Inmate Grievance Committee reversed this decision, but the matter was now before the Director for final adjudication, and the result was being awaited with some apprehension. The inmate attitude was cynical: "If we win, we lose" — meaning that if the Director upholds the Grievance Committee, punishment will be visited in other forms.

Quality of Facility Staff

The tremendous disparity between different medical personnel was stressed time and again. As one inmate put it: "I've had three shrinks. One was a screwball, one was an ass, and one was OK." The attitudes and wishes of the doctors are so different, one from the other, that each inmate becomes adept at discovering through the grapevine what information each doctor likes most to hear. "For one guy I talked about nothing but my parents. For another I now have to lob in a lot of sex. Whatever they want to hear, I give them."

The inmates also claim that they are constantly caught between the wishes and desires of the medical staff on the one hand and those of the custodial personnel on the other. The conflict takes various forms. For example, "A guy almost killed me — hit me in the head with something hard and I was out for a long time. He got 15 days in the hole. The guards wanted to throw away the key, and the doctors wanted him out earlier." Another inmate said: "They call this place therapeutic. It's going to be pretty therapeutic if I get my throat cut."[107] As a commentator on the therapeutic community has said, "The convicts see themselves trapped in a vise between, as one put it, 'the punitive nineteenth-century guard and the 1984 headshrinker.' "[108]

Education

The teaching, they claim, is poor. One example of lack of drive and imagination on the part of the prison personnel involves a course in "Great Books" which the inmates themselves initiated. It runs five nights a week with full attendance. For a long time participants taught it themselves. Then for a period they received help from someone outside the institution. But they have yet to obtain guidance, teachers or even enthusiastic encouragement from the Patuxent staff itself. Moreover, there is not nearly enough vocational training available to meet the demand.[109]

Post Release

Confinement at Patuxent also poses serious post-release problems. As one man said, "When I'm trying to get a job, I use every device I can think of to keep from telling where I've been. I can even say 'prison', and it's not so bad. But as soon as I say 'Patuxent', I'm dead. They think this is a nuthouse."

The Case of Edward Lee McNeil

Perhaps the institution's basic difficulties are best epitomized by the facts of *McNeil* v. *Director*.[110] Edward Lee McNeil is a 25-year-old black who was convicted in 1966 of assault with intent to rape and assault on a police officer. Despite the fact that this was his first conviction, that he had graduated from high school and was employed at the time of his offense, that he lived with his parents, and that no defense or evidence of insanity, drunkenness or drug addiction was offered at his trial, the court ordered that McNeil be examined by the Baltimore Medical Office. That examination revealed no sign of psychotic process, distortion of thought, organic deficit, or delusions. Nevertheless, McNeil was sent to Patuxent "for evaluation and treatment, if necessary," apparently because he vehemently denied that he committed the offense and because he had "a limited tolerance for anxiety and stress."

McNeil's sentence for his criminal offense was five years. If he had gone to prison, he would have been eligible for parole in a little over one year. When he arrived at Patuxent, because he feared that information given to the staff might be used against him either in a criminal proceeding or at the hearing to determine his confinement as a defective delinquent, he refused to cooperate with the evaluation process. For almost six years — four years and ten months after his minimum sentence had expired and almost a year after his maximum sentence had expired — this obstinate young man refused to talk. Therefore, the institution refused to evaluate him, left him on the receiving tier without treatment of any kind, and claimed the right to hold him, without a court hearing, indefinitely. Eventually, in June of this year, the Supreme Court ordered his immediate release,[111] and since then, more than half a dozen other inmates who had also refused to talk were released pursuant to the same ruling.

Staff Attitude

The important point for present purposes is not the maze of legalities surrounding the problem but rather what the case demonstrates about the attitude and mentality of those who operate Patuxent. First, it did not seem to occur to the authorities that since McNeil was claiming his Fifth Amendment rights, this presented a justiciable issue that could be settled at any time by the sentencing court. Instead of taking McNeil back to court as soon as it became clear that he would persist in refusing to answer questions, Patuxent chose to stand on the proposition, all the way to the Supreme Court, that McNeil could remain confined forever without a hearing of any kind.[112]

Secondly, instead of offering during those six years of confinement all of the remedial, educational and therapeutic services that its officials constantly claim for the institution, Patuxent simply left McNeil to rot for that entire period.[113] Those on the receiving tier are not "treated." At first blush, it would appear that an inmate could hardly be "treated" until the staff knew what was wrong with him, and since he refused to cooperate, the staff could not be expected to find out what his difficulties were. But there are two answers. First, in another case the court held that direct verbal communication with the inmate is not indispensable to an evaluation,[114] and in a third case Patuxent officials made an evaluation without the benefit of verbal communication after first telling the court that no evaluation was possible.[115] Secondly, a number of Patuxent's services do not require the inmate to reveal incriminating facts about himself. Yet McNeil was left without both the evaluation and the services for almost six years.[116]

McNeil's Aftermath

Ironically, the *McNeil* decision has led to some bitterness and cynicism on the part of many inmates at Patuxent. Those who refused to cooperate and have remained beyond their sentences have been released, and the argument will surely be made that those who have refused to cooperate and have been kept beyond a reasonable period for evaluation — probably six months[117] — should also be released. Yet those who chose to cooperate with the institution have been or will be evaluated, and instead of being released they will have to serve indeterminate sentences, potentially for life. It remains to be seen, in the light of this disparity of treatment, whether post-*McNeil* arrivals at Patuxent will agree to cooperate and what the results will be if they do not. Those with long prison sentences may opt for cooperation and the indeterminate sentence on the theory that they have at least a chance to cut their incarceration short, whereas those with short sentences may choose to refuse cooperation and serve out their sentences rather than take a chance on incarceration beyond their prison terms. It is the kind of gamble that many prisoners are extraordinarily adept at taking.

Conclusion

Thus, regardless of how the indeterminate sentence looks on paper, it becomes something quite different in the context of how a place like Patuxent actually operates. Some of what I was told undoubtedly was untrue or exaggerated. Much was self-serving. Some of it may even have been the product of the very illnesses the Patuxent inmates are supposed to have.[118] The important point, it seems to me, is that anti-therapeutic forces are at work at this institution — and presumably others like it[119] — that only a blind or incredibly insensitive person could fail to detect. Included among these forces are: fear of bodily harm from fellow inmates, hatred of the institution's top officials and selectively of others at all levels, distrust of the guards, a mind-boggling anxiety about an ever-indefinite release date, cynicism about psychiatry, therapy, rehabilitation and reform, and perhaps most important of all, an overriding feeling of unfairness about the entire endeavor, from the way the inmates were selected for Patuxent in the first place to the way the institution is operated and the requirements for release.

If the inmates thought that those who ran their lives were stupid, misguided and wrong — but fair — the therapeutic concept could perhaps get off the ground. But when there is a pervasive conviction among the offenders that virtually no one has their best interests at heart, that they are where they are solely so that they can be kept off the streets for as long as possible, that they never would have been sent to Patuxent if they had not been poor or black or both,[120] and that Patuxent is just as busy shamming them as they are busy shamming back, how much credence can be placed in the therapeutic concept, at least in the prison atmosphere?[121] Under these circumstances, does not therapy itself become a threat? If you do not attend, you do not get out; and if you attend and fail to tell them what they want to hear, your release is delayed. Whether or not this is true, the inmates believe it is true, and the attitude of the inmates is what therapy is trying to reach.

The point has been put in various ways by others:

> It is inhumane to commit a man with the intention that he will not be released until he is rehabilitated and then fail to provide him with rehabilitation. The offender sees himself as the victim of a sadistic hoax.[122]

> Quite aside from the point that the treatment envisaged by such a view is normally either unknown or not provided, it is highly questionable whether the commission of a reasonably harmless misdemeanor should subject the offender to the possibility of a lifetime of incarceration, be it in a hospital or anywhere else.[123]
>
> In recent years there has been a growing sympathy for restricting the indeterminate sentences for treatment to an even smaller proportion of offenders, since experience has shown how difficult it is to give a person a therapeutic treatment which he himself does not desire, and how difficult it is to decide how long such a treatment ought to continue.[124]

Against these kinds of problems, court rulings to the effect that involuntary inmates of non-prison facilities are entitled to "treatment" take on an added measure of complexity and concern.[125] For as one commentator has said:

> The "dangerous myth" of treatment is now disintegrating. But the policy which this myth protects — the policy of the indeterminate sentence — has been successfully embodied in law, in the power of paroling authorities, in treatment specialties, in public opinion.[126]

Do the courts mean that confinements — indeterminate, indefinite or definite — are constitutional so long as some form of treatment is attempted, or will they insist on treatment that offers some reasonable form of success? If the latter, by whose criteria is success to be judged — those at Patuxent and Vacaville who say they are succeeding, or those at the other end of the spectrum who say it is impossible?

Of one point I am reasonably certain. The indeterminate sentence is self-defeating as a rehabilitative device. Only by use of the indefinite sentence can any treatment stand a chance of success, for until an inmate knows for certain that he will be released at the very latest on a particular, known date, he will remain outside the purview of meaningful rehabilitation.[127] He may play the game to the point where the authorities are willing to take a chance on his freedom, but from the psychiatric standpoint he will be neither cured nor rehabilitated. The sooner society faces this fact the more quickly it can move on to solving the real problem of why these men had to be institutionalized in the first place. It is time we all stopped shamming.

Notes

*Reprinted with permission of the America Bar Association's Criminal Justice Section. This article originally appeared in the American Criminal Law Review. Vol. II, No. 1, 1972).

1. Under the Maryland Code:

   > [A] defective delinquent [is] an individual who, by the demonstration of persistent aggravated antisocial or criminal behavior, evidences a

> propensity toward criminal activity, and who is found to have either such intellectural deficiency or emotional unbalance, or both, as to clearly demonstrate an actual danger to society so as to require such confinement and treatment [at Patuxent], when appropriate, as may make it reasonably safe for society to terminate the confinement and treatment.

Md. Ann. Code art. 31b, § 5 (1967).

Patuxent has been described as "the only state institution which has been designed, constructed, and is operated for all types of sociopaths." *National Conference of State Trial Judges, Committee Report, The Sociopathic Offender and the Courts* 33 (1964) [hereinafter cited as 1964 *Report*]. As one commentator has pointed out, however, the use of the psychiatrically vague term, "sociopath," has largely disappeared from the more recent writings by officials of the institution. Crowley, "Maryland's Defective Delinquent Law – Nightmarish Prelude to 1984," at 1 (October 23, 1971) (speech delivered at Annual Meeting, Medical Correctional Association, New York, New York). As for the difficulty of treating sociopaths, whatever they may be, see Carney, "Some Recurring Therapeutic Issues in Group Psychotherapy with Criminal Patients," 26 *Am J. Psychotherapy* 34 (1972).

2. See Stanford, "A Model, Clockwork-Orange Prison," *The New York Times Magazine*, September 17, 1972, at 9, where a similar approach to the evaluation of Patuxent arrives at many of the same conclusions reached here.
3. Patuxent is under attack in both federal and state courts. See, e.g., *Murel* v. *Baltimore City Criminal Court*, 407 U.S. 355 (1972); *McNeil* v. *Director, Patuxent Institution*, 407 U.S. 245 (1972); *McCray* v. *Maryland, Misc. Pet.* No. 4363 (Montgomery Cty. Md. Cir. Ct., Nov. 11, 1971) (excerpted in 40 *U.S.L.W.* 2307), *appeal docketed*, No. 45 (Md., Sept. Term 1972).

   Patuxent is also under attack in the Maryland General Assembly where House Bill 10 (filed on May 22, 1972 for the 1973 session) seeks to repeal Maryland's Defective Delinquent law in its entirety. House Bill 10 is co-sponsored by 48 delegates to Maryland's 142 member House.
4. Boslow & Kandel, "Administrative Structure and Therapeutic Climate," 46 *The Prison Journal* 23 (1966).
5. *National Conference of State Trial Judges, Committee Report, The Sociopathic Offender and the Courts* 10, 11 (1966) [hereinafter cited as 1966 *Report*].
6. Note, "Use of the Indeterminate Sentence in Crime Prevention and Rehabilitation," 7 *Duke L.J.* 65, 83-84 (1958) [hereinafter cited as Note, "Use of the Indeterminate Sentence"] (pointing to an instance of prompt legislative response to an unreasonable construction of the statute by the courts).
7. Boslow & Manne, "Mental Health in Action," 12 *Crime and Delinquency* 22, 25 (1966).
8. *Report of the Commission to Study and Re-Evaluate Patuxent Institution* 24, 48 (1961) (prepared for Sen. George W. Della, Chairman, Legislative Council of Maryland) [hereinafter cited as *Commission to Study and Re-Evaluate Patuxent Institution*]. See also, *S. Rubin, Psychiatry and Criminal Law* 177 (1965); Schreiber, "Indeterminate Therapeutic Incarceration of Dangerous Criminals, Perspectives and Problems," 56 *Va. L. Rev.* 602, 607 (1970); 1964 *Report, supra* note 1, at 33-34.
9. Boslow & Manne, *supra* note 7, at 25; Boslow, Rosenthal, Kandel, & Manne, "Methods and Experiences in Group Treatment of Defective Delinquents in Maryland," 7 *J. Social Therapy*, 32 (1961); Manne, "A Communication Theory of Sociopathic Personality, 21 *Am. J. Psychotherapy* 797, 807 (1967); Address by

Jerome Robinson, Council of State Governments in Chicago, Ill., Dec. 5, 1958; *Commission to Study and Re-Evaluate Patuxent Institution, supra* note 8, at 8-9, 14, 20, 22-26. See also, *Report of the Commission to Study Medico-Legal Psychiatry,* 25 (submitted to Gov. William Preston Lane, Jr. and the Md. Gen. Assembly, Dec. 28, 1948).

10. *Commission to Study and Re-evaluate Patuxent Institution, supra* note 8, at 23-26. See also, *National Conference of State Trial Judges, Committee Report, The Sociopathic Offender and the Courts,* 3 (1965) [hereinafter cited as 1965 *Report*]; 1964 *Report, supra* note 1, at 34-35; *S. Rubin, supra* note 8, at 177. One report indicated that while the recidivism rate among the inmates of Maryland's prisons hovers around 70 per cent (see *Commission to Study and Re-evaluate Patuxent Institution, supra* note 8, at 23), only about 32 per cent of those paroled or placed on work release or leave programs from Patuxent are returned either for violation of the terms and conditions of their release or for the commission of new offenses. *Patuxent Institution Statistical Summary* (1970). These recidivism figures have been strongly attacked by others. E.g., Crowley, *supra* note 1, at 3-4; Schreiber, *supra* note 8, at 606, 619, 627-28; Stone, "Discussion of Crime Prevention by the Indeterminate Sentence Law" (1971) (speech delivered at Annual Meeting, American Psychiatric Association, quoted in the Association's official newspaper, Psychiatric News, Sept. 1, 1971).

    The inmates at Patuxent make great fun of the recidivism figures, claiming that many of their number who left prison and got into trouble never turned up on the institution's records as recidivists.

11. Boslow & Kandel, *supra* note 4, at 24. See also Boslow, Rosenthal, & Gliedman, *The Maryland Defective Delinquency Law: Psychiatric Implications for the Treatment of Antisocial Disorders under the Law* 11 (1966) (Patuxent Institution Publication).
12. Boslow & Kandel, *supra* note 4, at 24.
13. *Id.* at 26.
14. Boslow, Rosenthal, Kandel, & Manne, *supra* note 9.
15. Boslow & Kandel, *supra* note 4, at 26-27.
16. Boslow, Rosenthal, & Gliedman, *supra* note 11, at 12. See also 1964 *Report, supra* note 1, at 34.
17. Boslow & Kandel, *supra* note 4, at 28.
18. *Id.*
19. Boslow & Manne, *supra* note 7, at 26.
20. *Id.* at 27.
21. Hodges, "Crime Prevention by the Indeterminate Sentence Law," 128 *Am. J. Psychiatry* 291 (1971).
22. See Crowley, *supra* note 1, Stone, *supra* note 10.
23. Schreiber, *supra* note 8, at 607 *passim;* Note, "Defective Delinquent" and Habitual Criminal Offender Statutes – Required Constitutional Safeguard," 20 *Rutgers L. Rev.* 756, 760-87 (1966) [hereinafter cited as Note, "Defective Delinquent"]; Comment, "Post Conviction Problems and the Defective Delinquent," 12 *Vill L. Rev.* 545 (1966). See *Muriel* v. *Baltimore City Criminal Court,* 407 U.S. 355 (1972) (per curiam).

    In *Murel* the petitioners raised four constitutional issues which were decided against them in the lower federal courts, *Sas* v. *Maryland,* 295 F. Supp. 389 (D. Md. 1969), *aff'd sub nom. Tippett* v. *Maryland,* 436 F.2d 1153 (4th Cir. 1971). The petitioners contended that (1) Maryland's statutory standard for commitment to Patuxent was impermissibly vague; (2) they were entitled to put the state to the burden of proof beyond a reasonable doubt before they could be determined to be defective delinquents; (3) at the compulsory psychiatric examination prescribed by the statute they were entitled to have the assistance of counsel and to invoke the privilege against self-incrimination; and, (4) they were being denied a constitutional right to treatment.

In dismissing certiorari as improvidently granted, the Court found that the three remaining petitioners (one of the four original petitioners having been unconditionally released during the pendency of the appeal) were all subject to incarceration due to their original criminal sentences, and that none was subject to confinement due solely to the Defective Delinquent law, 407 U.S. at 357. The Court also noted that:

> . . . [T]he statutes governing civil commitment in Maryland are presently undergoing substantial revision, designed to provide greater substantive and procedural safeguards to committed persons. Accordingly, it seems a particularly inopportune time for this Court to consider a comprehensive challenge to the Defective Delinquency Law.

Id. at 358.

Mr. Justice Douglas wrote the only dissenting opinion. He addressed only the issue of the burden of proof which the State should be required to meet in defective delinquent hearings. *Id.* He believed that the decisions below should be reversed on this issue alone, without reaching the broader grounds tendered by the petitioners, since:

> . . . [A]n individual's personal liberty is an interest of transcending value for the deprivation of which the State must prove its case beyond a reasonable doubt.

Id. at 365.

In reaching his conclusion that the judgments below should be reversed, Justice Douglas specifically rejected the argument that the petitioners' commitments were civil proceedings, thus allowing the use of the preponderance of the evidence test employed in civil litigation. *Id.* at 364.

24. Goldfarb & Singer, "Maryland's Defective Delinquency Law and the Patuxent Institution," 34 *Bull. of the Menninger Clinic,* 223 (1970).
25. Crowley, *supra* note 1.
26. *McCray* v. *Maryland, Misc. Pet.* No. 4363 (Montgomery County Md. Cir. Ct., Nov. 11, 1971) (excerpts found in 40 U.S.L.W. 2307), *reviewed for compliance with order,* Misc. Pet. No. 4363 (Montgomery County Md. Cir. Ct., Feb. 24, 1972), *appeal docketed,* No. 45 (Md., Sept. Term 1972).

The petitioners in *McCray* brought individual suits seeking habeas corpus relief and alleging violations of the First, Fifth, Sixth, Eighth and Fourteenth Amendments. Their suits were consolidated by order of the Maryland Court of Appeals and brought as a class action on behalf of all persons confined at Patuxent who were subject to incarceration in the disciplinary (L-1 tier) or administrative (M-1 tier) segregation sections of the institution. The petitioners' primary complaints centered around the lack of procedural due process surrounding the transfer of an inmate to administrative or disciplinary segregation, the conditions which existed in the administrative and disciplinary segregation units and the institution's censorship of inmate mail, particularly mail to the inmates from their attorneys. See Joint Record Extract, vol. 1, at 11-18, 31, *Maryland* v. *McCray,* No. 45 (Md., Sept. Term 1972) [hereinafter cited as E.]

The petitioners also advanced ancillary claims that:

(1) Special diets should be provided for inmates whose religious beliefs required them (E. at 40);

(2) The custodial staff should receive special training in line with the

institution's treatment-oriented mission, since the major part of the inmates' time at Patuxent is spent in the custody of the custodial officers and not with the professional staff (E. at 4);

(3) Inmates confined in disciplinary or administrative segregation should receive intensive treatment rather than remaining in almost complete isolation (E. at 43-44);

(4) The overall treatment program at Patuxent should be immediately accelerated in all aspects (E. at 43);

(5) A drug addiction program should be instituted and the medical care program be improved (E. at 44-45).

Hearings began on July 22, 1971 with a walk through tour of the institution. On November 11, 1971 the court handed down an opinion and order in which it found that the physical conditions in the administrative and disciplinary segregation units constituted cruel and unusual punishment in violation of the Eighth Amendment. The court also ruled that the procedures used at Patuxent to place inmates in segregation constituted a denial of due process and that the procedures to censor the inmates' mail abridged their First Amendment rights. E. at 1-48.

The court ordered that a comprehensive set of regulations, set forth in the thirty-page appendix to the opinion, be adopted by the institution. These regulations centered on disciplinary proceedings, but also touched on almost every aspect of institutional life at Patuxent.

On February 24, 1972, Patuxent submitted regulations in almost complete compliance with the court's November order. There were only six areas in which Patuxent officials felt they could not comply and these are currently being appealed to the Maryland Court of Appeals. These areas are:

(1) The requirement that there be an independent hearing officer on the disciplinary board;

(2) The requirement that a correctional officer be assigned to the disciplinary segregation unit on a full-time basis;

(3) The requirement that a doctor make daily visits on the disciplinary and administrative segregation units;

(4) The promulgation of the correspondence rules in the November order;

(5) The requirement that dietary substitutes be provided for members of certain religious sects; and

(6) The requirement that accelerated treatment be provided those individuals confined to administrative segregation.

The McCray opinion points to the clear conflict between the Constitutional rights of the inmates and the therapeutic milieu approach to rehabilitation used at Patuxent. For example, the State's argument against having an independent hearing officer for disciplinary hearings urges that discipline is a distinct part of the treatment procedures and thus should not be subject to outside regulation. Brief for Appellant at 20, *Maryland* v. *McCray,* No. 45 (Md., Sept. Term 1972). Similarly, the State argues that Patuxent should not be required to accelerate treatment of recalcitrant inmates in administrative segregation, since the almost complete isolation of the inmate in this unit for an open-ended period of time serves as "negative reinforcement to motivate individuals into more positive behavior." *Id.* at 25-26. See Stanford, *supra* note 2, at 79.

27. There has been a good deal of confusion even about the phrase "indeterminate

sentence." Properly speaking, an indeterminate sentence is one in which no maximum term is established, and the appropriate authority has complete power to release the inmate at any time, with or without conditions, or to keep him incarcerated for life. S. Brakel & R. Rock, *The Mentally Disabled and the Law* 346 (rev. ed. 1971); S. Glueck, *Law and Psychiatry* 145, 146-49 (1962); S. Halleck, *The Politics of Therapy* 170 (1971). That is the type of sentence used at Patuxent.

An "indefinite sentence," on the other hand, is one in which there may be a minimum period of incarceration, but in any event there is a legislatively or judicially set maximum beyond which the inmate cannot be kept. The indefiniteness of the sentence arises from the fact that the authority can release the inmate prior to the expiration of his maximum term. E. Sutherland, *Criminology* 582 (8th ed. 1970); P. Tappan, *Crime, Justice and Correction* 432-33 (1960); Daunton-Fear, "Habitual Criminals and the Indeterminate Sentence," 3 Adelaide L. Rev. 335 (1970); Meure, "The Indeterminate Sentence in Tasmania," 3 *U. Tasmania L. Rev.* 329, 330 (1970); Note, "Use of the Indeterminate Sentence," *supra* note 6, at 71.

Unfortunately, these two phrases have on occasion been switched. E.g., L. Barbour, *The Indeterminate Sentence* 6-7 (1898). Often the term "indeterminate sentence" has been applied to sentencing procedures in which the court fixes a maximum and minimum sentence, e.g., *American Correctional Association, Manual of Correctional Standards* 117 (1966), or in which only a maximum term is established. See also, R. Clark, *Crime in America* 222 (1970); S. Rubin, H. Weihofen, G. Edward, & S. Rosenweig, *The Law of Criminal Corrections* 131-35 (1963).

There is also the "available" or "extendable" term, where a maximum sentence is imposed but can be extended in exceptional cases, and a minimum term may be authorized but not required. E.g., *Wis. Stat. Ann.* § 959.15 (Supp. 1967) (five year extendable sentence for "sex offenders"). See *ABA Project on Minimum Standards for Criminal Justice, Standards Relating to Sentencing Alternatives and Procedures* (Approved Draft, 1968) at 82-86, 110, 129-130, 142-143; Schreiber, *supra* note 8, at 631. For more of the confusion, see D. Thomas, *Principles of Sentencing* 273, 281-85 (1970). This article will use the phrase "indeterminate sentence" to include the indefinite sentence except when the distinction is important.

28. United Nations, *The Indeterminate Sentence* 12 (1954) (monograph). Interestingly, a Maconochie biographer notes that the originator would have been startled by the great powers now entrusted to administrative tribunals. Barry, "Alexander Maconochie," in *Pioneers in Criminology* 87 (H. Mannheim ed. 1960).
29. In other words, sentences should vary and be open-ended for prisoners who are freely able to correct their bad habits under proper tutelage. See Daunton-Fear, *supra* note 27, at 336.
30. *Id.*
31. P. Tappan, *supra* note 27, at 434.
32. *Id.*
33. Z. Brockway, *Fifty Years of Prison Service* 171 (1912); P. Tappan, *supra* note 27, at 434.
34. P. Tappan, *supra* note 27, at 434-35.
35. See Wilson & Snodgrass, "The Prison Code in a Therapeutic Community," 60 *J. Crim. L.C. & P.S.* 472 (1969).

For a discussion of the current English statutory scheme for sentencing mentally disordered and persistent offenders, see D. Thomas, *Principles of Sentencing* 257-83 (1970).

36. See S. Rubin, H. Weihofen, G. Edward, & S. Rosenweig, *supra* note 27, at 129.
37. See R. Clark, *supra* note 27, at 224-225. For a summary of which states now use some form of indeterminate or indefinite sentence, see *ABA, supra* note 27, at 101-03; S. Brakel & R. Rock, *supra* note 27, at 366-75; S. Rubin, H. Weihofen, G. Edward & S. Rosenweig, supra note 27, at § § 12-16, p. 134 n.91.

    The indeterminate sentence has found acceptance in a variety of forms in other countries. For a review of the famous Institute for Psychopaths at Herstedvester and the Horsens Klinick, both in Denmark, see J. Conrad, *Crime and Its Correction* 228-36 (1967); G. Stürrup, "Treating the Untreatable" 4-5 (1968); Frampton, "A Lesson From Denmark," 67 *The New Statesman* 161-62 (1964)."

    For a profile of indeterminate and extended sentences in other countries, including England, Canada, and Australia, see D. Thomas, *supra* note 27, at 257-83; N. Walker, *Sentencing in a Rational Society* 127 (1971); Goldfarb & Singer, *supra* note 24, at 234-35; MacDonald, "A Critique of Habitual Criminal Legislation," 4 *U. Brit. Colum. L. Rev.* 87 (1969); Meure, *supra* note 27; Price, "Psychiatry, Criminal Law Reform and the Mythophilic Impulse: On Canadian Proposals for the Control of the Dangerous Offender," 4 *Ottawa L. Rev.* 1 (1970).
38. For an exhaustive treatment of the arguments advanced in favor of Patuxent, see *Daniels* v. *Director of Patuxent Institution,* 243 Md. 16, 221 A.2d 397 (1966) (holding the Maryland Defective Delinquent statute constitutional on its face).
39. E.g., *ABA Project on Minimum Standards for Criminal Justice, Standards Relating to Sentence Alternatives and Procedures* 82 (Approved Draft, 1968); S. Halleck, *Psychiatry and the Dilemmas of Crime* 242 (3d ed. 1971); Reich, "Therapeutic Implications of the Indeterminate Sentence," 12 *Issues in Criminology* 7, 8 (1966).
40. E.g., Z. Brockway, *Fifty Years of Prison Service* 401 (1912); J. Conrad, *Crime and Its Correction* 233 (1967); Goldfarb & Singer, "Maryland's Defective Delinquency Law and The Patuxent Institution," 34 *Bull. of the Menninger Clinic* 223, 229 (1970).

    For descriptions of involuntary forms of treatment, see Conrad, *supra* note 37, at 235 (castration of sex offenders in Denmark); Weiner, "The Clockwork Cure," *The Nation,* April 3, 1972; Note, "Defective Delinquent," *supra* note 23, at 788 n.192 (lobotomy)
41. E.g., S. Glueck, Law and Psychiatry 145-46 (1962); Thomsen, "Sentencing the Dangerous Offender," 30 *Fed. Probation* 3 (1968); Note, "Defective Delinquents," *supra* note 23, at 756 (1966); Note, "Use of the Indeterminate Sentence," *supra* note 6, at 66.
42. Z. Brockway, *supra* note 40; Wilson & Snodgrass, "The Prison Code in a Therapeutic Community," *supra* note 35, at 472, 473-78.
43. E.g., L. Barbour, *The Indeterminate Sentence* 87-89 (1898); Schreiber, *supra* note 8, at 604 n.12, 606. See generally R. Clark, *supra* note 27, at 212-25.

    However, many commentators feel that indeterminate sentences, even where they are merely indefinite in nature, have the effect of prolonging incarceration. See. e.g., Rubin, "The Concept of Treatment in the Criminal Law," 21 *S.C.L. Rev.* 3, 4-5 (1968).
44. Cf. S. Rubin, *Psychiatry and Criminal Law* 186-89 (1965); Note, "Defective Delinquents," *supra* note 23, at 756.

    The legislation which created Maryland's Patuxent Institution was, in part, the result of the effort to find alternatives to capital punishment. See J. Ulman, *A Judge Takes the Stand* 273-85 (1933); Robinson, *supra* note 9, at 2; *Wash. Post,* Jan. 11, 1970, § C, at 1, Col. 4.

In 1931, Herman Duker was convicted of wantonly murdering a milkman during a robbery. Duker was found to be sane, but also of such "instability, abnormality and reduced mental and moral responsibility" as to be deemed a "psychopath" by a host of expert witnesses. Ulman, *supra,* at 278. Duker was sentenced to hang for his crime, even though the sentencing judge termed the sentence "a confession of social and legal failure." *Id.* The judge reasoned that Duker's psychopathic personality would have made him a very disruptive and dangerous life prisoner. Since there was no institution in the State of Maryland to which offenders with psychopathic personalities could be sentenced safely, Duker was given the death penalty. In 1948 his sentence was commuted to life imprisonment. Id. at 285. But the controversy surrounding his case helped lead to the legislation creating Patuxent.

45. See, e.g., L. Barbour, *supra* note 27; S. Glueck, *supra* note 27, at 152-59; J. MacDonald, *Psychiatry and the Criminal* 322 (2d ed. 1969); N. Walker, *Sentencing in a Rational Society* 129, 147 (1971); Mitford, "Kind and Unusual Punishment in California," 227 *Atlantic Monthly,* Mar. 1971, at 47. But see Thomsen, *supra* note 41, at 4.
46. See note 45, *supra.*
47. E. Sutherland, *Criminology* 583 (8th ed. 1970); Mitford, *supra* note 45, at 46-47; Schreiber, *supra* note 8, at 606.
48. Schreiber, *supra* note 8, at 604; Wilson & Snodgrass, *supra* note 35, at 472-73. See also Carney, *supra* note 1, at 38-39.
49. *ABA, supra* note 27, at 110; *American Correctional Association, supra* note 27, at 115; Z. Brockway, *Fifty Years of Prison Service supra* note 40; R. Clark, *supra* note 27, at 222; J. Conrad, *supra* note 36, at 233; S. Glueck, *supra* note 27, at 148-49; E. Sutherland, *supra* note 27, at 583; N. Walker, *supra* note 37, at 127-29; Note, "Use of the Indeterminate Sentence," *supra* note 6.
50. See, e.g., S. Rubin, *Psychiatry and the Law* 322-23 (2d ed. 1969); Daunton-Fear, *supra* note 27, at 352.
51. In Patuxent's eighteen year history only 115 patients have been released as cured. Stanford, *supra* note 2, at 80.
52. It is eloquently stated in R. Clark, *supra* note 26.
53. Daunton-Fear, *supra* note 27, at 353-56; MacDonald, *supra* note 37, at 108.
54. S. Brakel & R. Rock, *supra* note 27, at 353; Martinson, "The Paradox of Prison Reform," *The New Republic,* in four parts: *"The Dangerous Myth,"* April 1, 1972, at 23-25; "Can Corrections Correct?," April 8, 1972, at 13-15; "The Meaning of Attica," April 15, 1972, at 17-19; "Planning for Public Safety," April 29, 1972, at 21-23; Mitford, *supra* note 45, at 45-50. See Morris, "Impediments to Penal Reform," 33 *U. Chi. L. Rev.* 627 (1966). As one expert put it, " 'Treatment' is giving humanitarianism a bad name." Rubin, "The Concept of Treatment in Criminal Law," 21 *S.C.L.* Rev. 3 (1968).

    When an institution like Patuxent lacks adequate treatment facilities, it becomes "a mere device for warehousing the obnoxious and anti-social elements of society." *Sas* v. *Maryland,* 334 F.2d 506, 516 (4th Cir. 1964).
55. See S. Halleck, *Psychiatry and the Dilemmas of Crime* 333 (3d ed. 1971); T. Szasz, *Law, Liberty and Psychiatry* 97, 215-16 (1963). See generally discussion of "shamming" at note 71 *infra.*

At least one early advocate of the indeterminate sentence tried to explain away the problem by saying:

> It [the indeterminate sentence] concentrates the faculty of *finesse* (so common with convicts) and the use of the artifice upon persons charged with their curative treatment, thus securing actual and active contact of mind with mind, and bringing under immediate manipulation that element of character which should first be reached . . . When falsehood and strategy fail to deceive, as surely they will fail with a wise board, it secures heavy co-operation of the prisoners for the end in view . . . .

Z. Brockway, *supra* note 40, at 401-02.

56. S. Halleck, *supra* note 55, at 333; T. Szasz, *supra* note 55, at 97, 215-16.
57. Paper read by Professor Caleb Foote at the American Association of Law Schools Convention, San Francisco, Calif., Dec. 28, 1969. See also S. Halleck, *The Politics of Therapy, supra* note 27, at 171; Foote, "A Comment on Pre-Trial Commitment of Criminal Defendants," 108 *U. Pa. L. Rev.* 832, 833 (1960).
58. S. Halleck, *The Politics of Therapy, supra* note 27, at 172.
59. Mitford, *supra* note 45.
60. The true extent of the discretion exercised by the Patuxent Board of Review is illustrated by a recently published article in the *New York Times.* The board determined what actions are to be taken with regard to the patients appearing before it; whether, for example, a patient should be retained at Patuxent or put on work-release. When asked what standards are employed in determining if a prisoner is ready to move out into society, Dr. Boslow, the Director of Patuxent, replied, "It's a matter of experience and judgment." Stanford, *supra* note 2, at 80, 84. Sec K. Davis, *Discretionary Justice* (1970).
61. I have not dealt here with the problem of self-incrimination on the part of the "patient," but the problem remains. See Rubin, "Constitutional Aspects of the Model Sentencing Act," 42 F.R.D. 226, 232 (1966); Weiner, "The Clockwork Cure," *The Nation,* April 3, 1972, at 435. See also, Brief for Petitioner, *McNeil* v. *Director, Patuxent Institution,* 407 U.S. 245 (1972).
62. S. Halleck, *The Politics of Therapy, supra* note 27, at 172; S. Halleck, *Psychiatry and the Dilemmas of Crime, supra* note 55, at 332-33; Schreiber, *supra* note 8, at 626.
63. S. Halleck, *Psychiatry and the Dilemmas of Crime, supra* note 55, at 241. See also ABA, *supra* note 27, at 98, 104-05; J. MacDonald, *Psychiatry and the Criminal* 322-23 (2d ed. 1969); T. Szasz, *supra* note 55, at 106; T. Sarbin, "The Myth of the Criminal Type" (1970) (paper printed as No. 18 in a series of Monday Evening Papers of the Center for Advanced Studies of Wesleyan University).
64. Schreiber, *supra* note 8, at 614. According to one source, a recent breakddown of patients' crimes shows that there were inmates serving indeterminate sentences at Patuxent for crimes such as statutory rape (2), house breaking (14), rogue and vagabond (2), petty larceny (3), car theft (10), forgery (2), and writing bad checks (2). Stanford, supra note 2, at 72. It is interesting, however, that Arthur Bremer, the man convicted of attempting to assassinate Governor George Wallace, was not sent to Patuxent, despite his obvious mental difficulties.
65. Note, "Use of the Indeterminate Sentence," *supra* note 6, at 85.
66. See Ferrell, Tokstad, Listella & Jackson, "Influence of a Therapeutic Community on Behavior and Adjustment of Defective Delinquents," *Mental Retardation,* Dec. 1969, at 6 [hereinafter cited as Ferrell]; Meure, *supra* note 28, at 336.
67. *Cf.* S. Rubin, H. Weihofen, G. Edward & S. Rosenweig, *supra* note 27, at 131;

T. Szasz, *supra* note 55, at 213-14; N. Walker, *supra* note 37, at 127.

68. Reinert, Book Review, "The Manufacture of Madness, by T. Szasz," 35 *Bull. of the Menninger Clinic* 487 (1971); Weiner, *supra* note 61, at 436; Mitford, *supra* note 45, at 46.

69. The *ABA Standards on Sentencing Alternatives and Procedures, supra* note 27, in discussing the theory of the purely indeterminate sentence says:

> It is fortunate that no American jurisdiction has allowed such an Orwellian philosophy to dominate its sentencing structure.

Id. at 82. The prospect of the correctional system serving as a "Skinner box" for behavioral alteration is especially frightening in its possible political applications. See note 67 *supra.* The individual's right at least to hold political beliefs can be readily juxtaposed with the statement of at least one advocate of the therapeutic use of the indeterminate sentence that:

> I do not think I am overdramatizing when I say that at this point the criminal is faced with personal destruction, for cure implies that he must learn to see himself and his world and everyone in it in a new and different way, and it implies that the structure of the self must first be destroyed and then rebuilt.

Carney, *supra* note 1, at 39.

The cavalier attitude of Patuxent officials towards these problems is illustrated by a recent article in which a member of the staff noted that electroshock-aversive therapy was ended at Patuxent because, ". . . [W]e caught so much flak we had to drop it before we could even get going." Stanford, *supra* note 2, at 76. Due to the unrestrained power exercised over the inmates' freedom, Patuxent comes dangerously close to being a laboratory for experiments in behavioral alteration. See *id.* at 76, 78.

70. For a discussion of "shamming" and its implications, see note 91 *infra* and accompanying text. See also, Z. Brockway, *supra* note 40, at 401-02; Schreiber, *supra* note 8, at 626.

71. See P. Tappan, *supra* note 27, at 436-37; Stanford, *supra* note 2, at 76; Hall, "Psychiatry and Criminal Responsibility," 65 *Yale L.J.* 761 (1956).

72. S. Halleck, *The Politics of Therapy, supra* note 27, at 172.

73. Meure, *supra* note 27, at 331-338-41.

74. See Rubin, *supra* note 54, at 4-6.

75. See *ABA, Standards Relating to Sentencing Alternatives and Procedures, supra* note 26, at 161, 164-65 (25 year maximum sentence for recidivist); Stone, *supra* note 10, at 1-2. See also S. Rubin, *Psychiatry and the Criminal Law* 182-89 (1965) (comparing the maximum life sentence for habitual criminals under the *Model Penal Code* with the *Model Sentencing Act's* maximum of 30 years).

76. S. Brakel & R. Rock, *supra* note 27, at 342; Schreiber, *supra* note 8, at 606; Thomsen, "Sentencing the Dangerous Offender," *supra* note 41, at 3; Note, "Defective Delinquent," *supra* note 23, at 759-60; see *Eggleston* v. *State,* 209 Md. 504, 513, 523 A.2d 698, 702 (1956).

77. See T. Szasz, *supra* note 39, at 144-45; Martinson, "Planning for Public Safety," *supra* note 38, at 23. As one Patuxent inmate told me: "This isn't a mental institution; it's a hard core jail."

78. Mitford, *supra* note 45, at 45.

79. *Murel* v. *Baltimore City Criminal Court,* 407 U.S. 355 (1972), Joint Record App. at 132. A recent visitor to Patuxent also noted the institution's telltale appearance.

In one of Patuxent's many brochures, Dr. Boslow describes the institu-

> tion this way: "Dealing with nonpsychotic patients, it combines the functions of a mental hospital and a penal institution." To a visitor, the second function is immediately apparent. Patuxent is surrounded by a 30-foot chain-link fence fronted with a sheet of slick plastic "climb-proofing" and with barbed wire along the top. The guards in the towers carry high-powered rifles, and all the windows on the two main buildings in the compound come equipped with steel bars. (The buildings themselves — sprawling, three-story renditions of fifties institutional architecture — look as much like high schools as prisons, but that probably says more about high school, than anything else.) The mental hospital for nonpsychotics is, of course, not so obvious from the outside.

Stanford, *supra* note 2, at 9.

80. *Patuxent Patient Handbook,* ch. VIII, para. B(8) (April 1972).
81. *Id.* at ch. VIII, para. B(10).
82. *Id.* at ch. VIII, para. B(12).
83. *Id.* at ch. X, paras. A, C, E.
84. *Id.* at ch. XV, para. A(1) (b).
85. *Id.* at ch. XVI, para. B(1) (b).
86. *McCray* v. *Maryland,* Misc. Pet. No. 4363 (Montgomery County Md. Cir. Ct., Nov. 11, 1971) (excerpted in, 40 U.S.L.W. 2307), *reviewed for compliance with order,* Misc. Pet. No. 4363 (Montgomery County Md. Cir. Ct., Feb. 24, 1972), *appeal docketed,* No. 45 (Md., Sept. Term 1972). See generally *Landman* v. *Royster,* 333 F. Supp. 621, 646-47 (E.D. Va. 1971).
87. See note 26 *supra.*
88. E.g., *Daugherty* v. *Maryland,* 355 F.2d 803, 804 (4th Cir.), *cert. denied,* 385 U.S. 859 (1966); *Sas* v. *Maryland,* 295 F. Supp. 389, 397 (D. Md. 1969); *Director* v. *Daniels* 243 Md. 16, 40, 221 A.2d 397, 410, *cert. denied,* 385 U.S. 940 (1966); *McDonough* v. *Director,* 229 Md. 626, 630, 183 A.2d 368, 372 (1962); *Blizzard* v. *State,* 218 Md. 384, 386, 147 A.2d 227, 229 (1958). Fortunately, the Supreme Court has begun to bypass or ignore the civil-criminal distinction. *McNeil* v. *Director,* 407 U.S. 245, 257 (1972); *In re Winship,* 397 U.S. 358 (1970); *In re Gault,* 387 U.S. 1 (1967); *Specht* v. *Patterson,* 386 U.S. 605 (1967); *Kent* v. *United States,* 383 U.S. 541 (1966).
89. A California prisoner has been quoted as saying:

> I was sentenced to San Quentin on an indefinite term. The prisoner there has no notion during the entire first year regarding the term the parole board will set for him to do. At the end of that year the parole board fixes his maximum and may later reduce it. The first year is a perfect hell for the prisoner. He keeps asking others who were convicted of a similar offense about the details of their crimes and of their maximum sentences . . . . I figured that I will get between four and nine years. But I kept thinking and worrying about it, for every year in prison makes a big difference. My worry interferes with my work, and I get sent to the "hole" for inefficiency in work. That looks bad on my record and I wonder whether it will increase my maximum sentence. This worry drives a person mad. As soon as the sentence is fixed the prisoner can settle down to serve his time, and it is a great relief to have it settled.

S. Rubin, H. Weihofen, G. Edward, & S. Rosenweig, *supra* note 27, at 132, quoting from E. Sutherland, *Principles of Criminology* (1947). If this kind of uncertainty "drives a person mad" during his first year, one can imagine its effect during, say, 12 years at Patuxent.

90. As one commentator has pointed out:

> Unfortunately, there are some perplexing side effects to psychotherapy programs for men committed indeterminately. The patient can become so concerned with gaining his freedom that he forgets about everything else. He may focus all his efforts on trying to convince the therapist that he is improved or well. This makes it very difficult for him to experience the kind of therapeutic interactions that are essential for psychological growth.

S. Halleck, *Psychiatry and the Dilemmas of Crime, supra* note 55, at 332.32.

91. For the importance of staff understanding and guidance in a therapeutic community see Conrad, *supra* note 37, at 231; Wilson & Snodgrass, *supra* note 35, at 473.

One Patuxent inmate explained:

> I've read all this garbage about the personal relationship between the inmates and the guards. How they want to be so close and understanding. Good God, they don't have the simplest kind of relationship that would occur even to someone like me. For example, why not have the prisoners' basketball team play the guard basketball team. That would show more caring on a non-professional basis. But they'd never do it.

See also *McCray* v. *Maryland,* Joint Record Extract, vol. 1, at 41, *Maryland* v. *McCray,* No. 45 (Md., Sept. Term 1972) *supra* note 26, at E. 41, where the need for special training for custodial officers at treatment-oriented institutions is discussed.

92. See note 14, *supra.*
93. *Patuxent Patient Handbook,* ch. V, para. C. *supra* note 80.
94. I was told:

> For a long time, when the shrink kept wanting to know what I thought my sickness was, I told him I just stole because I wanted the money. I was getting nowhere; he made it clear that I wasn't cooperating. I caught on. You should hear me now. (He laughed and rolled his eyes.) Man, am I sick!

95. In a recent article describing four patient interviews by the Patuxent Board of Review, two of the patients seem to be following this same approach, or at least one very similar to it, in order to convince the board that they were ready to be released. Stanford, *supra* note 2, at 71-72, 74.
96. Carney, *supra* note 1, at 40.
97. For discussions of the California system, pro and con, see S. Glueck, *supra* note 27, at 154-57, and Mitford, *supra* note 45.
98. Reich, "Therapeutic Implications of the Indeterminate Sentence," 2 *Issues in Criminology* 11 (1966). A Patuxent inmate put the same thought in different words:

> There is a constant conflict between what they say and what they do. They say they want you to speak up and to speak out. Tell everything you think, no matter how crazy or far out it may be. But, man, if you *do* protest, or speak out, or tell all, the result can be anything from a report against you to the hole. There's no freedom of speech, much less understanding of what you're really all about.

99. *Id.* One is also reminded of the patient who had just undergone a lobotomy:

> He was still as mad as a March hare, only he was no longer talking about it, no longer telling relatives and doctors about his strange ideas, his crazy thoughts, or describing to them his hallucinations. Why should he? If you opened your mouth and talked about what was going on inside of you, someone was sure to pin you to a table and set an explosion going in your head, or perhaps cut out pieces of your brain. Better to pretend, to wear a mask, to pose as a normal citizen, to wear your blue serge with circumspection and outward dignity, to keep your secrets and to cover them over with the pretense of pressed trousers and gray fedora. Better, in short, to adjust.

R.Lindner, *Prescription for Rebellion,* 63-65 (1962).

100. Martinson, "The Meaning of Attica," *supra* note 54, at 18.

101. Not all are of this view. Said one inmate:

> Have I learned a lot about myself in here? Maybe not about myself, but I've learned a lot. I've learned how to steal a car, break into a house, and escape with a purse. That's what I've learned.

Another remarked:

> People get to hate so much in here that they're potential killers when they get out. They learn it here.

102. Another inmate said:

> They've tried various theories on me as to why I have to carry a weapon. But I know why I have to carry a weapon. I'm of the Jewish faith and grew up in an Italian neighborhood. Until I was 16, I had to run to and from school every day to stay safe. When I was 16, a friend gave me a gun. The first day after I got it I shot three kids on the way to school. Didn't kill anyone. But word got around and from then on I could walk to school.

103. Serious questions have been raised as to whether sexual psychopaths and sociopaths can be cured at all. E.g., S. Brakel & R. Rock, *supra* note 27, at 352; S. Rubin, *Psychiatry and the Law, supra* note 8, at 175-76; Carney, *supra* note 1, at 34. Others have questioned whether maximum security conditions and the so-called "therapeutic community" are inherently incompatible. E.g., Wilson & Snodgrass, *supra* note 35, at 478.

104. See, e.g., Goldfarb & Singer, *supra* note 24, at 230.

105. Another inmate said he asked to come to Patuxent because he was totally misled as to what the place was. He was shooting drugs and heard that Patuxent was a hospital where he could "get straightened out in my head." He described his incarceration at Patuxent as "pure hell" and worse than it would have been in prison (a subject on which he spoke with some authority).

106. Several alternatives to the indeterminate sentence were suggested by inmates. They all favored a limit beyond which the institution could not keep inmates confined. There were a number of remarks such as, "If they can't cure you in three years, they should release you back to prison." And surprisingly, many favored the New York "three-time loser" mandatory sentence.

107. Still another inmate said: "You attend a therapy session that is particularly unnerving. You come out of the session and slam the door. The guard reports you for slamming; the doctor comes out and wants to know why you slammed." Another gave a variation on the same theme: "The doctor makes you mad at therapy. You come out and the guard asks to see your pass. 'Up yours.' The guard says he's going to report you, and you get so mad you hit him.

Who's to blame – me or the doctor or the guard?"

108. Mitford, *supra* note 45, at 47.
109. See Crowley, *supra* note 1, at 3.
110. 407 U.S. 245 (1972). By appointment of the Court, the author served as counsel to McNeil.
111. *Id.* at 252.
112. *Id.* at 246.
113 *Id.* at 254.
114. *Davis* v. *Director,* Misc. Pet. No. 4410 (Cir. Ct. Montgomery County, Md., Dec. 11, 1971).
115. *McKenzie* v. *Director,* Law No. 39033 (Cir. Ct. Prince George's County, Md., July 7, 1970), aff'd, Md. Ct. Spec. App., No. 653, Feb. 11, 1971, *judgment vacated and remanded for consideration in light of McNeil* v. *Director,* 407 U.S. 245 (1972). On August 7, 1972 the Maryland Court of Special Appeals dismissed the case as moot since McKenzie had previously been released.
116. This is particularly tragic in view of the fact that the maximum usefulness of prison programs is probably within the first year, and the longer the term served, the more harmful the results. J. Andenaes, *The General Part of the Criminal Law of Norway* 89 (1965); S. Rubin, *Psychiatry and the Criminal Law, supra* note 8, at 174-75; "How a Revolutionary Plan for Prison Reform is Working," *U.S. News & World Report,* Mar. 13, 1972, at 60-61; Schreiber, *supra* note 8, at 604. See also N. Walker, *supra* note 37, at 126. As one commentator has said:

> Long prison terms not only do not deter, they have the opposite effect; numerous studies show that the longer a man stays in prison, the more likely he is to return to crime when released. Ergo, "rehabilitation" is a delusion; in fact, the committee [the California State Assembly Committee on Criminal Procedure] points out that "what is often neglected in official statements is not that prisons fail to rehabilitate but the *active* nature of destruction that occurs in prison."

Mitford, *supra* note 45, at 50. Thus, it has been suggested that instead of giving privileges to the top-tier inmates who are due to be released, they should be given to new arrivals and taken away only if the new arrivals cannot handle them. Crowley, *supra* note 1, at 3. See also, Wilson & Snodgrass, *supra* note 35, at 477-78. This suggestion is supported by one study showing that the freer the environment, the more quickly an inmate of a therapeutic community moves toward adjustment. Ferrell, *supra* note 66.

117. The strict holding in *McNeil,* that an inmate who has not been adjudged a defective delinquent may not be held at Patuxent beyond the term of his original criminal sentence, has been greatly expanded in lower state courts. See *Edens* v. *State,* Misc. Pet. No. 4494 (Montgomery County Md. Cir. Ct., July 13, 1972); *Coulter* v. *Director of Patuxent Institution,* Misc. Pet. No. 4467 (Montgomery County Md. Cir. Ct., June 29, 1972).

In the *Coulter* decision, the court found that an *ex parte* order issued without a hearing, resulting in six months further confinement on the receiving tier of Patuxent violated the Due Process Clause of the Fourteenth Amendment. Record at 11-12. The *Coulter* court found that, since an inmate on the receiving tier of Patuxent is denied all privileges and receives no treatment, confinement on this tier is actually more punitive than confinement in a normal correctional institution. Record at 7-8, 12. The heart of the *Coulter* decision, however, is that Section 7 of article 31B should be given mandatory effect. The pertinent language in this section reads:

> They [the examining board] shall state their findings in a written report to the court, not later than six months from the date said person was was received in the institution for examination, or three months before the expiration of his sentence, whichever first occurs.

Md. Ann Code art. 31B, § 7 (Supp. 1971)

In *Edens* the court reaffirmed its decision in *Coulter* that Section 7 should be given mandatory and not directory effect. The opinion in the *Edens* case emphasizes the need for a re-examination of the principles on which Patuxent was founded. With regard to those inmates "warehoused" on the receiving tier, the court noted:

> . . . [W]e are wasting four thousand [dollars] per man per year for every man that is being kept on the receiving tier in an unevaluated state, which is more than enough to pay his tuition at Harvard, if you please; more than enough to provide one teacher for every two inmates in the Maryland correctional system . . . .

Record at 34.

> So it is fair to say, I think, there is precious little being done in the name of rehabilitation in the Maryland correctional system, but that is better for society and for the inmate, in the court's view, than nothing at all which is the situation in the receiving tier at Patuxent Institution.

Record at 33.

The court concluded by noting:

> In fact, the Court believes that, on the basis of the results disclosed to it in various conferences, seminars, in which Dr. Boslow and others have participated, at the Maryland Judicial Conference and elsewhere, it [Patuxent] has been, if not an abject failure, at least a tremendous disappointment to those who conceived, established and have run it for the past 18 years.
>
> It was widely hailed nationally and internationally as a noble, ingenious and highly-motivated and well conceived experiment. Unfortunately, in this Court's opinion, it has not lived up to the advance notices and predictions made about it; nor does it bear out, on close analysis, the claims that are made of high rates of success.

Record at 37.

118. One doctor at Patuxent has written about four "issues" with which the inmates are concerned and which are symptoms of the inmates' "illnesses." Carney, *supra* note 1. One of these "symptoms" is concern about the "craziness" of other inmates and the danger involved in being confined with this type of inmate. (As others have noted, prison administrators rarely acknowledge that the system itself produces violence. E.g., Weiner, *supra* note 61, at 434). In dealing with another of these issues — the inmates' desire "to prove something to someone else" — the same doctor says, "The implication is that others sit in judgment on the patient's behavior, and that it is good behavior and successful adjustment which wins approval." Carney, *supra* note 1, at 39. These are examples of how inmate statements can be judged differently, according to your viewpoint. I would have thought that concern over the danger of others' "craziness" was all too natural and that the "implication" set forth by the good doctor was a quite accurate interpretation of the Patuxent situation.

119. For descriptions of the legal framework of particular institutional systems in New York, Connecticut, and Minnesota see *ABA*, *supra* note 27, at 86-90; S. Brakel & R. Rock, supra note 7, at 341 n.l., 342.

120. When these problems of therapy, combined with the indeterminate sentence, are placed in a racial context, they are greatly exacerbated, for the blacks at Patuxent are particularly resentful. As one said, "It's a spiritual crime in the first place to try to make a man change his whole life style. But it's even worse when a white psychiatrist has the power to force a black man to accept the white man's culture. Things that have always been normal to me, growing up in a ghetto, he doesn't even understand. He can't compare me with Henry White — but he does, and tries to make me conform."

121. As noted above, the problem of involuntary "treatment" has been pointed up by many others. For example:

> Psychoanalysts have long maintained that many criminals commit anti-social acts out of a sense of guilt. What they "neurotically" crave is punishment. By this logic, indefinite incarceration itself might be regarded as psychiatric treatment.
>
> At present, out publicly operated psychiatric institutions perform their services on the premise that it is morally legitimate to "treat" so-called mentally sick persons against their will. But if psychiatric treatment is compulsory, how can it be a right? I believe we ought to reformulate the problem posed by the neglect and mistreatment of the mentally ill by asking: What do involuntarily hospitalized mental patients need more — a legal right to receive treatments they do not want, or a legal right to *refuse* them?

Szasz, *supra* note 55, at 216.

See also Reich, supra, note 98, at 11, and authorities cited therein.

122. S. Halleck, *The Politics of Therapy, supra* note 27, at 173.

123. *ABA, supra* note 27, at 106.

124. J. Andenaes, *supra* note 116, at 90 (1965).

125. For a discussion of the current status of the right to treatment, see S. Brakel & R. Rock, *supra* note 27, at 347, 354-55; S. Rubin, H. Weihofen, G. Edward & S. Rosenweig, *supra* note 27, ch. 4 § 15 at 134; Drake, "Enforcing the Right to Treatment," 10 *Am. Crim. L. Rev* 587 (1972); Golten, "Role of Defense Counsel in the Criminal Commitment Process," 10 *Am. Crim. L. Rev.* 385, 406-07 (1972).

The questions raised by judicial implementation of the "right to treatment" in the field of mental health are discussed in Robitscher, "Courts, State Hospitals, and the Right to Treatment," 129 *Am. J. Psychiatry* 298 (Sept. 1972). After arguing that recent decisions have provided "justice for patients who have been denied justice," Doctor Robitscher concludes by warning:

> Psychiatrists at this time must deal with the problem of the camel whose snout is in our tent. We can recognize that there is a right to treatment. We can also insist that courts use simple yardsticks — which psychiatry will have to develop quickly — to keep the legal determination of treatment adequacy from usurping psychiatric authority and determining hospital policy.

Id. at 303.

126. Martinson, "The Meaning of Attica," *supra* note 54, at 18.

127. For the same reason, I am opposed to the fixed but "extendable" sentence, advocated by Schreiber, *supra* note 8, at 631-33. So long as the sentence is essentially open ended, it embodies the same anxiety and fear for the inmate, and the same potential for abuse by the authorities, as does the indeterminate sentence.

5. Justice and Parole: The Oregon Experience*

Ira Blalock

Background: A Growing Awareness

How do you make a fair release decision? That was the question that confronted me in July 1975, when first appointed to the Oregon Parole Board. My "innocence" was lost after attending one of my first hearings. It was the practice of the Parole Board at that time to meet in panels of three.[1] The panel would review each prisoner's case material prior to the hearing. This material, gleaned from the prisoner's file, included such items as a report from the institution, after-sentence reports from the judge and the district attorney, and psychiatric reports. The panel would review twenty or so cases every day; each prisoner would be brought before the panel and the panel members would take turns leading the interview. One exchange during deliberations following an interview illustrates some of the problems involved with traditional parole.

Because I was inexperienced at the time in parole matters, I was seated between two more experienced parole board members. Following the interview conducted by one of the other panel members, the interviewer suggested a reset of the parole hearing of twelve months. He said something like, "I'd set him to July of '76." The other panel member said, somewhat more harshly, "That isn't nearly enough, I'd set him to July of '77." They then looked to me who was apparently expected to resolve this dispute by coming down on one side or the other, or offering yet a third alternative, perhaps a compromise. I indicated that I really wasn't sure how to resolve the issue and appealed to them for suggestions.

One said, "Well, you just have to assess it on an individual basis." "I know," was my response, "But how long do you normally give a burglar in the first degree? This prisoner has committed a first degree burglary; what is an appropriate term for him?"

The other Board member replied, "It all depends." I persisted and said, "Yes, but isn't there a customary range? Do you keep a burglar ten years or two?" "It all depends," said one board member, "on the individual case. Each case has to be decided individually. We have to listen to and talk with the offender. You can't make up your mind until you actually have the prisoner sitting in front of you. Some offenders are ready for release early in their term. In fact, some are ready as soon as they are sentenced. Others don't get the message until they have served substantial portions of their sentence. You just can't tell in advance; each case is unique." I suggested that an approach, not unlike the U. S. Parole Commission's approach, should be adopted. "They have guidelines," I said, and "couldn't we model ourselves on what they are doing?" The other two Board members concurred and one suggested that I should put something together, that we could examine — something that would perhaps make our practice "more explicit."

At any rate, it was that simple and the guideline project in Oregon was underway. Up until July 1975, Oregon had been involved in traditional parole practices — parole defined as a conditional release from confinement. A dictionary definition fit the Oregon practice:

> Parole is not an act of clemency, but a penological measure for the disciplinary treatment of prisoners who seem capable of rehabilitation outside of prison walls. It does not set aside or affect the sentence; the convict remains in the legal custody of the state and under control of its agents, subject at any time for breach of condition, to be returned to the penal institution.[2]

In Oregon, release and revocation power has been and continues to be vested in the Board of Parole.[3] Oregon had adopted in 1971 a version of the Model Penal Code[4] which provides for a presumption of release at the first appearance. Release was to be ordered according to the Model Penal Code and under Oregon statute unless one of the following reasons was found by the Board to bar release (Model Penal Code, ORS 144.175):

> Whenever the State Board of Parole considers the release of a prisoner who, by its rules or orders, is eligible for release on parole, it shall be the policy of the Board to order his release unless the Board is of the opinion that the release should be deferred or denied because:
> (1) There is a reasonable probability that the inmate *will not*, after parole, remain outside the institution without violating the law and that his release is incompatible with the welfare of society; (2) There is a substantial risk that he will not conform to the conditions of parole; (3) His release at that time would depreciate the seriousness of his crime or promote disrespect for the law; (4) His release would have a substantial adverse affect on institutional discipline; or (5) His continued correctional treatment, medical care, or vocational or other training in the institution will substantially enhance his capacity to lead a law-abiding life when released at a later date.[3]

Oregon statutes further charged the Board in making its determination regarding release to look at the prisoner's personality, e.g., his maturity, stability, sense of responsibility, and any other personality attributes which would help him conform to the law. The adequacy of his parole plan was also a factor. Other considerations to be considered were: his willingness to undertake responsibilities; his past employment record; the type of residence; his use of narcotics and dangerous drugs; whether or not he made excessive use of alcohol; his mental and physical makeup; and his attitude toward the law. Finally, the prisoner's record of conduct in the institution was to be examined as well as any previous experience on probation or parole.

In granting or denying parole, the Oregon Board did not articulate its decisions through particularized written reasons. The Board did however, cite some of the reasons given in statute. A frequent comment was that the Board's first responsibility was to "protect the public"; the prediction of dangerousness or future criminality was a key concern, along with institutional misconduct and successful program achievement.

Due process at that time of the Board's history was limited essentially to an appearance before the Board. No one could appear in the inmate's behalf. The Board did not disclose the information used in making its determination. All of the file material and the material that the Board considered was kept from the offender. The offender had no opportunity to examine the information or its sources. The Board did, however, discuss most of the information with the offender at the hearing.

In short, at the start of the guideline development process, the Oregon Board was a traditional parole board. There was one difference, however, between the Oregon Parole Board and most other parole boards in the country; the Oregon Board of Parole was willing to examine its role and to adopt explicit criteria and rules to govern its decision making. In the few months between July 1975, and the early part of 1976, the Board developed and adopted explicit release guidelines and criteria.

In effect, Oregon parole practice moved in the direction of the "*justice model*."[5] David Fogel has written that "one of the more fruitful ways the prison can teach non-law-abiders to be law-abiding is to treat them in a lawful manner. The entire effect of the prison should be seen as an influence attempt based upon operationalizing justice. Fogel, along with Andrew von Hirsch, Don Gottfredson, Leslie Wilkins, and Peter Hoffman,[6] provided the underlying rationale of the reform. I, as well as members of the Oregon legislature, had read von Hirsch, Fogel, Morris, and others who were concerned about justice in sentencing and releases. Peter Hoffman and Andrew von Hirsch served as consultants to the Board and testified before legislative committees on legislative reforms. While the anecdotal approach of the first part of this chapter gives some life to the statutory and administrative scheme now operative in Oregon, a more systematic description is also in order. The logical place to begin is with the underlying philosophy behind the "Oregon Experience."

Philosophical Basis of Present Board Practice

The current philosophical foundation of Oregon parole practice is based in part, upon a failure; that is, the failure of the rehabilitation model.[7] There is a growing awareness among criminologists and correctional theorists that rehabilitation does not take place effectively within prisons. Presumably, the indeterminate sentence was designed to keep the inmate as long as rehabilitation required. The problem was that experience and research indicated that it was difficult, if not impossible, to determine when the "optimal" time for release had arrived. Consequently, prisoners have been incarcerated for disproportionately long periods of time for the sake of rehabilitation and treatment. Yet as Fogel, von Hirsch, and others have recognized, imprisonment is, no matter what else it may be called, punishment.[8]

Recognition of the fact that serving time in prison is punishment should promote fairer treatment for persons who are incarcerated. When a person is treated for physical or mental disorders, we prescribe what is, in the treater's judgment, helpful. Fairness has nothing to do with it. For example, in Ken Kesey's novel, *One Flew Over the Cuckoo's Nest,* the hero McMurphy manipulates his way from a determinate sentence in jail to an indeterminate mental hospital commitment. He does this for the obvious reasons: hospital life is perceived as easier and punishment is lacking — the hospital staff are clearly there to "help" and not to punish. For a while things go well for McMurphy and then the realities of his "treatment" become clearer to him. Instead of doing his jail time before he is released, McMurphy is first subjected to electroshock therapy and finally to a lobotomy. He is, quite literally, treated to death.

If imprisonment is hinged on treatment as its primary purpose, on treating inmate "patients," the concepts most integral to the due process ideal become moot. Institutional treatment, in other words, — its methods and "achievements" — lies in a world of subjective judgment and cannot be subjected to the constitutional standard of "cruel and unusual punishment." A "treatment", in short, may be painful (indeed, instilling pain may be regarded as a therapeutic necessity in some cases), but it may not be considered cruel according to the constitutional mandates. It is only when we talk of punishment as the major purpose of imprisonment that the conditions of such imprisonment become open to the objective scrutiny of procedural due process concerns. McMurphy, in effect, removed himself from the hands of the jurist and placed himself in the hands of treatment experts whose professional skills did not involve concepts of "rights" or "justice."

Inspired by a letter to an editor that urged treatment instead of punishment, C. S. Lewis, a leading lay theologian, commented upon the "humanitarian" theory of treatment:

> The author of the letter was pleading that a certain sin now treated by our laws as a crime should henceforward be treated as a disease. And he complained that under the present system the offender, after a term in jail, was simply let out to return to his original environment, where he would probably relapse. What he complained of was not the shutting up but the letting out. On his remedial view of punishment the offender should, of course, be detained until he was cured. And of course the official straighteners are the only people who can say when that is. The first result of the humanitarian theory is, therefore, to substitute for a definite sentence (reflecting to some extent the community's moral judgment on the degree of ill-desert involved, an indefinite sentence terminable only by the word of those experts — and they are not experts in moral theology nor even the law of nature — who inflict it. Which of us, if he stood in the dock would not prefer to be tried by the old system?[9]

Oregon Corrections and Parole have relied heavily upon rehabilitation rhetoric. The Corrections Division changed the titles of wardens to superintendents, guards to correctional officers, prisoners became inmates or residents, solitary confinement or punishment came to be regarded as security and isolation, and so on. But despite the ideals that grounded this rehabilitative perspective, the concept of fairness remained obscure. The "justice model" confronts this issue by stressing the recognition that serving time in prison as punishment may promote fairer treatment of the persons who are incarcerated. Further, "the justice model," as Fogel has written, "insists that, at least during the period of incarceration, the prisoner and the staff, as society's agents, will deal with the problems in strict fairness — something we expect of each other outside of prison. Further, it points to a way of engaging both the keeper and the kept in a rhetoric-free, manageable prison experience."[10]

There are other ways to look at the criminal justice system besides the rehabilitation model and the justice model. One can talk in terms of the models Herbert L. Packer calls "Crime Control" and "Due Process."[11] The crime control model, as the title implies, seeks to punish criminal conduct and to repress it. The procedures followed by everyone in the criminal justice system, from police to parole officer, should be designed to control and repress crime. The crime control model is compared to a conveyor belt on which the offender is processed as far as he needs to go. Each segment of the criminal justice system does its appointed duty, adding its particular input to the procedure, all with an eye toward efficient crime suppression. The due process model, on the other hand, is more like a steeple chase in which there are certain obstacles placed in the path of criminal justice officials. Official power, in order to protect the individual's rights, has to surmount certain procedural hurdles. Packer's analysis points up another way of looking at the whole issue of "doing justice," one that emphasizes procedures and rights. If we are going to intervene in the lives of citizens, it is imperative that our intervention be limited by some concept of desert, of justice. In other words, the ill-desert of the person is what justifies the intervention.[12] Recognizing ill-desert may sound harsh if corrections is to be thought of as a helping or reformative institution. Yet, C. S. Lewis' skepticism regarding the actual thrusts of "humanitarian" theory brings the idea of "ill-desert" into a clearer focus:

> [Don't be] deceived by a name. To be taken without consent from my home and friends; to lose my liberty; to undergo all those assaults on my personality which modern psychotherapy knows how to deliver; to be re-made after some pattern of 'normality' hatched in a Viennese laboratory to which I never professed allegiance; to know this process will never end until either my captors have succeeded or I grow wise enough to cheat them with apparent success — who cares whether this is called punishment or not? That it includes most of the elements for which any punishment is feared — shame, exile, bondage, and years eaten by the locust — is obvious. Only enormous ill-desert could justify it; but ill-desert is the very conception which the humanitarian theory has thrown overboard.[13]

If we recognize such realities as "ill-desert," certain procedural protections accrue to the offender. The ill-desert *both justifies and limits the intervention.*

Others have spoken of "just deserts." Under the concept of just deserts, criminal conduct should be sanctioned by a punishment which is deserved. Unlike the crime control model, the focus here is the past, not the future.[14] In other words, if the crime was serious, the punishment should likewise be severe; if the crime was less serious, the punishment should be less severe. Just deserts subordinates the crime control model to the due process model. Rehabilitation can and *should* be pursued, but not at the expense of justice. "When men are confined," David Fogel has written, "against their will . . . the bottom line of the arrangement of life for both the keeper and kept should be *justice as fairness.*"[15] Under

Oregon statutes, such justice considerations are now a limiting principle to the state's intervention.

This is consistent with *"justice as fairness."* Deterrence and incapacitation can still be considered in establishing a prison term. These considerations, however, are limited by justice principles. In other words, you may deter and you may incapacitate persons, but the deterrence and the incapacitation must be limited or bound by justice principles. The sanction imposed must not exceed what is deserved for the crime the prisoner chose to commit.[16] The Board may still predict future dangerousness, it may still try to deter crime by the imposition of sanctions, and it may incapacitate those whom it determines to be "dangerous," but only to the extent that the punishment imposed is commensurate with the crime committed. The impact of other considerations on time served must be modest. But whatever the Board does must proceed from an explicated set of reviewable standards and rules.

Background an Legislative Action

The first guidelines for the Oregon Parole Board were developed and implemented early in 1976 and followed the lead of the U. S. Parole Commission.[17] The Board worked with an interim committee of the Oregon legislature to draft legislation that would be submitted to the 1977 session of the Oregon legislature. House Bill 2013 was passed during 1977 and became effective on October 4th of that year. The new legislation accomplished several objectives. First, it delegated to the Parole Board the authority to fix sentences through parole decision making, regulating the length of prison terms. The Board was required to establish presumptive ranges to be given to an offender for each crime in the penal code. Second, the legislation removed the Parole Board's exemption under the State's Administrative Procedures Act and required the Board to follow the rule-making procedures of that act. Those rule-making procedures required the Board to give notice, hold public hearings, allow interested parties to propose rules on their own initiative, and required that the rules be published through the office of the Secretary of State, much as the federal rule-making procedures require that agencies use the Federal Register. These two procedures were directed toward reducing the disparity in prison terms that offenders actually served and making the rules explicit and public, and knowable. Offenders with similar criminal backgrounds and crimes were more likely to serve prison terms which were similar. Finally, the due process accorded to prisoners in the granting of parole was expanded.

Prior to the passage of the legislation, due process was essentially limited to an appearance before the Board at a hearing. Following passage of the law, several important and fundamental changes took place. The Board was required to disclose the material it was going to consider and give the inmate an opportunity to present evidence to rebut information the Board was utilizing. The law required written and particularized reasons for all actions, that is, boiler-plate reasons were not sufficient to justify deferral of parole. Another fundamental principle of due process is adequate notice. The quality of the notice the Board provides to prisoners has been greatly improved because the rules are explicit and make clear to the offender on what basis he will be judged. Yet another addition is the formalization and expansion of Administrative Review (appeal) provided to the prisoner following a decision by a panel of the Board. The review is conducted by the Chairman of the Board. If the chairman was involved in making the original decision, another member is assigned to conduct the review.

In addition to these changes, the legislature sought to enhance cooperation among the various sectors of the criminal justice system through the establishment of the Advisory Commission on Prison Terms and Parole Standards.[18] The Advisory Commission is composed of the five members of the Board of Parole and five members of the judiciary. The judicial members are trial judges who regularly hear trials and impose sentences in criminal matters. The legal counsel to the governor also serves as a member, but only votes when necessary, to break a tie on the commission itself. The purpose of the Advisory Commission is to advise the Board of Parole. The Commission has been involved in the guideline construction from the start. Modifications have to be considered by the Commission. This constitutes a unique system-building approach. The charge to the Advisory Commission and the principle of commensurate desert in term setting are set forth in the same statutory provision:

(1) The commission shall propose to the board and the board shall adopt rules establishing ranges of duration of imprisonment to be served for felony offenses prior to release on parole. The range for any offense shall be within the maximum sentence provided for that offense.

(2) The ranges shall be designed to achieve the following objectives:

  (a) Punishment which is commensurate with the seriousness of the prisoner's criminal conduct.

  (b) To the extent not inconsistent with paragraph (a) of this subsection:

    (A) The deterrence of criminal conduct; and

    (B) The protection of the public from further crimes by the defendant.

(3) The ranges in achieving the purposes set forth in subsection

(2) of this section, shall give primary weight to the seriousness of the prisoner's present offense and his criminal history.[19]

The objective of imposing a prison term as a sanction was delineated and rank ordered by the legislature. Parole boards, despite criticism levied against them, have always been concerned about equity and commensurate desert. In Oregon, Parole Board decision making has always been concerned with how much time is appropriate. The legislation made such concerns paramount. This clarification (rank-ordering) is unique and has been incorporated into the guidelines of the Board.

Heart of the Guidelines

Following the development process which began with the Board's own initiative and continuing with the Advisory Commission on Prison Terms

Table 1
Time To Be Served Under Rule 255-35-025

	Criminal History/Risk Assessment Score			
	11-9 Excellent	8-6 Good	5-3 Fair	2-0 Poor
Offense Severity Rating	(All ranges in Categories 1-6 shown in months)			
Category 1 (e.g., Welfare Fraud, Hindering Prosecution)	6	6	6-12 (4-8)*	12-22 (8-18)
Category 2 (e.g., Ex-convict in Possession of a Weapon, Burglary II)	6	6-10 (4-8)	10-18 (8-14)	18-28 (14-24)
Category 3 (e.g., Theft I where value exceeds $5,000, Forgery I)	6-10 (4-8)	10-16 (8-12)	16-24 (12-20)	24-36 (20-32)
Category 4 (e.g., Burglary on non-dwelling over $5,000)	10-16 (8-12)	16-22 (12-18)	22-30 (16-24)	30-48 (24-42)
Category 5 (e.g., less serious Rape and Robbery in 1st degree)	18-24 (12-20)	24-30 (20-26)	30-48 (26-40)	48-72 (40-62)
Category 6 (e.g., Rape I, Robbery I, Arson I)	36-48	48-60	60-86	86-133
Category 7 (e.g., Murder)				
Subcategory 2	8-10 yrs	10-13 yrs	13-16 yrs	16-20 yrs
Subcategory 1	10-14 yrs	14-19 yrs	19-24 yrs	24-Life

*Months in parentheses represent range for youthful offenders (21 or younger at time of conviction)

and Parole Standards, the matrix in Table 1 was developed. Two primary concerns are identified: one is the severity of the offense which runs from Category 1 through Category 7, and the other is prior criminal history. Prior criminal history is subcategorized under the terms "excellent," "good," "fair," and "poor." The two dimensions, seriousness of offense and prior criminal history, are plotted in a manner not unlike the mileage charts appearing on highway maps. One reads across one dimension to determine the criminal history in one of four categories and then turns to the other dimension which lists offense severity. At the intersection, two numbers appear, and the numbers refer to the range of time to be served in months.

Table 2
Board of Parole

Inmate (Name and No.)______________________________

Criminal History/Risk Assessment

Item	Score
(A) No prior felony or misdemeanor convictions as an adult or juvenile:	3
One prior conviction:	2
Two or three prior convictions:	1
Four or more prior convictions: (Do not count if over 20 years old)	0
(B) No prior incarcerations (i.e., executed sentences of 90 days or more) as an adult or juvenile:	2
One or two prior incarcerations:	1
Three or more prior incarcerations:	0
(C) Age at first commitment of 90 days or more:	
26 or older:	2
19 through 25:	1
18 or younger:	0
(D) Never escaped, failed parole or probation:	2
One incident of the above:	1
Any two or more incidents of the above:	0
(E) Has no admitted or documented heroin or opiate derivative abuse problem, or has no admitted or documented alcohol problem:	1
One or more of the above:	0
(F) Verified period of 5 years conviction free in the community:	
Prior to instant crime.	1
Otherwise:	0
Total History/Risk Assessment Score:	

Table 3
Aggravation/Mitigation under Rule 255-35-035

Aggravation	Mitigation
Production or use of any weapon during the criminal episode.	Victim(s) provoked the crime to a substantial degree, or other evidence that misconduct by victim contributed substantially to criminal episode.
Threat or violence toward witness(es) or victim(s).	Cooperation with criminal justice agencies in resolution of other criminal activity.
The prisoner knew or had reason to know the victims were particularly vulnerable (i.e., aged, handicapped, or very young).	Effort to make restitution or reparation, particularly before required to do so by sentencing.
Ability to make restitution or reparation and failure to do so.	The degree of property loss, personal injury [or threatened personal injury] was substantially less than is characteristic for the crime.
Violation of position of public trust or of recognized professional ethics.	Special efforts on the part of the perpetrator to minimize the harm and risk involved in the crime.
The degree of property loss, personal injury or threatened personal injury was substantially greater than is characteristic for the crime.	Peripheral involvement in the criminal episode (e.g., passive accessory).
There is a single conviction for a crime involving multiple victims.	Evidence of withdrawal, duress, necessity, lack of sustained criminal intent, or diminished mental capacity, e.g., mental retardation, which is insufficient to constitute a defense but is indicative of reduced culpability.
More than one concurrently imposed conviction, not arising out of the same criminal episode.	Sentence to pay restitution after a term of imprisonment.
Verified instances of repetitive assaultive conduct.	

Judge's sentence and reasons under rule 254-135-030(1) (d) and plea bargained offenses under rule 254-135-030(1) (c) may be considered as either an aggravating or mitigating circumstance.

Any aggravating or mitigating circumstances which constitute a defining element of the crime or subcategory of the crime of which the prisoner was convicted, or resulted in a lower history/risk score, shall not justify variation from the guidelines.

The actual computation of the history/risk score is done by scoring the items that appear in Table 2. If a prison term is not set within the presumptive range, written reasons are required of the Board. The reasons must cite aggravation and mitigation as appropriate. Factors in aggravation or mitigation are given in Table 3. These three tables comprise the heart of the Oregon guidelines for granting parole.

Empirical Assessment of the Operations of the Guidelines

The Board of Parole has recently completed an evaluation of the guidelines. The findings of that research are encouraging. Two samples were selected, the 1974 release cohort from Oregon penal institutions, and one half of those admitted to Oregon institutions in 1978. In separate phases, a validation of the predictive power of the history/risk score, and an evaluation of the impact of the matrix on time served and equity were completed.

The six items which comprise the history/risk score were all found to be related to return to incarceration within thirty-six months of release in a statistically significant manner (p VI .01). Collectively, as a single score, ranging from 0 to 11, these items were also significantly related with return to incarceration ($r = .23$). The magnitude of the correlation coefficient is probably a result of missing prior history data in some cases, as well as some missing disposition data in the follow-up period. Indications are that had these data been available, one could expect a correlation on the order of .30.

Time served prior to parole release in 1974 was compared with length of prison term imposed by the board for those admitted in 1978. While the median term has remained constant at 16 months, the average term has increased by about three months in 1978 over the severity and history/risk score with length of term imposed. While a statistical relationship existed between those variables in 1974, it was not significant. In 1978, however, the relationship was stronger and statistically significant. The variation in length of term imposed for offenders convicted of similar crimes with similar criminal histories has been significantly reduced under the guidelines.

A less detailed analysis of the matrix as it was applied in the calendar year 1977 has been completed. The results of this research reveal that of 1,448 prison terms established, 73.2% were within the guidelines, while parole was denied in 4.5% of the cases. The Board was more likely to establish a prison term "above" (longer than) the indicated matrix range (15.6%) than below the range (6.7%). Further review disclosed that this was probably due to the impact of consecutive sentences. Before legislation requiring the Board to sum the ranges in consecutive sentence cases, 40% of the terms established in such cases were "above" the matrix, while only 3% were below. After the practice of "summing" the ranges for consecutive sentences was initiated, only 10.6% of terms were set above the range while 6.1% were established below the range.

An examination of time served prior to the first release is enlightening. Exclusive of jail time credited against the sentence, inmates in Oregon correctional institutions served an average of 21.4 months prior to first release in 1974, 18.1 months in 1975, 18.7 in 1976, 19.3 in 1977, and 19.1 in 1978. There seems to have been no significant change in time served before first release. In the same time period, however, the percentage of first releases by parole rose from 67% in 1974 to 98.3% in 1978.

Other Guideline Development

The Oregon Board is moving toward the "justice as fairness" model in the area of parole revocation. Heretofore, with the exception of the Supreme Court decision in *Morrissey v. Brewer*,[21] little had been done to structure discretion in this area. Ironically, the reason for this may have been the Supreme Court itself. It stepped into the void and insisted upon minimal due process in revocation of parole decisions. Perhaps the Boards were busy responding to these demands; at any rate, little was done to improve the revocation process from the standpoint of rule making, explicit procedures, and guidelines.

This is a serious void, too long neglected by decision makers. Recently (June 1979) the Oregon Board structured their decision on revocations. Another two dimensional matrix was developed (see Table 4).

Along the vertical axis are four levels of violations, i.e., (1) Documented Technical Violations (less than 4); (2) Documented Major Technicals or Misdemeanor Conviction; (3) New Felony Findings; and most serious, (4) New Felony Conviction. The parole performance score is listed on the other dimension (horizontally: good, fair, poor). (See Table 5 for the scoring sheet.)

Some explanation of the violation severity levels is necessary. As can be seen from a review of the tables, minor technicals (rule violations) by themselves will not result in revocation. "Documented Technicals" (Item 1) is less than four technical violations not counting violations listed under "Major Technicals." Persistence on the part of the parolee is required for such violations to result in revocation.

"Documented Major Technicals" include: (1) four or more rule violations; (2) rule violation, which is itself a crime; (3) crime-related rule violation (e.g., a parolee with a conviction for sexual abuse of children, babysitting for strangers, in violation of the rules of his parole; or an alcoholic check writer in possession of checks and drinking in violation of his parole); and (4) a misdemeanor conviction.

"New Felony Findings" is only occasionally used. The Oregon practice emphasizes that new criminal misconduct should be subjected to the

Table 4
Oregon Parole Board's Customary Ranges (in months) for Parole Violators (includes jail time)

Parole Performance Score	Good (7-5)	Fair (4-2)	Poor (1-0)
Violation:			
1. Documented Technicals (Documents)	Record	Reprimand	Reprimand* or 0-4
2. Documented Major Technicals/Misdemeanor	Reprimand or 0-4	4-6	6-8
3. New Felony Findings**	6-10	8-11	10-14
4. New Felony Conviction	Recalculate Matrix Range		

*Reprimand may include program change, e.g., more intensive surveillance or halfway house placement. Numbers refer to incarcerative term in months.
**Incarceration for "felony findings" at Morrissey should not exceed the bottom of range for a new conviction or the ranges listed herein, whichever is smaller.

procedural protections and burdens imposed upon the state by a new trial. Lacking a trial the Board will, on occasion, impose a sanction under this heading. For example, a person on parole from a sentence for forgery who has absconded and in the process used a stolen credit card might be brought under this rule. "New Felony Conviction" and sentence to prison will result in the offender starting the process over with the range called for from Table 1.

The other dimension of the Table 4 matrix is "Parole Performance." A score of 0 to 7 is awarded using the factors in Table 5.

The parole performance scoring sheet has four items, A through D. Item A focuses on the original crime. From a strict justice perspective, the original crime probably should be accorded no weight. However, the Board was unwilling to disregard the original crime or believed they could justify giving this item some weight. In this scale, the original crime has one out of seven points. In accord with the belief that time on parole without a reprimand deserves consideration, Item B awards two points for over 18 months — no points if less than 9 months. Item C awards two points for incident-free (over 12 months) parole. Item D relates to program adequacy; a strong program, i.e., job, residence, supportive family or friends, or treatment program if necessary, is worth two points. A tenable program is worth one point if one of the elements of a strong program is present and the rest can be developed. If there are no community based program elements, the score is 0.

A parolee who receives 7 points will serve less time for a violation

Table 5
Parole Performance Scoring Sheet

A. Original Crime:		
Category 1, 2, or 3	Score 1 point	
Category 4, 5, 6, 7	Score 0 points	________
B. Time on Parole/Without Reprimand:		
Over 18 months	Score 2 points	
9 to 18 months	Score 1 point	
Less than 9 months	Score 0 points	________
C. Prior Difficulty:		
Not within 12 months	Score 2 points	
Not within 6 months	Score 1 point	
Within 6 months	Score 0 points	________
(Score 0 points if on parole 6 months or less)		
D. Program Adequacy:		
Strong program in place	Score 2 points	
Tenable program in place (or proposed)	Score 1 point	
Inadequate program	Score 0 points	________
	TOTAL	________

than a like-situated parolee who receives 0 points. These charts (Tables 4 and 5) represent Oregon's first attempt to make revocation policies explicit. Several functions are served. Field officers should be better able to formulate their recommendations to the Board. Needless incarcerations can be reduced. Sanctions will be scaled to the violation itself. The use of non-incarcerative sanctions can be expanded. Further, if the policies "work," other parole jurisdictions can learn from the experience in Oregon.

Perhaps similar guidelines can be developed to govern probation. Probation violators received in prison should benefit from more rational and explicit policies governing time served following a probation failure. If the failure is merely technical, then a lesser sanction may be called for than the rigid application of a prison term.

Conclusion

This writer is not in favor of retaining traditional parole. Parole boards have too often been arbitrary and capricious. They have deferred making the release decision until late in the term of the prisoner. The waiting and wondering that prisoners experience is cruel and counter-productive. However, abolishing parole entirely may not be the answer.

The evils of arbitrary and capricious decision making are not found in parole boards alone. The entire system needs to structure its discretion through explicit policies and rule making. Plea bargaining and sentencing, even the decision to arrest, are areas of discretion that are without much structure. As long as entry into the system is marked by unbridled discretion, it is helpful to retain parole boards but not, however, without fundamental changes.

Parole release is under attack because the concept of rehabilitation, with its indeterminate sentence, is intellectually bankrupt. The underlying rehabilitation rationale has been eroded by the realities of the real world. Research has sustained the disillusionment if, in fact, research did not cause this erosion of confidence. Simply put, it is impossible either to accurately predict dangerousness or determine if reformation has occurred.[22]

We have, really, no better alternative than adopting the "justice-as-fairness" approach that Fogel has championed, or, if you prefer, "Doing Justice" in the manner of von Hirsch. Both contain directions which put us on the road toward equitable policies of sentencing, incarcerating, and release. Such a system should incorporate the following:

1. The term of actual incarceration should be related to offense severity and criminal history.
2. The term itself should be established at or shortly after the sentence is imposed.
3. Supervision in the community should be limited and revocation decisions carefully structured. The practice of imposing long terms after a Morrissey hearing in lieu of prosecution should be eliminated. In other words, an administrative procedure offering less than the procedural protection of a new trial and imposing a lighter burden of proof on the state than "beyond a reasonable doubt" should not result in what, in effect, may be a new prison sentence.
4. The intervention of the state into an offender's life through fines, probation, incarceration, and release supervision should be parsimonious.

During a trial we treat defendants as willful and volitional human beings. Without delving into the vagaries of insanity defenses, "not guilty by reason of insanity" or "diminished capacity" means that the criminal conduct was not willful or volitional. If the defendant is found or pleads guilty, it is assumed that the insanity or mental defect defenses are not present. The offender is considered willful and volitional, and deserves punishment. Too often we have transformed the offender at the time of sentencing into a patient.[23] Following the guilty finding, the judge, more often than not, will slip into diagnostic categories. If the judge perchance doesn't, the system will; a "Diagnostic Center" may be called upon to make a pre-sentence assessment. The criminal thus may become a patient who needs our benevolent ministrations. We must rethink the fundamentals. A prisoner by legal definition is a responsible human being who deserves to be treated like one. Justice-as-fairness demands no less.

Notes

1. For an objective analysis and description of the Board's practices, see David M. Moule and John K. Hanft, Jr., "Parole Decision-Making in Oregon," *Oregon L. Rev.* Vol. 55, No. 3 (1976), pp. 303-347.
2. Black's Law Dictionary 1273 (4th rev. ed. 1968).
3. ORS 144.120, 144.125, 144.340, and 144.345.
4. American Law Institute, *Model Penal Code: Proposed Official Draft* (Philadelphia: American Law Institute, 1962).
5. David Fogel, "*. . . We Are the Living Proof . . .*" (Cincinnati: W. H. Anderson, 1975), p. 204.
6. Andrew von Hirsch and Peter Hoffman consulted with the writer and testified before the Oregon legislature on pending reforms. See, Andrew von Hirsch, *Doing Justice: The Choice of Punishments* (New York: Hill and Wang, 1976). See also, Don M. Gottfredson, Leslie Wilkins, and Peter B. Hoffman, *Guidelines for Parole and Sentencing* (Lexington, Mass.: Lexington Books, 1978).
7. See von Hirsch's *Doing Justice,* pp. 11-18, for discussion of the use of rehabilitation concepts as a basis for punishing. Andrew von Hirsch argues that justice should be paramount even if and where treatment was effective.
8. Fogel focuses on the prisoner's transition "from patient to plaintiff . . ." in Ch. 3 of ". . . We Are the Living Proof . . ." See also, von Hirsch, pp. 35-36, for a discussion regarding the use of the word "punishment."
9. C. S. Lewis, "The Humanitarian Theory of Punishment," in *Essays on The Death Penalty,* T. Robert Ingram (ed.) (Houston: St. Thomas Press, 1963), p. 5.
10. Fogel, p. 208.
11. Herbert L. Packer, *The Limits of the Criminal Sanction* (Stanford: Stanford University Press, 1968), pp. 149-173.
12. "Desert" is used by C. S. Lewis in the form "ill desert." The offender's ill desert accrues because of his wrong doing. See also, von Hirsch, pp. 46-55, for a discussion of using the word "desert."
13. C. S. Lewis, p. 6.
14. For a discussion on "Commensurate Deserts," see von Hirsch, pp. 67-76.
15. Prior criminal history is considered even though it has been sanctioned. Repetition raises the degree of culpability ascribed to the offender or prisoner (See von Hirsch, pp. 84-88, for a fuller discussion). While there is a difference of opinion among criminologists about the fairness of counting priors, in Oregon the decision is to increase time served for prior criminal conduct.
16. For current rules of the commission, see U.S. Parole Commission Rules § 2.12 in 42 Federal Register 39808, 39811 (1977).
17. ORS 144.775.
18. ORS 144.780.
19. In the course of writing this chapter, I discovered that the State of Washington has done some work in this area.

20. *Morrissey* v. *Brewer,* 408 U.S. 471 (1972).
21. Don M. Gottfredson has discussed the factors that have predictive power. These factors are largely known at sentencing or early in a prison term. Even if prediction is a critical element, the prison experience does not seem to change the prospects. See Don M. Gottfredson, "Assessment of Prediction Methods," Johnson, Savitz, and Wolfgang (eds.), *The Sociology of Punishment and Corrections,* 2nd ed. (New York: Wiley, 1970).
22. Judge Marvin E. Frankel, *Criminal Sentences*: *Law Without Order* (New York: Hill and Wang, 1973). This book provides an interesting overview of sentencing problems.

PART 3

Fairness in Juvenile Justice

Introduction

The two chapters in this section extend the discussion of justice as fairness to the operations of the juvenile justice system. The central issues in dealing with juveniles are essentially the same as those dealt with in earlier chapters on the adult justice system. First, what is the proper function of the juvenile court's disposition: treatment or punishment? Second, what is the appropriate range of dispositions that should be imposed as a response to criminal behavior? A related question then concerns the degree of discretion to be exercised by justice system officials in dealing with delinquent youth.

Chapter 6 by Charles Shireman, a professor of social work, describes the traditional juvenile court principle that the needs of the individual child are to be evaluated by professional diagnosis and observation so as to produce the appropriate disposition in the individual case. Treatment is to be provided according to the specific needs of the individual child, irrespective of the desires of the youth or whether a delinquent or status offense was committed. The tremendous amount of discretion exercised over delinquent youth caught up in the system extends into correctional institutions so that parole decisions in many jurisdictions rest with the institutional treatment staff.

Shireman identifies four major areas for juvenile justice reform: decriminalization of status offenses; diversion out of the system; increased emphasis on due process procedures; limitations on discretion. Clearly, as the author is aware, the effect of such reforms goes against traditional notions of the beneficent functions of the juvenile court and the place of the rehabilitative model.

Chapter 7 by David Chein and Joe Hudson illustrates many of the issues addressed by Shireman by reviewing the research literature. The central question addressed in Chapter 7 concerns the exercise of discretionary authority: what are the criteria used by juvenile justice officials to make decisions about detaining youth, referring them to court for adjudication, and in making disposition decisions? Based upon a literature review, Chein and Hudson conclude that no consistently used decision criteria are evident. They then turn to an examination of criteria used in making parole decisions about incarcerated youth. Again, a picture of inconsistency is revealed.

The third section of the paper by Chein and Hudson describes the use made of research done in Minnesota to partially eliminate and structure discretion of correction officials to release incarcerated youth. The release policy that has been adopted in Minnesota incorporates many of the principles enforced by Shireman, including proportionality and determinacy. The duration of the institutional stay is to be proportionate to the seriousness of the offense as well as specific and certain. In addition, status offenders are immediately returned from the correctional institution to the community, and visibility and accountability have been built into the parole decision-making process, along with the right to counsel.

6. The Juvenile Justice System: Structure, Problems and Prospects

Charles Shireman

The Juvenile Justice System

Although most industrial nations are concerned over what appear to be growing crime rates in recent years, crime seems more extensive and more corrosive of the quality of life in the U.S. than in any other Western country. Disturbingly, both our present concern and our anxiety over the prospects for the future are exacerbated by the fact that a major share of American crime appears to be attributable to the young. While we do not know precisely what that share is, we do have some data on the number of young people brought into contact with the juvenile or criminal justice system through arrests by police. In 1977 youth between the ages of 11 to 17, inclusive, constituted 13.0% of the U.S. population. They accounted for an estimated 23.2% of all arrests for that year. The situation is made more dramatically clear by narrowing our focus to the particularly vulnerable 15 to 17 age group and to the more serious crimes composing the F.B.I. Index. As shown in Table 1, in 1977 youth ages 15, 16, and 17 composed 5.8% of the total U.S. population. They accounted for 27.7% of all Index property crimes and 15.3% of all violent Index crimes, including 23.6% of all robberies.*

The recent years' increases in the youth population, the proportion of that population living in urban areas, the increasing number of minority youth and, perhaps, other changes in the character of American life bring in their wake increases in youth arrest. Thus in 1960, 586,700 youngsters under age 18 were arrested, comprising 14.8% of that year's total arrests. By 1977 the estimated number of arrests of persons under 18 had increased to 2,366,365, or 24% of the total.

The weight of contact with the justice system is not equally distributed among all juvenile population groups, as shown in Table 1. For Index crimes the 15, 16, and 17 year old group composes 19.8% of the juvenile population but contributes 73.0% of all juvenile arrests for violent crimes and 60.1% of those for property crimes. Males account for 80.6% of arrests of juveniles, compared to 19.4% for females. While blacks make up 14.7% of the under-eighteen population, their share of all property arrests is 27.7%, and that for violent crimes is 49.7%.

There are, of course, major weaknesses in the available data: they represent only a small fraction of all violative behavior on the part of juveniles. They are estimates based upon voluntary reporting to the F.B.I. on the part of several thousand law enforcement agencies. Data for minority groups other than blacks are not available, and that for blacks may be misleading, as the apparent disproportional contribution to juvenile arrests statistics by blacks may result in part from an actual preponderance of arrests among lower socioeconomic class youth. Arrest breakdowns by social class are not available. Adolescents live and perform in groups more than do adults, so many tend to be arrested in groups for the commission of a single offense. Young people may be more readily and more frequently apprehended for their violations than are adults. Nonetheless, any balanced analysis of the available data leads to the conclusion that a disconcerting number of Americans brought into the justice system by arrest are juveniles, and that among juveniles the problem is disproportionately acute among older adolescent, male blacks.

Official responsibility for coping with this disturbing tide of youth in trouble with the law is borne by the juvenile justice system. That system is now the target of considerable scholarly and popular criticism. This is in spite of the fact that the system's development was long hailed as one of the proudest achievements of the era of progressive reform sweeping the U.S. in the decades around the turn of the century. Of all the accomplishments of that era, none were more widely praised than the establishment in Illinois in 1899 of the first statutorily created juvenile court. This came about as one of the era's many steps toward the implementation of a growing solicitude for the youthful offender. The House of Refuge movement for the separation of institutionalized youth from adults had emerged as early as 1824. In 1869, Massachusetts laid the foundations for what was to become juvenile probation by authorizing an agent of the State Board of Charities to intervene in criminal cases concerning children and assist in finding suitable homes, opportunity for indenture, or other resources as alternatives to reformatory commitment (Rosenheim, 1962, pp. 2-4). As early as 1877, a New York statute prohibited placing a child under sixteen years "in any prison or place of confinement, or in any vehicle for transport in company with adults charged with or convicted of crime, except in the presence of proper officials" (Hurley, 1907, p. 14, quoted in Rosenheim, 1962, p. 4). In the creation of the juvenile court, these divergent but related streams were brought together to form an instrument that was meant to enable the state to deal with the child who broke the law as would a "wise and loving parent." An early, dedicated juvenile court judge wrote that, "the problem for determination by the judge is not, 'has this boy committed a specific wrong but *what* is he, *how* has he become what he is, and *what* had best be done in his interest and in the interest of the state to save him from a downward career.' [The Court's goal is] not so much

Table 1
Arrests of Juveniles for Index Crimes
By Population Group*
(1977)

	TOTAL U.S. POPULATION			POPULATION UNDER 18 YRS.				
	All Ages	Under 18	15-16-17 yrs.	Males	Females	15-16-17 yrs.	Whites	Blacks
Percent of Population Group	100	29.4	5.8			19.8	83.3	14.7
Total Arrests	9,845,529	2,366,365	1,574,885	1,860,461	508,896	1,574,885	1,789,851	525,075
	INDEX ARRESTS			PERCENT OF ALL JUVENILE INDEX ARRESTS				
	Total Juv.	% Juv.	% 15-16-17 yrs.					
All Property Index	1,740,500	46.2	27.7	80.6	19.4	60.1	70.4	27.2
Burglary	495,200	51.5	32.2	94.1	5.9	62.5	72.2	25.7
Larceny-Theft	1,098,000	42.9	24.2	71.7	28.3	56.4	68.5	29.1
Auto Theft	147,400	52.9	39.1	91.0	9.0	73.9	76.3	20.5
All Violent Index	421,700	21.0	15.3	89.7	10.3	73.1	48.2	49.7
Murder and Non-Neg. Manslaughter	18,700	9.7	8.5	91.7	8.3	87.1	46.4	48.8
Forcible Rape	28,100	16.5	12.3	97.5	2.5	74.6	44.5	53.5
Robbery	133,600	32.0	23.6	92.8	7.2	73.7	36.0	61.6
Aggravated Assault	241,300	16.3	11.7	85.1	14.9	71.3	62.0	36.3

*Source: See note, p. 158.

to punish as to reform, not to degrade but to uplift, not to crush but to develop, not to make him a criminal but a worthy citizen" (Mack, 1909, quoted in Silberman, 1978, p. 310).

The justice system emerging from these starry beginnings was conceived of as one which would deliberate with concern, compassion, and wisdom the unique needs of each child. "Individualized justice" was a watchword. Today, much of compassion, concern, and wisdom can undoubtedly be found in the juvenile court and the associated elements of the juvenile justice system. But the system's founders could hardly have imagined the enormous industry that it was to become: one that by 1975 received an estimated 2,170,000 arrests, resulting in an estimated 1,317,000 referrals to 2,879 juvenile courts (Juvenile Court Statistics, 1975, p. 5), perhaps a million youth a year being placed in detention in juvenile detention homes or adult jails (Sarri, 1974, p. 64), and the incarceration in 1978 of a daily total of 26,000 youth in state correctional institutions (Wilson, 1978). Of necessity, there has evolved a huge "people-processing system" composed of a multitude of societal institutions and agencies assuming enormous authority over the lives of young people, sweeping them willy-nilly into its field of power, deciding their futures upon the basis of criteria rarely stated and seldom studied, routing them into channels, leading some immediately back to their homes and family and others to incarceration, and ultimately discharging them with little knowledge of the manner or degree to which the process has shaped or misshaped them.

The major sub-processes composing the juvenile justice people-processing system are those of:

(a) Detection, arrest, and pre-judicial screening by police and other law enforcement officers.

(b) Detention, or placement in secure (locked) custody pending court disposition.

(c) Jurisdictional and dispositional adjudication. (The jurisdictional decision is that as to whether the allegations concerning the child are true and are such as to bring him properly within the purview of the law; the dispositional decision is that as to what to do with or for the person found to be within such purview.)

(d) Correction, or the implementation of the dispositional decision either by the "field services" of probation and parole, by correctional institutions, or by a variety of other less frequently available alternatives beginning to emerge in recent years.

Some brief description of the societal institutions performing those processes is in order. This will be followed by analysis of the issues confronting attempts to move the system toward a "justice model."

Police Work With Juveniles

The police are the gatekeepers of the juvenile justice system. A comparatively few youth may enter it through referral to the juvenile court from schools, parents, or other sources, but for most youth who become known as offenders, their first contact with the justice system is with a police officer. Further, it is a police officer, guided by whatever (often very little) available statement of law and public policy as may exist within his department, who will decide whether that contact is to result in an entirely unofficial handling and dismissal, or is to lead to arrest, referral to the juvenile court, or another disposition. Most modern police departments designate juvenile officers given at least some training in and presumed to have special skills in juvenile work. The juveniles who are seen as requiring attention beyond that which the uniformed patrol officer is capable of providing, are referred to these juvenile officers. However, patrol officers very generally initiate the police transaction with the juvenile and such contact does not progress beyond the patrol officer in a majority of cases (Reiss, 1971).

Juvenile work must thus be considered a function of the entire police department. As such, it tends to be assigned low priority. Patrolmen tend to regard juvenile cases as trivial, susceptible of no good solution, and not leading to recognition (Bittner, 1976). Nonetheless, police decisions loom large in the lives of the young people who are subject to them. Of all juvenile offenders known to have been taken into custody by police in 1976, 39% were handled within the police department and released, while 53.4% were referred to juvenile court jurisdiction, 1.6 to welfare agencies, 1.7 to other police agencies, and 4.4% to criminal or adult courts (Haskell and Yablonsky, 1978, p. 13, drawing from Uniform Crime Reports, 1976). Such data on nation-wide averages conceal enormous disparity in practice from jurisdiction to jurisdiction and from time to time. Further, no information is available regarding the undoubtedly large number of informal dispositions made by police without arrest.

There is also little information as to the criteria used by police in making their dispositional decision. Without question, very important to the decision-making process are a series of offense-related factors; what has the youngster done, how serious is it, what is his past offense record, if any, etc. But a series of studies suggest that a number of quite different factors may predominate in deciding whether or not a youngster's case is to result in an "adjustment by police" or a referral for further juvenile justice system processing. For instance, the presence or absence of an aggrieved citizen who is inclined to press his complaint against a youngster is one important determinant (Black & Reiss, 1970). Girls are much more likely than boys to be taken into custody for behaviors violating traditional societal expectations for girls; running away, ungovernability, or sexual promiscuity (Vinter, 1976, p. 23). A youngster's demeanor may also strongly sway the police judgment (Piliavin & Briar, 1964). The studies undertaken to date yield apparently conflicting findings as to the degree to which race and social class influence police decision making. Thornberry (1973), working from the data gathered on the careers of a birth cohort of 9,945 Philadelphia boys found that even after controlling for offense and prior record, police were more likely to arrest minority (particularly black) and low-income boys. But other investigators fail to find such bias (Black, 1970; Terry, 1967; Weiner & Willie, 1971). The lack of agreement in such findings means little more than that both socio-cultural conditions and police practices differ from community to community. It is all too apparent that the highest arrest rates occur in minority and low-income areas. In these areas reside large numbers of children who encounter the worst vicissitudes of American life: one parent families, inferior educational and employment opportunity, malnutrition and other environmental sources of biological impairment, and the growing self-doubt and despair that accompany minority status and economic disadvantage in the U.S. today. When confronted by misbehavior in such areas, police are expected to "do something." Some police officers may bring to the decision-making process the additional complicating factor of bigotry; others will not. In more disadvantaged areas the officer may find that there are simply no available resources other than referral to the court. In any event, whether police are biased or not, economically disadvantaged minority group youngsters from inner-city areas are sure to contribute more than their proportionate share to arrest statistics.

It is also evident that the initial decisions made by the juvenile justice system, those that determine whether or not youths are to receive the further attentions of the system and that may be of enormous importance in shaping their future lives, are made by police. These decisions are made without the benefit of widely recognized norms of judgment or an established body of technical knowledge. They are often made under pressure, in situations in which the policeman must act alone under emergency conditions and must not desist in the face of force. Bittner (1976) notes that:

> . . . It seems parodoxical, to say the least, that we do not insist on recruiting policemen from the most gifted, the most aspiring, and the most equipoised among us. All this may seem to be an outrageous exaggeration to those who know the police as they are. It is one thing to say that policemen ought to be better educated, but it is quite unrealistic to suggest that we recruit from among the cream of youth. Surely those who could be

physicians would not want to go into an occupation in which they may have to direct traffic, transport prisoners, type their own reports, work under the control of a sergeant, and so on. But suppose being a physician required doing the work that nurses, secretaries, and orderlies do, and following the orders of hospital administrators, in addition to saving lives? Would the choice be still clear-cut? Somehow, in appraising police work, 'realism' drives us to judge policing at the level of its most menial aspects and, in consequence, to entrust it to people who are deemed competent to operate at that level. We then hope that the more serious and important tasks will somehow get done with the least possible amount of trouble.

Juvenile Detention

For several decades, informed observers of the juvenile justice system have recommended that apprehended juvenile violators should generally be allowed to remain at home during the interval between referral to the juvenile court and adjudication, unless it seems very probable that their behavior in the interim would severely harm either themselves or others. During the pre-adjudicatory period, the youngster has not been convicted of a crime. Thus, detention is obviously inappropriate as a means of punishing him or in other ways "treating" him. Widely accepted standards of correctional practice promulgated by such agencies as the National Council in Crime and Delinquency have long affirmed this (Norman, 1971). Further, the same standards as well as the informed opinions of all students of the problem agree that the small proportion of juveniles who must be detained prior to adjudication should be detained only in a facility for juveniles — never in an adult jail. The country's jails have long been recognized as the disgracefully neglected shame of the American justice system, all too frequently characterized by filth, brutality, and the ever-present and too often quite justified fear of sexual or other assault by other inmates.

The standards supposedly prescribing correctional practice have been of little avail. On a given day in 1975, 11,089 juveniles were being detained in some 347 juvenile detention centers in the U.S. (U.S. Children in Custody, 1975, Table 7, p. 24, Table 5, p. 20). In a recent year, a total of almost 500,000 were so detained and, shockingly, another 500,000 were estimated to have been detained in adult jails (Sarri, 1974, p. 64). While standard-setting agencies such as the National Council on Crime and Delinquency have long recommended that no more than 10% of children arrested should be detained, the national average in a recent year was 32%, and in some jurisdictions approached 80%! While most youth (86.4% in a 1966 survey) remain in detention less than one month, the remaining 14% remained longer (Sarri, 1974, p. 20).

Admission to detention is most usually a result of police initiative, although in most jurisdictions a police decision to detain can be reversed by a detention home or court probation staff. Some few states (estimated by Wald, 1976, at p. 12) have in recent years instituted reforms calling for a hearing before a judge upon the issue of continued detention, usually within from 24 to 48 hours. However, in many jurisdictions, juveniles may be held for days, weeks, and sometimes for months while awaiting a court hearing, "diagnostic" studies, placement by overloaded child welfare agencies, or another disposition.

It can hardly be true that detention is reserved only for "dangerous" offenders. Data on the reasons for the apprehension and detention of youth in the country's detention homes and jails are not available, but occasional studies make clear that a proportion so large as to constitute a probable majority of all detainees are "status offenders": that is, they are accused of actions such as running away, truanting, being ungovernable, or other acts not criminal if performed by adults (Sarri, 1974; Ferster, Snethen, and Courtless, 1969; Beale, 1973).

Finally, standards of care vary, but observations from various studies were summed up by the National Assessment of Juvenile Corrections: "Throughout the U.S. conditions in jails and most detention facilities are poor; they are overcrowded and lack basic necessities for physical and mental health. Supervision and inspection are inadequate, and little or no in-service training is provided. The lack of supervision is especially problematic for jailed youth since they can be abused by adult prisoners" (Sarri, 1974, pp. 65-66).

Adjudication: The Juvenile Court

Young violators go through a variety of screening processes before someone decides that their behavior is so severe or has been so frequently repeated as to require referral to a juvenile court. As has been previously noted, much of such behavior does not come to the attention of the authorities at all. When it does, the matter is frequently handled unofficially. Usually, only when a youngster's behavior arouses particular concern for the welfare of the child or of the community does a referral to the juvenile court result. Nonetheless, in 1975, the nation's 2,879 juvenile courts disposed of an estimated 1,317,000 delinquency cases, excluding traffic charges. While some few of these may have resulted from multiple referrals of the same child in the same year, some picture of the incidence of court referral may be gained from the fact that the courts disposed of about 40 cases for every 1,000 of the nation's 1975 population ages of 10 through 17. By contrast, in 1960 juvenile courts disposed of 510,000 cases, or about 20 for every 1,000 youth ages 10 through 17 (Juvenile Court Statistics, 1975, p. 11, Table 6).

While little data is available on the nature of the disposition of this enormous number of court cases, we do know that an estimated 678,023 (51%) were adjusted by a judge, referee, probation officer, or other officer of the court without formal court action, while 638,927 resulted in formal action (*ibid.*, pp. 3 and 5).

Although national data on the nature of juvenile court intake and dispositions is scant, we do have a revealing study of a national multiple-stage probability sample of 367 courts, done as a part of the National Assessment of Juvenile Corrections. For the total delinquency intake of these courts, reasons for referral were as follows (Hasenfeld, 1976, p. 68):

Table 2*

Offense	Percent of Total Intake
Offenses against persons	7.3
Offenses against property	36.2
Sex Offenses	1.0
Liquor violations	6.3
Drug violations	7.3
Truancy	7.2
Curfew, runaway, incorrigibility	22.7

Reasons for Referral of Juveniles Referred to a 367-Court Sample of U.S. Juvenile Courts.

*This table is drawn from data reporting the average (mean) proportion of each intake category for each of four sets of juvenile courts: those serving small, medium, large, and very large jurisdictions. In order to summarize for the entire national sample, the mean of the means of the four sets is presented. The results should not be expected to add to 100. (For details, see Hasenfeld, *ibid.*, pp. 61-2.)

Following the national pattern, the courts sampled handled about 50% of their cases unofficially (non-judicially). The dispositional pattern in the national sample is shown in Table 3 (*ibid.*, p. 70)

Clearly, the court serves as a major instrument in the filtering process that begins on the street where the youth and the law, in the form of a policeman, first confront each other: by one estimate "of every 500 possible juvenile arrests it is estimated that there are two hundred police contacts resulting in 100 arrests. Of these, only 40 youths are taken in, only twenty appear before a judge, and only 2 or 3 are sent to a correctional facility" (Nejelski, 1976).

The country's nearly three thousand juvenile courts are established under state statutes and are usually administered as county or city entities. Variation among them is enormous. Most standard setting agencies call for juvenile court jurisdiction until the child reaches eighteen years of age, but this is an often legislated issue. As of 1977, in six states (including New York), youngsters came under adult criminal court jurisdiction

Table 3

Disposition	Percent of Total Dispositions
Non-judicial Handling	
Dismissed	20.7
Referred to other agencies	7.8
Counseled, warned and released	22.6
Informal probation	13.0
Judicial Handling	
Dismissed	12.1
Formal probation	21.7
Commitment to correctional institution	6.8
Waived to adult court	1.2
Total	100.0

Dispositions of Cases of Juveniles Referred to a 367-Court Sample of U.S. Juvenile Courts

at the age of sixteen. In eight states the upper age limit was seventeen, in thirty-six states it was eighteen, and in one it was nineteen (in many states, once jurisdiction is achieved the court may retain it until age twenty-one). Between 1972 and 1977, ten states changed the age for delinquency jurisdiction. Six of these raised the age to the national modal figure of eighteen. One lowered it to seventeen and two lowered it to sixteen (Zimring, 1978, pp. 45-46).

Most juvenile courts have jurisdiction over delinquent, neglected, abused, and dependent children. Delinquency tends to be defined very broadly, including both all acts defined as criminal when committed by adults and a wide range of behaviors generally thought to be undesirable and illegal only if performed by the young: incorrigibility, ungovernability, truancy, running away from home, or simply being "beyond control." Indeed, in most states, almost any child could at one time or another be found to be so comporting himself as to be within the court's jurisdiction. It is commonly argued that such breadth of definition is justified by the protective and rehabilitative purpose of the juvenile court: its purpose is not to punish but to help, and thus the broader the definition the more youth that may be helped. It is further argued that the nature of the help to be given must vary with the diagnosed need of the individual child: the court must be free to order such remedy as is indicated, without the necessity of reference to the severity of the violation bringing the child before it. Thus, the concept prevailing in criminal law to the effect that the degree of interference with the citizen's liberty possible to the state should be proportional to the severity of his offense, has not traditionally applied in the juvenile court. The fundamental operating concept has been that of statutorily decreed, institutionalized benevolence. Little attention has traditionally been paid the fact that such benevolence is exercised with almost complete discretion in a legal institution having nearly unbridled authority to intervene in the life of the child and the family.

Not until the 1960's was the issue of due process in the juvenile court raised to the extent that it received serious nationwide attention and Supreme Court consideration, as will be noted in later sections of this chapter. In the meantime, the idea prevailed that the delegation to a judge of almost unlimited authority, together with instructions that such authority be used paternally, would assure wisdom, compassion, and the positive remaking of the lives of children and families. Numerous wise and compassionate juvenile court judges there have been. But nothing in the process of their selection assures that they will be thus. Judges reach the juvenile bench in a variety of ways dictated by state law and variously evolved practice. Some are elected to it, some are appointed by governors, and many — probably a majority — are elected to courts of general jurisdiction and then designated as juvenile court judges, frequently on a rotating basis. This melange of appointment processes has produced many eminent juvenile court judges. But the juvenile court is often not regarded as a pathway to judicial recognition and preferment and does not always attract the most outstanding members of the bench. While findings of the 1967 President's Crime Commission are not wholly applicable today, it is instructive to note that at that time the Commission reported half of all juvenile court judges then sitting had no undergraduate degree, a fifth had no college education at all, and a fifth were not members of the bar. Almost three quarters devoted less than a quarter of their time to juvenile and family matters, and juvenile hearings in which the future lives of children were at issue often lasted from ten to fifteen minutes (quoted in Haskell and Yablonsky, 1978, p. 45).

The juvenile justice complex is not only a people-processing system. It was also designed as a people-changing system, one that was "not so much to punish as to reform — to make [the errant child] not a criminal but a worthy citizen." This goal was to be accomplished by uniting, under the auspices of juvenile corrections, paternal compassion and the wisdom of the then-emerging "sciences" of psychiatry, psychology, and sociology. Thus, according to one juvenile court judge, "I, the judge, and the bailiff and the other court attendants are like those in a hospital staff, dressed in white. We are there to diagnose, investigate, counsel, and advise. We are specialists in ways and means to correct conduct and help reorient wayward youngsters to a life cognizant of responsibilities to the community" (quoted in Silberman, 1968, p. 314). The major tool available to the court for the accomplishment of these awesome tasks is the correctional system: probation and the juvenile correctional institution, with its aftercare function of parole.

Juvenile Probation

Probation is a term used to define both a *legal status* and a *service delivery program.* As a legal status, it is a condition of limited and conditional freedom conferred by a court upon an offender. After adjudication of guilt, the offender is permitted to remain in the free community, but on condition that he refrain from further violative behavior and, very often, with some degree of continuing surveillance by a probation officer. As a service delivery program, probation provides that surveillance. It is also commonly defined as adding two further and immensely complicated functions:

(a) Service brokerage, or mustering on behalf of the probationer such needed educational, medical, or social services as are available and are pertinent to assisting the probationer's successful community functioning.

(b) Counseling, designed to assist the probationer, and very often his family, in understanding and coping with the demands that the court and social living have placed upon him.

Probation is by far the most common disposition of all juvenile cases officially dealt with by the juvenile court. While national statistics are not available, it was the recourse in somewhat more than 40% of the cases handled by the national sample of courts studied by the National Assessment of Juvenile Corrections. A further 18% resulted in "informal probation," an arrangement by which youngsters and their families voluntarily agree to a degree of surveillance and counseling on the part of a probation officer (Hasenfeld, 1976, p. 70). The degree to which such "voluntary" agreement results from implicit threat of official court action is unknown.

In actual practice, in many courts probation has become as much a "mass production industry" as have most juvenile justice functions. In 1967, the President's Commission on Law Enforcement and the Administration of Justice found that the average probation officer was expected to maintain a caseload of from 75 to 100 probationers, conduct pre-sentence investigations, keep up with extensive paperwork, and perform other functions as well (President's Commission, 1967, p. 5). The current situation seems essentially unchanged. The National Assessment of Juvenile Corrections reports that the probation officers in its national sample carried a median caseload of 55 juveniles, with some reporting loads of over 100. The modal frequency with which probationers were seen was once a month, and the median length of time per contact was 30 minutes (Sarri, 1976, pp. 158-9). These data should not obscure the fact that many dedicated probation officers devotedly spend long hours with some youth; the fact remains that for most youth, probation does not represent the sort of dedication of effort promising of help in the solution of life problems.

Further, present policies regarding recruitment and training of probation officers in many agencies seem to suggest faith that any well motivated person can effect change in human attitudes and behavior; less than half of the probation officers in the sample courts had professional training in criminal justice, corrections, or social work, and they reported receiving little help or special training in handling problem cases. They tended to perceive community expectation of them to be to remove serious offenders and to "protect the community at any cost," and were thus likely to emphasize control and punishment over the treatment and education of youth (*ibid.*, pp. 159-165).

In spite of these problems, it seems probable that probation will remain a useful tool. While data is sparse and most jurisdictions make little study of the success rates achieved by various dispositional methods, a number of studies do report modal success rates of about 75%. It is clear that that a considerable majority of youth found delinquent by our courts can and do survive in the community without becoming re-involved with the justice system. It is not clear whether or not this process is frequently materially aided by the presence of a probation service. Research upon this point is limited and fragmentary, yielding no conclusive findings. To any diligent observer of the juvenile correctional scene, it is evident that there are in the probation service many officers of surpassing skill and sensitive ability to help. But repeated findings of the prevalence of impossible caseloads, absence of training, and lack of available resources to meet the problems of youth and their families provide little basis for optimism about the general effectiveness of that service in reducing the problem of juvenile delinquency and rehabilitating delinquent youth.

Juvenile Correctional Institutions

On a given day in 1975, 34,255 juveniles were housed in public long-term juvenile correctional facilities: training schools, ranches, forestry camps, farms, halfway houses, and group homes. Another 26,460 were living in privately operated long-term facilities (Children in Custody, 1977, pp. 18-19).

Long-term trend data on county and local or on private long-term institutions is available only until 1975. However, the state training school remains the cornerstone of the correctional system for delinquents thought to need custodial care. Yet estimates derived from a *Corrections Magazine* survey of such institutions indicate a population decrease in them from 34,200 in 1965 to 26,000 in January, 1978 — and this in spite of enormous increases in youth arrests (Wilson, 1978). The reasons for this trend are not wholly clear, and recent repeated calls for a "get-tough" policy may well reverse it. But a major factor in the trend has surely been the recent years' growing disillusionment in many quarters with the idea that the large juvenile institution can ever be expected to serve as a rehabilitative factor in the lives of many juveniles. Added to this is the disrepute brought upon juvenile correctional institutions in general by periodic revelations of gross abuses within a few of them. In 1974, for example, uncontradicted testimony concerning conditions within Mountain View and Gatesville, institutions operated by the Texas State Youth Corrections Agency, revealed a sordid story of routine beatings, regular use of tear gas and mace, and a variety of physical and psychological tortures. Of these, the court found that "Staff brutality is not ignored, but encouraged by those in authority" (*Morales* v. *Turman*, 383 F. Supp. 53 1974).

As training school commitment is the most restrictive alternative available to the juvenile court, one would expect that the residents of such institutions would represent a carefully screened selection of the most dangerous and violent juvenile offenders. There are dangerous and violent offenders in the training schools, to be sure, but there are also numerous youngsters who could hardly be so described. In the national sample of juvenile correctional institutions studied by the National Assessment of Juvenile Corrections, 27% of all boys and 54% of all girls detained were found to be status offenders: youngsters "convicted" of offenses not considered crimes when committed by adults (Vinter, 1976, p. 34).

The proper role of training schools in juvenile corrections is a subject of current dispute. There is fairly general consensus that the traditional institution housing several hundred youth should be abandoned, as is shown by the recommendations of successive prestigious national study commissions: the President's Commission on Crime and the Administration of Justice (1967), the National Commission on the Causes and Prevention of Violence (1969), and the National Advisory Commission on Criminal Justice Standards and Goals (1973). The central criticisms of these institutions have been summarized by Miller and Ohlin (1976):

> . . . the basic ideology of the traditional training schools was destructive and doomed to failure. Such a system might elicit a surface conformity from youth in the presence of adult authority — but only there. Such coerced conformity could only obscure identification of the real problems preventing a more construc-

> tive social adjustment. The punitive sanctions of the training schools simply displaced the blame on individual youth for the failure of staff and programs. The availability of sanctions reduced staff motivation to cultivate other forms of authority in dealing with youth, ones based on loyalty, knowledge, emulation, respect, and affection. The sanctions also constituted a punitive threat which other authorities could employ in dealing with the adjustment problems of children in their homes, schools, or neighborhoods. By providing a custodially secure dumping ground for rebellious youth, the training schools encouraged communal authorities to weed out recalcitrants in order to induce greater conformity in others and to divert attention from basic defects in family life, the school system, the church, the employment market, and other essential socializing and control agencies.

One state, Massachusetts, summarily closed all its traditional training schools in 1971, replacing them with a network of community-based residential and non-residential services, some state-operated and others secured on a purchase of service basis. As should be expected, the Massachusetts program has not proved to be a panacea. A follow-up study of a cohort of youngsters discharged from the new community system reveals a slightly higher recidivism rate than a cohort discharged from the earlier institutional program. However, the study took place in a time of generally rising arrest rates. Boys released to the new program tended to have been somewhat older, more experienced delinquents than former groups. Even so, in the state administrative regions in which the planned broad spectrum of community placement resources actually was developed, recidivism rates were down. In the regions in which resources did not permit discriminating placement in community-related programs according to youths needs, recidivism was comparatively high (Coates *et al.*, 1978). More recently, a "Task Force on Secure Facilities" com posed of twenty-one persons of diverse professional and political backgrounds was appointed by an incoming director of the State Department of Youth Service (DYS) in response to widely expressed fears that too many dangerous youth were being set free. It reported that "the vast majority of DYS youth can be effectively and appropriately placed in the broad and diverse range of non-secure community-based settings and alternatives without detriment to public protection" (Wilson, 1978).

The Massachusetts Task Force judgment would seem to find support from other, less radical ventures. While retaining its training school program for the youths who appear to be the most threatening, Illinois has, since 1974, been assigning selected serious delinquents who would otherwise be committed to institutions to the state's Unified Delinquency

Intervention Service's (UDIS) program. About three quarters of the 200 to 300 youth in UDIS at any one time live at home. Most are assigned "advocates" or counselors, who are responsible for keeping in extremely close contact with their charges. The remainder live in group homes or foster homes in their own communities, or, for less than five percent of the total, in out-of-town residential placements. Through a purchase of service program, most care is privately provided. The precise relative success of UDIS and state training school graduates is a matter of sharp controversy at present, but at the very least it is clear that well-planned community intervention can meet the needs of many youngsters who would otherwise be incarcerated (Krajick, 1978).

In actuality, the long debate as to how to shape the mass-custody juvenile correctional institution into a therapeutic agent is probably past. Such institutions are not hospitals, and will not become treatment institutions. Their remaining justification is generally perceived more simply as the incapacitation of a small core of particularly threatening offenders, particularly those who have been violent, and the preservation of the deterrent power of the law. The urgent need of our time is for a thoughtful study of means by which such care can be made as non-criminogenic and as positive as possible. This involves the creation of custodial care that is expressive of decent relationships that breathe understanding, concern, and respect combined with strength, and that strive creatively to offer on non-coercive terms the opportunity for growth and change.

Justice in the Juvenile Justice System?

The problems of assuring that the child will find justice within the justice system are many. Not the least of them is the presence of a variety of definitions of what constitutes "justice." The system operates within a governing framework of law and societal expectation. *Any balanced analysis leads to realization that this framework is built upon a number of theories and concepts that are at several vital points in direct opposition to each other.* Thus there are created a variety of almost unresolvable built-in contradictions and tensions. While it is possible that roughly the same statement might be made of many or most large-scale societal institutions, the resultant problems are particularly disturbing in an institution designed to intervene authoritatively and aggressively in the shaping of the lives of children and youth. Such intervention must be done without the aid of generally understood and agreed definitions, either of the methods to be followed or the ends to be achieved.

Among the inherent contradictions upon which the juvenile justice system is built are:

1. The concept of individualized justice v. the rule of law.

2. Varying definitions of the nature of man as a rational being operating on the basis of relatively free will v. behavioral science conceptions of human behavior as the result of discernible antecedent causes, many of which originate from without the personality.
3. Conflicting expectations that the justice system should promote the rehabilitation of the child and at the same time should protect society by controlling behavior.
4. The assumption of ability on the part of the justice system to understand, predict, and control human behavior v. apparently demonstrated present inability to do any of these things surely and satisfactorily.

The task of the continuing development of juvenile justice law and policy is largely one of the resolution of the tensions arising from these fundamental contradictions. In a democratic society, the ever-present necessity is the avoidance of rigid extremism and the finding of compromises enabling the definition of ends and means best expressive of the dignity of man under the ever-changing conditions of a given era. Clarification of this position requires some further examination of each of the inherent contradictions noted above.

"Individualized Justice" v. The Rule of Law

The Anglo-Saxon legal system has as one of its fundamental assumptions the necessity of the exercise of the enormous authority and power of the state within the rule of law, rather than by the variable whim of fallible man. A system of abstract laws and rules is established. These laws and rules define the behaviors which place the individual at risk of the intervention of the state into his life. They also define the degree to which and manner in which that intervention may take place. These principles are difficult to apply in the juvenile court and the associated elements of the juvenile justice system. At every level and in every process, that system grants to its operators enormous discretionary power over the lives of the children and families who are its clientele. This is best exemplified at the level of the juvenile court. Most states' statutes are so broadly written as to make possible the court's assuming jurisdiction over an array of youth behaviors so extensive as to include many engaged in at some time by most youth. Once jurisdiction is achieved, judges and other functionaries are to operate on a basis of "individualized justice." This entails inquiry into the particular personal, familial, and social circumstances of the child and the requisites for his rehabilitation. Such circumstances and needs will inevitably be perceived by a judge in a manner dictated by his personal background, beliefs, and ethical system, as well as by varying bureaucratic and system preservation pressures and an infinite variety of other idiosyncratic factors. Inevitably, decisions central to the welfare of children reflect these considerations, rather than an agreed body of statutes and rules. The dangers in such a situation are enormously exacerbated when, as is almost characteristically the case, judges and those appearing before them come from widely differing social, racial, economic, and cultural backgrounds.

Rehabilitation v. Control

The juvenile court is generally instructed to act in the best interest of the child *and* of society. From the rehabilitation perspective, the young offender is seen as "malfunctioning" or as a victim of unfortunate circumstance which an agent of society must alter. The interests of the youth may demand a wide variety of helping functions directed at promoting personal growth or expanding the opportunities available. But the interests of society demand that controls upon the behavior of its members be imposed. The freedom of the child is precious, but necessary limits upon his propensities to deprive others of their freedoms are equally important. Thus, from a control perspective, the offender is viewed as a threat to society and his behavior arouses condemnation. It may be necessary to resort to incapacitation by institutionalization, or to impose other curbs on his freedom. Punishment may be indicated in order to deter repetitions of offensive behavior or to reinforce the general deterrent power of the law. Such treatment may be necessary to serve the best interests of society. It will rarely be perceived by the youngster involved as being in the interest of his "rehabilitation" — and his perception may be quite realistic.

Opposing Definitions of the Nature of Man

The law, and societal organization itself, must almost of necessity assume that the individual citizen is a rational, choosing being, capable of determining his own behavior and responsible for his choices. Behavioral control thus becomes a matter of imposing a measured set of sanctions upon violative behavior. The issues become those of procedural fairness in the determination of guilt and the meting out of sanctions. Such guidelines as "just desert" and proportionality of punishment become controlling. But most contemporary social scientists view the assumption that man is completely in control of his own destiny quite differently. They quote Dickens' Mr. Bumble: "If the law supposes *that,* it is an ass, an idiot." In the view of many behavioral scientists, man's attitudes and his behavior are the natural products of antecedent causes. Such causes stretch in a long chain to man's social and biological inheritance and to the totality of his experiences in the family and society in which he has been reared. The concept of causality in human behavior leads to the concept of social guilt joining that of individual guilt. Thus, as the offender stands alone before the bar of justice, "just desert" and "proportionality" become less satisfactory ends of the justice system. Instead, the necessarily dominant processes emphasize the provision of help in the solution of the personal or environmental problems thought to have led to behavior, and/or the institution of social reforms.

The Ability of the State to Control Behavior

The injunction that the juvenile court should set en train societal treatment of the offender so calculated as to cause him to grow to conforming citizenship rests upon assumptions to the effect that a beneficently intending arm of the state can be depended upon to alter and control human behavior and to direct it into desired channels. This assumption may not be justified. "Nothing works" is a phrase frequently used in the ardent discourse over efficacy of various rehabilitative methods. Yet this denouncement may not be completely accurate. The evidence from numerous rather carefully documented studies reveals that many programs have demonstrated the rather remarkable feat of achieving positive change in the lives of some people. In the community setting, this seems to have been done, for example, for some subjects through intensive counseling and guidance, using a sort of community center approach and relying to a considerable degree upon counselors coming from the same cultural background as the youth served (Hunter, 1968; Bohnstedt, 1978); by parole supervision, resource mobilization, and counseling, at least somewhat guided by theory based upon the assessment of degree to which youth were able to function socially with appropriate interpersonal maturity skills (Palmer, 1974); by a combination of vocational counseling and psychological therapy (Massimo & Shore, 1963; Shore & Massimo, 1972); by some "wilderness adventure" programs (Kelly & Baer, 1971); and by probation officers carefully trained in family therapy (Bohnstedt, 1978). Within juvenile correctional institutions, similar accomplishments appear to have been demonstrated by vigorous pressing toward a "therapeutic community" concept permeating all intra-institutional relationships (Jesness, 1965) and by carefully implemented behavior modification and transactional analysis programs (Jesness, 1972). Success seems most likely to be achieved under conditions in which service programs are reasonably small, are not highly bureaucratized, and are administered by staff imbued with creative enthusiasm for an exciting venture, conditions obviously not always replicable.

Successful intervention thus does seem possible under *some* circumstances, for *some* individuals, confronting *some* personal or social problems. But for most endeavors to date, failure seems to be almost as frequent as is success. Current knowledge about what helping methods may most effectively be used, under what circumstances, with what sort of persons or problems is woefully weak. We are unable to specify which offenders are likely to be helped and which are likely to remain unaffected or even to be harmed by our efforts. Thus, no programs have demonstrated a degree of effectiveness general enough or consistent enough or sufficiently replicable to serve as a basis for broad public policy (Robison and Smith, 1971; Lipton *et al.*, 1975; Bailey, 1966; Martinson, 1974).

The problem of inadequately demonstrated treatment effectiveness is enormously exacerbated by the present primitive state of experimentation and research regarding methods of assisting juvenile offenders in becoming more positive citizens. In spite of many creative efforts, even the best of endeavors to fashion and evaluate experimental programs suffer from three flaws, any one of which is potentially crippling:

1. They have been applied indiscriminately to undifferentiated groups of offenders confronting unspecified personal and/or environmental problems. It is almost as if the expectation was that some sort of universal cure-all should emerge. Thus, findings of no or limited average impact upon a treated group may indicate general ineffectiveness or may result from the fact that efforts were applied to a wide variety of persons and problems. Some individuals may be helped, others harmed, and others remain relatively untouched. An average result for the total group tells little. (The much-discussed California Community Treatment Project series represents one of the few attempts to date to overcome this problem: Palmer, 1974).

2. The actual helping effort applied is almost always described only in broad conceptual terms, without the degree of specificity necessary to an understanding of what actually went on between the helper and the persons to be helped. Under such circumstances the degree to which any interventive theory has actually been tested remains unclear. Further, the sort of replication so necessary to the scientific method becomes impossible.

3. Interventive programs have generally been imposed upon groups of youngsters designated only as offenders, without consideration of their awareness of any problem for which help may be needed, their depth of concern about such problem, or their motivation to work toward change in their circumstances or behavior. There is in such a perspective a type of unreal "illusion of omnipotence," a sense that one should be able to "take charge" of an offender's destiny and do so in such manner as to produce, at will, major changes in personality, life

situation, or behavior. The preponderance of evidence suggests that this is simply not true.

The problem is enormously complicated by the danger that isolating, defining, and stigmatizing a youngster as a delinquent or criminal may result in the creation of a self-fulfilling prophecy. Arrest, court referral, court processing, and the official "finding" of delinquency, with referral to the correctional agency and confinement are hardly neutral life experiences. They may go far to create for the child a private self-concept and a public reputation as one set apart from the conventional world, as one who is dangerous and is to be watched with suspicion. Thus, out of the treatment of the original violative behavior may be born further, "secondary deviance." The considerable body of literature upon this point remains generally speculative in nature (Mahoney, 1974), but the position has intuitive appeal as a description of one set of forces that may be brought to bear upon the identified offender.

"Next Steps" Toward Juvenile Justice

The past decade's growing awareness of the inequities and inadequacies of juvenile justice law, policy, and performance may have brought into being a phenomenon rare in the history of social institutions: a climate in which inertia and entrenched interest may be compelled to yield to a growing tide of dissatisfaction and general awareness of the need for change. The necessity for growth and change does not dictate the abandonment of a juvenile justice system separate from and differing from that for adults. Our culture does recognize the diminished capacity of the immature to fully appreciate the cost of their actions to themselves or to others. We accept childhood and adolescence as developmental stages particularly vulnerable to pressures toward violative behavior. We will continue to endeavor to facilitate growth beyond that vulnerable period without creating permanent stigma or isolation from the broader society. But unless the juvenile justice system moves so as to accomplish these goals with greater emphasis upon fairness and with realistic assessment of "the art of the possible," it is in danger of being washed away by the tide of history.

Four major areas of opportunity for reform provide the focus for much of today's active discourse:

1. The decriminalization of status offenses.
2. The diversion of increasing numbers of youthful offenders away from the justice system and to voluntary services.
3. Remedying common deficiencies in due process so as to assure

greater fairness in the transaction between the state, the family, and the juvenile offender.

4. Limiting the enormous discretion now granted courts in the sentencing of juveniles.

Decriminalization of Status Offenders

The problem of the child who offends parental and societal authority by behaviors not criminal when performed by adults is currently the focus of considerable attention throughout the juvenile justice system. Two issues currently provide the focus for much of that concern: (a) the juvenile court's jurisdiction over status offenders, and (b) the present common practice of placing status offenders in secure detention facilities and in correctional institutions.

Juvenile Court Jurisdiction

In order that all who might profit from its beneficent offices be effectively reached, the founders of the juvenile court extended its jurisdiction far beyond the minor who engaged in acts defined as crimes when committed by adults. The court's reach was to a wide range of other behaviors considered undesirable on the part of youth and possibly indicative of the danger of their "growing up in a life of idleness and crime." The list has grown to include truancy, running away from home, being disobedient of parents or school authorities, being sexually promiscuous or otherwise "endangering morals," using drugs or alcohol, or simply acting in a manner "injurious to self or others."

There is a certain rationality in the juvenile court's jurisdiction over these non-criminal misbehaviors. The use of the power of the state to back up parental authority is not inherently wrong. Parents cannot always limit the world in which today's youth may move and they cannot combat all the negative influences that exist outside the family. The persistent runaway or truant, the sexually promiscuous teen-ager, or the adolescent drifting into drug addiction or alcoholism may need understanding and support, but may also truly need coercive intervention. The complete abandonment of the juvenile court's authority to intervene in the interest of the child in such situations would be a rejection of a long tradition of American family law, unless such authority were simply to be transferred to some other court — a doubtful benefit.

Yet, the persistently disobedient child has proved one of the most difficult sorts of cases known to either courts or social agencies. Voluntary but effective community services adequate to his needs are often nonexistent. In its frustration (and often its resultant anger) over its inability to control the errant child or to produce ideal solutions, the court often turns to simply punitive treatment. Thus status offenders tend to be treated in the same manner as are juveniles who violate the criminal law. The runaway very often finds himself confined with and subjected to the same sanctions as the repeated recidivist robber. The status offender referred to the juvenile court has the same if not higher probability of being committed to correctional institutions as juveniles involved in more serious offenses. In fact, two national studies have shown, respectively, 33% and 35% of all inmates of juvenile correctional facilities to be status offenders (Hasenfeld, 1976, p. 67).

It may well be that in a frightening proportion of status offense cases the judicial system is "incapable . . . of effectively managing, except in a very gross sense, so delicate and complex a relationship as that between parent and child" (Goldstein, Freud, and Solnit, 1973, quoted in A.B.A. — I.J.A., 1977a, p. 11). It may too often have been demonstrated that "The law is simply inept as a corrective of the kinds of family dysfunction that these cases most frequently involve . . . Using legal compulsion to restore (or provide) parent-child understanding and tolerance and to build up mechanisms for conflict-resolution within the family unit is akin to doing surgery with a spade" (*ibid*).

Further, the assumption that the court is responsible for the provision of such services may suggest to parents, to schools, and to the voluntary social service structure that they may be absolved from efforts to deal directly with youth problems. "Thus, for example, when children fail in school and are officially defined as delinquent because of behavior frequently resulting from such failure (i.e., truancy, incorrigibility), the schools are relieved from having to deal with the very causes of their failure" (Hasenfeld and Sarri, 1976, p. 213).

The President's Commission on Law Enforcement and the Administration of Justice (Task Force Report, 1976), the National Council on Crime and Delinquency (1964), the American Bar Association — Institute of Judicial Administration Juvenile Justice Standards Project (1977a), and the U.S. Department of Health, Education, and Welfare have recommended the curbing of juvenile court jurisdiction over status offenses and the development, in its stead, of a system of voluntary referrals to services outside the justice system.

The problem is difficult to resolve. It is probable that some provision must be made, as in the Juvenile Justice Standards Project proposals (*ibid.*, p. 77) for carefully restricted and time-limited official intervention in certain kinds of cases involving youth in immediate jeopardy — those who run away and are in need of alternative living arrangements, which they and their parents cannot agree upon, those who face substantial and immediate physical danger, or those who are in need of emergency medical services. Statutes might be so drawn as to create a firm legal presumption that no coercive intervention is possible, such presumption being rebuttable only in the presence of a formal, written finding by the court, with due process of law, detailing specific "clear and present dangers" to the immediate health or welfare of the child. But the possibilities for coercive intervention will have to be rigidly limited. No solution is ideal:

> Inevitably, some cases will be lost to help and some youth will go unassisted who might have been aided if the formal scheme of coercive intervention in cases of noncriminal misbehavior were kept. It is believed, however, that their numbers will be relatively few, and that the social costs of retaining the status offense jurisdiction as it now exists far outweigh the relatively small benefits. In the great majority of cases, it is to be expected that voluntarily based services will be accepted and will prove far more effective than warship and court-ordered commitment (*ibid.*, p. 20).

Status Offenders and Secure Custody

Short of the complete decriminalization of status offenses and their removal from the jurisdiction of the juvenile court is the recent years' growing concern about the frequent practice of confining status offenders with delinquents in both secure detention quarters and in long-term correctional institutions. In response to this concern, a number of states have removed status offenders from that class of juvenile offenders labeled "delinquent" and created for them a new nomenclature: "children," or "minors," or "persons in need of supervision" (Chins, Mins, Pins), etc. Frequently, such designations are accompanied by provisions forbidding the placement of youth so designated in adult prisons or jails, in secure detention facilities, or correctional institutions for delinquents. This goal has been vigorously pursued by the federal government. The federal program was mandated in 1974 by the passage of the Juvenile Justice and Delinquency Prevention Act, administered by the Law Enforcement Assistance Administration (LEAA). The Act provided that in order to receive federal funds for juvenile corrections programs the states would have to guarantee that status offenders were never to be locked in secure institutions. When it was necessary to hold them, it was to be only in home-like shelter facilities. As such alternatives would have to be developed in most states, two years were allowed to come into compliance. However, the tradition of ready incarceration of disobedient children and youth has proved difficult to overcome. The majority of states were unable or unwilling to comply with the standard, at least within the time given. Thus in 1977 Congress loosened the standards and stretched the deadlines, creating exceptions to the rule that status offenders could be placed only in shelter facilities and extending the time limit to three years. Some progress has been made. LEAA has financed a number of demonstration projects, making it possible for some states to develop alternatives to correctional placement. But movement is slow. As of 1977, thirty-four states still had laws allowing status offenders to be placed in correctional institutions (Moskowitz, 1978). In too many states, the fourteen year old runaway and the seventeen year old robber may still be incarcerated together and treated identically in the same maximum security institution, the one told that the purpose is benevolent "help" and the other for the purpose of societal protection and punishment.

Diversion from the Juvenile Justice System

The widespread disillusionment with the capacity of the justice system to rehabilitate young offenders has led to recommendations by various study groups, beginning with the 1967 report of the President's Commission on Crime and the Administration of Justice, that informal, non-justice system handling of the cases of many juvenile violators would be preferable. This trend was confirmed in the Juvenile Justice and Delinquency Prevention Act of 1974, which provided support for programs diverting delinquent youth to "community-based" facilities, defined as including foster care and shelter homes, group homes, halfway houses, homemaker and health services, volunteer and crisis counseling for youth remaining at home, home probation, and vocational, social, and psychological guidance or other rehabilitative services. The concern has clearly been both to remove juveniles from the juvenile justice system, in general, and to remove them from detention or correctional institutions, in particular. Thus, diversion takes various forms: a police department alternative to court referral, a probation agency alternative to court processing, or a court alternative to institutional commitment. In a sense diversion might be better defined as minimizing penetration into the continuum of criminal justice.

During the past approximately ten years a great many projects have been implemented in the diversion of juveniles from the justice system and their referral to voluntary sources for help needed. Undoubtedly, such programs have done much to reduce negative labeling and stigmatization, provide increased access to conventional social roles, and make available to disadvantaged and endangered youngsters community, social, educational, psychological, and other services.

The diversion movement is an important element of modern social policy toward the youthful offender. It should and probably will become more widely available and more widely used. However, in recent years it has also become clear that diversion, like any other social policy, must be applied thoughtfully and discriminatingly. Otherwise, such programs all too often produce unintended negative consequences. Most often identified among these is a phenomenon currently referred to as "widening the net." This refers to the practice whereby police or other decision makers may offer a community referral with the threat of official action if it is not accepted. Thus, an aggressive diversion program could result in more, rather then fewer juveniles being coercively placed under a degree of control of the state. For example, a study by Bohnstedt (1978) of 3,871 youth clients diverted to a sample of eleven diversion projects thought by the author to be representative of many such, seems to show quite clearly that 49% of the cases served would not have received justice system processing beyond court intake in any event. This 49% was involved in more processing then they would have otherwise received. In some diversion projects, juveniles have simply been offered a choice between detention or acceptance of a referral and, in addition, have been required to admit their guilt in order to avoid official processing. Thus youngsters become labeled as delinquents, with the danger of stigmatization. In these circumstances a meaningful degree of coercion is used without traditional protections (already frequently all too feeble) against the abuse of discretionary authority.

The problem is complex. The fact that some youngsters not traditionally involved with the justice system are served by community resources brought into being by diversion projects does not automatically mean that a negative "widening of the net" has taken place. The critical issue is probably whether or not recourse to legal sanctions remains available once diversion has been made. Clearly stated, broadly understood safeguards, probably in statutory form, will become necessary. Among them:

1. The diversion of a youth from the justice system and his referral to an alternative program should be a substitute for all further processing and adjudication. Youngsters thought in need of a degree of continuing official control should be made probationers, by judicial decision and with continued judicial oversight.
2. The agencies to which youth are diverted should be outside the formal jurisdiction of the justice system.
3. Diversion efforts should focus only on youngsters who would normally progress at least as far into the justice system as juvenile court intake. Youth normally screened out of the system and released by police should receive no further disposition.

Due Process in the Juvenile Court

For the purpose of this discussion, due process is defined as the presence of the traditional procedural safeguards guaranteed by the Bill of Rights of the U.S. Constitution in order to protect individual liberties and to restrict the actions of the state (Sosin and Sarri, 1976, p. 181). The goal of provision of due process so defined might be expected to be a conservative one. After all, these constitutional protections fix only constitutional minima. They need not be used to fix maxima, and complete fairness in the transaction between the state and the individual before the bar of justice may often require transcending them. But even the modest goal of general achievement of the minima remains at some distance.

Prior to approximately the end of World War II, the issue of due process protections for youthful offenders was not generally thought to be very substantial. Benign custody of the child was perceived as a much more evident and pressing right than was liberty. The juvenile court and the juvenile justice system were designed to protect, not to punish the child. No particular need to protect the child from his protectors was discerned. The prevailing attitude might be illustrated by an oft-quoted Pennsylvania decision denying certain due process protections in a juvenile court case:

> . . . it is important that the powers of the court, in respect to the care, treatment and control of dependent, neglected, delinquent and incorrigible children should be clearly distinguished from those exercised by it in the administration of the criminal law . . . [appeals to due process] overlook the fact, hereafter to be noticed that it [the juvenile court act] is not for the punishment of offenders, but for the salvation of children, and points out the way by which the state undertakes to save, not particular children of a special class, but all children under a certain age, whose salvation may become the duty of the state in the absence of proper parental care or disregard of it by wayward children (*Commonwealth v. Fisher,* 213 Pa. 48 1905).

Approximately the same assessment was made by the Supreme Court of the United States when in 1955 it refused to hear an appeal alleging want of due process in a juvenile case in Philadelphia: "Since juvenile courts are not criminal courts, the constitutional rights granted to persons accused of crime are not applicable to the children brought before them" (*In re Holmes,* 109 A 2d 523 (L935), cert. denied, 348 U.S. 973. Quoted in Haskell and Yablonsky, 1978, p. 34). Not until the 1960's was the issue of due process in the juvenile court raised to the extent that it received serious nationwide attention and Supreme Court reconsideration. The subsequent years have seen considerable revision in the thinking of legal scholars, in the holdings of competent courts, and in some statutes. They may even have brought some changes in this nature of the court experience accorded many children. Spurred by evidence of gross abuses of unbridled discretion and by the increasing criticism of legal scholars (see, for example, Tappan, 1949; Rosenheim, 1962), the Supreme Court began to lay down at least some of the landmarks designating the path that the juvenile justice system was to follow, often tardily and hesitatingly. In *Kent* v. *U.S.* (1966) it mandated that a right to counsel and a proper hearing were necessary in cases involving waivers to adult courts. In *In re Gault* (1967) the Court ruled that at the adjudication stage in a case involving risk of commitment to an institution for delinquents a child has the right to:

1. Notice of the precise charge against him.
2. Counsel, and proper notification of this right.
3. Protection against self-incrimination (the right to remain silent).
4. Confrontation and cross-examination of witnesses.

A variety of Supreme Court rulings have followed. In *In re Winship* (1970) the court denied that the juvenile proceeding is essentially a civil one and declared that "proof beyond reasonable doubt" is required in delinquency hearings. In *Breed* v. *Jones* (1975), the ruling was to the effect that transfer to and prosecution in a criminal court following an adjudicatory hearing in juvenile court constitute impermissible double jeopardy. However, the court has also revealed its continuing conviction that not all procedural protections applicable to the criminal court can be transferred to juvenile proceedings, in a ruling that juveniles need not be granted jury trials. In *McKeiver* v. *Pennsylvania* (1971), the court stated: "There is a possibility, at least, that the jury trial, if required as a matter of constitutional precept, will remake the juvenile proceeding into a fully adversary process and will put an effective end to what had been the idealistic prospect of an intimate, informal, protective proceeding."

It is not clear precisely how we are to move in the future in efforts to achieve essential and evident fairness and still retain the "idealistic prospect of an intimate, informal, protective proceeding." There is much yet to be done. The protections granted in *Gault* cover only the adjudication stage. Thus, at the arrest stage, at court intake, and at the point of disposition, the protections of counsel, of confrontation of witnesses, and against self-incrimination are not assured. The court's assumed therapeutic mission results in "social studies" by probation departments, which result in the invasion of privacy by the collection of information irrelevant to actual charges. As long as status offenses remain a matter of court jurisdiction, youths may be placed in jeopardy upon vague charges. The issue as to who may place youths in detention remains clouded. Probation social study reports may influence judges' dispositional decisions in major ways, but their accessibility to juveniles, parents, or counsel remains uncertain. The rights to counsel and to the appointment of counsel at hearings concerning the revocation of probation and the nature of such hearings are by no means clear.

In sum, it is evident that even if all pertinent statutes and guiding court rulings were adhered to, present definition of *due process* would not assure *a fair process*. Thus the National Assessment of Juvenile Correction concluded from its study of its national sample of juvenile courts that the Supreme Court rulings on the juvenile court had produced formal more often than full and substantial compliance and that "There has been no due process revolution. . . . It is clear that there must be more positive action toward the implementation of the rights of individual juveniles in all phases of case processing than has occurred in the vast majority of juvenile courts in the U.S." (Sosin and Sarri, 1976, pp. 205-206).

Sentencing in the Juvenile Court

The fundamental difference between the juvenile correctional system and the child welfare and related systems is the former's capacity to impose coercive dispositions on children and youth. The heart of this process is the juvenile court's sentencing power, usually referred to in the juvenile court as its "dispositional" function. The exercise of this power is a relatively little-studied phenomenon. Just as in the adult criminal court, juvenile court sentencing is carried out with little statutory guidance, with considerable confusion and disagreement as to the fundamental social purpose sought to be achieved, and with slight or no feedback as to the ultimate impact of the process upon its subjects. Only recently have the elements of a "justice model" which might guide the juvenile court's dispositional function begun to emerge. The endeavor to accomplish this end has been aided by the work of thoughtful study groups such as the Task Force on Sentencing Policy Toward Young Offenders formed by the Twentieth Century Fund (Twentieth Century Fund, 1978) and the Institute of Judicial Administration — American Bar Association Joint Commission on Juvenile Justice Standards (A.B.A. — I.J.A., 1977). Both of these groups have contributed to illuminating the issues and both have produced rather detailed recommended standards. The complexity of the problem is illustrated by the fact that at certain key points the two sets of standards are in sharp disagreement. However, from these and other studies, a series of issues has surfaced. For none of these issues are final answers apparent; necessary to their resolution will be further discourse and experiments and findings in different jurisdictions. But the general direction in which movement is beginning to take place is reasonably clear.

The resolution of the sentencing problem which will eventually emerge in the juvenile court will probably be just as strongly oriented toward striving for true and evident fairness as will those which must be developed in the criminal court. They will differ in some respects from those developed in that court for the very reasons that we have a separate juvenile justice system: our belief that children and youth have a somewhat diminished responsibility due to their presumably lesser capacity to count the present and future cost of their actions to themselves or to others; their particular vulnerability to peer pressures; the sense that societal failure is often at least contributory to juvenile misbehavior; and our desire not to permanently stigmatize and isolate the developing future citizen. We desire to preserve "room for reform." However, in the instance of the particularly serious offense involving criminal violence on the part of an offender over the age of, say, fifteen or sixteen, provision will continue to be made for waiver, with due process of law, to the criminal court. Otherwise, both the Task Force on Sentencing Policy and the Juvenile Justice Standards Project recommend that the juvenile court have jurisdiction over children committing offenses before their eighteenth birthday. With regard to such youth, the following principles and issues are emerging as a contemporary consensus:

1. The fundamental purpose of juvenile justice system sanctions curbing liberties normally available to youth not involved with the justice system is societal protection, not the rehabilitative treatment of offenders. The emphasis will inevitably be upon maintaining the reality of the threat of punishment and upon the temporary incapacitation of a small core of youth who pose serious threats to the safety of the persons and property of their fellow citizens.

We are unable to demonstrate that we can with any degree of reliability promise to successfully treat or rehabilitate the delinquent, or that we can predict who will respond favorably and who unfavorably to rehabilitative efforts. Thus we can not justly deprive youngsters and families of their freedom for the purpose of rehabilitation. This does not mean that "rehabilitation is dead" or that efforts to assist in the solution of personal and/or societal problems impeding the reintegration of the offender into the broader society must be abandoned. Such efforts are a fundamental obligation of a democratic society to the hurt and therefore hurtful children in its midst. The youngsters placed in a correctional institution or in other states of limited freedom should be offered every needed treatment and educational or environmental assistance possible. But such assistance is not the purpose of and should not be used as the justification for the justice system sanction.

It will be evident that the principle here enunciated leaves wide scope for the judgment of those forming statutes governing the sentencing of juveniles or implementing them in the juvenile court. The exclusion of rehabilitation as the purpose of custodial sanctions is only a first step. We may know less than we would wish about rehabilitation, but the harsh fact is that we know as little or less about how to bolster the deterrent power of the law, how to predict which offenders will be dangerous, or how to incarcerate without increasing eventual dangerousness. This uncomfortable fact dictates the necessity of considerable humility and of careful restraint in the employment of the sanctioning power of the state. These considerations dictate to a large extent the further principles emerging from current discourse.

2. Curbs must be placed upon the present almost completely indeterminate sentencing practices of most juvenile courts. The general dispositional pattern today makes it possible for the court to commit a juvenile to the custody of the state correctional system or to some other private or public agency. That system or agency then decides when to release the youth. Unless the court further intervenes, it may not be required to do so until the youth reaches his majority. It was this system that made it possible to commit fifteen year old Gerald Gault to the Arizona State Industrial School "for the period of his minority [until age 21] unless sooner discharged" for the crime of making a somewhat indecent telephone call. An adult convicted of the same offense could have been jailed for no more than sixty days (*In re Gault*, 1967). Actual practice in most states is for most institutionalized juveniles to remain in custody for a period of a few months. Some, however, "fail to adjust" or to "achieve maximum benefit" and are kept much longer. Once released, they may remain under parole supervision for years. It is the presence of the threat of these abuses that exists as a subtle poison throughout the entire juvenile justice system.

3. While the precise degree of sentencing determinacy to be striven for is the subject of considerable current debate, it is becoming widely agreed that the maximum duration of all coercive dispositions should be determined at the time of sentence.

Agreement beyond this principle is hard to achieve. Some scholars and practitioners would turn from the present over-broad discretionary system to one that would call for sentences of a fixed duration set by the court at the time of sentencing within the limits established by the legislature (I.J.A. — A.B.A., 1977b, p. 23). Under such proposal, the receiving administrative agency could do no more than, at most, make some slight provision for "good time." Other students of the problem would establish presumptive sentences by statute, fixing both maximum and minimum sentences for specified offenses within rather narrow ranges. Among the central issues here is the important one of "proportionality." Obviously, if a sense of justice is to pervade the juvenile justice system there must be an evident relationship between the seriousness of the offense committed and the severity of the sanction imposed. "Like sentences for like offenses" is a necessary goal. However, it is a goal that can be statutorily achieved only within a degree of approximation. Both the specific violative acts of juveniles and the circumstances surrounding them vary widely. Inflexible, highly specific statutory definitions of offenses would provide some degree of comforting illusion of rationality to some legal scholars but would too frequently bear little relationship to reality — and this would be perfectly evident to the youth involved. Further, statutory inflexibility would result in distortions of charges brought by police and states' attorneys in attempts to escape rigid sentencing structures. For these reasons, it may be realistically impossible to accomplish more by statute than to establish a system by which:

a. Maximum sentences for quite broadly defined classes of offenses would be statutorily established. Such maxima would cover both time spent in custodial care and time under state supervision upon release.

b. Judges would fix maximum sentences within the statutorily established maxima.

c. Commitment would be to a centralized correctional authority, which would be empowered to set a release date short of the maximum.

The plan here suggested is essentially that proposed by the Twentieth Century Fund study group (Twentieth Century Fund, 1978, p. 12). It would change practice in many states only in its fixing of maxima. Admittedly, it creates the continued danger of considerable sentencing disparity. But this problem probably cannot wholly be counteracted by statute, and the plan would preserve the flexibility that may be necessary in work with juvenile offenders.

4. In designing sentencing codes and in the judicial selection of dispositions, the governing principle should be the employment of the least restrictive category and duration of disposition appropriate to the seriousness of the offense, taking into account the circumstances of the particular case and the age and prior record of the juvenile. This principle accepts the very real danger of the correctional process to the future life of the child. Unfortunately, it leaves unresolved the question as to what a "least restrictive alternative" policy should mean in practice. The Twentieth Century Fund Task Force (pp. 13-17) suggests a meaningful approach to the provision of such a definition:

> a. For all property offenses except burglary of a dwelling, an administrative presumption should be established that juveniles who have not previously been arrested for a serious offense

should be handled informally. Formal handling by petition to the juvenile court would then remain possible if the administrative agency (police, probation intake, etc.) feel that the circumstances of the offense or the situation surrounding it so indicate. Otherwise reliance should be placed upon the shock of arrest, official warning, and such referral to other community services as seems indicated. This principle recognizes the enormous proportion of juvenile offenses constituting relatively minor property violations and the fact that such acts do not necessarily predict further serious delinquency. Thus the avoidance of unnecessary stigmatization and of "flooding" the court's function with a sea of cases in which major intervention is contra-indicated become realistic goals.

b. Burglary of a dwelling, or a second arrest for other serious property crime should result in formal adjudication. A presumption against custodial confinement and in favor of less drastic sanctions would still hold for first convictions for property offenses. For repeated or very severe property offenders a one year limit upon custodial confinement and a two year limit upon total state-imposed control might be reasonable.

c. For violent offenses, the establishment of three grades is suggested. The first and least serious would include assaults not involving serious threat to life or robberies in which the defendant did not use a deadly weapon or inflict grave bodily harm. For this class, a maximum of eighteen months' custodial confinement or a longer but limited period of non-custodial control is recommended. A second, more serious class of offenses against the person would result in a two year maximum or a presumption of waiver to the criminal court for repeat offenders. In this class would fall robbery with a deadly weapon or bodily harm, aggravated battery, voluntary manslaughter, attempted rape, etc. A third, most serious class of offenses would include murder and attempted murder, forcible rape, and arson with intent to commit bodily harm. For such offenses, a relatively low maximum of two and one-half years would be set, with the provision that cases for which more severe sanction might be considered if guilt is established should be waived to criminal court.

5. Meaningful application of the foregoing principles will necessitate the availability of a wider range of sanctioning possibilities than those currently available to most juvenile courts. In its dispositional decision the court must too often swing ponderously from the extreme of commitment to a secure institution to the other extreme of return to the community in a condition of restriction of liberty which exists only in theory and is hardly apparent to many youthful offenders. A variety of experiments in widely scattered jurisdictions suggest that this situation

need not necessarily obtain. Among possible alternatives are restitution orders, symbolic restitution in the form of assignments to community work projects for a designated number of hours, fines, intermittent custody on week-ends or after school or work, and day custody in centers providing educational or other training program opportunities. None of these are widely developed in the U.S., but imaginative examples of all of them are available (for a brief summary of such examples see A.B.A. — I.J.A., 1977c, pp. 42-57, 65-66). All such programs present the danger of abuse in the form of too ready expansion of the use of coercive dispositions. However, the presence of such alternatives is also of value in rendering meaningful a carefully supervised "least restrictive alternative" policy.

6. Recourse to programs providing psychotherapeutic services calculated to intervene in youths' attitudes, feelings, emotional patterns, and psychological states should be on a voluntary basis. The prospect of coercive intervention in the offender's psyche is ever-tantalizing. It beguiles even the generally very realistic authors of the A.B.A. — I.J.A. Juvenile Justice Standards Project, who would "permit coercive imposition of community programs, such as vocational training, special education courses, and *various types of therapy, including individual or group counseling or analysis, as a dispositional alternative*" (A.B.A. — I.J.A., 1977c, pp. 58-59). But the prospect of controlled, predictable, coercive altering of the psyche is a mirage — one that not only is unachievable in the present state of knowledge but which too frequently leads into a quicksand of unintended consequences in the form of "treatment" designed to be therapeutic but in practice proving to be highly punitive. (For a deeply moving account of the manner in which coercive programs, planned as examples of the promotion of behavioral change within an atmosphere of respect and dignity, deteriorate into hostility and intimidation, see Bartollas, Miller, and Dinitz, 1976.)

7. The utilization of the "purchase of service" mechanism to extend the range of resources available to the court's dispositional function. The frequently trying, attacking, rejecting youngsters enmeshed in today's juvenile justice system not infrequently do find compassion and long-term commitment to their welfare. But these qualities are difficult to sustain in the bureaucratic structure of the large public agency. The functionaries of such agencies tend to "burn out" under the years-long assault of large caseloads, limited resources, and the most difficult of client groups. The commitment to formalized merit system selection, permanent career lines, promotion by seniority, and job protection by statute and/or union negotiation make for depersonalized service patterns. They do not provide a climate in which the often highly individualistic, creative personality with a "flair" for flexible work with youthful offenders is

comfortable over the long haul. Often needed are a variety of small, highly personalized programs, many of which will creatively experiment with and then further develop or discard particular services. The use of state funds which can be supplied on an as-needed basis through a market economy may be a much sounder device than is "freezing" services into a state budget.

The foregoing analysis suggests four major themes which seem to be emerging as powerful determinants of the directions in which the juvenile justice system of the future will move:

a. Provision for the imposition of statutorily defined sanctions in the instances of serious offenses by juveniles, particularly, serious violent offenses. The purpose here is the clear establishment of negative consequences for violative behavior as an aspect of legal and social reality.

b. Introduction of statutory and procedural limitations upon the broad discretion to intervene coercively in the lives of youth and families traditionally exercised by the juvenile justice system.

c. Endorsement of the quest for real and evident "fairness" in all relations between the state and the offender.

d. Continuing endeavor to achieve through non-coercive means the benign, helping goals traditionally important to the juvenile justice system.

To many, these principles seem to spell an end of the "era of the rehabilitative ideal" in juvenile justice. This is a false perception. We do argue that subjection of the child to the justice system sanction should be justified only by the goal of societal protection — not as a means of instituting "treatment." But this does not spell the limits of society's obligation to the troubled child in its midst. The youngster placed in a status of limited freedom must be offered help in envisioning the termination of such status and the alternatives available to him. The societal obligation extends to providing the child on a free-choice basis with the greatest possible opportunity to grow to his full potential and to achieve positive relationships with society. This task, if meaningfully pursued, involves the provision of services that are real, that are perceived as such by their intended recipients, and that are offered on terms acceptable to them. Such provision calls for the ultimate in concern, compassion, and depth of understanding that constitute the resource of the helping professions. Herein lies the challenge to the helping professions and to the "rehabilitation of the rehabilitative ideal" within a continuum of justice.

References

*All data in this section on arrests are taken from U.S. Department of Justice, Federal Bureau of Investigation, *Uniform Crime Reports* (Annual, 1960-1977). However, it is too infrequently noticed that in these annual volumes the population bases used in tabulating arrests vary from year to year, as well as from table to table within each volume. This is due to the fact that for various data items, varying numbers of jurisdictions have reported to the F.B.I. Therefore, for the purpose of this paper the populations reported to be covered by the jurisdictions reporting have been compared with the total U.S. population. Estimates of total numbers of arrests have then been extrapolated for each table. Population data are derived from U.S. Department of Commerce, Bureau of the Census, *Current Population Reports,* Series P. 25 (Annual). This analysis is from a paper to be published by Troy Armstrong, Senior Research Associate, National Center for the Study of Alternatives to Juvenile Justice Processing, University of Chicago.

American Bar Association, Institute of Judicial Administration, Juvenile Justice Standards Project, *a. Standards Relating to Non-criminal Misbehavior, b. Standards Relating to Juvenile Delinquency and Sanctions, c. Standards Relating to Dispositions* (Cambridge, Mass.: Ballinger Publishing Co., 1977).

Bailey, Walter C., "Correctional Outcome: An Evaluation of 100 Reports," *Journal of Criminal Law, Criminology, and Police Science* (June, 1966), pp. 153-60.

Bartollas, Clemens, Stuart J. Miller and Simon Dinitz, *Juvenile Victimization: The Institutional Paradox* (New York: The Halsted Press, 1976).

Beale, David, *Juvenile Justice in New Jersey* (Princeton, N.J.: Center for Analysis of Public Issues, 1973).

Bittner, Egon, "Policing Juveniles: The Social Context of Common Practice," In Margaret K. Rosenheim (ed.), *Pursuing Justice for the Child* (Chicago: University of Chicago Press, 1976).

Black, Donald and Albert Reiss, "Police Control of Juveniles," *American Sociological Review* (February, 1970), 35, pp. 63-77.

Bohnstedt, Marvin, "Answers to Three Questions about Juvenile Diversion," *Journal of Research in Crime and Delinquency* (January, 1978), 15, pp. 109-23.

Coates, Robert, Alden D. Miller, and Lloyd E. Ohlin, *Diversity in a Youth Correctional System: Handling Delinquents in Massachusetts* (Cambridge, Mass.: Ballinger Publishing Co., 1978).

Ferster, Elyce Zenoff, Edith Nash Snethen and Thomas F. Courtless, "Juvenile Detention: Protection, Prevention or Punishment?" *Fordham Law Review* (1969), 38, pp. 161-96.

Hasenfeld, Yeheskel, "Youth in the Juvenile Court: Input and Output Patterns," in Rosemary Sarri and Yeheskel Hasenfeld (eds.), *Brought to Justice? Juveniles, the Courts and the Law* (Ann Arbor, Michigan: National Assessment of Juvenile Corrections, University of Michigan, 1976).

Haskell, Martin R. and Lewis Yablonsky, *Juvenile Delinquency,* 2nd ed. (Chicago: Rand McNally Publishing Co., 1978).

Hunter, E. Farley, *RODEO: Reduction of Delinquency through Expansion of Opportunity* (County of Los Angeles, Probation Department Research Report No. 33, 1968).

Hurley, Timothy D., *Origin of the Illinois Juvenile Court Law,* 3rd ed. (Chicago: Visitation and Aid Society, 1907).

Jesness, Carl F., William J. DeRisi, Paul M. McCormick, and Robert F. Wedge, *The Youth Center Research Project* (American Justice Institute and California Youth Authority, 1972).

Jesness, Carl F., *Comparative Effectiveness of Behavior Modification and Transactional Analysis Programs for Delinquents* (December, 1974). Mimeographed.

Kelly, Francis J. and Daniel J. Baer, "Challenge As a Treatment for Delinquency," *Crime and Delinquency* (1971), 7, pp. 437-45.

Krajick, Kevin, "Illinois: A Blow for the 'Get Tough' Side," *Corrections Magazine* (September, 1978), 4, pp. 19-22.

Lipton, Douglas, Robert Martinson, and Judith Wilks, *The Effectiveness of Correctional Treatment* (New York: Praeger Press, 1975).

Mack, Julian W., "The Juvenile Court," *Harvard Law Review* (December, 1909), 23, pp. 104-122.

Mahoney, Anne Rankin, "The Effect of Labeling on Youths in the Juvenile Justice System: A Review of the Evidence," *Law and Society Review* (1974), 8.

Martinson, R., "What Works? Questions and Answers about Prison Reform," *The Public Interest* (1974), pp. 22-54.

Massimo, Joseph L. and Milton F. Shore, "The Effectiveness of a Comprehensive, Vocational-Oriented Psychotherapeutic Program for Adolescent Delinquent Boys," *American Journal of Orthopsychiatry* (1963), 33, pp. 634-42.

Miller, Jerome and Lloyd E. Ohlin, "The New Corrections: the Case of Massachusetts," in Margaret K. Rosenheim (ed.), *Pursuing Justice for the Child* (Chicago: University of Chicago Press, 1976), pp. 154-75.

Moskowitz, Daniel B., "The New, Flexible J.D. Act," *Corrections Magazine* (September, 1978), 4, pp. 29-31.

National Council on Crime and Delinquency, "Jurisdiction Over Status Offenses Should Be Removed From the Juvenile Court – Policy Statement," *Crime and Delinquency* (April, 1975), 21, pp. 97-99.

National Council of Juvenile and Family Court Judges, *Juvenile Court Statistics* (Pittsburgh: The Council, 1975).

Nejelski, Paul, "Diversion: Unleashing the Hound of Heaven?" in Margaret K. Rosenheim (ed.), *Pursuing Justice for the Child* (Chicago: University of Chicago Press, 1976), pp. 94-119.

Norman, Sherwood, *Guide for Use of Detention and Shelter Care for Police, Probation and Courts* (New York: National Council on Crime and Delinquency, 1971).

Palmer, Ted. "The Youth Authority's Community Treatment Project," *Federal Probation* (March, 1974), pp. 3-14.

Paulson, Conrad G. and Charles H. Whitebread, *Juvenile Law and Procedure* (Reno, Nevada: National Council of Juvenile Court Judges, 1974).

Piliavin, Irving and Scott Briar, "Police Encounters with Juveniles," *American Journal of Sociology* (September, 1964), 70, pp. 206-14.

Reiss, Albert J., *The Police and The Public* (New Haven: Yale University Press, 1971).

Robison, James and Gerald Smith, "The Effectiveness of Correctional Programs," *Crime and Delinquency* (January, 1971), 17, pp. 67-80.

Rosenheim, Margaret K. (ed.), *Justice for the Child* (New York: Free Press, MacMillan, 1962).

Sarri, Rosemary, "Service Technologies: Diversion, Probation and Detention," in Rosemary Sarri and Yeheskel Hasenfeld (eds.), *Brought to Justice? Juveniles, the Courts and the Law* (Ann Arbor: National Assessment of Juvenile Corrections, University of Michigan, 1976), pp. 151-75.

Sarri, Rosemary C., *Under Lock and Key: Juveniles in Jails and Detention* (Ann Arbor: National Assessment of Juvenile Corrections, University of Michigan, 1974).

Shore, Milton F. and Joseph L. Massimo, "After Ten Years: A Follow-Up Study of Comprehensive, Vocationally-Oriented Psychotherapy," *American Journal of Orthopsychiatry* (January, 1973), 43, pp. 128-32.

Silberman, Charles E., *Criminal Violence, Criminal Justice* (New York: Random House, 1978).

Sosin, Michael and Rosemary Sarri, "Due Process — Reality or Myth," In Rosemary Sarri and Yeheskel Hasenfeld (eds.), *Brought to Justice? Juveniles, the Courts, and the Law* (Ann Arbor: National Assessment of Juvenile Corrections, University of Michigan, 1976), pp. 176-206.

Tappan, Paul W., *Juvenile Delinquency* (New York: McGraw-Hill Book Co., 1949).

Terry, Robert M., "The Screening of Juvenile Offenders," *Journal of Criminal Law, Criminology, and Police Science* (1967), 58, pp. 173-81.

Thornberry, Terrence P., "Race, Socioeconomic Status and Sentencing in the Juvenile Justice System," *Journal of Criminal Law and Criminology* (1973), 64, pp. 90-8.

Twentieth Century Fund, Task Force on Sentencing Policy Toward Young Offenders, *Confronting Youth Crime* (New York: Holmes and Meier, Inc., 1978).

U.S. Department of Justice, Federal Bureau of Investigation, *Uniform Crime Reports* (Annual).

U.S. Department of Commerce, Bureau of the Census, *Current Population Report*, (Annual).

U.S. Department of Health, Education, and Welfare, Office of Youth Development, *Model Acts for Family Courts, and State-Local Children's Programs* (Washington, D.C., U.S. Government Printing Office, 1974), pp. 14-15.

U.S. Department of Justice, Law Enforcement Assistance Administration, *Children in Custody, Advance Report on the Juvenile Detention and Correctional Facility Census of 1975* (Washington, D.C.: U.S. Government Printing Office, 1977).

U.S. National Advisory Commission on Criminal Justice Standards and Goals, *Community Crime Prevention* (Washington, D.C.: U.S. Government Printing Office, 1973).

U.S. National Commission on the Causes and Prevention of Violence, *To Establish Justice, to Insure National Tranquility: Final Report* (Washington, D.C.: U.S. Government Printing Office, 1969).

U.S. President's Commission on Law Enforcement and the Administration of Justice, *The Challenge of Crime in a Free Society* (Washington, D.C.: U.S. Government Printing Office, 1967).

U.S. President's Commission on Law Enforcement and the Administration of Justice, *Corrections* (Washington, D.C.: U.S. Government Printing Office, 1967).

Vinter, Robert D., *Time Out: A National Study of Juvenile Correctional Programs* (Ann Arbor: National Assessment of Juvenile Corrections, University of Michigan, 1976).

Wald, Patricia, "Pretrial Detention for Juveniles," in Margaret K. Rosenheim (ed.), *Pursuing Justice for the Child* (Chicago: University of Chicago Press, 1976), pp. 119-38.

Weiner, Norman L. and Charles V. Willie, "Decisions by Juvenile Officers," *American Journal of Sociology* (September, 1971), 77, pp. 199-210.

Wilson, Rob, "The Long-Term Trend Is Down," *Corrections Magazine* (September, 1978), pp. 3-11.

Zimring, Franklin E., "Background Paper," in Twentieth Century Fund, Task Force on Sentencing Policy toward Young Offenders, *Confronting Youth Crime* (New York: Holmes and Meier, Inc., 1978), pp. 29-120.

7. Discretion in Juvenile Justice*

David B. Chein & Joe Hudson

The interpretation of norms by justice system officials plays an important part in the administration of law. Vague, imprecise statutes allow for considerable discretion in how, when, and against whom sanctions are to apply. This is especially the case with delinquency statutes and the administration of juvenile justice. While suffering from some recent slippage, the predominant aim of juvenile justice remains the rehabilitation of delinquent youth through the use of purportedly beneficent treatments. Clearly, however, the ambiguity of most delinquency statutes and the broad discretionary authority given to juvenile justice officials suggest that decisions made about youth caught up in the system are likely to be made on a variety of grounds, over and above the delinquent behavior itself.

In this chapter we assess the criteria used by justice system officials in dealing with delinquents. We first review evidence from studies in this country concerning the disposition and adjudication of delinquents, including the decision to place a juvenile in a detention facility, the decision to refer to court for a formal hearing, and the disposition decision. Our aim is to determine which, if any, criteria consistently relate to processing decisions by juvenile justice officials. The second section of this chapter then describes the research methods and findings of a recent study in Minnesota on the criteria used by corrections officials in making decisions about incarcerating and paroling adjudicated delinquents. The final section briefly describes how the research was used in Minnesota for the development of structured parole release guidelines for juveniles.

Contradictory Goals of Juvenile Justice

It is not surprising that discretion plays a central role in the administration of juvenile justice. To begin with, the same factors giving rise to discretion in the adult system — overcrowded courts, ambiguous laws, bureaucratic pressures, and so on — are also present in the juvenile justice system. In fact, the very purpose of establishing a separate system of justice for juveniles was to permit more informal and personal handling of delinquency cases (Platt, 1969). The belief was, and to a large extent still is, that juveniles are not set in their behavior patterns and given the proper environment and moral education, they can be deflected from potential criminal careers. The state "intervenes" in the life of the child to provide structure and guidance (whether this be expressed in the form of a lecture from the judge or by more formal means such as probation or institutionalization) without giving the child the stigma and trauma of adult criminal proceedings.

If the court is acting on behalf of the child, and if its actions are defined as beneficial, then it must do more than determine guilt or innocence. It must determine what, within the bounds of the general social welfare, is best for the child's well-being. This, in turn, involves consideration of the alleged offense as well as such factors as the child's attitude, educational needs, the quality of the home environment, and so on (Cicourel, 1968).

How the juvenile's future is conceived by the court is commonly the key to the disposition of the case. For example, Robert Emerson has suggested that the juvenile court is primarily concerned with the potential, not the past, dangerousness of the youth — with his or her character or condition rather than with the offense (Emerson, 1969). At the same time that the court must concern itself with the juvenile's needs, it also must protect the interests of society. After all, the court is an agency of social control, and as such is obligated to remove dangerous offenders from the street. While proponents of the juvenile court philosophy see rehabilitation as the main reason for institutionalizing juveniles, they are also aware that some juveniles have to be removed from society to insure public safety. In short, the court and those individuals responsible for making decisions about juveniles are faced with two contradictory tasks — serving and helping youth, on the one hand, and protecting society on the other (Langley, 1972).

The question to be addressed here is how this dilemma of role definition is resolved by agents of juvenile justice in their decisions about how particular cases are to be handled. If the juvenile court and its related institutions of probation and institutionalization are acting simply as agents of social control, one would expect studies that have examined court actions to find that such actions are based primarily on the offense and prior offense record of the juvenile. If, on the other hand, the court is operating with the goal of serving youth, one would expect to see more idiosyncratic psychological and social factors central to the disposition of cases. Variables such as the sex, age, race, socioeconomic status, and demeanor of the juvenile might also be related to the handling of juvenile delinquents if viewed by decision makers as important in assessing the treatment needs of juveniles.

It is possible that juvenile justice officials have not adequately resolved the issue of conflicting goals and continue to proceed on a case-by-case basis, sometimes invoking the needs of the individual and sometimes the need to protect society as justifications for decisions. In this event, no clear pattern of criteria used in decision making is likely to emerge from previous studies and current research. Rather, the decision-making process would appear to be arbitrary and inconsistent.

Decision Criteria in Juvenile Justice

Many studies have attempted to uncover the criteria used by juvenile court judges and probation officers in making decisions concerning juveniles. In this section we will examine three central points in the juvenile justice system — detention, referral to court, court disposition — and look at the relationship of decisions made at these points to such variables as sex, race, age, socio-economic status, offense, family environment, and the juvenile's demeanor.

Sex

In recent years considerable attention has been focused on sexual biases in the administration of justice — particularly juvenile justice. For example, in a study of juvenile court dispositions in a midwestern community between 1958 and 1962, Terry (1967) found that 67.7% of female dispositions resulted in institutionalization as compared to 59.7% of male dispositions. This was found to be the case even though females tended to have less extensive records of prior delinquent behavior. Similarly, Cohn (1963), in a study of 175 pre-sentence investigation reports in the Bronx, New York in 1952, found that girls were three times as likely as boys to be recommended for institutionalization. Similar findings were reported by Chesney-Lind (1973), in a study of adolescents referred to juvenile court in Honolulu in 1955, 1960, and 1964, by Kratcoski (1974), in a study of youth referred to juvenile court in a midwestern state in 1971, and by McDonald, et al., (1977), in a study of court dispositions of 3,000 cases in a district juvenile court in North Dakota between 1965 and 1974. In a cross-sectional study of institutionalized juveniles in Connecticut, Rogers (1972) found that 80% of the institutionalized females were status offenders as compared to 18% of the males, and that the average length of stay was seven months for females and five months for males. Similar findings were reported by Hudson (1972) in a study of institutionalized juveniles in Minnesota.

Contrary evidence has also been reported, however. For example, Thomas and Cage (1977) in a study of 1,552 juveniles who appeared in court in a southeastern metropolitan area between 1966 and 1973 reported that males were likely to receive more severe dispositions than females, even when prior record and offense severity were held constant. Thomas and Sieverdes (1975), in a study of 346 juvenile court dispositions in a small southeastern city between 1966 and 1969, found only a slight relationship between sex and court disposition. Meade (1973), in a study of 439 juvenile court cases in a large Southeastern metropolitan area between 1968 and 1970, reported no significant relationship between the juvenile's sex and the decision to retain the youth for a formal hearing. Cohen (1975a), in a comparative study of dispositions in 1972 in Denver County, Colorado, Memphis and Shelby Counties, Tennessee, and Montgomery County, Pennsylvania, found no relationship between sex and the severity of dispositions.

In terms of detention decisions, Cohen (1975b), studying the same three counties in Pennsylvania, found that females were more likely to be detained in Memphis-Shelby Counties, but no sex-related differences were found in the other two counties. Sumner (1971) observed juvenile detention hearings in California and found no relationship between sex and the likelihood of being placed in detention. Pawlak (1977) studied detention decisions in 66 county courts of an unidentified state between 1966 and 1968. He observed that females convicted of "juvenile" offenses were more likely to be detained than were male "juvenile" offenders. The reverse was true among "personal" offenders. Rates of detention for those arrested for "property" and "victimless" crimes did not differ significantly according to the juvenile's sex. A similar relationship between sex, offense, and disposition was reported by Dungworth (1977) in a study of detention decisions pertaining to 500 cases in Calhoun County Juvenile Court in Michigan in 1975. Males were more likely to be detained for felonies and misdemeanors than were females, but female status offenders were more likely than male status offenders to be detained.

Interaction effects among sex, offense, and case outcome were also reported in a study of juvenile court dispositions conducted by Datesman and Scarpitti; (1977) in a medium-sized eastern city during an unspecified seven month period. In analyzing records of 1,103 juveniles appearing before the family court, it was found that females were given more severe dispositions than males for status offenses, but less severe dispositions for felonies and misdemeanors. This finding remained when the number of prior offenses and the juvenile's race were controlled, although sex differences in the severity of dispositions were most pronounced among those with prior offense records and among whites.

The majority of studies thus indicate that offenses committed by females (particularly status offenses) tend to be perceived as more serious than offenses committed by males and, as a result, females are processed further through the juvenile justice system than are males.

Race

The relationship of race to decisions made by juvenile justice officials has also been extensively explored with inconsistent results. The studies by Terry (1967), Cohn (1967), and Cohen (1975a) discussed above found no relationship between the juvenile's race and case dispositions when other variables were controlled. Thomas and Sieverdes (1975) found only a slight tendency for blacks to be given more severe disposition than whites. Similarly, in an analysis of juvenile court records and observation of court cases in "Affluent County" in 1968 and 1969, Ferster and Courtless (1972) found no relationship between race and disposition. Scarpitti and Stephenson (1971), in a study of 1,210 adjudicated delinquents in a large eastern metropolitan county, found that with prior offense records controlled, blacks were less likely than whites to be sent to a reformatory. Meade (1973) found no relationship between race and the decision to refer a youth to a formal hearing. Similarly, in an analysis of referral patterns of 295 juvenile males in Philadelphia between May, 1971, and January, 1973, Rosen and Carl (1974) found no relationship between race and the likelihood of referral to the juvenile court when seriousness of offense was controlled.

Langley (1972), in a study of pre-trial detention in Tennessee from 1966 to 1970, reported no relationship between the juvenile's race and the likelihood of being detained. Pawlak (1977) found no significant differences on detention rates among males, but among females, whites were slightly more likely than non-whites to be given detention. Dungworth (1977) found negligible relationships between race and detention decisions among felons and misdemeanants, but he found that among status offenders, blacks were more likely than whites to be detained.

There are several studies, however, that do show discrimination effects. Sumner (1971), for example, found that blacks were more likely than whites to be given detention. Using data derived from an earlier cohort analysis of all boys born in 1945 who lived exclusively in Philadelphia between the ages of 10 and 18 (Wolfgang, et al., 1972), Thornberry (1973) found that non-whites were more likely than whites to be referred to court for trial and more likely to be institutionalized. Again, these differences remained when other variables were controlled. Somewhat supportive of this finding is a study reported by Arnold (1971) in which a review of juvenile court files in a medium-sized southern city in 1963 and 1964 revealed that blacks were more likely than whites to be sent to court and be institutionalized. The differences, however, existed only for those youths who had committed serious offenses or had a history of two or more prior offenses.

Confusing the issue further is the study reported earlier by Thomas and Cage (1977). This study found that cases involving blacks were significantly more likely than cases involving whites to be dismissed. However, blacks were almost twice as likely as whites to be committed to institutions, a finding which remained significant when prior record and offense severity were held constant.

In summary, the findings regarding the relationship between the juvenile's race and decision making are inconsistent and do not permit generalizations about the existence or non-existence of a racial bias in the administration of juvenile justice.

Age

The relationship between the age of the juvenile and discretionary decision making within the administration of juvenile justice has been the subject of only a few research studies. Scarpitti and Stephenson (1971) found that 17 year old males were more likely than younger adjudicated male delinquents to be sent to a reformatory. Dungworth (1977) reported a positive relationship between age and the likelihood of receiving detention among felons and misdemeanants, but very little relationship between age and detention decisions for status offenders. Meade (1973) found no relationship between age and the likelihood of being referred to a formal hearing, and Ferster and Courtless (1972) found that age was not related to court disposition. McDonald (1977) found an inconsistent relationship between age and court disposition in North Dakota. Between 1965 and 1969, younger juveniles received more severe dispositions; in 1970 and 1971, older juveniles received more severe dispositions; and between 1972 and 1974, no significant relationship between age and either detention or disposition was found. Thus, there is insufficient evidence to support the contention that the juvenile's age is an important factor in the handling of delinquency cases.

Socio-Economic Status (SES)

While many theorists have argued that the criminal justice system is biased against lower class citizens (Quinney, 1970, 1973, 1977; Chambliss and Seidman, 1971), the evidence pertaining to juvenile justice does not consistently support this claim. Terry (1967) found no relationship between socio-economic status and disposition of cases when the frequency and severity of offense was controlled. Similarly, Cohen (1975a and b) found no relationship between social status and either detention decisions or case dispositions. No relationship between court disposition and socio-economic status was reported by Thomas and Sieverdes (1975), although in this study family stability was found to be related to disposition. Meade (1973) found no relationship between socio-economic status and referral to a formal hearing. Birdsall (1974), in a questionnaire given to 23 intake officers at a juvenile detention center in Arizona, found socio-economic status to be an unimportant consideration in decision making.

In contrast to these studies, Thornberry (1973), using the Wolfgang

Philadelphia cohort, found a greater rate of referral to court trial and placement in an institution for lower class boys, even when offense severity, offense history, and race were controlled. Scarpitti and Stephenson (1971) found lower status juveniles over-represented in reformatories, as were children from broken homes and welfare families. Finally, Thomas and Cage (1977) found an inverse relationship between socio-economic status and disposition (i.e., the lower the status, the more severe the disposition) among felons and status offenders, but no such relationship was found among misdemeanants.

It appears, therefore, that there is contradictory evidence regarding class bias in the processing of juvenile delinquents and that no firm conclusions can be drawn from the evidence gathered to date. It should be noted, however, that these studies deal with populations of juveniles at the point of referral to the court system. Police discretion may well be diverting middle and upper status youth and leaving a population of largely lower status youth for court processing (Wolfgang, et al., 1972; Chambliss, 1973).

Family/Home Environment

Although there is contradictory evidence about the relationship of socio-economic status to decision making within the juvenile justice system, more consistent evidence is available to show that the quality of the home environment is a factor given a great deal of consideration. For example, Cicourel (1968) reported that juveniles from lower class homes were over-represented in juvenile institutions, but he suggested that this was attributable to other factors in the family/home environment, such as marital discord, lack of supervision, and so on. In a similar vein, Emerson (1969) has argued that the crucial difference for the juvenile court is not between middle and lower class families but between the family life of the "respectable" and "disrespectable" poor. In support of this point, Cohn (1967) found that children recommended by probation officers for institutionalization were more likely than children recommended for probation to have come from fatherless homes and to have had a poor relationship with their parents. Similarly, Monahan (1957) found that a greater proportion of institutionalized delinquents as compared to delinquents placed on probation came from broken homes. Monahan concluded from this finding that juveniles from broken homes are more seriously delinquent than children from intact homes, but an equally plausible explanation is that officials are more likely to assign delinquents to institutions if they come from broken homes. Thomas and Cage (1977) reported more severe dispositions for children from broken homes, a finding that persisted even when offense severity was held constant. Dungworth (1977) reported that detention was more likely when the juvenile came from a broken home and when the home was categorized by caseworkers as "unstable.'"

Rosen and Carl (1974), however, found that broken homes increased the likelihood of court referral only when the offense was minor. Meade (1976) found no relationship between referral of the youth to a formal hearing and family disruption. Cohen (1975a) found no relationship between family stability and disposition when other variables were controlled, but he did find a positive relationship in two of the three counties studied between the likelihood of being held in detention and coming from a broken home (Cohen, 1975b).

Emerson (1969) concluded from his study that a broken home as such is not used by probation officers as an indicator of a more serious delinquency problem on the part of the youth, but that the parent's inability to control and supervise the child is. Thus, a mother on welfare would be defined as acceptable if she maintains control in the home, disciplines children properly, attempts to keep them neat and clean, and so on. In contrast, a mother who drinks and entertains men and does not control her children is regarded as "someone producing a breed of criminal-like delinquents."

It appears, then, that there is evidence of a relationship between the youth's family/home environment and the handling of cases, but once again the finding is not universal, and the measure of what constitutes a "broken home" or an "unsuitable" home environment is not uniform.

Offense and Offense History

The variables given the most attention by research studies are the juvenile's immediate offense bringing him or her to the attention of the court or other adjudicating body, and the history of previous offenses. Indeed, many studies have found that the juvenile's offense plays an important role in decision making. Studies by Scarpitti and Stephenson (1971), Cohen (1975a and b), Birdsall (1974), Thomas and Sieverdes (1975), Sumner (1971), Pawlak (1977), McDonald (1977), Thornberry (1973), Rosen and Carl (1974), and Langley (1972), all found that either the seriousness of the present offense or the prior record of the juvenile — although not necessarily both — were heavily considered by decision makers and/or were positively correlated with more severe dispositions at various levels of the juvenile system. Clearly, however, in only a few of these studies was offense found to be the only factor related to the decision, and in several of them it was not the most important factor. Thomas and Cage (1977) reported, surprisingly, that those with multiple prior offenses were more likely to have charges against them dismissed as compared to those with no prior offenses. On the other hand, those with multiple prior offenses were more likely to be institutionalized than those with no prior offenses.

In contrast, several studies have found that status offenders receive just as severe or more severe handling by the juvenile system than do criminal offenders. For example, Meade (1973) found no difference in the likelihood of being referred to a formal hearing between status offenders and serious offenders. Lerman (1971) found that among boys sent to juvenile correctional institutions in New York, those who had committed criminal acts spent an average of 10.7 months in institutions, whereas those who were designated as "persons in need of supervision" (PINS) spent an average of 16.3 months in institutions. Lerman also re-analyzed data from the U.S. Children's Bureau from 19 of the 30 largest cities in 1965 and found that 23% of those juveniles who committed a serious crime, 18% of those who committed a less serious crime, and 26% of the juvenile status offenders were committed to institutions.

Other studies corroborate Lerman's findings. Ferster and Courtless (1972) found that status offenders received more severe dispositions from the court than did serious offenders. Cohn (1967) found that probation officers were more likely to recommend institutionalization for offenses committed against the family (including running away and truancy) than for offenses against life or property. Zimmerman and Chein (1977) reported that among 150 juveniles appearing for the first time in a midwestern metropolitan area juvenile court during two time periods, 1961-1963 and 1967-1970, status offenders were significantly more likely than serious offenders to be adjudicated delinquent and to be placed under formal supervision (usually probation). Stapleton and Teitelbaum (1972), in a study of the effect of lawyers on juvenile court dispositions, report data indicating that juveniles with no previous court experience received more favorable dispositions than those with court experience. However, in one of the two cities studied, status offenders received more severe dispositions, while in the other city there was no relationship between offense type and disposition. Dungworth (1977) reported a slight negative correlation between severity of offense and the likelihood of receiving detention. Pawlak (1977) found that female status offenders were more likely to be placed in detention homes than female criminal offenders, whereas among males, status and personal offenders were more likely to be placed in detention than were those arrested for property or "victimless" offenses. Finally, as noted earlier, Cicourel (1968) observed that the offense itself is not crucial in court dispositions, but that the offense is interpreted by court and probation personnel in the light of the prior delinquent history, home situation, and demeanor of the juvenile.

Taken as a whole, therefore, the studies fail to yield consistent results regarding the relationship between the severity of the offense committed by the juvenile or the prior offense record and the processing of the case by the juvenile justice system.

Attitude and Demeanor

The juvenile's attitudes and demeanor have received more systematic study in relation to police decisions on whether to arrest a juvenile than in relation to decisions made by the juvenile court (Piliavin and Briar, 1964; Black and Reiss, 1970; Hufford, 1974; Sullivan and Siegel, 1972). However, police-citizen encounters involve special situations in interpersonal relationships geared around the officer's relationship to authority (Skolnick, 1966; Bittner, 1970; Sykes and Clark, 1974) and may not be typical of decisions made about juveniles by other officials in the system.

Beyond the arrest decision, there is less direct evidence about the relationship of attitude and demeanor to decision making. Gross (1967), using a questionnaire mailed to 70 probation officers in Minnesota, reported that the "child's attitude toward the offense" was rated as the most important criterion used in making recommendations. Both Cohn (1967) and Emerson (1969) have suggested that the cooperation shown by the youth with the probation officer and the deference and remorse expressed to the court are significant factors considered in the disposition of cases. Cicourel (1968) has presented several case studies in which the poor attitudes and demeanor of juveniles led to their being institutionalized, and Platt (1969) has discussed the role of the juvenile's attitude as a determinant of case dispositions in the juvenile court. It appears, then, that there is some support from field research for the contention that the demeanor of the juvenile is related to the handling of cases by the juvenile justice system, but this relationship has not been subject to statistical analysis. This is understandable, given the absence of data on demeanor in court records and the difficulty of operationalizing the concept in a manner that would make it amenable to statistical analysis.

Parole Decisions

Very little research has been conducted on the question of what factors influence the decision to parole a juvenile. We mentioned earlier the findings that females stay longer in institutions than do males (Rogers, 1972) and that status offenders stay longer than criminal offenders (Lerman, 1971).[1] The only empirical study to date of juvenile selection for parole was conducted by Hussey (1976) on 424 juvenile males released during one year from one institution for juvenile delinquents. The study is described as preliminary by the author, and no details as to when and where the study was conducted are given, and no statistical data are presented. The author summarizes his results, noting that most background variables are not significantly related to the number of days spent by the juvenile in the institution prior to parole and that those variables which are related differ in their bearing on length of institutionalization according to the race of the juvenile. Prior escapes, criminal history of the father, and offense severity were found to be predictive of length of incarceration for blacks. For Mexican-Americans, severity of offense and age at first commitment were variables found to relate to length of incarceration. For whites, however, offense related variables did not predict length of incarceration, but parental education, psychological problems of the juvenile, and social class did have bearing. On the basis of these findings, Hussey suggests that minorities are more subject to a legalistic interpretation of length of incarceration, whereas "treatment" considerations are applied to whites to determine their readiness for parole.

Because of the preliminary nature of Hussey's study and the absence of any other thorough investigations of the parole decision, no firm conclusions can be made at the present time concerning factors which are influential in determining when to parole a juvenile.

Summary of Previous Research

We initially suggested that the absence of a clear pattern of criteria used in decision making would indicate that the juvenile justice system has not resolved the dilemma of conflicting goals and essentially proceeds on a case-by-case basis. This seems to be the situation. Previous research summarized in Table 1 indicates a general inconsistency of findings related either to detention, referral to an adjudicatory hearing or dispositional decisions for adjudicated delinquents.

The majority of the studies show that age, race, and socio-economic status are not in themselves important factors in decision making about juveniles, but that juveniles who come from broken homes or unsuitable home environments (variously defined) tend to be handled more severely. While several studies reported interaction effects among the variables studied, these do not follow a consistent pattern and therefore do not cause us to modify our depiction of the decision-making process as inconsistent.

It may be that the differences in results are due to different methods of recordkeeping and data collection used in different studies. Surely, however, some consistent patterns of criteria used in decision making would have been expected to emerge despite minor variations in data

TABLE 1

Summary of Results of Previous Research Studies on the Processing of Juvenile Delinquents

Variable	Type of Decision		
	Detention	Referral	Disposition
Juvenile's Sex	1 study reports no relationship; 1 study reports females more likely to be detained in one county and no relationship in the other two counties; 2 studies report males more likely to be detained for serious offenses and females more likely to be detained for status offenses.	1 study reports no relationship; 2 studies report females more likely to be referred.	2 studies report no relationship; 5 studies report more severe dispositions for females; 1 study reports more severe dispositions for males; 1 study reports more severe dispositions for female status offenders and male criminal offenders.
Juvenile's Race	2 studies report no relationship; 1 study reports blacks more likely to be detained; 1 study reports black status offenders more likely to be detained, but no relationship among criminal offenders; 1 study reports white females slightly more likely to be detained, but no relationship among males.	2 studies report no relationship; 1 study reports blacks more likely to be referred; 1 study reports whites more likely to be referred; 1 study reports black serious or repeat offenders more likely to be referred, but no relationship among non-serious first offenders.	5 studies report no racial differences; 3 studies report more severe dispositions for blacks; 1 study reports more severe dispositions for black serious or repeat offenders, but no differences among non-serious first offenders.

TABLE 1 (cont'd)

Variable	Type of Decision		
	Detention	Referral	Disposition
Juvenile's Age	1 study reports no relationship; 1 study reports that older juveniles are more likely to be detained for criminal offenses, but no differences among status offenses.	1 study reports no relationship.	2 studies report no relationship; 1 study reports more severe dispositions for older juveniles; 1 study reports inconsistent results over time.
Socioeconomic Status of Juvenile's Family	1 study reports no relationship.	2 studies report no relationship; 1 study reports that lower SES juveniles are more likely to be referred.	3 studies report no relationship; 2 studies report more severe dispositions for lower SES juveniles; 1 study reports more severe dispositions for higher SES felons and status offenders, but no relationship among misdemeanants.
Juvenile's Family Environment	1 study reports higher detention rates for juveniles from poor environments; 1 study reports higher detention rates for juveniles from poor environments in two of three counties studied, no relationship in the third county.	1 study reports no relationship; 1 study reports that juveniles from poor family environments who commit minor offenses are more likely to be referred, but no differences among serious offenders.	1 study reports no relationship; 2 studies report more severe dispositions for juveniles from poor family environments.

TABLE 1 (cont'd)

Juvenile's Offense and Offense History	4 studies report greater likelihood of detention for juveniles committing more serious offenses; 1 study reports greater likelihood for less serious offenders; 1 study reports greater likelihood of detention for less serious female offenders, but no relationship among males.	1 study reports no relationship; 3 studies report greater likelihood of referral for juveniles committing more serious offenses; 1 study reports greater likelihood of referral for juveniles committing less serious offenses.	6 studies report more severe dispositions for juveniles committing more serious offenses; 5 studies report more severe dispositions for juveniles committing less serious offenses.
Juvenile's Attitude or Demeanor	no studies conducted	no studies conducted	4 studies report general field observations that poor demeanor results in more severe disposition; 1 questionnaire reports that juvenile's demeanor is important criterion in case dispositions.

collection. It might be, on the other hand, that the differences are real and merely reflect the fact that there is regional or temporal variation in the decision-making process. Yet analysis of the limited number of studies that have been conducted reveals no consistent patterns based on the time data was collected, region of the country under study, or whether the study was conducted in a large metropolitan area or a non-metropolitan area.

Decision Making in Juvenile Institutions: Research Setting and Method

In an effort to further explore factors influencing decisions in juvenile justice, a study of decision making in another setting — juvenile correctional institutions — was undertaken. This research was conducted during 1974 and 1975 at the three state operated institutions for juvenile delinquents in Minnesota: The Minnesota Home School (MHS), which received juveniles from counties in the western half of the state; the State Training School (STS), which received juveniles from counties in the eastern half of the state; and the Minnesota Metropolitan Training Center (MMTC), which at the time of this study received juveniles from the three major counties of the Twin Cities metropolitan area.[2]

In common with most of the states (Levin & Sarri, 1974), adjudicated delinquents in Minnesota can be committed by the Juvenile Court Judge to the state Department of Corrections for purposes of evaluation and assessment. Formal admission to the treatment program at each institution is then determined by the staff at each of them so they have the ultimate decision-making power regarding the incarceration of juveniles. In Minnesota the system worked as follows: juveniles committed by the courts to the Commissioner of Corrections were placed in one of the three institutions where they were subjected to a four week "diagnostic evaluation," at the end of which time a "staffing conference" was held and a decision made to either admit youth to the regular institutional program or return them to the community on probation status. In turn, the staffing team decision was reviewed by an "action panel" composed of three rotating representatives of the institutions and juvenile probation services. Action panels could confirm, reject, or modify staff recommendations but in practice they concurred in over 95% of the cases reviewed during the time of this study. If the decision was made to retain youth in the regular institutional program, they were held for an indeterminate length of time with special reviews held on an annual basis.

The purpose of the present study was two-fold: first, to assess criteria used by staff in making the initial decision to retain or release youth and, second, to assess the criteria used in arriving at the decision to parole youth after exposure to the institutional treatment program. In short, both key decision points were to be assessed.

Three research methods were used. First, direct observation of the decision-making process was undertaken. These observations were useful for guiding the construction of a staff questionnaire and in interpreting the written staffing reports. As a second research method, a questionnaire was administered to all staff who participated in the decision-making process at each of the three institutions (n = 172) in order to determine staff perceptions of the factors relevant to the decision-making process (both the intake and the parole decision).[3] Staff members were asked to rate 33 different criteria in terms of their importance for both the initial decision and the parole decision. (See Table 2 for a list of the criteria and the related data.)

A third research method consisted of a content analysis of official staffing reports. These reports were actually a conglomeration of reports written by caseworkers, group leaders, and counselors at the institutions as well as social history reports prepared by probation officers, psychological reports prepared by staff psychologists, and educational reports prepared by teachers at the institutions. Finally, recommendations of the staffing team and the reasons for the recommendations were also included in the reports. A stratified random sample of 211 reports, or 25.5% of all juveniles committed for evaluation between January 1, 1973 and June 30, 1974, was selected for analysis.

Information was gathered on the juvenile's age, sex, race, offense, offense history, psychological and intellectual functioning, school aptitude, behavior, and place of residence. Also, when available, information on the occupation and education of the juvenile's parents was included. More qualitative information was gathered on the quality of the juvenile's family/home environment (a scale consisting of items dealing with parental presence in the home, parental discord, parental control over the child and emotional support for the child, parental drinking, sibling fighting, the physical condition of the home, and the probation officer's overall evaluation of the home environment), and the juvenile's demeanor (a scale measuring the juvenile's attitude toward authority, cooperativeness, behavior in the cottage, and acceptance of responsibility for and insight into behavioral problems).[4] Finally, information was gathered on the decision made by the institutional staffing team whether to admit the juvenile to the institutional treatment program or release the youth to the community on probation. As a measure of the parole decision, the length of time the juvenile remained in the institution was also coded. Chi-square and analysis of variance were used to measure the significance of each of the factors to the two decisions.[5]

Staff Perceptions of the Decision-Making Process

Staff had considerable difficulty pinpointing specific criteria as more important than others in making decisions about juveniles. Often when the purpose of the research was explained, staff members responded with such comments as "good luck" or "if you find out, let me know." One staff member observed that "people who are making decisions are really making decisions about what they feel, not what they know." On the questionnaire, the staff rated most of the 33 criteria as important factors they considered in their decisions. This is illustrated in Table 2. Staff were asked to rate each item as "very important," "somewhat important," "of little importance," or "not important at all." These responses were scored 4, 3, 2, and 1 respectively. Thus a score above 3.00 for an item suggests that the majority of the staff members feel that the item is an important criterion.

TABLE 2

Staff Ratings of Criteria Used to Make Decisions About Juveniles

	Initial Decision		Parole Decision	
Variable	Mean Rating	Rank Order	Mean Rating*	Rank Order
The extent to which the youth has learned to accept responsibility for his (her) actions	3.720	1**	3.885	1
The seriousness of the offense committed by the youth	3.720	1**	3.100	19
The degree to which the youth is open and honest in dealing with problems	3.707	3	3.808	3
The attitude of the youth toward the offense he has committed	3.663	4	3.746	5
The number of court and institutional contacts prior to this commitment	3.645	5	2.923	24
The availability of acceptable community placements	3.538	6**	3.669	7
The extent to which the youth has gained insight into his (her) behavior	3.538	6**	3.705	6
The extent to which the youth has matured and exhibited personal growth	3.533	8	3.853	2

TABLE 2 (cont'd)

	Initial Decision		Parole Decision	
	Mean Rating	Rank Order	Mean Rating*	Rank Order
The recommendation of the probation officer	3.527	9	3.331	18
The ability of the youth's parents to properly supervise the youth	3.484	10	3.392	15
The quality of emotional support received by the youth from his (her) family	3.452	11	3.385	16
The family's feelings about the youth staying at home	3.419	12	3.515	11
The fact that the youth has a job or school placement in the community	3.394	13	3.585	8
The extent to which the youth has successfully accomplished personal goals that were set up for him (her)	3.391	14	3.754	4
The juvenile's desire for a certain disposition or treatment plan	3.330	15	3.485	13**
The youth's attitude toward the staff and other authority figures	3.326	16	3.554	9
The extent to which the youth has successfully accomplished any educational goals that were set up	3.275	17	3.523	10
The youth's behavior in the cottage	3.272	18	3.512	12
The psychologist's report on the youth's personal adjustment problems	3.267	19	2.953	22**
The youth's behavior in school	3.239	20	3.369	17
The psychologist's report on the youth's anti-social tendencies	3.231	21	2.953	22**
The treatment recommendation of the psychologist	3.187	22	2.876	26
The age of the juvenile	3.151	23	2.485	28

TABLE 2 (cont'd)

Variable	Initial Decision Mean Rating	Initial Decision Rank Order	Parole Decision Mean Rating*	Parole Decision Rank Order
The youth's school attendance record	3.098	24	2.899	25
Recommendation of other members of the youth's treatment group	3.096	25	3.485	13**
The community's attitude toward the juvenile and his (her) offense	3.032	26	3.038	20**
The general condition of the youth's home environment	3.000	27	3.038	20**
The youth's grades in school	2.707	28	2.731	27
The marital status of the youth's parents	2.613	29	2.385	29
The size of the community in which the juvenile's family resides	2.086	30	2.140	30
The race of the juvenile	1.742	31	1.508	32
The sex of the juvenile	1.739	32	1.465	33
The occupation of the juvenile's parents	1.677	33	1.752	31

*Ratings were assigned on the following basis to responses on a Likert scale: very important = 4; somewhat important = 3; of little importance = 2; not important at all = 1. A double asterisk denotes a tie in rank order ratings. N = 92 for initial decision and 129 for parole decision.

Twenty-seven of the 33 items received a rating above 3.00 on the initial staffing decision and 21 of the 33 items were rated above 3.00 on the parole decision. In fact, the only variables which received low ratings for both decisions were categorical variables such as the sex, race, and socio-economic status of the juvenile. The following comments by staff members further illustrate their difficulty in defining the purpose of their institution and pinpointing the basis for their decisions:

> We offer treatment, but in the meantime, we have to exercise the other options like keeping them off the streets.
>
> To me, the major thing is what the kid's been into, his attitude, the seriousness of past offenses, and the type of treatment he needs, not necessarily in that order.

Despite the staff belief that nearly everything is important, it is still possible to rank the importance of the variables on both decisions. Table 2 reveals that the items ranking highest on the *initial decision* are those relating to the offense and the attitude of the youth. Following in descending order of importance are variables concerning the availability of community placements, the youth's maturing and progress on goals (presumably during the diagnostic phase), the quality of the youth's home environment, the youth's psychological profile, the youth's behavior in school and in the cottage, and recommendations from the probation officer and the psychologist.

The variables ranked highest in the *parole decision* (Table 1) are mostly attitudinal and adjustment variables, including the amount of progress the youth has made on his or her goals (ranked fourth on the parole decision, fourteenth on the initial decision). The seriousness of the offense drops from a tie for first on the initial decision to nineteenth on the parole decision, and the number of prior court and institutional contacts drops from fifth to twenty-fourth.

It appears, therefore, that the juvenile's attitude and demeanor, including the degree to which he accepts responsibility, his honesty and openness in dealing with his problems, and his self-insight were perceived by staff to be the most important in initial decisions, but not in parole decisions where the youth's maturation and attitudinal and behavioral changes were defined as most important.

These results suggest that staff members did not have a clear rationale for the purpose of institutionalization. On the one hand, staff consider the youth's behavior, most notably the offense and prior offense history, and in this respect consider the need to protect society. On the other side, factors relating to the youth's family and psychological problems were also viewed as important. The attitude and demeanor of the juvenile was important to both decisions because it is an indicator of the potential dangerousness of the youth and the youth's need for treatment. The data, then, suggest a certain ambiguity. In the view of staff, youth may be institutionalized either to protect society or to help the juvenile deal with problems, develop self-insight, learn to be responsible, and so on. Once institutionalized, however, the central criteria for determining parole were perceived to be the juvenile's attitude, maturation, and social progress as defined by the staff and the institutional treatment program.

Analysis of Case Outcomes

Analysis of actual case outcome is consistent with staff opinions in the sense that no clear pattern of decision making emerges. Table 3 shows a general absence of relationships between a juvenile's social and behavioral attributes and the initial decision to institutionalize. In all, the decision was made to accept the juvenile into the institution's treatment program in 78.8% of the cases. A general belief was noted on the part of the staff that most juveniles could be helped by the institution's treatment program. Although staff members recognized that in some cases alternative placements could also serve the needs of the juvenile, they were reluctant to recommend such a placement unless they knew more about it. Usually, no one thoroughly researched the different group homes, foster homes, youth camps and ranches, and private residential settings. As a result, the staff felt more comfortable with their own program, where most youth would "surely" benefit, especially educationally, and where society would be protected from dangerous youth.

A key figure in determining placement is the probation officer. If the probation officer attended the staffing with a community placement in mind, and had worked out some of the details of having the juvenile accepted there, the chances were greater that the staff would recommend such a placement. But if, as was often the case, the probation officer believed that the juvenile should be institutionalized and attended the staffing with no alternative plan, institutionalization was the likely outcome.

One of the few statistically significant findings in Table 3 shows that juveniles at one institution (MMTC) were less likely to be admitted to the institutional treatment program than juveniles at the other two institutions. (The finding approaches significance — $p = .06$. When MMTC is compared with STS and MHS combined, the difference is significant at $p = .005$). This can probably be explained by the presence of a caseworker at MMTC, whose responsibilities included exploring alternative placements and making recommendations to the other staff. Greater availability of community programs in the Twin Cities Metropolitan Area is another likely reason for this finding.

TABLE 3

Percent of Juveniles Admitted to the Institutional Treatment Program According to the Juvenile's Characteristics

Variable	Value	% Institutionalized	Statistics*
Institution	MMTC	70.9	Chi-square = 5.48; p = .06;
	STS	85.9	Cramer's V = .16; n = 211.
	MHS	82.0	
Race	White	80.5	Chi-square = .49; p = .49;
	Non-white	75.3	phi = .06; n = 211.
Age	12-15 yrs. old	73.8	Chi-square = 1.51;
	16-17 yrs. old	81.9	p = .22; phi = .10; n = 211.

TABLE 3 (cont'd)

Variable	Value	% Institutionalized	Statistics*
Sex	Male	82.2	Chi-square = 4.45;
	Female	66.7	p = .03; phi = .16; n = 211.
Size of Home Community	Under 30,000	80.4	Chi-square = .34; p = .56;
	30,000 or more	76.0	phi = .05; n = 208.
Father's Occupation	Manual	87.5	Chi-square = .01; p = .91;
	Non-H.S. grad	85.0	phi = .03; n = 68.
Father's Education	Non-H.S. grad	91.7	Chi-square = .02; p = .89;
	H.S. grad	100.0	phi = .16; n = 34.
Intelligence	I.Q. 100 or more	81.4	Chi-square = .05; p = .82;
	I.Q. below 100	77.8	phi = .04; n = 115.
Reading Aptitude	Behind	80.8	Chi-square = .38; p = .83;
	Average	77.8	Cramer's V = .05; n = 186.
	Ahead	76.0	
Math Aptitude	Behind	80.9	Chi-square = 1.92;
	Average	62.5	p = .38; Cramer's V = .10;
	Ahead	71.4	n = 188.
School Behavior	Good	72.7	Chi-square = .64; p = .42;
	Poor	79.5	phi = .07; n = 186.
Personality Functioning	Normal or mild problems	76.3	Chi-square = .93; p = .63;
	Emotionally disturbed	83.9	Cramer's V = .07; n = 202.
	Sociopathic	80.0	
Commitment Offense	Status offense	66.7	Chi-square = 4.87; p = .03;
	Serious or drug offense	82.5	phi = .17; n = 211.
Most Serious Offense	Status offense	76.5	Chi-square = .01;
	Serious or drug offense	78.4	p = .94; phi = .02; n = 211.
Prior Treatment Experiences	None	84.3	Chi-square = 1.50; p = .22;
	One or more	75.9	phi = .10; n = 211.
Alleged Use of Drugs	No	75.9	Chi-square = .36; p = .55;
	Yes	80.3	phi = .05; n = 209.
Family/Home Environment	Good	77.1	Chi-square = .44; p = .51;
	Poor	82.7	phi = .06; n = 209.
Attitude/ Demeanor	Good	75.9	Chi-square = .52; p = .47;
	Poor	81.0	phi = .06; n = 208.

*Number of cases (n) varies because of missing information. Chi-square used for all variables (corrected for continuity for 2 x 2 tables); p values reported for all variables. (A p vaue of .05 or less is generally regarded as indicating a statistically significant difference.) Phi and Cramer's V, measures of association based on chi-square, were used for 2 x 2 and larger tables respectively.

Table 3 reveals that most attributes of the youth were not related to diagnostic decisions. Neither race, age, size of the juvenile's home community, father's occupation or education, I.Q., school aptitude or behavior, or the child's psychological problems is related to the staff decision. There is, however, a significant relationship between the juvenile's sex and the decision. Contrary to much of the evidence discussed earlier, males referred to institutions for evaluation were more likely to be institutionalized than females. Table 4, however, reveals that this difference existed only at MMTC, where 60.1% of the females, compared with 20.6% of the males, received probation. It appears, then, that the leniency shown to females was not characteristic of Minnesota institutions in general, but resulted from the greater availability of community resources in the Twin City Metropolitan Area.

TABLE 4

Disposition of Diagnostic Evaluation According to Sex Controlling for Institution

	MMTC				STS				MHS			
	Male		Female		Male		Female		Male		Female	
	No.	%	No.	%	No.	%	No.	%	No.	%	No.	%
Disposition												
Probation	14	20.6	11	61.1	7	13.5	2	16.7	8	18.6	3	16.7
Institution-alization	54	79.4	7	38.9	45	86.5	10	83.3	35	81.4	15	83.3
	chi-square = 9.45 p = .002 phi = .36				chi-square = .03 p = .86 phi = .04				chi-square = .03 p = .85 phi = .02			

Further elaboration on the relationship between the juvenile's sex and the placement decision is found in Table 5, which controls for the commitment offense.

Table 5 reveals that the greatest percentage difference between males and females occurred among serious and drug related offenders. Among this group, only 15.2% of the males versus 40% of the females received probation. Among status offenders, however, females were slightly more likely than males to be institutionalized. This finding of interaction is in accordance with studies discussed earlier by Pawlak (1977), Datesman and Scarpitti (1977), and Dungworth (1977). It may be, then, that a girl who is incorrigible or sexually promiscuous is seen as needing greater supervision and treatment than an incorrigible or sexually promiscuous boy, but a female thief is not seen as a potential adult criminal and does not require the treatment and control deemed necessary for a male thief.

TABLE 5
Disposition of Diagnostic Evaluation According to Sex Controlling for Seriousness of Offense

Disposition	Commitment Offense							
	Serious and Drug Offenses				Status Offenses			
	Male		Female		Male		Female	
	No.	%	No.	%	No.	%	No.	%
Probation	22	15.2	6	40.0	7	38.9	10	30.3
Institution-alization	123	84.4	9	60.0	11	61.6	23	69.7
	Chi-square = 4.21*; p = .04 phi = .19				Chi-square = .10*; p = .76; phi = .09			

*Expected frequency too small for valid chi-square.

Table 3 reveals that the juvenile's commitment offense is significantly related to the initial decision, but the differences are not large. Furthermore, breaking down this relationship by institution (Table 6) reveals that the differences are only significant at MMTC.

Again, it is suggested that the greater availability of community resources in the Twin Cities metropolitan area protected many status offenders from prolonged incarceration.

Further evidence that offense is not an important determinant of decision making comes from other variables contained in Table 3. The most serious offense alleged to have been committed by the juvenile, the number of prior treatment experiences, and the alleged involvement of the juvenile in drug use or drinking were not significantly related to the initial placement decision.

Neither the youth's score on the family/home environment scale nor the score on the attitude/demeanor scale were related to the initial sion. This suggests that even an in-depth assessment of these variables to an extent not attempted in previous studies does not show them to be related to decision making.

In short, the data presents a picture of inconsistency with respect to the initial decision to retain youth for an indeterminate length of institutional treatment or to release them on probation after a three week evaluation. Those relationships which were found may be explained, in part, by the greater availability of community alternatives to institutionalization in the Twin Cities area of the state.

TABLE 6

Disposition of Diagnostic Evaluation According to Commitment Offense Controlling for Institutio

	MMTC				STS				MHS			
	Serious and Drug		Status		Serious and Drug		Status		Serious and Drug		Status	
Disposition	No.	%	No.	%	No.	%	No.	%	No.	%	No.	%
Probation	12	19.4	13	54.2	7	13.7	2	15.4	9	19.1	2	14.3
Institution-alization	50	80.6	11	45.8	44	86.3	11	84.6	38	80.9	12	85.7
	Chi-square = 8.55 p = .004 phi = .34				Chi-square = .09 p = .77 phi = .02				Chi-square = .00 p = .98 phi = .05			

Parole Decisions

Looking at the decision to parole, Table 7 indicates that the only variables related to length of incarceration (number of days in the institution) were the institution to which the juvenile had been sent and race. The mean length of stay was 250 days at STS, compared with 155 days at both MHS and MMTC during the time of this study. This was undoubtedly due to the nature of the "guided group interaction" program at STS which staff believed required a longer length of time to produce maximum benefits. What is most interesting, however, is that juveniles were sent to STS, not because it was felt that they would be helped most by a guided group interaction program, but because they lived in the eastern half of the state. The greater length of stay for STS juveniles is consistent across all race, sex, and offense categories.

The shorter period of incarceration for non-whites than whites is contrary to most of the prior research on court decision making. This trend is characteristic of all three institutions and cannot be attributed to the existence of more community programs for non-whites in the metropolitan area. Two explanations for this can be suggested. The first is that staff were conscious of the race issue and worked to ensure that blacks and Native Americans were not discriminated against. The second possibility is that minorities adjusted better to the institutions, progressed more rapidly, and were paroled sooner. It is not possible to arrive at a definite explanation of this finding on the basis of this research.

None of the other variables, including offense, are significantly related to length of incarceration. Although not statistically significant, the mean

TABLE 7
Length of Institutionalization According to the Juvenile's Characteristics

Variable	Value	Mean No. of Days in Institution	Statistics*
Institution	MMTC	155.4	F = 12.94; n = 166;
	STS	249.9	p less than .001
	MHS	155.1	
Race	White	205.5	F = 7.30; n = 165;
	Non-white	153.2	p = .008
Age	12-15 yrs.	198.0	F = .88; n = 166;
	16-17 yrs.	179.8	p = .35
Sex	Male	186.4	F = .00; n = 166;
	Female	187.4	p = .96
Size of Home Community	Under 30,000	196.3	F = 1.37; n = 166;
	30,000 or more	174.2	p = .24
Father's Occupation	Manual	214.4	F = .93; n = 65;
	Non-manual	187.1	p = .34
Father's Education	Non-H.S. Grad	208.4	F = 1.43; n = 32;
	H.S. Grad	164.5	p = .24
Intelligence	I.Q. 100 or more	225.9	F = .01; n = 91;
	I.Q. below 100	223.7	p = .93
Reading Aptitude	Behind	200.5	F = .77; n = 148;
	Average or ahead	184.3	p = .38
Math Aptitude	Behind	196.1	F = .10; n = 150;
	Average or ahead	185.0	p = .75
School Behavior	Good	165.7	F = 2.71; n = 144;
	Poor	197.6	p = .10
Personality Functioning	Normal or mild problems	190.5	F = .87; n = 158;
	Emotionally disturbed	156.2	p = .42
	Sociopathic	191.5	
Commitment Offense	Status offense	210.2	F = 1.64; n = 166;
	Serious or drug offense	186.0	p = .20
Most Serious Offense	Status offense	193.9	F = .05; n = 166;
	Serious or drug offense	186.0	p = .82
Prior Treatment Experiences	None	176.6	F = .62; n = 166;
	One or more	192.1	p = .43
Alleged Use of Drugs	No	187.2	F = .00; n = 166;
	Yes	186.2	p = .96
Family/Home Environment	Good	180.9	F = .47; n = 164;
	Poor	194.1	p = .49
Attitude/ Demeanor	Good	175.9	F = 1.14; n = 163;
	Poor	196.1	p = .29

*Number of cases (n) varies because of missing information. F statistic based on one-way analysis of variance. p values are reported for all variables. A p value of .05 or less is generally regarded as indicating a statistically significant difference.

length of stay in the institutions is 30 days longer for status offenders than for serious and drug offenders. This is not surprising, since, as described by the staff in their responses to the questionnaire items, the parole decision is based on factors relating to progress on goals and general maturity. Since it was impossible to obtain reliable information on these variables from the files, it is not possible to substantiate that hypothesis. However, the fact that none of the pre-diagnostic evaluation variables, except for institution and race, were related to length of incarceration lends general support to that proposition.

The consequence of this pattern of parole decision making was most keenly felt by status offenders who were institutionalized not because they committed a heinous offense or presented a threat to society, but as a result of perceptions on the part of decision makers that they needed help. Such offenders were then judged by the same standards as were serious offenders when it came to the release decision. Thus, although no serious crime was committed, the status offender must mature, must show progress on treatment goals, and must learn to respect authority, develop self-insight, and accept responsibility, in order to be released. While the achievement of such conditions may be desired for all juveniles, the crucial issue is whether youth should be coerced to pursue them in a correctional institution simply because they have had difficulties in their relationships at home.

Use of Research Findings

The research findings described in the previous section were presented to Department of Corrections administrators. These seemed to confirm what was already suspected: different staff at the institutions used different criteria at different times to make decisions about retaining or releasing youth committed to them. In practical terms this meant that a lot of staff time and energy were being wasted in an elaborate decision process that was essentially based on subjective interpretations of vague criteria. Even more importantly, youth were being incarcerated for a relatively long time, six to eight months, most often for offenses that probably would not result in imprisonment if committed by adults. If imprisoned at all, adults would serve much shorter sentences. Policy specifying the purpose and role of state institutions needed to be established and, along with this, procedures developed to carry out the policy in respect to staff decisions about releasing youth committed to them.

If only because it defied the commonly held notion that research findings are rarely used, this research was exceptional. The findings stimulated the discomfort felt by administrators about the purpose of juvenile institutions and the releasing decision. A task force was appointed with a mandate to review the research and make recommendations for action. Composed of representatives from the institutions, probation and parole services, planning and research divisions of the Department of Corrections, the committee set to work. The group process soon settled into a dialogue — often heated — between two different views. On the one side, were those who held to more of a rehabilitation approach to juvenile corrections institutions and, on the other, were those who held to a just deserts approach. The main points at conflict were defining the purpose to be accomplished by the institutions and, following from the resolution of that issue, the specific procedures to be used in making decisions about releasing youth from these institutions. The linkage between the two issues was obvious and it was apparent that the way the first issue was answered would have implications for answering the second. If juvenile institutions operate for the purpose of punishing youth, releasing decisions should be most appropriately based on the instant offense and, perhaps, on prior adjudications. A rehabilitative purpose, on the other hand, would rely more upon criteria based upon the youth's amenability to treatment, especially as reflected by the youth's attitude and behavior within the treatment setting. A compromise policy was arrived at holding that the protection of the public was the single most appropriate basis for institutional commitment. Clearly, this begged the question as to the means to be used for reaching such a goal.

The task force discussion about release procedures to be used with youth committed to the institutions again reflected two different perspectives. The proponents of the rehabilitation view argued for probation, parole, and institutional staff being provided with wide latitude to exercise their discretionary authority to make release decisions. In contrast, the just deserts view held for the elimination of discretionary decision making and the use of flat time sentences. Again, a compromise of sorts was worked out with the release procedures providing for structuring the exercise of staff decision-making authority. Three categories of youth were defined and specific release procedures established. Status offenders were to be returned immediately home from the institution. Youth committed for crimes against property could remain in the institutions for up to three months while person offenders could remain up to five months from the admission date. Exceptions were provided for but the burden of proof was reversed: the onus was placed on staff to give grounds for recommending a longer period of confinement, not on youth to show why they should be released.

A Hearing Officer Panel was established at each institution composed of institutional, probation, and parole staff and empowered to make release decisions. Finally, a review panel made up of department managers not connected to the institutions was set up to hear appeals about decisions made by the Hearing Officer Panel. Appeals could be made by the youth themselves, parents, legal advocates, or the institutional and field services staff.

What happened to the release procedures once they hit the institutional worlds and what effect did they have on incarcerated youth? The procedures went into effect in late 1976, and on the basis of monitoring the movement of youth admitted to the institutions since that time, a number of trends are evident. First, the guideline lengths of stay have generally been followed: approximately seven out of every ten youth were released within the three and five-month maximums. Those youth who were handled outside of the guidelines remained in the institutions an average of approximately six additional weeks. The reasons for extending the length of stay were, in order of frequency, the unsuccessful completion of program goals that had been contracted by the youth and staff, running away from the institution, and problems in placing the child in a substitute care program in the community. The average length of institutional stay for youth released during the two years in which the guidelines have been in effect was reduced by approximately four weeks at one institution and nine weeks at the other (Minnesota Department of Corrections, 1977, 1978).

Conclusion

Reducing and structuring the discretionary authority of officials in the justice system is a key ingredient of the justice model (Fogel, 1975). The aim of such an approach is the imposition of sanctions in a fair and equitable way. Accordingly, theoretical assumptious about the cause of criminal or delinquent behavior or the rehabilitative needs of the offender are seen as having little place in the determination of punishments.

Both the studies reviewed in the first section and the data presented in the second, suggest that officials in the juvenile justice system characteristically exercise discretionary authority in an inconsistent way. Agreement on system goals is likely to help a lot in the consistency with which such a system might operate. But the extent to which such a system might still be characterized by the exercise of unstructured discretionary authority by officials in it, still remains an issue. In the last section we briefly described the use to which the research done in Minnesota was put. The release guidelines established in that state are a step in the direction of relieving what may well be a sense of injustice on the part of young people in conflict with the law.

Notes

*The research reported on here was supported by Grant Number 4700000374 from the Minnesota Governor's Commission on Crime Prevention and Control. The points of view and opinions expressed herein are those of the authors.

1. Because juvenile institutional commitments are indeterminate in most jurisdictions, and because there is usually no parole board hearing common to adult decisions, it is not possible to study the factors which differentiate juveniles who are paroled at a point in time from those who are not. Hence, the only way to measure the parole decision is indirectly, via length of incarceration. The question is not whether a juvenile will be paroled, but when.
2. Historically, the State Training School was the state facility for institutionalizing male delinquents and the Minnesota Home School served a similar purpose for females. The Minnesota Metropolitan Training Center was re-named from the Minnesota Reception and Diagnostic Center and served as the initial residence for juveniles committed to the Department of Corrections from throughout the state. Here, youth would undergo intensive evaluation, and if further institutionalization was deemed necessary, they would be sent to one of the other institutions. In 1972, the system was reorganized. Juveniles were assigned to institutions on a geographical basis. All three institutions became co-educational and all three took on both diagnostic and regular treatment program responsibilities. Subsequent to this research, the Minnesota Metropolitan Training Center was converted to an adult minimum security pre-release center, and juveniles from the Twin Cities metropolitan area were sent to the State Training School.
3. Staff members were instructed to rate the criteria only if they were involved in the decision-making process. This resulted in an n of 92 for the initial decision and an n of 129 for the parole decision. Overall, 172 out of 182 staff members responded. Three refused, three were on sick leave or vacation leave, and four never responded despite several urgings and reminders from the researcher.
4. In order to assess the reliability of coding, both intra-coder and inter-coder reliability were assessed. Intra-coder reliability was measured by recoding a random sample of 10% of the cases. Since 214 cases were coded over a six month period, it is doubtful that the coder remembered how the cases were first coded. In addition, a random sample of a second 10% of the cases was coded by a different coder and the two codings were compared in order to determine inter-coder reliability. The overall reliability as measured by the percent of items in agreement was found to be quite high for both tests — 95% for intra-coder reliability and 88% for inter-coder reliability with no items lower than 65% agreement for both intra- and inter-coder reliability.
5. A multiple regression analysis was also performed at each of the two decision points but in both cases, the standardized regression coefficients were not significant, nor were the regression equations that were generated.

References

Arnold, William R. (1971) "Race and ethnicity relative to other factors in juvenile court dispositions," *American Journal of Sociology* 77:211-227.

Birdsall, William M. (1974) "Juvenile Justice in Arizona II: Detention," *Arizona Law Review* 16:264-292.

Bittner, Egon (1970) *The Functions of the Police in Modern Society*, (Washington, D.C.: U.S. Government Printing Office).

Black, Donald J. and Albert J. Reiss, Jr. (1970) "Police Control of Juveniles," *American Sociological Review* 35:63-77.

Chambliss, William J. (1973) "The Saints and the Roughnecks," *Society* 11:24-31.

Chambliss, William J. and R. B. Seidman (1971) *Law, Order and Power* (Reading, Pa.: Addison-Wesley).

Chase, Edward (1973) "Schemes and visions: a suggested revision of juvenile sentencing," *Texas Law Review* 51:673-706.

Chesney-Lind, Meda (1973) "Judicial enforcement of the female sex role: the family court and the female delinquent," *Issues in Criminology* 8:51-69.

Cicourel, Aaron V. (1968) *The Social Organization of Juvenile Justice,* (New York: John Wiley).

Clark, John P. and Richard E. Sykes (1974) "Some Determinants of Police Organizations and Practice in a Modern Industrial Democracy," in Daniel Glaser (ed.), *Handbook of Criminology* (New York: Rand McNally), pp. 445-494.

Cohen, Lawrence E. (1975a) *Delinquency Dispositions: An Empirical Analysis of Processing Decisions in Three Juvenile Courts,* (Washington, D.C.: United States Government Printing Office).

Cohen, Lawrence E. (1975b) *Pre-adjudicatory Detention in Three Juvenile Courts,* (Washington, D.C.: United States Government Printing Office).

Cohn, Yona (1963) "Criteria for the probation officer's recommendation to the juvenile court judge," *Crime and Delinquency* 9:262-275.

Datesman, Susan K. and Frank R. Scarpitti (1977) "Unequal protection for males and females in the juvenile court" in Ferdinand, Theodore N. (ed.), *Juvenile Delinquency: Little Brother Grows Up,* (Beverly Hills, Sage Publications), pp. 59-77.

Dungworth, Terence (1977) "Discretion in the juvenile justice system: the impact of case characteristics on prehearing detention" in Ferdinand, Theodore N. (ed.), *Juvenile Delinquency: Little Brother Grows Up,* (Beverly Hills: Sage Publications), pp. 19-43.

Emerson, Robert M. (1969) *Judging Delinquents: Context and Process in Juvenile Court,* (Chicago: Aldine Publishing).

Ferster, Elyce Z. and Thomas F. Courtless (1972) "Predispositional data, role of counsel, and decisions in a juvenile court," *Law and Society Review* 7:195-222.

Fogel, David (1975) ". . . *We Are the Living Proof* . . .", *The Justice Model for Corrections,* (Cincinnati: W. H. Anderson).

Gross, Seymour Z. (1967) "The prehearing juvenile report: probation officers' conceptions," *Journal of Research in Crime and Delinquency* 4:212-217.

Hudson, Joe (1972) "An Experimental Study of The Effects of Differential Exposure to Parole Supervision of a Group of Male and Female Juvenile Parolees," *Ph.D. Dissertation, University of Minnesota.*

Hufford, Henry M. (1974) "Juvenile Justice in Arizona I: Intake," *Arizona Law Review* 16:239-263.

Hussey, F. A. (1976) "Perspectives on parole decision making with juveniles," *Criminology* 13:449-469.

Kratcoski, Peter C. (1974) "Differential treatment of delinquent boys and girls in juvenile court," *Child Welfare* 53:16-22.

Langley, Michael H. (1972) "The juvenile court: the making of a delinquent," *Law and Society Review* 7:273-298.

Lerman, Paul (1971) "Child convicts," *Trans-Action* (July-August): 35-44, 72.

Levin, Mark M. and Rosemary C. Sarri (1974) *Juvenile Delinquency: A Comparative Analysis of Legal Codes in the United States* (Ann Arbor: The University of Michigan).

Matza, David (1964) *Delinquency and Drift,* (New York: John Wiley).

McDonald, Thomas D., Jeri J. Thilmony and Eldon C. Schriner (1977) "Rural delinquents: a ten year assessment of their disposition patterns" in Ferdinand, Theodore N. (ed.), *Juvenile Delinquency: Little Brother Grows Up,* (Beverly Hills: Sage Publications), pp. 45-57.

Meade, Anthony (1973) "Seriousness of delinquency, the adjudicative decision and recidivism — a longitudinal configuration analysis," *Journal of Criminal Law and Criminology* 64: 478-485.

Minnesota Department of Corrections, *Analysis of Juvenile Release Criteria 1978, 1979,* St. Paul, Minnesota.

Monahan, Thomas P. (1957) "Family status and the delinquent child; a reappraisal and some new findings," *Social Forces* 35:251-258.

Pawlak, Edward J. (1977) "Differential selection of juveniles for detention," *Journal of Research in Crime and Delinquency* 14:152-176.

Piliavin, Irving and Scott Briar (1964) "Police encounters with juveniles," *American Journal of Sociology* 69: 206-214.

Quinney, Richard (1970) *The Social Reality of Crime,* (Boston: Little, Brown).

——— (1973) *Critique of the Legal Order: Crime Control in a Capitalist Society,* (Boston: Little, Brown).

——— (1977) *Class, State and Crime: On the Theory and Practice of Criminal Justice,* (New York: David McKay).

Rogers, Kristine O. (1972) "'For her own protection . . .': conditions of incarceration for female juvenile offenders in the state of Connecticut," *Law and Society Review* 7:223-246.

Rosen, Lawrence and Arlene Carl (1974) "The decision to refer to juvenile court for a judicial hearing," in Reidel, Marc and Terence P. Thornberry (ed.), *Crime and Delinquency: Dimensions of Deviance,* (New York: Praeger), pp. 154-166.

Scarpitti, Frank R. and Richard M. Stephenson (1971) "Juvenile court dispositions: factors in the decision-making process." *Crime and Delinquency* 17:142-151.

Skolnick, Jerome H. (1966) *Justice Without Trial,* (New York: John Wiley).

Stapleton, W. Vaughan and Lee E. Teitlebaum (1972) *In Defense of Youth,* (New York: Russell Sage).

Sullivan, Dennis C. and Larry J. Siegel (1972) "How police use information to make decisions: an application of decision games," *Crime and Delinquency* 18:253-262.

Sumner, Helen (1971) "Locking them up," *Crime and Delinquency* 17:168-179.

Terry, Robert M. (1967) "Discrimination in the handling of juvenile offenders by social control agencies," *Journal of Research in Crime and Delinquency* 4:218-230.

Thomas, Charles W. and R. J. Cage (1977) "The effect of social characteristics on juvenile court dispositions," *Sociological Quarterly* 18:237-252.

Thomas, Charles W. and Christopher M. Sieverdes (1975) "Juvenile court intake: an analysis of discretionary decision-making," *Criminology* 12:413-432.

Thornberry, Terence P. (1973) "Race, socioeconomic status and sentencing in the juvenile justice system," *Journal of Criminal Law and Criminology* 64:90-98.

Wolfgang, Marvin E., Robert M. Figlio and Thorsten Sellin (1972) *Delinquency in a Birth Cohort,* (Chicago: University of Chicago Press).

Zimmerman, Mary K. and David B. Chein (1977) "Social characteristics, offense and the attribution of responsibility: decision-making in juvenile court," Paper presented an the Annual Meeting of the Society for the Study of Social Problems.

PART 4

Fairness in the Prison

Introduction

The three chapters in this part move the discussion of justice as fairness into the internal world of the prison. Included are chapters on formalizing inmate participation in the operation of the prison, non-coercive institutional programming, and the changing role of the prison guard.

Chapter 8 by Phyllis Jo Baunach, a social psychologist, reports on research into inmate self government. Baunach notes that prisons have traditionally been operated in a totalitarian manner with inmates and line-level staff denied formal opportunities to participate. As alternatives to this type of top-down form of administration, a typology of participatory management is presented covering what Baunach defines as token, quasi-governmental, governmental, and full participation approaches. While noting that the full participation model has never been fully implemented, the author traces four approximations in the work of Alexander Maconochie, Thomas Mott Osborne, Howard Gill, and Thomas O. Murton. The common characteristics of these schemes for inmate participation are seen as the provision of opportunities for self determination through sharing decision-making authority.

Normalizing the work environment of the prison is the focus of Chapter 9 by Jack Schaller. On the basis of extensive experience conducting research and providing technical assistance to state prison industry programs, Schaller is able to provide a comprehensive review of the evolution and current status of prison industrial operations.

Major changes in the rationale for prison work are traced by Schaller. First, is the justification of work in prison as a remedy for idleness to a concern for profits, use as a treatment tool, and the more recent emphasis on profitability. Clearly, however, the growing concern for profits differs from that of the earlier era largely as a result of the changing character of private industry and the movement of the courts into the prison setting. With the exception of some state corrections agencies, convict slave labor is no longer seen as either feasible or desirable. Instead, Schaller argues that normalizing the prison work setting is contingent upon inmates being dealt with as volitional and responsible human beings.

The extent to which contemporary developments in prison industry programs reflect elements of justice as fairness is considered in the final part of Schaller's chapter. Largely on the basis of federal funding initiatives, seven states are participating in efforts to upgrade their industrial operations through the "free venture" program. The aim is to apply free world business practices to prison industrial operations. Decent wages are to be provided, workers freely hired and expected to work in accordance with production needs, vacation and sick time provided. If fully implemented, such a scheme has the potential to be operationally linked with a system of restitution as described in Chapter 3 by Hudson and Galaway.

The final article in this part by Jess Maghan deals with the changing work of the prison guard. Primary consideration is given to the potential for achieving justice as fairness for the prison guard through three significant developments: the standards and accreditation movement, centralized training, and the prison guard union movement. Maghan describes the potential for line level staff participation in the governance of the prison and notes that the rights of prisoners are inseparably linked with improvements in the working environment of the guard.

8. Participatory Management: Restructuring the Prison Environment

Phyllis Jo Baunach

Participatory Management and the Justice Model

Traditionally, prison management has entailed a totalitarian regime with the warden as the ruler. Despite efforts at prison "reform" or the prevailing treatment orientation, the warden has been invested with absolute authority from the state to control the operations of the institution. In general, the result has been the emergence of a hierarchical structure with the warden at the top, the line staff beneath the administration and lastly, at the bottom, the inmates. In this regard the flow of decision-making authority has been from the top down, with the inmates simply following orders rather than having any real decision-making authority over their own lives or those of staff or other inmates. The net effect has been that the three disparate elements of what has been called the prison community[1] have been traditionally polarized. Relationships among these factions have been strained and oftentimes hostile, as during riots or disturbances. In these situations, inmates have expressed their disapproval with the nature and structure of management practices as inadequately addressing their needs. Similarly, the formation of guards' and inmates' unions may be considered a manifestation of dissatisfaction with the lack of a voice to articulate their needs and demands in the prison community.

Despite this traditional antipathy, however, there have been a few brief instances in which the three factions of the prison community have been joined together in varying degrees to make decisions that affect one another. Alexander Maconochie in Australia, Thomas Mott Osborne in New York, Howard Gill in Massachusetts, and Thomas O. Murton in Arkansas all demonstrated the feasibility of recasting traditional prison management practices with an eye to "engagement of the governed in their own governance."[2]

The concept of true participatory management, to be explored in this chapter, rests upon several assumptions that are consistent with the Justice Model.[3] Both approaches assume that offenders are sent to prison *as* and not *for* additional punishment and that they should therefore be treated in a humane and fair manner. Secondly, both specify that the keepers and the kept must join forces to resolve mutual problems in the prison community. This assumption, the keystone of the Justice Model, provides "justice-as-fairness"[4] for both staff and inmates. Further, both indicate that the prison environment should be conducive to the development of a sense of responsibility among offenders.[5] Offenders should be given a chance to "wield lawful power."[6] Conversely, both offenders and staff assume the responsibility for the powers vested in them. Moreover, both orientations postulate that the opportunity for self-governance should be available, but that neither offenders nor staff should be coerced into participation. With respect to the participation of inmates, Fogel notes that "opportunities for self-improvement should be offered and not made a condition of freedom."[7] Similarly, Murton points out that "decision making infers the right of the individual to determine for himself his amount of participation; or not to participate at all."[8]

In essence, then, both true participatory management and the Justice Model suggest the alleviation of tensions among traditionally disparate elements of the prison community through the joint "management" of the prison. However, as will be elaborated in a subsequent section of this chapter, the two approaches differ as to the nature and extent of power granted to staff-inmate coalitions and the manner in which representation may be granted.

With rare exception, the literature in this area presents a confusing picture of the manner in which inmates have been involved in decision-making processes in the institution. Baker, for example, notes that there were nearly 100 examples of democracy within prisons.[9] Scharf, similarly, discusses Osborne's Mutual Welfare League as an instance of democracy in prisons.[10] However, neither of these authors provides a clear definition of the dynamics underlying or the elements that comprise the "democracy." Enabling inmates to have voting privileges does not necessarily entail true participatory management.

In order to articulate the conceptual framework for various participatory management approaches, the Murton Foundation for Criminal Justice, Inc. undertook the development of a continuum or typology of models of participatory management with a small grant from the United States Department of Labor. The major goal of the study was to identify and examine the nature and extent of participatory management in adult American prisons. The methodology included a review of the literature; the development of a typology of councils based upon this review; a mail survey of adult American correctional institutions; and on-site visits to several institutions in which councils operated at the time of the study.[11]

The typology of participatory management developed in this study provides a springboard for further discussion of the characteristics of participatory management and their relationship to the Justice Model.

Parameters of Participation

In delineating the concept of participatory management, the investigators identified two major factors: "decision-making power" and "representation" in the decision-making process. The investigators believed that the partial or total absence of either of these elements would result in a managerial system which falls short of a full participatory management approach.

More specifically, "decision-making power" was defined conceptually as the authority to make decisions which affect the lives of the decision maker and/or others, either directly or indirectly, through legitimate or illegitimate means. Within penal institutions power may be exercised by staff, inmates, or both groups, and its extent may be determined by the effects of decisions on both staff and inmates. Although decision-making power theoretically embraces legitimate and illegitimate power, the concept of participatory management excludes illegitimate power since the use of tactics such as sabotage, manipulation, and coercion are not reflective of joint, cooperative efforts in decision making.

"Representation" entails the eligibility of all staff and inmates to be involved in the electoral process, and minimal interference in seeking offices.

"Participatory management as defined in the study, included both involvement in the decision-making process as well as representation of the largest number of staff and inmates. Thus, "participation" entails the real opportunity for both staff and inmates of all ranks and classifications to become candidates for council positions and/or to exercise voting rights in the elections.

In essence, then, participatory management involves a joint effort of all elements of the prison community — the administration, staff, and inmates — working together. These disparate elements may be viewed as individual, albeit interrelated parts of the entire prison community. As opposed to the competitive, adversary relationship usually operative among these factions, there is a more cooperative, unified effort to work together as a team, to further one's own interest and the common good. In this regard, the process of participation in elections and/or council activities is more important than the actual council itself.

Inmates may participate, however, in the operations of the institution in ways which do not reflect true participatory management because they do not include either decision making or representation. That is, inmates may exercise either legitimate or illegitimate power, but may not represent the interests of the general inmate population or staff. For instance, inmate guard systems, such as those that have existed in Mississippi, Louisiana, and Arkansas empowered inmate trusties with a great deal of authority, including life or death power over other inmates. However, since the administrator, rather than the inmates, selected trusties, this system lacked representation of the inmate population and thus does not reflect true participatory management.

Similarly, inmate riots, strikes, or other disturbances may be brought about by a small group of inmates who do not represent the wishes of the majority of the population. In addition, power usurped in such cases is not legitimate. Finally, the representation of the administration and the democratic process for selecting leaders is lacking in these instances.

Thus, despite the fact that the inmates may indeed be in command of the decision making regarding the operations of the institution during a riot, the manner in which they assume power and the fact that administration and staff are not involved in the selection process or represented in the resulting coalition of power indicates that this approach is also not a reflection of true participatory management.

A Typology of Institutional Management Models

In developing the typology of institutional management models, the investigators focused on two elements considered important aspects of management models: function and structure. In terms of the two factors characteristic of participatory management, power and representation, the functions of the council are a manifestation of its power, and the structure of the council is a manifestation of the extent of representation of the various elements of the prison community and the process by which these elements become a part of the council.

Using the elements of power (function) and representation (structure), three major types of councils were identified from the literature review. In order of their increasing levels of participation, these models include "Token," "Quasi-Governmental," "Governmental." A few of the councils reviewed did not fit into any of these categories as they contained elements approximating more closely a "pure" participatory management model. Thus, a fourth classification, called "Full Participation" was devised.

The typology of participatory management devised in the study is illustrated in Table 1. This Table reflects variations in the dimensions of power and representation and the resulting models.

As the Table indicates, there are three types of powers. Executive powers include developing policies, assigning work for staff and inmates, promoting and classifying staff and inmates, and assuming general managerial functions. Legislative powers include devising rules that govern both staff and inmates. These powers entail developing regulations covering creature comforts, services, commodities, internal control, and judicial sanctions. Judicial powers include the authority to discipline staff and inmates for violations of institutional rules and to determine the legitimacy of the rules and regulations.

TABLE 1

Typology of Participatory Management Models*

Power (Function):	Token	Quasi-Governmental	Governmental	Full Participation
1) Executive (i.e., carrying out policies; "policing" loosely defined; work assignments; classific) determination for:	Staff = No Inmates = No	Staff = No Inmates = Yes	Staff = No Inmates = Yes	Staff = Yes Inmates = Yes
2) Legislative (i.e., rules; creature comforts; recreation/housing) determination for:	Staff = No Inmates = Some	Staff = Some Inmates = Some	Staff = Some Inmates = Yes	Staff = Yes Inmates = Yes
3) Judicial (i.e., sanctions) determination for:	Staff = No Inmates = No	Staff = No Inmates = No	Staff = No Inmates = Yes	Staff = Yes Inmates = Yes
Representation (Structure): 1) Elected (vs appointed).	Staff = No Inmates = No	Staff = No Inmates = Yes	Staff = No Inmates = Yes	Staff = Yes Inmates = Yes
2) *Staff* participation in elections.	No	No	No	Yes
3) *Inmates'* participation in elections.	No	Yes	Yes	Yes

*Taken from Murton Foundation for Criminal Justice, Inc., Final report, 1975, p. 13.

Similarly, as the Table indicates, representation (structure) includes the manner in which staff and inmates are selected for the council and the involvement of staff and inmates in the selection process. Selection mechanisms include election by their peers or appointment by the prison administrator. As noted previously, true participatory management entails minimal administrative interference in office seeking and the election of staff and inmates to council positions, with all staff and inmates eligible to participate in the electoral process.

Token Model

The most significant characteristic of the Token model is that only a small portion of the institution's operations rather than the entire institution is affected by the council's decisions. Hence, the term "token participation" was selected to describe this approach. Within the Token model, inmate involvement is limited by the duration of the council's existence, the topic of concern or the physical area affected by council decisions. These limitations suggest three sub-classifications of token participation.

The first sub-classification is task forces or ad hoc committees devised to handle one or more problems within the institution. Often, these committees are formed by the warden in response to an institutional crisis and thus are of limited duration. The purpose of the committee in this instance is to involve the inmates in assisting to alleviate the crisis. Following its resolution, inmate participation ends as the task force is terminated.

A second sub-classification of token participation is inmate councils with authority to handle specific topics of concern such as recreation or entertainment.

A third sub-classification of token participation is those groups that have authority which is restricted to a specific geographic area within the institution. For example, honors cottages may have some degree of authority in governing the inmates within their own unit, but have no authority over the rest of the institution. Within the framework of general institutional policies and rules, the inmates may devise rules and regulations which affect the cottage itself.

The Just Community implemented in one cottage unit of the Connecticut Correctional Institution for Women at Niantic at the time of the study is an example of this approach. Essentially, this model entailed using a group problem-solving process to handle personal (as opposed to managerial) problems of women within the cottage. Decision-making activities were limited to the cottage. In addition, certain discipline problems were referred to the institution's disciplinary committee. In this respect, the model operated within the context of the institutional policies and rules.[12]

An additional characteristic of this approach is the relatively limited role of the staff. Staff members are usually assigned to track and report the activities of the council to the warden.

Quasi-Governmental Model

As suggested by the title of this approach, the appearance but not the essence of participatory management is maintained: true staff or inmate participation in the management of the institution does not occur. The structure closely resembles that of the Governmental model, yet the functions differ. Whereas the latter delegates authority to the inmates, the former involves little delegation of power to the inmates. The power of the Quasi-Governmental council includes primarily holding meetings, developing proposals, and making recommendations for changes to the administration.

Frequently, this model is initiated by the staff or warden in response to an institutional crisis. Moreover, the council may be suggested as a means of preventing additional problems by providing a forum for discussion of problems between the administration and the inmates. However, inmates may demand more powers than those delegated to them.

One example of the Quasi-Governmental model examined in the study was the resident government council at the Washington State Penitentiary in Walla Walla. This council was created in 1971 in response to an institutional crisis. The council had a relatively elaborate constitution and committee system for areas such as hospital and elections. The primary responsibility of the council was to promote understanding and cooperation among inmates, administration, and community. The council reviewed major grievances affecting the inmate community and referred those it could not resolve to the superintendent. In addition, the council promoted public relations and issued press releases to keep the public informed of conditions and events occurring within the institution. However, as stated in the constitution, the superintendent had final approval or veto power over all council actions or recommendations. Thus, the extent of responsibility and influence in institutional management exercised by the council was limited. Council members may have had some power to make recommendations concerning institutional rules, but seem to have had minimal effect on the inmate or staff discipline. With respect to the subcategories of power indicated in Table 1, councils within the Quasi-Governmental model, such as the RGC at Walla Walla, may have some executive and some legislative powers but no judicial powers.

With respect to representation, staff neither vote in council elections nor serve on the council. Thus, as with the power (function) of the council, its representation (structure) is limited to inmates.[13]

Governmental Model

The Governmental model resembles both the Quasi-Governmental and Full Participation models in some ways. The structure parallels that of the Quasi-Governmental model. For both models, staff are not represented on the council and do not vote for council members. Inmates, however, are represented on the council and do participate in the elections.

With respect to the Full Participation model, the manner and involvement of inmates in the electoral process are similar. The difference in the structure between the two approaches is the active involvement of staff in electing and serving on the council in the Full Participation but not in the Quasi-Governmental model. However, the primary difference between the two models lies in the decision-making authority of the inmates. One of the distinguishing characteristics of the Governmental model is the council's limitations in handling institutional management beyond matters directly relevant to inmate welfare. The council may discuss issues and make recommendations to the administration regarding staff-related matters. However, they remain relatively uninvolved in policies pertaining to staff. As with the previously discussed models, final decisions rest with the warden.

Generally, within the Governmental model, the council is delegated few legislative or judicial responsibilities. Their powers extend to creature comforts for inmates and are carefully monitored. Consequently, inmates and staff involved in the council perceive and may actually have very little impact on the actual management of the institution.

Moreover, the warden's reliance upon staff input in making decisions may reinforce inmates' perceptions of "inferiority" to staff and may strain the relationship between these two groups. This strained relationship may mitigate any sense of trust and cooperation between staff and inmates which is characteristic of the Full Participation model.

An example of the Governmental Model revealed by the literature review was the Effort League established in 1917 at the Westchester County Penitentiary in East View, New York. The inmates drafted and the warden approved a constitution. The functions of the League included responsibility for inmate conduct in the cellblocks, mess hall, and corridors. In addition, the League made classifications in the grading system and recommendations to the warden regarding assignments of trusties. Within the grading system used by the institution, only the top three grades were permitted to participate in the League.

One of the significant features of the League was the Inmate Court.

Initially, the Court was limited to reprimanding and expelling inmates from the League. However, later the Court was invested with greater authority to draft a penal code and determine the boundaries for its jurisdiction. In addition, the League created a probation system to handle first offenders. Given these additional judicial responsibilities, this council exemplifies the Governmental Model.

The Effort League falls short of a Full Participation model because of the limitations in its function and structure. The League and Inmate Court were empowered with some executive and judicial functions. However, the latter was limited, since not all complaints were handled by the Court. In addition, the League had no legislative powers but could only make recommendations to the warden. Thus, in terms of institutional management, the League was primarily advisory, although it had some control of inmate affairs.

With respect to structure, staff involvement in the League was informal and minimal; staff members were not elected but honorary. Moreover, as mentioned previously, only the top three grades of inmates were allowed to participate in the League. Thus, inmate participation was also restricted. The Full Participation model, as will be discussed more fully in the next section, entails unrestricted inmate eligibility for involvement in the electoral process.

Full Participation Model (Hypothetical)

The Full Participation model entails the greatest degree of shared decision making among administration, staff, and inmates. The primary distinction between this model and the others is that in this model administrators, staff, and inmates collectively share the decision-making authority and responsibility for decisions made. The councils devised along the lines of this model share executive functions such as determining work assignments, staff hiring and firing, and security classifications; legislative functions include making rules regarding creature comforts, recreation or housing; and judicial functions include determining disciplinary rules which affect staff and inmates alike.

With respect to structure, all segments of the prison community are represented on the council. Staff and inmates of all ranks and classifications have voting rights. In turn, representatives elected by staff and inmates are directly responsible to their constituents.

One of the direct benefits of this approach lies in the potential remolding of staff-inmate interactions. Since the council makes decisions which affect everyone in the prison community and since the representatives are responsible to their constituents, staff and inmates may perceive the council as actually working for them to better their welfare. Thus, they may bring matters of great concern before the council, and may develop a vested interest in its continuance. If both staff and inmates do so, a dialog may be created between these traditionally polarized factions. Thus, a cooperative working relationship may evolve.

An additional distinctive feature of this hypothetical model is the manner in which it is implemented. Although the warden may have initially devised the idea for the council, the development of the structure and function and its implementation hinge upon the joint endeavors of administration, staff, and inmates. The warden, of course, must initially extend the hand of trust to staff and inmates in this joint venture. However, the council is never forced upon staff and inmates by the administrator. In this regard, coercion is non-existent in the Full Participation model.

Although the Full Participation model has never been operationalized, there have been at least four examples wherein several characteristics of the Full Participation model have been implemented. These case studies include the works of Alexander Maconochie in the British penal colony on Norfolk Island, near Australia between 1840 and 1844; Thomas Mott Osborne and the Mutual Welfare League at Sing Sing, New York between 1914 and 1916; Howard Gill and the development of his committee system at Norfolk, Massachusetts between 1927 and 1934; and Thomas O. Murton and the establishment of the Farm Council in Arkansas in 1967 and early 1968. These case studies are described here briefly to provide illustrations of the manner in which inmates, and to some extent, staff in the case of Gill, have been involved in the decision-making process. Although they differ in structure, each of these cases captures the essential elements of participatory management.[14]

Alexander Maconochie (1787-1860)

Captain Alexander Maconochie of the British Royal Navy was appointed superintendent of the penal colony on Norfolk Island off the coast of Australia in 1840. In establishing his "Social Management" theories of prison administration, he replaced the brutal, oppressive practices of previous administrations with those built on responsibility and self-determination.

Small six-man groups of inmates were responsible for one another's conduct, and thus, release from prison. When the groups had earned 12,000 marks, they were paroled to the mainland. Maconochie considered these small groups as moral units of mutual caring and concern for themselves and others. All other institutional activities revolved around these units. On small plots of land, inmates raised food to sell to free islanders and were allowed to retain the money in their possession.

Initially, inmates chose their own group members. However, following some complaints of unjustified punishment of the entire group for the unacceptable behaviors of one inmate, the selection procedure for group composition was modified.

In a less formal way, Maconochie involved the inmates in the administration of the prison. He allowed them to observe court actions inside the prison. Although thwarted by a prohibitive law from enabling inmates to sit as jurors, Maconochie often sought testimony and advice from them on disciplinary matters.

Maconochie delegated custodial power to inmates appointed to an inmate police force. They patrolled the island day and night and provided general law enforcement functions for the prison. As Maconochie later observed:

> And my Police [force] was composed of men selected by me from the general body of prisoners, furnished only with short staves . . . instead of a large free and probationer force armed with cutlasses, and in some cases pistols, that has since been maintained.
>
> If, then, with this inferior physical force, I was able to preserve perfect order, submission, and tranquility, it seems to me to follow incontestably either that my measures were most singularly adapted to attain their end or, as a general proposition, that restraints founded on self-interest, persuasion, exhortation, and other sources of moral influence, are in every case more stringent than those of brute force, even in dealing with the worst of men.[15]

In this way, Maconochie's plan combined inmate selection for reorganization into small groups with his own intuitive selection of inmates for responsible positions to assist in management of the institution.

Shortly after his appointment, Maconochie released the entire prison population for one day as a "holiday." Despite staff warnings of widespread disorder, looting and pillaging, all 1800 inmates returned to the prison on time. No accidents, ". . . theft or disorder had disgraced the day"; the inmates had acted responsibly.

During Maconochie's four years as warden, only 3% of the 1450 prisoners discharged were re-convicted. Of 920 doubly convicted inmates, only 2% were re-convicted of a crime. Inside the prison, there was only one killing, four escapes, and no uprisings during this same period.

Maconochie's impact on the penal colony is best summarized in his own words:

> I found the island a turbulent, brutal hell, and left it a peaceful, well-ordered community . . . the most complete security alike

> for person and property prevailed. Officers, women, and children traversed the island everywhere without fear. [To which Judge Barry, his biographer, added, "all reliable evidence confirms his statement."][16]

Maconochie was fired and the subsequent administration was one of partial regression to the conditions which had existed prior to his intervention.

Thomas Mott Osborne (1859-1926)

Following a series of riots and fires and the subsequent resignation of the warden, Thomas Mott Osborne was appointed warden of Sing Sing Prison in 1914. He believed that an inmate's permanent reformation would occur only if he were able to exercise meaningful decision making within the prison. Thus, as warden, Osborne set about creating an environment in which inmates could develop a sense of responsibility through self-determination.

In order to achieve his objectives, Osborne established the Mutual Welfare League. All inmates automatically belonged to the League. Every six months, two delegates were elected from each shop by secret ballot. From the Board of Delegates, an executive board was selected. The executive board selected a clerk and a sergeant-at-arms.

A judiciary committee was devised to handle all disciplinary infractions. The warden's court, composed of the warden, the principal keeper, and the prison doctor, handled appeals. Inmates' responsibilities increased and inmate morale improved greatly when Osborne replaced guards in the shops and mess halls with civilian foremen and delegates elected from the League, respectively.

In addition to creating the League, Osborne set up committees to handle every aspect of prison life including such areas as:

> . . . sanitation, athletics, entertainment, . . . finances, ways and means, reception of visitors, religious services, reception of new prisoners, employment, fire company, prison graveyard, a bank, and a parole board.[17]

Statistical evidence regarding Osborne's efforts is minimal. However, some observations suggest a measure of his success in restructuring the prison environment. For example, the impact of Osborne's efforts were reflected in the inmates' attitudes towards themselves and the institution:

> Since the League started, these men find it easier to be law-abiding; they find their self-respect restored as their belief in their own manhood grows stronger; they feel responsible for the acts of the community as well as for their own individual acts.[18]

Moreover, during his tenure, the number of wounds treated by the prison hospital dropped by two-thirds. In each of the three years prior to Osborne's administration, an average of 35 inmates had been committed to Dannemora State Hospital; under Osborne's administration, this figure dropped to 19 inmates.

Industrial production increased 21%. In the first 13 months of his administration, there were three escapes. In previous years, there had been ten escapes in 1913, six in 1912, four in 1911, seventeen in 1910, and nineteen in 1909.

According to Obsorne:

> In Auburn prison for more than two years, in Sing Sing prison for more than a year, the new system has been in operation and the thing works. The truth of that fact no reluctant official and no stupid politician can argue out of existence. It is a rock which affords a solid foundation for the future of prison reform.[19]

Osborne's appointment was short-lived. Following indictment by the Westchester County grand jury, he resigned because of political pressures. Despite his own professional demise, Osborne's innovations had successfully demonstrated that inmates afforded the opportunity to make meaningful decisions would do so responsibly.

Howard G. Gill (1889-)

Howard B. Gill was appointed as superintendent of a new prison at Norfolk, Massachusetts, in 1927 and given a free hand to design the facility and create a new prison environment. Gill espoused what he referred to as the "small group principle." Fifty inmates and two officers were housed together in what he called his "community prison."

Although Gill did not believe in inmate government as such, he did create an inmate council with numerous committees which advised the superintendent on all aspects of the prison, including construction. Gill saw this as "joint participation and joint responsibility." Eventually there were sixty inmates and thirty officers working on twelve committees.

After corruption of the council occurred, Gill decided that candidates would have to be cleared in advance for the position by the superintendent. The council was recalled by the entire population and subsequently councils included staff members.

> . . . [T]he real and most crucial accomplishments of the council system lay in the intangibles. It was a spirit of armistice where the two factions of social warfare forgot the gun and the instruments of vengeance to live together in amity to think out and put into practice a plan that would reduce the need for these conflicts.[20]

Construction productivity for the new facility doubled after a joint committee on construction was created and inmate foremen were involved in supervising the work. During the five years of construction, only 35 of about 700 inmates ran away from the minimum custody facility, although there was no security perimeter.

But movement into the new facility removed the personal contact between inmates and the superintendent and eliminated the "homey" atmosphere that characterized the construction stage. Simultaneously, there was a rapid expansion of population and staff.

> Like the early Christian church, which was truest and noblest in the days of its adversity, the council system of Norfolk was at its best when it was diligently forging the new plan, and the men involved in its creation were called upon to make sacrifices.[21]

Gill believed that his principles applied to a select tractable, cooperative segment of the population rather than to all prisoners. He chose these tractable inmates to build the new institution. Gill was less concerned with reduction of recidivism than with changing prisoners. Nonetheless, his efforts demonstrated that involving the staff and inmates jointly in prison management has the potential to reduce tension and incidents, and increase production.

Later Gill commented on the effectiveness of inmate participation in prison management:

> Instead of letting it become the means whereby men can achieve anything they want, it is to be the means of teaching them what they should have. We have got to have certain standards of decency, order, quietness, industriousness, and patience which we must insist be the standard of the meanest, the most undesirable men in the place.
>
> On the other hand, with the proper plans, I think it has been demonstrated that the whole tone of an institution can be raised by this kind of participation of exchange of ideas, of expression as contrasted with repression. We see men's faces light up and become normal, and that very atmosphere becomes a part of our therapy, because unless we meet that normal human feeling on the part of our men, we cannot do good case work with them. We cannot do the thing which we have set out to do . . . that is, to help them to help themselves.[22]

Gill's tenure as warden was terminated on April 5, 1934; he was fired following a political battle which lasted five months.

Thomas O. Murton (1928-   )

In February, 1967, Tom Murton was hired as warden of Tucker Prison

Farm in Arkansas by Governor Winthrop Rockefeller who had been elected on a prison reform platform. Murton's first acts were the abolition of corporal punishment and torture, and the removal of sadistic guards.

During the first few months of his tenure, there were a rash of escapes. Inmates in whom Murton had established a relationship of confidence suggested that he reactivate the position of Inmate Sheriff. In addition, Murton utilized inmate talents in the creation of the Farm Council.

Murton's belief that the democratic process was far more important than the product impelled him to take especial care in educating inmates for the Council:

> The process would have made all subsequent decisions suspect, and there was no assurance that the superintendent could select the proper inmates. Moreover, such a method would have negated an essential ingredient of the Council: the inmates had to become personally involved in the process if they were to have any commitment to the outcome. Finally, since the representatives were chosen by the inmates, they had credibility, were accountable to the inmate body and indirectly the general population was thus required to share the responsibility for managerial errors in the future.[23]

The first councils dealt with creature comforts, but subsequent councils devoted their efforts to classification and discipline. To make the operation more efficient, the council was split in half. Three inmates and the warden comprised the Classification Committee; the other three inmates and the warden composed the Disciplinary Committee. Although Murton retained veto power, he never used it.

The Classification Committee determined job assignments and custody grades. Since inmates comprised the guard force at Tucker, job assignments included deciding which inmates were to carry weapons. With inmate input into job assignments, erroneous decisions were often avoided. For example, although Murton favored a job change for one inmate, the Council unanimously denied it because they knew that he would attempt to escape to solve a domestic problem.

The Disciplinary Committee met weekly to hear rule infractions and complaints filed by both free world and inmate staff members. Very often inmates were acquitted because of a lack of evidence or intent. Committee members were also personally interested in many cases. One sixteen year old youth who had spent much of his sentence in the hole, "was paroled" to an older inmate who believed that he could alter the inmate's attitude. The older inmate had a personal interest in the youth's performance because he had agreed to forfeit his job as barracks orderly should the plan fail. As Murton suggested, "Commitment without personal jeopardy is a meaningless intellectual exercise." The plan succeeded, and the youth was eventually paroled and has stayed out of prison.

Following the creation of the Farm Council, there were no assaults, no fights, and only one escape (from a homosexual assault). No inmate classified minimum custody ever escaped from the farm during Murton's last five months at Tucker. No condemned prisoner ever attempted to escape even while outside the prison. Women and children freely mingled with the inmates and were never threatened or assaulted. However, as Murton observed:

> The most significant change was in the attitude of the inmates. Fear had disappeared, a new community had been created, and despair had been replaced by hope.[24]

Murton's reflections on the involvement of inmates in meaningful decision making in the institution provide an assessment of the experience:

> In review, it should be noted that the first requisite for change was that the superintendent did not consider himself omnipotent. Second, the idea for change had to emerge from the inmates. Time was devoted to really involving the inmates in a legitimate self-help effort. Success fostered success and confidence. A by-product of the farm council was the redirection of traditional hostility from the superintendent to the inmate body. The sharing of decision making with the inmates carried with it the implicit collective responsibility for the decision made.
>
> Confidence was established through meticulous procedures and credibility. Flexibility was the custom. I did not last long enough to test the final phase wherein the superintendent becomes an advisor and relinquishes the veto power. The true success of inmate government can only thus be validated. The correlation with recidivism would require additional experimentation beyond the institution.[25]

Despite his successful efforts to involve inmates in meaningful decision making in the institution, Murton was fired on March 7, 1968.

Some Common Threads

Several common threads characterize these efforts to restructure the prison environment. The prison was seen as a place to modify behavior, but only if it approximated the free world. Experience in meaningful decision making was available in the prison in order to involve the inmates in self-determination.

In attempting to restructure the prison environment, each administrator initiated the first step in reducing the suspicion and hostilities of the inmates by entrusting them with decision-making authority. In this respect, each warden risked the possibility that the inmates might act irresponsibly in learning to act responsibly.

Involving the inmates in the decision-making process forced them to share in the responsibility for the decisions made. Collective decision making resulted in meaningful participation and a coalition of interests towards common goals. In addition, this involvement also heightened the participants' vested interests in the process and increased the credibility of the election process and the viability of the councils.

Although data was not collected systematically on the effects of these approaches, some evidence suggests that during the councils' operations, the numbers of fights, escapes, and general institutional tensions were alleviated. These limited observations suggest that while operational, the councils were successful.

Despite the fact that none of these case studies exemplifies the Full Participation model, some aspects of this model are evident. With respect to representation (structure), Gill involved both staff and inmates in his committee system; Maconochie, Osborne, and Murton[26] involved only inmates. However, staff were non-voters in Gill's approach. In terms of power (function), these approaches entailed real decision making, since the inmates were involved in sharing responsibility for their own lives as well as the lives of the other inmates in the prison.

Even the limited record of success with these approaches suggests that implementation of participatory management may prove effective in reducing tensions within the prison, in significantly reducing the polarization between staff and inmates, and in providing an environment more conducive to the development of a sense of responsibility and positive growth among the inmates. In this respect, ideally, the implementation of participatory management might better prepare inmates to resume their responsibilities upon release from prison.

Reflections on Participatory Management

The typology of participatory management outlined briefly here has some advantages and some limitations. Perhaps its greatest value lies in the provision of an alternative conceptual framework within which to view the prison environment. The typology suggests a means to analyze and discuss possible mechanisms to restructure the prison environment in order to involve inmates and staff in various levels of decision making. Similarly, it suggests an approach to determine the extent to which currently functioning councils may involve inmates and staff in joint prison management efforts. Moreover, in an analysis of participatory management in terms of management theory, Bloomberg[27] suggests that the latter provides a schema to integrate the expertise of related fields into the traditionally isolated realm of prison management practices. Within this context, the typology of participatory management provides a specific perspective with which to view the extent of communication and cooperation among administrators, staff, and inmates. In this regard, the typology is a contribution to correctional management theory.

The single most important limitation of the typology, however, is the subjectivity which must be exercised in classifying any council within one of the categories. The crucial element of "responsibility" is not easily conceptualized or measured. Similarly, the elements of "power" and "representation" may not be delineated clearly enough to allow for ease in the classification of councils within one category as opposed to another. For example, the distinctions between the Governmental and Quasi-Governmental models may be difficult to assess empirically. The differentiating factor between these two models seems to be extent of legislative powers the council has which affect inmates' welfare; this characteristic may be difficult to quantify.

Conceptually, participatory management as used in this context and self-government as proposed in the Justice Model share some common features. In both orientations, as noted earlier, the concept of fairness to staff and inmates is paramount. Consequently, both groups share in the joint responsibility of providing information to the administration for the management of the institution. In addition, neither approach envisions the council as a group of "warden's boys."[28] Both approaches suggest beneficial effects on the management of the institution and the prison environment as a result of the joint involvement of staff and inmates in the decision-making process.

Perhaps the major differences between the two approaches lie in the extent of power granted to the councils and the manner in which individuals are selected for participation on the council. With respect to the former, true participatory management requires that decisions should be made jointly by staff, inmates and administration.[29] In the Justice Model, however, final decisions rest with the administration alone:

> The inmate-staff serves as a program planning and grievance mechanism. It is not, as were some earlier models, an internal court. The administration retains its veto power over proposals brought to it from the council.[30]

In this regard, councils in a Justice Model framework serve primarily in an advisory capacity. The potential under the Full Participation model, however, is that the councils are actual decision making bodies.

Furthermore, an essential element of participatory management is the election of both staff and inmates to the council. The Justice Model may include the appointment of individuals to the council: "The seats on the council may be filled in several different elective and *elective-appointive* formats."[31]

In addition, although the Justice Model stipulates that the council's "vitality and credibility will be established by the range of tasks with which it is permitted to deal,"[32] it does not delineate what this range of tasks includes. However, in true participatory management, the range of tasks clearly specifies legislative, judicial, and executive aspects. In some fundamental respects, then, these two positions diverge.

Despite these discrepancies, the question remains as to whether or not either of these self-governance proposals are indeed viable prison management alternatives. Some authors have noted that inmates involved in governing other inmates do so primarily to further their own interests.[33] Baker contends that this behavior often results in the formation of what wardens may perceive as a "gimme group": inmates incrementally seek additional benefits until the warden refuses to grant any more. Thereupon, the council declines in prestige and importance in the institution. Baker further argues that reliance upon charismatic leaders as opposed to carefully training staff in the dynamics of self-governance eventually led to the downfall of previous efforts to implement the concept:

> All of the self-government systems reviewed depended on a central figure and rapidly expired when that person departed. Apparently little, if any, effort was made to indoctrinate the staff and lead them to an acceptance of this concept of managing prisoners.[34]

Other writers point out additional operational defects in self-governance proposals. Lindquist, for example, cites two additional arguments raised by critics of self-government:

> (1) an absence of credibility among inmates and a tendency of administrators to view self-governance as merely an experiment . . . and
> (2) confusion over both the goals to be achieved . . . and the parameters of the governance system . . . .[35]

Lindquist, himself, favors involving inmates in resolving inmate grievances[36] and in institutional management and planning.[37] Formally involving inmates in the management process of the institution, he argues, would alleviate "institutional stagnation and injustice."[38] As his discussion focuses primarily on inmate involvement and only briefly on the involvement of both staff and inmates, it is difficult to determine the exact nature, structure, and operations of the self-governance model he proposes.

Still others have argued that successful implementation of any self-governance mechanism can only be achieved given sweeping reforms of the current system. Recommendations for these reforms have included redesigning the physical prison environment to make it more conducive to the goals of democracy,[39] extending full citizenship, including due process and voting rights to incarcerated felons, and transforming the prison into an economic enterprise in which the inmates share in the profits, may form unions and strike if necessary.[40] The extent to which these measures might causally influence the course of true participatory management, however, seems questionable.

Implementation of true participatory management is in itself a reform. Given the elements of power and structure outlined previously, however, one of the greatest obstacles to its implementation is that the concept is antithetical to the dictatorial philosophy and structure of current management practices. Consequently, the implementation of true participatory management may portend the demise of the current system. Thus, the concept may be perceived as threatening to commonly acknowledged and accepted prison practices and therefore unfeasible, despite the fact that where participation has been tried, there have been beneficial effects.

Additional research is thus required to more fully substantiate the impacts of participatory management and other self-governance approaches on such outcomes as staff-inmate interactions, institutional tension levels, and the attitudes of all segments of the prison community towards one another and the management process. In addition, since the evaluation of the council itself and the process whereby council members are selected are essential elements in the development of a participatory management approach, careful assessments of the evolution and nature of these processes over a period of time should be done.

As the overcrowding in adult American prisons continues, as tension levels heighten, and as "reform" rhetoric and efforts lead to more of the same, the potential for another Attica holocaust appears as a spectre on the horizon. Although participatory management is not proposed as a panacea for the ills of prison, it offers a challenging means to restructure the prison environment, to alleviate the traditional hostilities which fractionize the prison community, and to effect *real* reform efforts.

Notes

*The views expressed here are those of the author and do not reflect the opinions of the National Institute of Justice or the United States Department of Justice.

1. Donald Clemmer, *The Prison Community* (Boston, Massachusetts: Christopher Publishing House, 1940).
2. David Fogel, . . . *We Are the Living Proof* . . . (Cincinnati, Ohio: W. H. Anderson Company, 1975), p. 209.
3. *Ibid.*, pp. 204-214.
4. *Ibid.*, p. 204.
5. Thomas O. Murton, *Shared Decision-Making as a Treatment Technique in Prison Management* (Minneapolis, Minnesota: Murton Foundation for Criminal Justice, Inc., Final report for the U.S. Department of Labor, Grant Number 21-27-74-29, March 19, 1975). In this research effort, the present author was significantly involved in the development, execution and synthesis of materials. For a summary of the study see Thomas Murton, "Shared Decision-Making as a Treatment

Technique in Prison Management," *Offender Rehabilitation,* Volume 1, Number 1, Fall, 1976, pp. 17-31.
6. *Op. Cit.,* n. 2, Fogel, p. 206.
7. *Ibid.,* p. 204.
8. *Op. Cit.,* n. 5, Murton, 1975, p. 129.
9. J. E. Baker, *The Right to Participate, Metuchen* (New Jersey: Scarecrow Press, 1974).
10. Peter Scharf, "Thomas Mott Osborne and the Limits of Democratic Prison Reform," *The Prison Journal,* Volume LVII, Number 2, Autumn-Winter, 1977, pp. 3-15.
11. *Op. Cit.,* n. 5, Murton, 1975.
12. For a more detailed discussion of the Just Community approach at the Niantic Institution at the time of the study, see *Op. Cit.,* n. 5, Murton, 1975, pp. 98-107. In addition, for information regarding the Just Community approach, see L. Kohlberg, K. Kauffman, P. Scharf, and J. Hickey, *Just Community Approach to Corrections* (Cambridge, Massachusetts: Harvard Graduate School of Education Press, 1975).
13. For a more detailed description of the Resident Government Council (RGC) at Walla Walla at the time of the study, see *Op. Cit.,* Murton, n. 5, pp. 107-116. An additional description of the RGC appears in G. T. Stasney, and C. I. Stasney, "The Changing Political Culture of a Total Institution: The Case of Walla Walla", *The Prison Journal,* Volume LVII, Number 2, pp. 43-55.
14. The excerpts on these four case studies are taken from *Op. Cit.,* Murton, n. 5, pp. 34-38. For a more complete discussion and analysis of all four case studies, see T. O. Murton, and P. J. Baunach, "Shared Decision-Making in Prison Management: A Survey of Demonstrations Involving the Inmate in Participatory Government," in Herman, M. G. and Haft, M. G., Editors, *Prisoners' Rights Sourcebook* (New York, New York: Clark Boardman Company, 1973), pp. 543-573.
15. John Vincent Barry, *Alexander Maconochie of Norfolk Island* (London, England: University Press, 1958), p. 166.
16. *Ibid.,* p. 167.
17. Frank Tannenbaum, *Osborne of Sing Sing* (Chapel Hill, North Carolina: University of North Carolina Press, 1933), p. 130.
18. Thomas Mott Osborne, *Society and Prisons* (New Haven, Connecticut: Yale University Press, 1917), p. 230.
19. *Ibid.,* pp. 22-23.
20. Carl R. Doering, Editor, *A Report on the Development of Penological Treatment at Norfolk Prison Colony in Massachusetts* (New York, New York: Bureau of Social Hygiene, 1940), p. 86.
21. *Ibid.,* p. 86.
22. *Ibid.,* p. 182.
23. Tom Murton, "Inmate Self-Government", *University of San Francisco Law Review,* Volume IV, Number 1, Oct. 1971, p. 94.
24. Tom Murton, "One Year of Prison Reform", *The Nation,* New York, Jan. 12, 1970, p. 14.
25. *Op. Cit.,* n. 23, Murton, p. 101.
26. In the Arkansas prison system, there were very few free world staff during Murton's tenure. Inmates still retained functions otherwise carried out by free world staff.
27. S. Bloomberg, "Participatory Management: Toward a Science of Correctional Management", *Criminology,* Volume 15, Number 2, August, 1977, pp. 149-164.
28. *Op. Cit.,* n. 2, Fogel, p. 215.

29. *Op. Cit.*, n. 5, Murton, p. 129.
30. *Op. Cit.*, n. 2, Fogel, p. 214.
31. *Ibid.*, p. 214, emphasis added.
32. *Ibid.*, p. 214.
33. President's Commission on Law Enforcement and the Administration of Justice, *Task Force Report: Corrections*, "The Legal Status of Convicted Persons" (Washington, D.C.: Government Printing Office, 1967), p. 49.
34. J. E. Baker, "Inmate Self-Government", *Journal of Criminal Law and Criminology*, Volume 55, 1964, pages 46-47.
35. Charles Lindquist, "Inmate Participation in Correctional Institution Governance: An Analysis of Inmate Grievance Mechanisms", Paper presented at the annual Academy of Criminal Justice Sciences Conference, New Orleans, Louisiana, March 8-10, 1978, p. 8.
36. *Ibid.*, p. 13.
37. *Ibid.*, p. 23.
38. *Ibid.*, p. 24.
39. David Marrero, "Spatial Dimensions of Democratic Prison Reform", *The Prison Journal*, Volume LVII, Number 2, Autumn-Winter, 1977, pp. 31-42.
40. *Op. Cit.*, n. 10, Scharf, pp. 13-14.

Bibliography

Baker, J. E., "Inmate Self-Government". *Journal of Criminal Law and Criminology*, 1964, 55, 39-47.

__________, *The Right to Participate*. Metuchen, New Jersey: Scarecrow Press, 1974.

Barry, John Vincent, *Alexander Maconochie of Norfolk Island*, London: Oxford University Press, 1958.

Bloomberg, S., "Participatory Management: Toward a Science of Correctional Management", *Criminology*, 1977, 15, 2, 149-164.

Clemmer, Donald, *The Prison Community*. Boston: Christopher Publishing House, 1940.

Doering, Carl R., Editor, *A Report on the Development of Penological Treatment at Norfolk Prison Colony in Massachusetts*. New York: Bureau of Social Hygiene, 1940.

Fogel, David, . . . *We Are the Living Proof* . . . Cincinnati: W. H. Anderson Company, 1975).

Kohlberg, L., Kauffman, K., Scharf, P., and Hickey, J., *Just Community Approach to Corrections*. Cambridge: Harvard Graduate School of Education Press, 1975.

Lindquist, Charles, "Inmate Participation in Correctional Institution Governance: An Analysis of Inmate Grievance Mechanisms", Paper presented at the annual Academy of Criminal Justice Sciences Conference, New Orleans, Louisiana, March 8-10, 1978.

Marrero, David, "Spatial Dimensions of Democratic Prison Reform", *The Prison Journal, LVII*, 2, Autumn-Winter, 1977, 31-42.

Murton, Thomas, "Shared Decision-Making As A Treatment Technique in Prison Management", *Offender Rehabilitation, 1*, 1, Fall, 1976, 17-31.

Murton, Thomas O., *Shared Decision-Making As A Treatment Technique in Prison Management*. (Minneapolis: Murton Foundation for Criminal Justice, Inc., 1975.)

__________, and Baunach, Phyllis Jo, "Shared Decision-Making in Prison Management: A Survey of Demonstrations Involving the Inmate in Participatory Management", in Herman, M. G. and Haft, M. G., Editors, *Prisoners' Rights Sourcebook* (New York: Clark Boardman Company, 1973, 543-573.

Murton, Tom, "One Year of Prison Reform", *The Nation,* New York, Jan. 12, 1970.

———, "Inmate Self-Government", *University of San Francisco Law Review, VI,* 1, Oct., 1971.

Osborne, Thomas Mott, *Society and Prisons.* New Haven: Yale University Press, 1917.

President's Commission on Law Enforcement and the Administration of Justice, *Task Force Report: Corrections*: Washington, D.C.: Government Printing Office, 1967.

Scharf, Peter, "Thomas Mott Osborne and The Limits of Democratic Prison Reform", *The Prison Journal, LVII,* 2, Autumn-Winter, 1977, 3-15.

Stasney, G. T., and Stasney, C. I., "The Changing Political Culture of A Total Institution: The Case of Walla Walla", *The Prison Journal, LVII,* 2, 43-55.

Tannenbaum, Frank, *Osborne of Sing Sing.* Chapel Hill: University of North Carolina Press, 1933.

9. Normalizing the Prison Work Environment

Jack Schaller

Work in prison is as old as the American penitentiary itself. Work was in fact the core of the penal experience both at Eastern State Penitentiary, the first such institution in the United States, and at Auburn in New York, Eastern's earliest counterpart. Justifications for the emphasis on work were largely moral, with much stress on the reformative potential of hard labor. Whether through individual labor at a bench in a permanent solitary confinement cell, or through congregate labor in brutally managed "silent" shops, the work ethic was seen as the essential ingredient in the reformation of America's criminals.

Prison officials of the early nineteenth century quickly became aware of the need for some kind of daily activity for their institutional populations. This was as necessary to offset the significant expense of boarding prisoners for extended periods of time as it was to forestall the onset of serious physical and emotional disability that was seen as an inevitable by-product of long-term idleness. Many people, most notably the Pennsylvania Quakers, held that "the routine of labor might serve to rehabilitate the offender, transforming him into a hard-working citizen."[1] The Pennsylvania plan for imprisonment, as practiced at Eastern State Penitentiary, began with the prisoner subjected to a period of total isolation. Following this, the prisoner would be given tools and would be permitted to work at a bench in his cell. In this context, labor was seen not as a punishment, but as a welcome diversion. It was asserted that, over the period of the sentence, regularity and discipline would become a matter of habit, replacing the prisoner's former vices. Ultimately, the convict would be returned to the community cured of vice and idleness.[2]

Idleness has indeed been advanced as a "cause" of crime since at least the dawning of the penitentiary movement in this country. The very structure of the earliest penitentiaries gives evidence of concern for idleness. The most ardent supporters of the penitentiary diligently held that the tougher the institutional work regimen, the more positive the results. As one proponent said:

> The object of prison discipline is to induce (the convict) not merely to form good resolutions . . . but to support himself by honest industry. The only effectual mode of leading him to do this, is to train him . . . to accustom him to work steadily and dili-

> gently from 8 to 10 hours a day, with no other respite . . . . The discipline best adapted to such men, is that which inures them to constant and vigorous toil.[3]

Prisoner reformation and reduction of idleness, however, were hardly the exclusive purposes of prison work; concern for profits permeated practically every prison factory. With the expansion of imprisonment as this country's dominant penal sanction, profitable work programs took on even greater significance: the self-sufficient prison became practically every warden's goal: "In former times, the success or failure of many wardens depended on their ability to meet this test, and many of them met it successfully even though they may have failed in all else."[4] The effect of this emphasis was to transform labor "from any moral beneficence it may have contained for guiding the indolent into an exploitative revenue producing program for state legislatures."[5]

The New York prisons led the nation in profiting from its prison system. The advent of the Industrial Revolution in this country, along with the rise of the merchant-capitalist class, paved the way for large-scale prison-based industrial operations. Both Auburn and Sing Sing prisons claimed to be self-sufficient by 1828. Other states quickly followed the New York model of contract labor, impressed by the financial benefits of such a system.[6] Connecticut, Massachusetts, and Maryland all were proudly announcing annual profits from their industrial programs by 1835.[7]

As prison labor expanded, so too did opposition from private industry. Almost from its inception, prison labor had been perceived as a threat to private industry. As early as 1801 New York cabinetmakers and shoe manufacturers had been successful in effecting the passage of restrictive legislation aimed at reducing competition from the prisons. By 1870, private industry resistance to prison labor had influenced the firing of wardens (many of whom were replaced by men who would "establish a different industry"), had depressed prison production goals, had blocked the acquisition of new equipment, and had in some instances led to the passage of compulsory purchase laws.[8]

The first attempt at federal restrictive legislation for state prison work programs was introduced into the House on May 22, 1888, by Representative John J. O'Neill of Missouri, at the request of a group of manufacturers. The legislation, which passed the House by a four-to-one margin, was actively supported by the American Federation of Labor. The bill failed to pass the Senate, where it was effectively killed by senators from the "contract labor" states at the request of the governors and the prison boards of those states. Undaunted, the various manufacturing groups, especially those representing the garment and cordage industries, continued to battle for federal restrictions on prison labor. The A.F.L. was a frequent ally of the manufacturers in these battles.

Federal restrictive legislation finally was passed in 1929. This legislation prohibited the interstate commerce of prison made goods. Strengthening legislation was passed during the '30's, the effect of which was ultimately to destroy the prison as a center of industrial activity. Idleness in prisons soared as a result.

Creation of so-called "state use" laws, which attempted to define specific markets for prison industrial products, were not adequate to bring back the large-scale work effort in the American prison that preceded the restrictive legislation. With the exception of the WWII years, when restrictions were temporarily removed, idleness was a severe problem in most typical American prisons. According to federal government statistics, the percentage of prisoners productively employed during this period never exceeded 45%;[9] even this figure has been labeled as a "gross exaggeration of the true state of affairs."[10]

With the emergence of the "treatment ethic" in the post-war years, important questions regarding the future of work in American prisons came to the forefront. Was work a treatment? Was it for training, or was it for production? Who runs "programs"?

In the 1950's prison work ultimately did become part of an overall treatment scheme. In this vein then, work became a *vehicle* rather than an end in itself. Principal justifications for prison industry "programs," in many instances explicit goals for such programs, were training and attitude change. A conscious policy of industrial diversification was the very real product of a training emphasis; this policy also helped protect prison systems against potential protests from free world industries concerned with undue competition. Attendant decreases in productive capacity, as a result both of diversification and of the practice of periodic job assignment rotation, were of little concern to prison administrators. Prisoners were being employed, and idleness was consequently being reduced. This general attitude led to many parallels between prison industry programs and vocational education programs. Many states operate these two ostensibly very different programs in such similar fashion that the two are often hard to distinguish.

The emphasis on treatment in prison work programs brought about three very noticeable shifts in the nature of those programs. First, emphasis shifted from concern for the *product* to concern for the *worker*. Second, concern moved from a focus on *profits* to a focus on *training*. Third, interest in *industrial self-sufficiency* was supplanted by interest in developing the *future employability* of inmate workers. In short, business goals were abandoned in favor of treatment goals.

The shift from business to treatment as the *modus vivendi* for prison industries allowed prisons to continue to meet another important institutional goal: reduction of prison idleness through the maximum assignment of prisoners to work programs.

In the past few years prison industry operations around the country have begun to move away from an explicit treatment orientation. In its place the work ethic has reappeared. This recent transition has probably occurred for two reasons. First, much recent writing and research has seriously discredited the efficacy of prison-based treatment programs; prison industries are simply following the lead of the corrections field in general in abandoning rehabilitative goals. Second, treatment-oriented prison work programs have become too expensive to operate. In an era of increasing fiscal stringency, annual state subsidies to offset supervisory and raw material expenses associated with prison-based manufacturing enterprises have become increasingly less acceptable. Operations that have the capacity, at least in principle, to function as self-sufficient entities are once again being expected to do so. Profits have again become a central concern of prison industry administrators.

This is not to say, however, that prison labor is experiencing a one hundred year regression. Having spent much of this century moving away from concerns for profitability and its concomitant exploitation of prison labor, it is very unlikely that Auburn's brutal silent shops will be resurrected in the immediate future. If nothing else, the involvement of the nation's courts in correctional matters would forestall such an occurrence. Contemporary prison industry operations geared for profit can no longer afford to ignore at least the rudimentary under pinnings of worker dignity. The costs of exploitation, in terms of equipment sabatoge, diminished productivity, excessive absenteeism, chronic disciplinary violations, and general strikes are more than any profit-oriented enterprise can bear, whether prison-based or private.

The world of private enterprise has changed enormously over the past hundred years, as well. Prison competition with private industry today, in those states where such competition is allowed, is a far cry from that which occurred in the 1870's. In today's market the small private manufacturer, the "mom and pop" type operation that served as the principal competition for prisons in the last century, has been largely replaced by the giant corporation and the industrial conglomerate. Those large manufacturers have no reason to fear competition from the small production outlets that typically operate in a prison setting. Nationwide marketing strategies, along with the vastly improved transportation systems available to today's manufacturer, have so broadened a producer's sales potential that limited competition within the confines of one state poses no threat to business at all.

In some states private enterprise has defined the prison industrial operation as an ally rather than an adversary. Having pursued a conscious policy of increasing the capital intensivity of industrial production for many years, American enterprise finds itself increasingly less capable of effectively — and profitably — operating labor intensive production shops. Private industry in Minnesota and in Kansas has effectively employed state prisoners to the benefit of their industry, the prison system, and the prisoners themselves. Prison systems in Washington state, Nevada, and Indiana are in some stages of the process of considering private industry involvement in their prisons. For many years now labor intensive industrial operations have been fleeing the United States in search of cheaper, third world labor forces. As previously noted, some manufacturers have identified the American prison as an attractive alternative to the sometimes expensive move to foreign based production; indeed, some labor intensive operations are entirely unsuitable for relocation overseas, often because of the excessive shipping expenses involved. It is not at all unrealistic to assert that, in the future, prison manufacturing operations will pose a greater threat to Hong Kong and Seoul than they do to Detroit or Pittsburgh. Jeremy Bentham's principle of "lesser eligibility" has thus been turned inside out, with American prison labor's status enhanced at the expense of the foreign worker.

How does a prison industrial operation function in the setting of the contemporary American prison along lines consistent with the principles inherent in the Justice Model? This question is the focus of the next section of this chapter.

The two key concepts that link prison-based manufacturing operations with implementation of the Justice Model are *responsibility* and *volition.* At the heart of the justice-as-fairness approach is the notion that prisoners must be seen as responsible for their own behavior, and treated accordingly, during the period of their incarceration. This concept is certainly consistent with the needs of a modern prison industrial program. To be fully productive in a "real world" sense, industry administrators must inevitably delegate some production responsibilities to the workers. Indeed, the very notion of production *expectations,* intrinsic to any efficient manufacturing operation, implies some level of responsibility delegation.

Volition, a second key concept of the Justice Model, is also of prime importance to the successful operation of a profitable and productive industrial venture. Coerced participation in prison work activities paves the way for worker exploitation and its attendant by-products as mentioned earlier: sabotage, diminished production, disruptive behavior, and work stoppages.

Perhaps the greatest contribution that the re-emerging emphasis on prison labor has made to the environment of the contemporary correctional institution is the "normalization" of the work setting. The Justice Model attempts to do the same for the prison environment as a whole, and thus is in basic accord with contemporary approaches to prison industry.

How does "normalization" of prison work programs occur? It begins with a basic re-evaluation of the industrial program's *structural* and *operating* characteristics. The principal structural characteristics of traditional industry programs, which shape the system's design, are sales markets and capitalization levels.

Since the passage of federal restrictive legislation in 1929 and subsequent enforcement acts in 1935 and 1940, prison industry programs have typically been confined to "state use" sales markets, with a few notable exceptions. This means that state governments, and in some instances municipal and non-profit agencies within the state, are by law the sole customer of the prison industrial operation. Such a market limitation exerts a powerful influence on the design of the industrial program. It need not, however, as some have asserted, doom the operation's very existence. Government at all levels has mushroomed over the past two decades, and as a consequence so too has government's need for products and services. The first task, then, in evaluating contemporary industrial programs is an analysis of prison industry *markets*. Market analysis should uncover a list of products and services capable of being provided by the prison; further, it should pinpoint those which can most effectively fulfill the dual goals of maximum possible prisoner employment and adequate profit.

Further, market analysis should not be a "one-shot" task, but should be performed on a regular basis. The case of license plate manufacturing is a good example of the need for regularity. Manufacturing of license plates has historically been both a profitable and a productive business for prison industry. In recent years, however, the nature of the market has changed dramatically, largely due to technological advances in the durability of the raw materials utilized. As a result, many states now issue plates only every three to five years, rather than annually. This has severely depressed the prison-based license plate industry, and has led to a need for market exploration and equipment re-tooling to effectively use the production capability present in the plate manufacturing equipment. Few states to date have successfully addressed this problem.

An analysis of markets should lead to an examination of the second structural characteristic: capitalization. Prison Industry has long suffered from undercapitalization compared to similar operations in the free world. Further, what equipment is available is often outdated or otherwise inefficient from the viewpoint of contemporary production standards. Prison Industry can, however, offset its lack of capital with an abundant supply of labor. In some free world industries, scarcity of labor has been a real factor in increasing capitalization; thus the abundance of labor in the prison setting somewhat mitigates the need for capital in prison industrial operations. This does not mean, however, that prison industries have no capital needs. A prison work program that relies solely on inmate labor, with no mechanization, must either be unprofitable or exploitative: unprofitable because the industry cannot begin to approach free world standards of productivity, or exploitative because the reward structure for prison labor cannot provide adequate compensation for the labor provided.

Market analysis and assessment of capital requirements and resources, then, define the industrial program's basic structure. The next phase in the "normalization" process is an evaluation of the program's *operating* characteristics.

While structural elements determine the *design* of the industrial system, operating characteristics define the way in which the system is *maintained*. Principal among these are the following:

1. hours of production
2. compensation
3. relations with other prison programs
4. staffing

Hours of Production

Industrial operations in prison have traditionally been scheduled around the needs of the prison in general. Thus, the typical work day begins and ends in conformance with institutional dining needs. The lunch period is also determined by the dining hall schedule; in some instances a noon count of inmates must also be accomplished at this time. Hours of production in an industrial program so influenced, then, generally vary from a low of 4.5 to a high of 6.5 hours. This period of time would be generally unacceptable to a competitive free world industry that must remain profitable to survive. Over the past few years many states have begun to grasp this fact and have adopted a variety of solutions to the problem of the short work day. Bag lunches have been tried in some states to eliminate the noon visit to the dining hall completely; under such an arrangement the lunch period is under the total control of industry management. Other states have been able to create "express line" meal service for industry workers in the institutional dining hall. Still other states have discussed the possibility of constructing a separate industry workers' cafeteria adjacent to the industrial plant. Franchise food service operations have also been considered for placement inside the walls as an alternative to the institutional dining hall.

The relation between structure and operation must be stressed here, however; an industry that lacks an adequate market, or the necessary means of production to capture an acceptable portion of the market, has little reason to lengthen the hours of production.

Compensation

A second element intrinsic to the definition of a prison industrial program's operation is the form and level of compensation provided to prisoner-workers. Some prison industry operations, such as those in Texas and Arkansas, pay no wages at all, but instead reward workers by deducting fixed amounts of time from their sentences. This approach to prisoner compensation is inadequate for several reasons. First of all, it is "negative compensation," in that it rewards by diminishing a punishment. Further, this "reward" is highly manipulable, both overtly and covertly. If the time earned as compensation is not vested, it can be taken away at the whim of industrial or correctional administrators. If it is vested, it can be effectively neutralized as a reward by judges and legislators, who can increase sentence lengths to the point where "earned time" merely insures that prisoner-workers will not serve *longer* sentences than their counterparts in other states. Earned time can be further neutralized by parole boards. Roughly two-thirds of all prisoners released from correctional institutions in this country are released via parole. Thus, a parole board that chooses to do so can significantly undermine the compensation structure of a prison industry program simply by denying parole to prisoner-workers at the expiration of the minimum sentence. Despite the best intentions of industrial management, who may sincerely believe that they are offering the most effective incentive to their work force, "earned time" compensation dilutes industrial management's control of its own operation by letting too many factors unrelated to production influence the real level of compensation.

There are additional arguments that can be marshalled against earned time compensation systems. In terms of fit with the Justice Model, earned time payments emphasize "prison" rather than "industry" in the prison industry program, and, therefore, do little to facilitate the "normalization" approach intrinsic to the model. In the justice-as-fairness approach, corrections and industries interact only in that they share a common environment; neither should unduly influence the other in carrying out its mission.

Earned time is too subjective a compensation system. There is no quantifiable relationship between production levels and profits and time off a prisoner's sentence; consequently, an accurate calculation of time off as a function of the worker's individual contribution to shop performance can not be made. Money, as the common denominator, allows such a compensation to be made accurately; under a wage system, the worker's contribution can be *precisely* rewarded.

Finally, earned time provides absolutely no benefit to anyone other than the worker. A wage system of compensation makes the prisoner-worker a taxpayer, can allow for family support, and provides an opportunity for the prisoner to make restitution payments to crime victims. Further, a time-based system does nothing for the released offender other than release him earlier (perhaps). A monetary compensation system provides the released worker with a pool of funds to augment the typically inadequate (and sometimes non-existent) gate money payment made to all released prisoners. Numerous studies in the past few years have underscored the importance of some minimal level of financial stability for the newly released offender to forestall his rapid resumption of criminal activities.

Given these factors, it is reasonable to assert that a wage-based compensation system is superior to one that rewards via sentence reduction. It remains, however, to determine appropriate levels of monetary compensation.

Many institutions provide to all prisoners, or in some instances all prisoners involved in institutional programs, a weekly support payment sufficient to allow the purchase of basic personal necessities. Industrial wages should not be linked with this institutional "welfare" payment in the sense that such a payment *becomes* the wage. As in the free world, the minimum industrial wage should be set at a level above this welfare payment, to insure that it does in fact constitute a legitimate incentive to work. Further, the industrial wage should be paid from industrial revenues, and not from general correctional appropriations.

Clearly the most equitable way to construct a compensation system is to parallel prison industrial wages with wages paid for similar work in the free world. Such a method would then establish the federal minimum wage as the salary floor for most industrial shops. This relatively high wage for prison labor would be sufficient to allow deductions for taxes, room and board, family support, and restitution payments as appropriate. In terms of fairness, as well as to facilitate the sense of responsibility basic to the Justice Model, free world wages for prison labor is the ideal approach. Some variant of this approach has been implemented in the prison industry operations in Minnesota and in Iowa.

There are implications to this approach which need to be considered, however. In establishing a high wage formula with multiple deductions, prison industry operations are in effect subsidizing other correctional programs. Through room and board payments, industrial revenues are being used to offset the expenses incurred in operating a correctional facility. Restitution payments, when deducted from prisoners' wages, are also subsidized by the fruits of industrial activity.

In most states, prison industry revenues are generated as a result of products and services sold to other state agencies; these agencies in turn obtain the funds to purchase these goods and services through state appropriation. In a sense, then, the state is supporting a complicated series of transfer payments from the purchasing organization through the industrial operation to the correctional system. Thus, to use an example, legislative appropriations to the state department of transportation are to some extent subsidizing the department of corrections as well, when the transportation department purchases highway signs from prison industry. If the correctional "charge-back" reverts to the state general fund, the transfer payment completes the circle and returns to the source from whence it came. This seems cumbersome, at best. Further, such indirect subsidies are probably not at all consistent with the intent of a legislative funding authorization. There are at least some legislators who would be dismayed to learn that their approval of a community development agency's budget will result in a subsidy for the operation of a correctional facility.

There is also a question of fairness which is germane to the construction of a charge-back system. The state corrections department is charged with the responsibility for housing and sustaining individuals sentenced by the courts to a period of incarceration; legislative appropriations are made to the department to allow the discharge of this responsibility. It seems unreasonable to require some individuals, by virtue of their labor, to reduce the state's financial responsibility for their shelter when those individuals have no voice in the circumstances of their shelter; this is especially so when the number of individuals required to contribute is small in relation to the total number of non-working prisoners who receive exactly the same amenities at the total expense of the state. The state levy is patently unfair when the "amenities" purchased constitute a cell in a typical American correctional institution. It is hypocritical to create an attractive wage plan that seemingly awards a high level of personal compensation for work performed when in fact a portion of that compensation is returned, without the worker's consent, to the organization that disburses the wage. Such a system calls to mind the "company towns" created by the large mining companies. Mr. Peabody's coal company is hardly a respectable model for contemporary corrections.

Without room-and-board and restitution payment deductions, it is unlikely that legislatures, or society generally, would tolerate minimum wage-level salaries for prisoners. Indeed, it is not clear that payment of the minimum wage to prisoners serves any purpose beyond facilitating the formation of incredibly large, and while incarcerated unspendable, nest eggs for prisoner-workers. A philosophy of wages in the free world holds that a salary paid in compensation for a given amount of work represents the minimum acceptable level of payment necessary to insure that the work is adequately performed by an individual with the requisite skills. The federal minimum wage attempts to establish a floor for compensation such that even the lowest wage is sufficient to provide the basic necessities of life.

This purpose is not relevant to prisoner-workers, given that prisoners are either provided with the basic necessities of life at state expense, or are unable to purchase such necessities as a consequence of their incarceration. A wage plan for prison industry workers, then, should be created to meet criteria relevant to labor in the prison setting. Five general criteria for prison wage plans come to mind:

1. The wage should constitute a sufficient incentive for creating and maintaining an acceptable level of worker productivity.
2. The amount should be affordable by the industrial operation, expressed as a percentage of gross revenues.
3. The minimum industrial wage should be set at a level above the basic institutional "welfare" payment, to insure sufficient interest in the operation to maintain a stable work force.
4. Workers' earnings should allow for enough savings to be accumulated to assist in the transition period when the prisoner returns to the free world.
5. The wage plan should be generally congruent with institutional and political realities.

Relations With Other Prison Programs

Another important element in analyzing the operation of a prison industry program is the nature of the "fit" between industrial work and other prison programs and services. The typical prisoner-worker encounters a variety of institutional infringements on his time in the shop. Group therapy, individual counseling, education, visits, medical care, haircuts, etc., all must compete for the prisoner's time during normal production hours. Thus, the already minimal hours of production available to the industry as a consequence of general institutional scheduling policy are further eroded as individual workers are called from the shops.

In recent times, some states have begun to address the problem of interruptions to production. Some solutions to the problem have entailed the rescheduling of other institutional services into non-production hours; needless to say, this has not been enthusiastically received by staff providing these services.

In Minnesota, the industrial program at Lino Lakes clearly takes precedence over all other institutional activities at that facility. In order to provide services to industrial workers, counselors at Lino Lakes work a 1-to-9 schedule instead of the more common 9-to-5 work day. The Fremont Correctional Center (Medium Security Unit) in Canon City, Colorado, has likewise re-scheduled social workers and psychologists onto a second shift to service industry workers after the end of the work day. In Connecticut, social workers service the prison labor force in the shops rather than in individual offices, drastically cutting back on production time lost. Some states have re-arranged their commissary schedule so that industry workers can have special access to the commissary during non-working hours; other states have instituted a "pre-order" system for workers, so that commissary purchases are bagged and delivered to the prisoner in the shop.

Preferential treatment for the industrial operation in terms of scheduling is a clear indication of the emergence of work as "top dog" in the institutional regimen. This has in some instances led to the formation of a "treatment vs. work" confrontation as a replacement for the classic "treatment vs. custody" dichotomy.

Staffing

The fourth item mentioned as indicative of an industry's operating practices is the manner in which prisoners are selected for work in the industrial shops. Industrial staffing has traditionally taken place through a classification or "assignment" committee, which may or may not have industrial representation. Staffing levels, as well, have more often than not been determined by non-industrial administrators; total institutional population and percent idle have generally been more important staffing criteria than production needs.

A modern, prison-based industrial venture cannot afford to operate in this manner. Labor must be viewed as a factor in the production process that both incurs expenses and generates revenue, and consequently must be controllable by industrial management. The problem of prisoner idleness can hardly be ignored by anyone in the institution, given the volatile potential of a largely idle prison population. The industrial operation, however, must be free to deal with the problem in a manner that does not violate its own purpose. Prison industry can best deal with the problem of prisoner idleness through more aggressive marketing of products and constant exploration of potential new markets. Such a thrust creates a need for expanded production capability, and thus additional workers become essential to the operation. Indiscriminate addition of workers to static operations only diminishes individual productivity and increases industrial costs.

How does the foregoing theoretical discussion relate to contemporary events in prison industry programs around the country? The following discussion will attempt to answer this question.

Clearly, some states have begun to act on at least some of the issues discussed above. Over the past five years, the Law Enforcement Assistance Administration (LEAA) has been very active in influencing change in prison industry operations, through its funding of the Free Venture prison industry program. At its most basic level, the Free Venture program attempts to replicate the outside world of business within the confines of a correctional institution, and in so doing, to provide a meaningful work experience that enhances the prisoner's employment potential upon release. Change in prison industry practices has not been confined to states receiving federal grants, however; dissatisfaction with "traditional" practices and attempts to apply modern business principles to prison industry have been in evidence in practically every part of the country.

Seven states have been funded by LEAA to implement Free Venture industry programs as of this writing. Each state has chosen a slightly different approach to implementation, but all participating states expect to have a successfully operating program at the conclusion of their respective grant periods. In Connecticut, a microfilming/graphics plant, a tire recapping facility, and an upholstery shop have been established with LEAA funding; also, a low cost office furniture line has been designed and a production line for furniture manufacture will be established. This latest operation represents a shift in orientation for Connecticut's furniture factory, largely the result of an extensive survey of the office furniture market.

Minnesota initiated its Free Venture program at the Lino Lakes facility, a medium-to-minimum custody institution to which prisoners are transferred from Stillwater and St. Cloud. The Lino Lakes institution is heavily work oriented, with much work being performed by the industry program under contract with private industry. Bell Telephone Co. and Toro, Inc., have contracted with Minnesota Prison Industries for a variety of jobs; prisoners are not private industry employees, however. They are employed by the state of Minnesota. Free Venture operations have been initiated at Stillwater as well.

After a shaky beginning, Illinois has begun to experience some limited success with its Free Venture operations. Serious correctional problems throughout the Illinois system dominated the attention of correctional administrators at the program's outset, preventing any focused attention on the problems of Illinois Correctional Industries. New leadership within both the Department and the industry program, however, has served to elevate prison industries to a more prominent role in the Department, with positive results. Stateville, Joliet, and Sheridan have all made progress in recent months in running productive, profitable industrial operations.

In Colorado, the state legislature has been extremely interested in prison work programs. The Colorado Senate has passed a bill mandating work for all able-bodied prisoners, and has given the industry director control over all work programs, including food service and maintenance details. The Prison Industry staff will attempt to operate all work programs from the Free Venture viewpoint.

Washington state has just begun to move in the direction of the Free Venture program. The state has made some tentative selections for new industries, and has now begun to conduct a series of market surveys to assess the feasibility of the selections. The Washington legislature has recently passed a bill that would allow private industry to set up shops inside the walls of Washington's correctional institutions.

The state of Iowa has taken a very different approach to Free Venture implementation. Some Iowa prison industries have been set up in an industrial park in Des Moines, and prisoners are bused to the work site from a nearby institution. This operation probably represents the first state-owned, community-based prison industry plant in the United States.

South Carolina is operating the Free Venture program on a pilot basis at one institution; a large furniture manufacturing and reupholstery plant at the Kirkland facility is the site for implementation activities. A second shift operation has been created at Kirkland to increase the yield from present equipment. South Carolina hopes to use its experience at Kirkland to guide the development of industrial ventures at two new institutions scheduled for completion in the immediate future.

As mentioned above, change in prison industry practices is not confined to "Free Venture" states. Many other states are altering at least some facets of their industrial operations. The Idaho legislature, for instance, has enacted legislation allowing Idaho prison industries to sell their products and services on the open market. Idaho has also been successful in implementing a full work day in industry shops, and has all but eliminated the problem of call-outs that are so disruptive to production.

In Oklahoma the Department of Corrections is working with the Osage Nation in developing an industrial park adjacent to the Hominy correctional facility; the industrial park hopes to attract private industry that will employ both Osage Indians and Oklahoma prisoners, each on a separate shift.

Maryland's prison industry program has undergone extensive redefinition over the past few years. Maryland is now attempting to put together a plan to link institution-based vocational training programs with the industrial operation's need for production-ready workers.

Alaska has recently commissioned a criminal justice master plan, a significant part of which focused on assessing the feasibility of a prison industry program for the state. The industry study included a series of market/feasibility analyses for various candidate industries, an analysis of present institutions as prospective sites for industrial operations, and a series of specific implementation considerations, including a legislative package, a wage plan, a management organization plan, and a discussion of industrial-institutional "fit."

The above examples give some indication of the direction in which contemporary prison industrial programs are moving. Market identification has been a major thrust of prison industries throughout the country. Attempts to maximize productivity, both by lengthening the work day through scheduling changes and by minimizing worker call-outs, has likewise been a consistent concern of most states. Many states have begun to recruit management personnel from private industry to administer the prison industry program, rather than follow the traditional practice of promotion from within. This has in some instances had profound effects on both industrial and institutional staff attitudes toward the industry operation, with reaction ranging from strongly positive to extremely hostile. Capitalization, a serious problem in any industry whether prison-based or private, has been provided by LEAA in some states; this has been enormously helpful in up grading the industrial operation. The structural and operating characteristics delineated in the previous section of this chapter, then, do have specific relevance to contemporary attempts to transform state prison industry programs. While not all occurring simultaneously, or in the same order, or with the same emphasis, in every state, these factors are of obvious importance to present day efforts at change.

The prison industry operation that wants to contribute to the "normalization" of the prison environment, then, has a fairly clear path to follow. The program should focus first on the markets for its potential products, and then assess the capital resources necessary to effectively compete in those markets. From there the system's operating characteristics can be reviewed both to determine how those characteristics constrain the operation's ability to compete in the markets, and to analyze how those characteristics can be modified to enhance productive capacities.

A "Justice Model" prison industry program would be a profit oriented business housed in a prison environment. It would attempt to attract a work force through a system of wage incentives, and would freely hire and fire prisoners according to their work performance and the needs of the business. It would set production expectations for the prisoner work force and would reward workers exceeding those expectations with wage bonuses or through a profit-sharing scheme. The work day would be defined by production needs, and workers would be expected to take care of personal matters outside of normal working hours. Promotions and salary increases would be available based on individual merit. Paid "vacation" and sick time would be accrued. Benefits would be paid by the employer (workers' compensation, unemployment insurance, etc.) and workers would be liable for taxes on income. In short, the "normal" world of work would impose itself upon the prison for at least eight hours each day, and prisoners employed therein would daily have the opportunity to mentally "escape" from the drudgery and meaninglessness that is the normal lot of those incarcerated.

Notes

1. Rothman, David, *The Discovery of the Asylum* (Boston: Little, Brown and Co., 1971), p. 92.
2. Rothman, p. 86.
3. Gray, Francis, quoted in Rothman, p. 103.
4. U. S. Department of Justice, The Attorney General's Survey of Release Procedures, Vol. V: Prisons (Leavenworth: Federal Prison Industries, Inc., Press, 1940), p. 210.
5. Fogel, David, *We Are the Living Proof* (Cincinnati: W. H. Anderson Company, 1975), p. 44.
6. Barnes, Harry Elmer, and Negley K. Teetus, *New Horizons in Criminology* (Englewood Cliffs, New Jersey: Prentice-Hall, Inc., third edition, 1959), p. 528.
7. Lewis, Orlando F., Ph.D., *The Development of American Prisons and Prison Customs, 1774-1845* (Montclair, N.J.: Patterson Smith Co., 1967), p. 133.
8. Howard G. Gill in *Technical Proposal for a Study of the Economic and Rehabilitative Aspects of Prison Industries* (Entropy Limited), 1974, pp. 6-7.
9. U. S. Bureau of Labor Statistics, *Prison Labor in the United States: 1940,* U.S. Government Printing Office, Washington, D.C., 1941.
10. Flynn, Frank T., "Employment and Labor," in Paul W. Tappan, Editor, *Contemporary Corrections* (New York: McGraw-Hill Book Co., Inc., 1951), p. 238.

10. Guarding in Prison

Jess Maghan

The job of the prison guard has remained essentially the same for the past 150 years—custody and control. The desired ways of performing this job, however, have undergone considerable stress and role definition in the development of modern penology. Today there is a new and significant interest in the prison guard. This interest is long overdue and is being stimulated by major social forces affecting contemporary corrections. These forces are largely the by-product of the great social changes in American society in the post-World War II era.

The civil rights movement, union movement in the private and public sectors, the growth of bureaucratic systems in government and industry, and the related need for sophisticated human resources and technical training have permeated the corrections world at all levels. These have impacted on the world of the contemporary correctional officer usually with the consequence of confusing the officer in his attempts to maintain his central job function of custody and control: prison guard unions have emerged, riots have occurred, bold attempts at new roles and/or job titles for the prison guard have been applied. The prison guard is all too frequently left standing in the middle, faced with the necessity of maintaining custody and control in a work environment of rapidly changing and diminishing power and authority.

When the ways of performing a job are dramatically changed and yet the job itself remains essentially the same, significant problems of role identity and confusion are likely to occur. The prison guard remains today as in the past, "the other prisoner." It is the prison guard who remains, while inmates come and go, while administrative changes are invoked, policies implemented, revised and reversed, administrative rules and regulations set by the courts, and a constant barrage of new programs established. It is the guard who is expected to somehow accommodate to all of these changes and in the process, maintain a concern for custody and control.

The problems of guarding in prison have become more complex with the advent of civil rights litigation, the development of various treatment and leisure time activity programs, and the centralization of management and administrative authority in a headquarters staff usually located outside of the prison at the state capital. The very social structure of the contemporary prison has changed drastically around the issue of race and with it an internal atmosphere of "*Us* vs. *Them*" held by both inmates and guards. Furthermore, there is a new type of inmate: typically young, predominantly Black or Latino, with a self-image of being a political prisoner.

The available literature on the prison guard is very limited in scope. Gordon Hawkins has presented a succinct review of the problem observing that "when writers on the prison have seen prison guards, when they have seen them at all, they have seen them as involved in corrupt alliances with inmates, as ignorant and prejudiced functionaries of a corrupt system, or as featureless robots performing purely mechanical functions."[1] Hawkins points out the implications of this bias for limiting our understanding of the prison world and the future of imprisonment.

One can trace through the literature the confusion about the role of the guard, especially as prison operations moved through various eras of assumed change. Fogel, for example, has noted:

> The fate of the keeper has always been linked to that of the kept. In colonial days, when the criminal-sinner was being detained and worked, the keeper was called upon to merely watch him. With the advent of the humanitarian reduction of death penalties, the elimination of mutilations and the accompanying rhetoric of reformation, the guard began a long journey of role obfuscation. The humanitarians did not deliver humanity to convicts. Quite to the contrary, the convict was brutalized and in this calculated schema the guard was brutalized by having to administer the program. Under the tutelage of the [19th Century wardens], and reformation was the first mistake. [Many of the early wardens were] not confused — [and] had no pretentions about reformation — but after [they were] swept out of office the guard was still holding the whip, cellular confinement was still the order of the day and reformation remained the rhetoric![2]

The same social forces that have brought confusion about the basic role of the guard are also partly responsible for bringing about a new interest in the function and place of the guard within the total context of the prison. Thus, the role of the prison guard is emerging as a legitimate subject for research. Scholars are beginning to consider the guard as an essential component for a credible and complete analysis of the experience of imprisonment and the operation of the prison. Most recent criminal justice higher education textbooks now devote at least a chapter to the role and function of the guard; numerous professional journals contain papers examining the role of the guard, as well as articles on security staffing systems, training issues, union movements, recruitment, and retention.

If properly perceived and accepted, the influx of structural and operational changes brought about by inmate rights litigation, affirmative action, accreditation, and standard setting procedures, and centralized training, can provide the guard and inmate with a "lawful and rational arena" for change. This is beginning to happen with the growth of due process in administrative review boards for inmate disciplinary hearings, *Miranda* warnings on all charges and discipline tickets issued, access to law libraries, uncensored mail, affirmative action, monitoring for cell and work assignments, and court intervention to monitor medical, dietary, recreational, and religious programs. All too frequently, corrections has seen these developments imposed as a result of administrative compliance with court orders. Inmates have very little official voice or control over such matters except, of course, by recourse to the courts. Prison guards, on the other hand, are required to help implement these new program components often without being offered underlying reasons for them or the purposes to be accomplished. The result is that all too frequently the prison guard and the prison inmate become more polarized about the "solution" to a problem than previous to program introduction. The prisoner is perplexed and soured because all of the court mandates were not implemented as quickly or effectively as anticipated, and the guard is confused and resistant because of a lack of information and training.

Such situations have developed not only as the result of the inmate rights movement. Since World War II, more subtle but equally significant forces have also affected the world of the guard. The civil rights movement, for example, had a dramatic impact on the nation's prisons. The sense of solidarity among Black and other minority inmates and their increasing numbers among prison populations shifted the traditional relationship between inmates, and between inmates and guards, resulting in drastic changes in the manner guards attempted to maintain custody and control.

The traditional roles of inmate clerks, inmate runners, or "keyboys," dwindled; thus, power negotiated by control of information and favors informally given by the guard was drastically reduced and altered. Inmates and officers found it more difficult to rely upon their previous informal arrangements; a "no man's land" evolved in place of the traditional arena of officer-inmate relations. Consequently, the guards' systems for maintaining security and custody, role identity, power and authority were directly affected:

> The parole of the old cons, the rising proportion of minority inmates, and the increasing inmate turnover all contributed to the demise of the traditional inmate social system. Some of the best jobs in the prison were abolished. Shorter prison terms gave less reason to find a good job. The "rat" system died when the old cons left. The intricate accommodation system that had

> joined guards and inmates together deteriorated. New racial consciousness made cooperation between guards more problematic. The few privileges that once attracted inmate cooperation became fewer and less valued. The booming economy on the outside pumped more money into prisoners' hands than ever before.[3]

With these changes the prison guard became increasingly alienated from both supervisors and inmates. Morale suffered. As officers observed inmates achieving greater civil rights within the prison along with more programs and services, resentment followed. This was further compounded by the practice of central administrators taking more policy and decision-making authority away from the warden and ranking security staff. For example, inmate grievance mechanism procedures permitting central office review might reverse disciplinary tickets written by line officers. The prison guard subsequently began to feel a loss of traditional support from the warden and senior officers and retreated into a state of normlessness. These changes and reforms induced a state of anomie not only among the guards, but with administrators and senior correctional officers as well. The power of the new centralized prison bureaucracy, union stewards, ombudsmen, prisoner advocates, and other external prison constituency groups affecting the internal interests of the inmates and guards caused alarm and further confusion for the prison guard:

> In the [officer's] eyes, the interests and welfare of the officers have been sacrificed by the self-interests of their superiors and the inmates. The result is a general feeling that they are unsupported by their superiors, and that the disciplinary process makes them look like fools to the inmates they are expected to supervise. In consequence, the officers define their rule enforcement function in a highly personal manner. Each officer constructs his role in a manner so as to cause himself the least trouble. They view themselves not as a team working together to ensure security and control, but as individuals whose function is to minimize disorder and trouble in their individual areas of responsibility, even at the expense of overall institutional security. The officers are not working for the inmates: they are working for themselves.[4]

The emergence of the bureaucratic prison system has brought with it the need to reassess the internal support systems to maintain the guarding function. Security staff deployment models, unit management systems, officer-inmate panels, officer-administration panels, and training delivery systems are but a few of the approaches that have been considered.

Supporting Forces for the Contemporary Prison Guard

Three important factors have emerged during the last decade that, potentially, at least, can provide the support necessary for structuring and rationalizing equity for the guard in the management of the modern prison. These are the standards and accreditation process for corrections, centralized training, and the union movement. Through union representation, prison guards are achieving access to management so as to ensure justice in terms of job expectations. Through centralized training, the administration has authority to instruct and expect accountability so as to ensure justice for inmates and as much efficiency as possible in operations and management. At the same time, the standards and accreditation process can focus the field upon commonly held aspirations and help monitor operations and services throughout the system.

These factors have the potential for more clearly defining the obligations of the prison system to the guard and for providing services to the inmate as mandated by the courts and legislatures. These three factors, standards, centralized training, and the union movement, also have the potential for providing some modicum of equity and justice for prison staff in relation to perennial problems associated with the political nature of prison systems and the rapid turnover in administrators.

Standards and Accreditation

The formulation of standards and an accreditation process provides an external constituency for the prison guard and inmate in the form of a complementary support system. If given appropriate policy development and authority at the management level, accreditation can reach the very fabric of a prison system. The necessity to meet standards and the monitoring network that results should help to neutralize some of the inherent contradictions between custodial and treatment goals. Accreditation should also bring about more quantifiable goals and objectives resulting in a less ambiguous role definition for the prison guard.

The adoption of standards and an accreditation process is perhaps the most practical vehicle to bring separate groups in the prison into a joint effort for achieving fairness for inmates and staff. An appropriate way to secure standards is through training. In this sense, training could be responsive in a quantifiable manner for system-wide shared objectives and itself be tested in course content and on-the-job application. Training can serve as a common denominator for the standards and accreditation process as well as represent an important and signal feature for facilitating required changes for the agency.

Centralized Training

With the emergence of a correction academy as a system-wide institution in a prison system, the heretofore parochial nature of training inherent in most prison systems can be lessened. As Cohen writes: "Training, therefore, is no longer left in the control of the individual institution and cannot be utilized to perpetuate the tradition of the institutional autonomy resulting in an estrangement between essentially urban minority clientele and rural, non-minority staff."[5]

Centralized training gives supervision of the course content and of the trainee to the academy. "The academy represents an alternative to the traditional process by which guard recruits [are] socialized into their occupation. The civilian instructors at the academy prepare recruits to meet certain resistances among the old guards, and provide them with a professional reference group that is, to an extent, an alternative to the peer reference group inside the prison."[6] But this view of the corrections academy as an institution providing guards and other employees with a viable reference group is contingent on the academy itself achieving a stable and significant role within the prison system. In this sense, the corrections training academy must initially overcome the problem of survival in a system during an era of scarce resources. While no one argues with the importance of training, it has become an issue of priority and a resource to be controlled within a prison system. Maintaining a priority on training becomes difficult relative to the ever-present prison manpower needs caused by understaffing, absenteeism, overtime, hospital-funeral-writ duty, and the pressing reality of emergencies, such as hostages or riot situations. Further, the viability of training is usually weakened by the deeply entrenched negative attitudes emanating from "old school" supervisory and line custody staff who question the need for centralized training at all.

Jay Cohen's comparison of the State of New York and the State of Illinois Corrections Academies considers several factors essential to the development and future of the academy as the newest "Criminal Justice System Institution." It seems that the training function, however it may be structured, must necessarily focus on the guard and other custodial/security staff. Despite initial and deliberate attempts to develop training academies with a balance of philosophy and training content that go beyond the basics of custody and security, these skill areas are emphasized in most of the training being provided in Illinois and New York. No matter how one tries to dress up the curriculum euphemistically, the training needs of guard staff will pull it back to the basics of security.

Undergirding the curriculum content is the credibility given to a corrections training academy in the overall prison system, especially the attitude of top management toward training and requirements for staff participation. As noted in the first external evaluation project on the Illinois Corrections Academy: "Training is an aid, a supporting program, a resource at the disposal of the Department. Training does not make policy decisions, or change operations, or direct line programs . . . the burden of reforming and improving training cannot be put on training, with the operating units free to carry on as before. Training cannot do what management cannot do. But it can facilitate what management wants to do."[7] This view recognizes training as a support system for the prison guard and other staff. Training becomes a matter fundamentally accountable to the corrections administrator. The requirement that employees continue training through on-the-job application represents the administrator's substantive commitment to training as an "essential" in prison operations. Training then becomes a work assignment, another "duty post" and will be viewed accordingly in the resource allocation process. This constitutes the successful integration of training in part with other levels of prison operations.

The concern over the survival and status of corrections academies as new and separate institutions is a serious issue, however. Inherent in the question of survival is the ultimate nature of the institution itself. Most academies as initially conceived in grant applications to LEAA and through planning within correction agencies were designed to have a broad philosophy of bringing security and other program functions together, to develop ties with academia and to become correctional learning centers. In reality, however, the demands for basic security training have eventually produced a program more in line with Law Enforcement and Police Academies. The nature of the Corrections Academy has yet to fully evolve.

Other more pertinent forces also are affecting the development of the corrections academy concept: limited time and funds for training, lack of strong or appropriate support for training from top administrators, and most importantly the inability (or perhaps unwillingness) of management to conceptualize the significance of centralized training. The issue of survival appears somewhat more settled, however, for as previously noted, the complexity of the forces affecting the operations of modern day prisons dictates the necessity of training. Academies can expand into correctional learning centers for all levels of staff, if administrators acknowledge training as essential to managing the prisons.

It is the larger issue of the ability to conceptualize the purpose and uses of centralized training and develop programs consonant with such purpose that will determine the utility of the training provided. The perception by prison officials of the corrections academy as a separate institution with the primary purpose of serving as a vehicle for staff development and agency goal attainment should significantly open up possibilities for integrating Justice Model components in the world of the guard. There are some encouraging signs for this view. The academy concept as a model for centralized training in prison systems is now national in scope. One interesting aspect to this new and national network of state training centers is the use of academies as locales for national field training projects. For example, the American Correctional Association used state training academies in four regions to offer "Training of Trainers" workshops; registration was open to all states in a particular region and the host academy provided its facilities as a laboratory for the training content. The National Institute of Corrections has also sponsored programs utilizing and supporting these new institutions for training. NIC will fund the first National Directors of Training Seminar shortly. The American Association of Correctional Training Personnel has long advocated such a forum. Considerable exchange of information between the academies is underway. The Law Enforcement Assistance Administration has conducted follow-up evaluations and several academies have been cited for "Exemplary Project" status. This activity at the national level further strengthens state training efforts and adds variety through specialized seminars with renowned experts in the field participating.

New Developments in the Training Field

Training in both the private and public sectors has experienced a technical revolution in the past two decades. This, coupled with the growth of adult education and new research into the psychology of the adult learner, has generated a remarkable increase in sophisticated training styles, subjects, and delivery systems that are particularly adaptable for guard training. Role-play simulations, group dynamics, and other adult learning methods are being applied to the concept of "training as therapy." Cohen, for example, has noted:

> It may be that one of the most important effects of the academy movement is simply giving the demoralized rank-and-file guards a sense that they are important and a target of concern independent of the content of the training program itself. An opportunity to get away from the institution may be a healthy experience for persons who work in chronically tense environments. . . . The 'therapeutic potential' of guard training could be realized by bringing guards in small groups to the academy or other 'retreats' for group experiences, which would allow them to discuss and share their problems.[8]

The techniques of Transactional Analysis and Transcendental Meditation are being applied, especially with in-service officers, for stress awareness and reduction, communications, and in human relations seminars. Other examples of new trends in guard training are centralized field training models for linking work units and academy programs; team-trainer systems utilizing institutional trainers and central training personnel; assessment and role identification instruments in preparing curriculum; innovative uses of audio/visual equipment and techniques such as shoulder-pack TV cameras for taping actual incidents and/or operations demonstrations for viewing in the training classroom. A considerable product market in training films has developed in subject areas exclusively for guard training and prison operations. This activity has drawn the status of training to a higher level of credibility among its consumers — guards and administrative personnel.

Mention has already been made of the American Association of Correctional Training Personnel; this affiliate, along with the ACA's Committee on Personnel and Training, carry membership with national representation and serve as a strong lobby group for guard training. ACA is currently revising its Correctional Officer Training Guide and in so doing has solicited all current curricula in the fifty states as an exchange and accuracy base for content. ACA continues to publish monographs in topic areas germane to guard training and staffing. The National Street Law Institute and ACA's Correctional Law Project are entering their fourth year of nationally sponsored training programs for administrators and guard trainers. More recently, many other officer oriented training programs have emerged through market competition, which in itself has become a supporting force for the further growth of prison guard training. Other programs either federally funded, sponsored by ACA or by private foundations are also underway. Examples of these are the NIC — American Arbitration Association's Grievance Arbitration and Contract Administration training programs and the NIC — Law Enforcement Training and Research Association's Crisis Intervention and Hostage Situations Training Programs.

The Prison Guard Union Movement

Unionization is perhaps the most significant force for bringing about change in the role of the prison guard. It is in the interest of the union to champion training and other modernization efforts in corrections. The union steward system and management-union meetings help monitor conditions in the prison. In addition, unions are becoming involved in lawsuits in the interest of inmates and guards.

> In 1976, Council 82 [AFSCME] linked its interests with those of the prisoners in a federal lawsuit charging that severe over-

crowding in the New York State prison system constituted cruel and unusual punishment for the prisoners and thereby forced officers to violate prisoners' Eighth Amendment rights. AFSCME, asserting the rights of guards and prisoners, sought an injunction against any reduction in the number of corrections officers or in the budget, which might decrease the ratio of guards to inmates. It also requested a court order requiring the Department of Correctional Services to allocate sufficient expenditures to provide adequate, decent, and safe physical facilities.[9]

Union contracts for prison guards and other staff invariably include training as mandatory, and some have expanded to include definitions of contraband and other safety and security issues. Inmate writs increasingly demand that guards and other staff be trained in such areas as firearms use, safety and certification in first aid, (CPR) cardiopulmonary resuscitation, correctional law, report writing, and human relations. Of special note in relation to guard unions and training was the resolution o fthe Spring, 1979 prison guard strike in the State of New York. The New York agreement provides for stipends of two and three hundred dollars, respectively, for participation in pre- and in-service training. Additionally, the training is subject to union review in terms of content and delivery. This constitutes a totally new era for the concept of centralized training. The union with such a provision has effectively institutionalized a continuing forum for prison staff development, a forum that is not subject to either the sole whim of management or changing administrations.

Related Issues

Interest in the prison guard is also reflected in the attention given to such issues as recruitment and qualifications for employment and the hiring system itself, especially as it involves civil service exams, the use of merit boards, or direct hiring by institutions. The way this issue is resolved will have profound effects on the calibre of prison guards hired and the ability to train and retain them. The matters of entry salary, increments, overtime and hazardous duty pay, pension plans, and whether prison guards are duly recognized as Peace Officers by state law will also have important effects on recruitment and retention. Some state corrections systems are considering hiring psychologists to serve officers in the areas of job stress and alcohol abuse. Large police departments have had such programs for some time and such proposals are emerging in union contracts for prison guards.

Recognition of prison guards as an employee group with particular needs has made considerable progress in the last decade. Not unlike the situation with inmates and their newly gained civil rights, this has been achieved as a result of exigencies external to the prison itself. The courts acted where legislatures and prison administrators left vacuums. Improvements are in some instances still marginal and it will take much time, good will, and effort to be fully achieved. There are indications, for example, that the courts are more closely scrutinizing inmate petitions. A saturation point may have been reached in litigation, especially since key constitutional rights for the incarcerated have been spelled out by the courts. If, indeed, a "back to basics" conservatism is beginning to emerge in the land, it will most likely be reflected in the management of America's prisons as well. The progress made in establishing an "arena of fairness" for the prison guard and inmate might, therefore, be threatened. Priorities could become reset in such a manner as to concentrate on security, custody, and control, at the expense of other approaches to humane management of the prisons.

Future Trends

Precedents are being established as the result of new forces impacting on both the prison guard and the inmate world. The necessity for a cooperative custody climate is being seriously considered as the constitutional rights of the incarcerated continue to be enlarged. Giving prisoners a significant sense of participation in prison management has been successfully tried in New York State, with the active support of a prison guard union.

> The implementation of a prisoners' grievance procedure demonstrates that the guard union will not automatically oppose reform and may indeed make reform easier to achieve, at least, when the interests of guards are also protected . . . .The committee consisted of two inmates, two line officers, and a chairman/mediator, who could be either a prisoner or a staff member. Procedures permitted inmates with complaints about institutional matters to take them before the committee and to appeal decisions that did not satisfy them . . . . The present system allows an inmate with an unresolved complaint to file a formal grievance . . . The very existence of this complex grievance procedure gives prisoners significant participation in prison management . . . . With respect to the scope of grievable issues, the department and the union rejected specific charges against a corrections officer and agreed that only rules, practices, and generalized complaints would be brought before the committee.[10]

Another example of a total prison program involving considerable inmate participation in custody management is the Vienna Correctional Center in the State of Illinois. The Vienna experience, now twelve years in the making, has created an open-custody, community climate sustained through the uniqueness of the institution's architecture, through its programs, its involvement with the surrounding community, and most of all through the remarkable dexterity of management and philosophy of the former Warden Vernon Housewright.

> It is the nature of the relationship between inmates and staff that is mainly responsible for Vienna's success. "You can talk to staff here," residents say: "they really listen, and they try to help." The help is substantial — first-rate job training and education, as well as counseling to deal with personal and familial problems . . . inmates recognize the fact that disorder could easily and rapidly undermine the community acceptance Veinna has gained — hence, they make sure that new residents are socialized into an inmate culture that emphasizes the value of cooperation . . . . Concentrating tractable prisoners in some institutions means that rebellious inmates are concentrated in the rest. Without the stabilizing influence of the first group, the whole burden of control is placed on the guards and administration.[11]

The development of an inmate classification system managed on an agency-wide basis and giving reduced custody assignments to deserving inmates creates a climate that helps to relieve tension while providing options and accountability to all segments of the "tripolar prison" — inmates, administrators, and guards.

The relationship of custody officers with program staff in Vienna is designed to deliberately create role diffusion: officers actively participate in inmate program team assignments and other non-security functions; a zone management system has been invoked and the training to support this system includes all staff, security and programming, for each zone. It is significant to note that many of the senior officers in the prison guard corps of the Vienna Correctional Center are career officers and have been employed previously at the major traditional maximum security institutions in Illinois (e.g., Stateville, Joliet, Pontiac, or Menard). These officers have more than adequately adjusted to the Vienna open-custody and security system and are now responsible for transmitting this to their subordinates and newly hired staff.

> The justice model is based upon rhetoric easily understood by the personnel who will be the dominant force in prisons for the foreseeable future — the custody staff. The guard can understand simple fairness and reasonableness. He can also understand the need to build structure to insure justice. Measuring prisoners' progress by their lawful behavior is as plausible to the guard as is measuring his own work program and upward mobility by his lawful behavior.[12]

The Vienna experience, at work now for over a decade, represents an attempt to embody many elements of the Justice Model.

Prisoners' rights and the guards' working environments are inseparately linked. Improvement in one affects the other. In getting both to see their community of interest lies the promise of adding meaning to attempts to reduce the tension, confusion, and danger they mutually face. The hope for the future is that as the guard learns to be more self-determining through training, unionization, and the acquisition of a new sense of dignity, he will also free himself from his previously narrowly conceived status as a part-time prisoner.

Notes

1. Gordon G. Hawkins, *The Prison,* p. 106.
2. David Fogel, "*. . . We Are the Living Proof . . .*", p. 103.
3. James B. Jacobs, *Stateville: The Penitentiary in Mass Society,* p. 58.
4. Leo Carroll, *Hacks, Blacks, and Cons,* pp. 54-55.
5. Jay Cohen, *The Corrections Academy,* p. 186.
6. Jacobs, p. 124.
7. Cohen, p. 189.
8. Cohen, p. 198.
9. James B. Jacobs and Norma Meachem Crotty, *Guard Unions and the Future of Prisons,* p. 44.
10. Jacobs & Crotty, pp. 46-47.
11. Charles E. Silberman, *Criminal Violence, Criminal Justice,* pp. 423-425.
12. Rudolph J. Gerber, *Contemporary Issues in Criminal Justice,* pp. 127-128.

References

Carroll, Leo, *Hacks, Blacks, and Cons: Race Relations in a Maximum Security Prison.* Lexington, Mass.: D. C. Heath & Co. (A Lexington Book), 1974.

Cohen, Jay, "The Corrections Academy: The Emergence of a New Institution in the Criminal Justice System," NCCD Journal, Vol. 25 No. 2. (April, 1979).

Fogel, David, ". . . We are the Living Proof . . .". Cincinnati: W. H. Anderson Co., 1975.

Gerber, Rudolph J., *Contemporary Issues in Criminal Justice: Some Problems and Suggested Reforms.* Port Washington, N.Y., Kennikat Press Corp. (1976).

Hawkins, Gordon, *The Prison.* Chicago: University of Chicago Press, 1976.

Jacobs, James B., *Stateville: The Penitentiary in Mass Society.* Chicago: University of Chicago Press, 1977.

Jacobs, James B. and Norma Meachem Crotty, *Guard Unions and the Future of the Prisons.* Ithaca, N.Y.: Institute of Public Employment, New York State School of Industrial and Labor Relations, Cornell University (August, 1978).

Silberman, Charles E., *Criminal Violence, Criminal Justice.* New York: Random House, 1978.

PART 5

Overseeing Fairness

Introduction

The two chapters in this section deal with scrutinizing the discretion exercised by justice officials so as to extend fairness in the system. Chapter 11 deals with the development, current status, and role of the corrections ombudsman while Chapter 12 reviews recent developments in prisoner rights litigation.

Following in the illustrious footsteps of his mentor, Professor Walter Gellhorn, political scientist Stanley Anderson has become this nation's leading authority on ombudsmanry. Although the ombudsman as an institution has been operational in the Scandinavian countries since early in the nineteenth century, it has begun to take hold in this country only during the last fifteen years, and in American prisons, only during the past decade. As with other institutions that invade a formerly private bureaucratic realm, the reception of the ombudsman in American corrections has ranged from hesitancy to rejection. Even in states where it was initiated by corrections administrators, the process of acceptance was slow, uneven, and at times fearful.

Only a decade after our two biggest states rejected the Ombudsman Office in 1971, many states have adopted various forms of the concept. The growing acceptance of the Office is probably the result of prison rioters' claims that they had no other lawful way to redress grievances, the post-Watergate ethos of the public's demand for more access to governmental processes, and new levels of oversight of prisons growing out of corrections case law.

Corrections leaders greeted the ombudsman something like the police have greeted the concept of police review boards. The police, having historically been more responsive to oversight, wondered "Why single us out?" In a sense they have been right. Why indeed only the police when other public and private agencies, particularly in the 1970's, became the targets of public attack. What has not been generally understood is that the ombudsman-type of investigatory office has existed in this country since the birth of the Republic. The Continental Army had an Inspector General, an office which survives to this day with greater powers than the originators of the ombudsman envisioned. Similarly, the Government Accounting Office deals in much the same manner with civilian agencies as the Inspector General does in the internal realm of the military. In a sense, the ombudsman-like agency is as American as apple pie, but its establishment in a corrections institution had to wait until 1972.

Simply put, the ombudsman is a way of receiving and remedying grievances of sorting out the spurious so that, as Warren Burger has said, "the valid grievances can be remedied." The office in its purer form stands independently between the aggrieved and the government. It has the power to investigate the public agency and upon verification of a grievance, suggest a remedy, or suggest and negotiate a modification of agency procedure. Publicity and/or referral for prosecution in the absence of redress is the greatest power available. Professor Anderson's chapter details the history of corrections ombudsmanry in America from initial rejection to its current status.

The National Prison Project of the American Civil Liberties Union is the leading group in the American legal profession pursuing corrections reform through prison litigation. Alvin Bronstein, author of Chapter 12, is the director of the National Prison Project and perhaps this nation's foremost correctional case law expert. His contribution to this volume updates and summarizes developments in prison case law. As he points out, the course of prison litigation is not always an upward spiral of progress. For example, in *Bell* v. *Wolfish*, the Supreme Court in 1979 reaffirmed the traditional "hands off" doctrine:

> The problems that arise in the day-to-day operation of a corrections facility are not susceptible of easy solutions. Prison administrators therefore should be accorded wide-ranging deference in the adoption and execution of policies and practices that in their judgment are needed to preserve internal order and discipline and to maintain institutional security.

With such deference accorded correctional administrators, one would expect a certain timidity if not fearful constraint on the part of the litigants in bringing officials to court. But the opposite seems to be closer to the truth.

Despite the Supreme Court's admonishment, litigation flourishes on an unprecedented scale. Bronstein traces the types of constitutional issues raised in litigation. Particularly important in his discussion is the recent approach of dealing with the totality of conditions within a prison or prison system. In the states of Alabama, Ohio, Maryland, Colorado, Rhode Island, Oklahoma, and Mississippi, the plaintiffs challenged not individual conditions such as due process in disciplinary hearings, censorship, and medical care, but rather all the prison operations which combined to create unconstitutional conditions. Massive judicial intervention was seen as necessary.

Mr. Bronstein details the gains, losses and likely future of corrections litigation. He agrees with other researchers by suggesting that only modest gains in correctional reform can be expected through litigation. However, given what Norval Morris has referred to as the "glacial case" of correctional progress, the National Prison Project has probably been largely responsible for keeping a constitutional floor under correctional practice by forceful litigation.

11. The Corrections Ombudsman

Stanley Anderson*

Warren Burger, Chief Justice of the United States Supreme Court, tells us that "every penal institution must have . . . the means of having complaints reach decision-making sources through established channels, so that the valid grievances can be remedied and spurious grievances exposed."[1] This chapter is mainly about one such channel — the Ombudsman institution in prisons. It examines two kinds of offices, one in which the Ombudsman stays behind his desk and the other in which he ventures into the field. The original Ombudsman offices in Scandinavia handle complaints from prisoners much as they do other complaints.[2] Grievances are received and investigated mostly through correspondence. During the past six years, a new kind of office has sprung up in North America, one whose work is limited to places of incarceration. Prison Ombudsmen do much of their work face-to-face, inside the prisons.

This study grows out of the failure of two correctional Ombudsman proposals in 1971. The first was embodied in a bill adopted by the California Legislature (following extensive hearings in which David Fogel and I participated)[3] and was vetoed by Governor Ronald Reagan. The second was a counter-proposal to rebellious Attica inmates put forward by the Commissioner of the New York State Department of Correctional Services, Russell Oswald, and was never implemented.[4] Opposition to the proposals in California and New York cannot be explained by mere partisan labels. The Ombudsman idea cuts across the ideological spectrum, and has been identified with both major political parties in the United States.[5]

Because there were no Ombudsman offices anywhere at that time whose field of responsibility was limited to places of incarceration, the justification for the California proposal had necessarily to be based considerably upon speculation. When an Ombudsman for Corrections was appointed in Minnesota in 1972 and when a deputy for prisons was hired in the Iowa Ombudsman office in 1973, it occurred to me that the best way to allay the misgivings of those who feared that an Ombudsman in prison might be disruptive was to present the experience of these new offices, so that one would not have to rely on speculation.

The experience is reassuring. Indeed, management has benefitted as much as the inmates from the presence of an Ombudsman, because the Ombudsman is a useful control device for upper echelons, while employees down the line can use the Ombudsman as a means of focusing the attention of their superiors on problems which the lower ranks would like to have solved. The Ombudsman office is not "just another layer of bureaucracy," but is instead a monitor for bureaucracy. It is an instrument for controlling the quality of quality-control instruments. Grounded in the common law case-by-case method, it is much more effective in policing day-to-day administrative activity than courts, legislators, or governors. The complaints which properly pertain to an Ombudsman are those related to administrative action. He screens other matters which come to him, and he refers them to prison officials, legal aid offices, public defenders, and social service agencies. Without these alternative resources, the Ombudsman might drown in a deluge of requests.

Only one criminologist, Professor David Fogel, has made the prison Ombudsman an integral part of his approach.[6] Otherwise, the Ombudsman notion cuts across the current strands of debate in penology, and the Ombudsman institution is congenial to any humane philosophy of imprisonment. While an atmosphere of prison reform is not essential to the operation of an Ombudsman office, such an atmosphere is conducive to it. In a climate of prison reform, each new program or service provides a possible new subject of controversy. Because the correctional Ombudsman idea itself is a reform measure, with a primary focus on the grievances of individual prisoners, it is part of the ferment which currently surrounds prisoners' rights and remedies.

During one of my visits to American state prisons in connection with this study, I chatted with an official who could remember when an inmate had to take his hat off at a respectful distance and ask permission to speak to a guard by saying "Sir!" During the nineteenth century, convicts in some American prisons were not allowed to communicate with one another, let alone with the outside world. Until fairly recently in this country, it might be said that prisoners had neither rights nor remedies. They were "slaves of the state," completely subject to the warden and his subordinates.[7] Individual institutions were autonomous, and there was no appeal to a higher authority. The past twenty years have seen the emergence of rights and the development of remedies. In contrast to the "slave of the state" doctrine, we are moving toward the position that "A prisoner retains all the rights of an ordinary citizen except those expressly, or by necessary implication, taken from him by law."[8]

A crucial initial step in the process of translation of rights into reality is to open lines of communication outside the prison walls. Most states have followed the example set by the Federal Bureau of Prisons in allowing inmates to correspond with friends and family and in permitting prisoners to write "uncensored and unopened letters to public authorities, the courts, and members of the House and Senate."[9] Normally, an inmate may send a letter or a "kite" to any official within a given prison. Among the other authorities to whom an inmate may write are those in the chain of command above the warden, i.e., the head of the department of corrections and the head of the umbrella agency which may house the department. This avenue is valuable, but it "does not assure a convict that his grievance will be evaluated by a thoroughly impartial authority."[10]

While appeals to elected officials outside the system may add impartiality, the office holders contacted usually lack the capacity to carry out an independent investigation.[11] Also, some legislators who otherwise welcome constituent complaints may not want to be bothered with convicts. I spoke to one Governor's aide who said that he always waited several weeks or more to reply to an inmate letter because a prompt answer would generate a spate of letters from the inmate and his companions. The aide said that he did not want to encourage such "pen pals."

An aggrieved inmate who is frustrated by the reaction of the executive and legislative branches is likely to turn to the courts for judicial redress. In the past twenty years, there has been a veritable flood of litigation in two main areas: post-conviction appeals and challenges to the conditions of incarceration.[12] The latter stems from the discrediting of the hands-off doctrine, which held that the "courts are without power to supervise prison administration or to interfere with ordinary prison rules or regulations."[13] The gates in the dam of this kind of a judicial abstention have been opened by the newly construed constitutional prohibition against cruel and unusual punishments[14] and the recent reinterpretations of the meaning of the due process and equal protection clauses.[15] Whatever the reasons, prisoners now petition more than ever before. The flow for prisoner redress has stabilized, statistics show, but the volume of complaints remains high.[16] There is some reason to believe that too many complaints to courts are frivolous and, in two states, Maryland and North Carolina, prisoner litigation has been curtailed in the state courts by interposing a mandatory administrative procedure which includes an opportunity for hearing before an Inmate Grievance Commission. At the federal level, however, the United States Supreme Court has directed the District Courts to take cases from prisoners even though state remedies have not been exhausted, pursuant to the Civil Rights Act of 1871, which protects against "the deprivation of any rights, privileges, or immunities secured by the Constitution and laws."[17]

If the tide of lawsuits cannot be stemmed, it must be channeled. The underlying problem is one of screening papers which have not been prepared by lawyers.[18] A special committee of the Federal Judicial Center, composed of five federal judges, has made the following preliminary recommendations for handling prisoner complaints:

centralized processing by expert "intake" or "writ" clerks;

subsequent screening by law clerks or magistrates;

the use of a standardized complaint form.[19]

There is no evidence that Ombudsmen have reduced inmate litigation, but they do assist in the screening process. In Iowa, for example, the Deputy Ombudsman for Corrections gave sealed and confidential testimony in chambers in a federal suit filed by an inmate at the Iowa State Penitentiary.[20] In Connecticut, a federal judge referred a complaint to the Correctional Ombudsman "with instructions to investigate and report its findings to the court."[21] This particular dispute was resolved without requiring further action by the court.

Overall, the direct interplay between courts and Ombudsmen has been minimal. While there is some overlap of functions, which is probably wholesome, each has its own distinct role to play. An Ombudsman could not effectively attack a grossly deficient prison system, as did a federal judge in Arkansas.[22] According to a study sponsored by the American Bar Association on the Arkansas case:

> [T]he number of, and consequent level of supervision by free world employees increased significantly, thereby improving inmate safety. The general level of sanitation improved markedly. Significant strides were made in reducing racial discrimination and race relations improved as a result. Health services and recreation were expanded considerably. Corporal punishment was stopped, and a measure of procedural regularity was introduced into prison discipline.[23]

An Ombudsman might have been able to cope with one or two of these problems, but he would not have been able to attack them all at the same time. Thus, courts can help to establish the basic preconditions for the successful operation of a prison Ombudsman office.[24] By the same token, Ombudsmen should handle minor complaints which have a potential for clogging the courts. (We do not know if those who complain to an Ombudsman would otherwise have gone to court, and we do not know if those who go to court would have been satisfied with an Ombudsman.) For substantial relief of the regular courts, it seems to be necessary to set up an administrative court. Such tribunals can have an Ombudsman component, as they do in Maryland and North Carolina.

The first American State Ombudsman office went into operation in Hawaii in 1969. Since then, three additional statewide offices have been established, in Iowa (1970), Nebraska (1971), and Alaska (1975). The jurisdiction of all four offices includes prisons. As far as size is concerned, however, we move from small to smaller: the largest of these states, Iowa, has about the same population as New Zealand. Comparing the general operation of these four offices with that found elsewhere, I am much more impressed by similarities than by differences. In Australia, Canada, New Zealand, Scandinavia, and the United States, the Ombudsman officers are independent, staffed by impartial and expert Ombudsmen and assistants, widely accessible to their populace, with plenary power of investigation, but no power to command, and who must consequently rely upon reasoned persuasion with only the threat of publicity as a weapon.

In transferring the Ombudsman institution to the New World, the development of specialized prison offices has clearly been the most significant innovation. There are now six correctional Ombudsman offices in the United States, in Minnesota (since 1972), Connecticut (1973), Iowa (which added a prison deputy in 1973), Kansas (1975), Michigan (1975), and Oregon (1977). In terms of size, only Michigan is on a par with Sweden, the most populous of the Scandinavian countries. The prison population of Michigan, however, is proportionally much greater, and the inmates are concentrated in a single institution which is the largest in the United States, and perhaps the largest in the world.

The prison Ombudsman idea was one of many put forth by David Fogel during his tenure as Commissioner of Corrections in Minnesota. The proposal met with a positive reaction when, as Fogel states:

> Initial anxiety melted when each of the state's institutional administrators and their executive staff met, analyzed, and modified the proposal.[25]

Previous to Fogel's proposal, however, an Ombudsman for corrections had been appointed, upon nomination by a broadly based ten-member Ombudsman Commission, by the then-Governor Wendell Anderson. Theartrice Williams, a black and the son of a Mississippi sharecropper, has served as Ombudsman for Corrections in Minnesota since July, 1972. He holds a Master's degree in social work from the University of Pennsylvania, and had previously been director of a community center in Minneapolis.

Yet Fogel's proposal brought the need for the creation of a formal Office of Ombudsman for the Minnesota State Department of Corrections into clear focus. The result of his proposal was a law enacted by the Minnesota Legislature in 1973, creating such an office. The statute was amended in 1976 to make the office permanent, by repealing the previous automatic expiration date of July, 1977. These amendments also gave the Ombudsman subpoena power and immunity from suit or compulsory testimony, while extending the jurisdiction of the office to include regional facilities (but not local jails).

The Ombudsman serves "at the pleasure of the Governor" (Minn. Stats.

241-41). Except for the manner of appointment and the absence of a fixed term, the Minnesota Ombudsman office differs from other Ombudsman offices only in that its jurisdiction is limited to correctional matters. Indeed, with these important exceptions, the Minnesota law is taken in great part from Walter Gellhorn's Annotated Model Ombudsman Statute.[26] It costs about $210,000 a year to run the office. Initially, it was partly supported by grants from the Law Enforcement Assistance Administration, and it has also received money from the Bush Foundation. (For their first two years, the Ombudsman offices in Iowa and Nebraska were supported by grants from the Office of Economic Opportunity.)

In addition to the Ombudsman and his Deputy, the Minnesota office has three Field Investigators and a Research Analyst — men and women of diverse ethnic backgrounds, with Bachelors' or Masters' degrees in the social sciences or in social work. Two former staff members were ex-offenders, as was one of the ten interns who have passed through the office. The six professional staff members serve about 1,800 inmates in eight adult and juvenile institutions and another 2,300 parolees. Half of the work of the office is directed to the 900 men held in the maximum security prison at Stillwater, about 20 miles from the Ombudsman's office in St. Paul.

Prison inmates in Minnesota have access to the telephone, but it is just as easy to lodge a complaint directly with a representative of the Ombudsman's office on the premises. At first, "the overwhelming majority of the complaints were written and came through the mail."[27] Now, only about 20% are initiated in writing, while 30% are started by telephone, and 25% are made in person. The remaining 25% are indirect referrals, which often lead to an interview.

During the fiscal year 1972-73, the Ombudsman received 935 complaints. By 1978-79, this had climbed to 2,207 complaints, on the basis of which the Ombudsman opened 1,733 cases, averaging nearly 150 a month. The Ombudsman takes up a handful of cases — eight in the fiscal year 1978-79 — on his own initiative. During most of these years, there were two complaints for every three inmates, which puts Minnesota at the top of the list of per capita inmate complaints received:

Minnesota	1 complaint for every 1.5 inmates
Iowa	1 complaint for every 5 inmates
Hawaii	1 complaint for every 9 inmates
Denmark	1 complaint for every 13 inmates
Sweden	1 complaint for every 17 inmates
Norway	1 complaint for every 20 inmates

Nebraska	1 complaint for every 30 inmates
New Zealand	1 complaint for every 40 inmates

In screening complaints, the Minnesota Correctional Ombudsman does not apply a strict test of exhaustion of remedies:

> Complainants are encouraged to utilize existing resources at the various institutions or within the Department of Corrections to resolve their grievance. The problem with this, as a hard and fast rule, is that the resources for resolving grievances are not well defined. As the resources are better defined and the complainants gain confidence in them, the Ombudsman can become more insistent upon their use.[28]

The subject matter of inmate complaints in Minnesota is much the same as that found in other Ombudsman jurisdictions. The 1,130 cases whose consideration was concluded in 1975-76 were categorized as follows:

221	Rules	101	Legal
210	Parole	24	Records
162	Program	17	Threats
109	Placement	7	Discrimination
107	Property	66	Miscellaneous[29]
106	Medical		

When he concludes his investigation, the Ombudsman does not characterize complaints as justified or unjustified. He does claim that he is able to find a satisfactory resolution, in whole or in part, about 75% of the time (see Table 1).

TABLE 1
The Minnesota Ombudsman for Corrections*

Case Resolution

Resolution	*Cases*	*Percent*
Full	821	68.3
Partial	96	8.0
None	39	3.2
Withdrawn	71	5.9
Dismissed	107	8.9
Referred	68	5.7
	1,202	100.0%

*Source: 1977-78 Annual Report, p. 17.

For the first six months of 1979, the Minnesota Ombudsman presents a more detailed breakdown of substantiated and unsubstantiated complaints, in which claims of faulty prison recordkeeping have the highest validity (70%), while claims of discrimination have the lowest (28.6%) (see Table 2).

TABLE 2

The Minnesota Ombudsman for Corrections*

Complaint Validity

(Complaint Cases Closed January 1979 — June 1979)

	Substantiated (%)	*Unsubstantiated (%)*	*Total*
Parole	65 (56.5)	50 (43.5)	115
Medical	34 (49.3)	35 (50.7)	69
Legal	17 (65.4)	9 (34.6)	26
Placement	35 (59.3)	24 (40.7)	59
Property	16 (66.7)	8 (33.3)	24
Program	39 (59.1)	27 (40.9)	66
Discrimination	2 (28.6)	5 (71.4)	7
Records	14 (70.0)	6 (30.0)	20
Rules	72 (58.1)	52 (41.9)	124
Threats	15 (55.6)	12 (44.4)	27
Other	41 (64.1)	23 (35.9)	64
TOTAL:	350 (58.2)	251 (41.8)	601

*Source: 1978-79 Annual Report, p. 21.

The complainants' perceptions of satisfaction have been somewhat less sanguine. In a 1973 survey conducted by the Law School at the University of Minnesota, half of the inmates at Stillwater Prison felt that the Ombudsman helped them,[30] while a 1974 appraisal carried out by the Governor's Commission on Crime Prevention and Control shows that "less than half (45.5%) of inmates at all the institutions were satisfied with the Ombudsman's efforts on their behalf."[31] Part of the lack of enthusiasm by inmates was attributed to the absence of a formal procedure for notifying clients of the conclusion of the Ombudsman's investigation. This lapse has since been corrected.

The Crime Commission study found the administrators were "basically satisfied with the Ombudsman's performance," while staff personnel "were supportive."[32] It concludes that:

> Generally speaking, it seems that those who were initially *least* enthusiastic about the concept (administrators and guards) are now the most satisfied with his efforts, while those who were originally *most* enthusiastic about the concept (inmates) are now least satisfied with his efforts.[33]

The Crime Commission study also found that "[t]he Ombudsman has made fifty-six policy recommendations and approximately one-half of these have been implemented."[34] Twenty-two of the 56 (including 12 of the first 14) had to do with procedures governing parole hearings, grievance mechanisms, and disciplinary decisions. Among recent recommendations which have been rejected are ones which would have had the Department of Corrections "create a judicial subdivision that would be responsible for administering the disciplinary hearings at all adult institutions" and another which would have required that "the prison maximum custody classification committee be chaired by a staff member from the Department of Corrections central office."[35]

The Ombudsman's successful intervention in crisis situations has helped to establish his credibility. For example:

> In October, 1972, T. Williams and Commissioner Fogel were able to secure the release of a guard who was being held hostage, after hours of talk with three inmates, two of whom had previously had contact with the Ombudsman.
>
> In 1973, the Ombudsman's investigation of a fight between several black and white inmates at St. Cloud Reformatory established that the origins of the dispute were not racial[36] and thereby helped prevent the incident from escalating into a major racial conflict.
>
> In 1973 and 1974, the Ombudsman's investigation of a series of inmate suicides helped allay misgivings that the deaths might have racially motivated killings.[37] In the most dramatic of these, Mr. Williams recorded the dying statement of an inmate who had taken poison and set his cell on fire.

These explosive incidents reveal a new dimension of prison Ombudsman activity, that of riot prevention and control. Former Governor Anderson states that:

> One of the main reasons I appointed an Ombudsman for the prisons is that if you're going to avoid Attica-type riots, you have to have a channel for inmates to express grievances so they don't feel they have to riot.[38]

The cooling function of an Ombudsman office can be specific, as in the occurrences just related, but it can also be general. Former Stillwater Warden Bruce McManus alludes to the latter when he says:

> The Attica thing scared everybody in corrections. These joints are impersonal, but the Ombudsman gives prisoners a little individual attention. If nothing else, it provides a catharsis for the men.[39]

After an initial period which was generally harmonious, relations between McManus and Williams reached a low point in March, 1973, following the use of tear gas in the segregation block while Deputy Ombudsman Melvyn Brown was inside. McManus still denies Williams' charge that excessive force was used. Since then, Warden McManus has stated:

> I was uptight. He was uptight. And our staff fought him. We went from suspicious holding off to a serious confrontation. But I think Williams learned a lot. He and I have learned a lot together. [Williams has a] willingness to see both sides. He's a straight professional . . . an honest man. . . . At least he understands our problems and how we think. He may not buy it, but he understands.[40]

The then Minnesota Corrections Commissioner Kenneth Schoen goes even farther in praising the Ombudsman office, saying, "I don't know how we operated without it."[41]

Crisis intervention is dramatic, but the more pervasive impact comes from numerous uncelebrated contacts. The 1,130 complaints considered by the Minnesota Correctional Ombudsman during 1975-76 were lodged by 693 different individuals. This represents an average of 1.6 complaints for each complainant. Only about 50 of the nearly 700 complainants — one out of 14 — could be called querulants, defined as those who complain four or more times a year. Even the most persistent complainer averaged less than one complaint a month.

Many more matters are handled informally. According to Paul Keve:

> The [Minnesota] experience has shown the great importance of starting the program with a patient, tolerant, adaptive, low-key approach that will encourage the Ombudsman's credibility in the view of both inmates and staff.[42]

The first time we met, T. Williams told me that one prison reform group had been quite disappointed at his refusal to join with them in a frontal attack on the Minnesota prison system. Similarly, in Iowa, when asked if he would demolish walled prisons, prison deputy Ombudsman Raymond Cornell replied, "I am not by nature a man who seeks to destroy." Like general-purpose Ombudsmen, those who specialize in prisons are incrementalists.

In population, the two largest Ombudsman jurisdictions mentioned to this point have been Sweden with eight million and Michigan with nine million inhabitants. It is a substantial jump to the appointment of a prison Ombudsman in Canada, with a population of twenty-two-and-a half million inhabitants. There are about 8,500 inmates in federal institutions, under sentences of two years or more. (Shorter sentences are served in Provincial gaols.) This is fewer inmates than in Michigan, but they are spread over a much vaster territory. Except for a greater interval between visits to prisons, necessitated by the greater distances, the operation of the Canadian Correctional Investigator is nearly indistinguishable from that of the prison Ombudsman offices in the United States. Structurally, however, the office is precarious, as it depends upon an annual renewal by the Solicitor General. It should be made into a statutory office. The Canadian experience suggests that prison Ombudsmen could function effectively in American states of comparable population, such as California or New York. In California, however, there are nearly 25,000 prison inmates. Can an Ombudsman handle three times as many potential clients as there are in Canada?

There are four basic ways to attack the problem of size: (1) having more than one Ombudsman, as with the plural offices in Sweden, Finland, New Zealand and Australia; (2) decentralization, as exemplified by the regional Ombudsman offices in the Canadian Provinces of Alberta (branch in Calgary) and Quebec (branch in Montreal), Australia (Canberra, with branch offices in each State capital), and in New Zealand (branches in Auckland and Christchurch); (3) specialization, of which military Ombudsmen and prison Ombudsmen are the foremost examples; and (4) filtering, by denying the public direct access to the Ombudsman.

This last technique, used in France and Great Britain (each with a population of more than 50 million inhabitants), requires that complaints be forwarded by members of Parliament. Great Britain has since retreated from this line. Medical care was excluded from the purview of the Parliamentary Commissioner for Administration when the office was founded in 1967. Later, when the P.C.A. was given a separate and additional assignment as Health Service Commissioner in 1973, he was empowered to receive complaints directly from the public. This is a far superior solution. But, if specialization alone is insufficient to carry the burdens of size, then some other means should be found than the erection of artificial barriers.

Decentralization is such a device. The Health Service Ombudsman has separate mandates for England, Scotland, and Wales. There are also separate local government Commissioners in England and Wales. The Stormont in Northern Ireland established its own Commissioner for Complaints in 1969. In Britain, then, as in Canada, we find both specialization and regionalization. The same tack might be followed elsewhere. In New York, for example, the prison Ombudsman proposal of the Correctional Association of New York would have divided the State into four regions. Decentralization should not be carried too far, however. There should not be a separate office for each prison:

> [L]iving, working, eating on a daily basis with the staff, the Ombudsman would become but one more person working at the prison. . . .[43]

In the structure of their prison work, there are four main types of statutory Ombudsmen in the United States:

1. general purpose offices (Alaska, Hawaii, and Nebraska);
2. general purpose office, with specially designated prison deputy (Iowa);
3. correctional offices, with the Ombudsman appointed by the Governor (Minnesota and Oregon), the Legislature (Michigan), a special board (Kansas), and a private philanthropic institution (Connecticut); and,
4. Inmate Grievance Commissions, with an Executive Director who functions as a correctional Ombudsman (Maryland and North Carolina).

All of the Ombudsmen whose jurisdiction is limited to corrections hold office at someone else's pleasure. Perhaps the caution implicit in this limitation can be attributed to the particularly sensitive nature of prison administration. There is an understandable reluctance to do anything which might undermine security. For three reasons, however, tenured prison Ombudsmen would not threaten security: (1) careful selection; (2) removability for cause; and (3) the fact that the Ombudsman may not compel obedience to his recommendations.

What is missing is a prison Ombudsman removable only for cause who serves a set term, like other Ombudsmen do. As with judicial appointments, tenure in office is meant to buttress independence. None of the removing agencies has yet interfered with the work of a prison Ombudsman, but a new Governor in Minnesota or a different majority in the Michigan Legislature, for example, could bring instability or loss of independence. While the lack of a term of years is precarious, it is also open-ended and could lead to the retention of a relatively ineffectual Ombudsman simply because his employment had no date of termination. It is easier not to renew an appointment than it is to fire someone. On either count, the prison Ombudsman statutes should be amended to provide fixed terms for incumbents.

Great care has been exercised in the selection of prison Ombudsmen. It took a year or more to seek, screen, and select the office holders in Connecticut, Kansas, and Michigan, respectively. Less time elapsed in Minnesota — about five months — but a nominating panel was used composed of six members appointed by the Governor (including at least one woman and two representatives of racial minorities) and the following office holders or their designees: the Commissioner of Corrections, the Attorney General, the State Public Defender, and the Commissioner of Human Rights.[44]

Jails have been excluded from this chapter on the assumption that conditions are so bad that an Ombudsman could not function.[45] Basic reforms would have to come first; order would have to replace chaos. This may have been accomplished in Connecticut, where the six regional jails, called Correctional Centers, are under the jurisdiction of the Department of Corrections. So far, Correctional Ombudsman James Bookwalter has gone to work in only one of the six, the largest, in Hartford. He receives proportionally fewer complaints from the jail inmates, and his investigations are more frequently terminated by the discharge of the complainant. Perhaps the Ombudsman should complete his investigations even though the complainant has left. The work of Ombudsmen in jails deserves further study. The statewide offices in Iowa and Hawaii have jurisdiction over jails, as do the Canadian Provincial Ombudsman offices. The urban Ombudsmen in Jackson County, Missouri, and Seattle, Washington, appear to have been effective in monitoring their county or city jails. The New York City Board of Correction has been carrying out an Ombudsman function in addition to its other duties.[46]

The American contribution to prison Ombudsmanry is not in the invention of specialized offices as such. That had already been done with the establishment of Military Ombudsman offices in Sweden (1915), Norway (1952), West Germany (1957), and Israel (1972). The peculiar American contribution is in bringing the Ombudsman to the inmate. This is now done mainly by correctional Ombudsmen and deputies, but it could also be done by all-purpose Ombudsmen and deputies (as in Iowa) who nonetheless go to prisons frequently — at least once a week to maximum security institutions and once a month to most others — in order to carry out their investigations. By concentrating on prisoners, correctional Ombudsmen have for the first time effectively extended the outreach of the Ombudsman office to poor people. Otherwise, the main beneficiaries have been members of the middle class.[47]

Presence on the premises is what defines the work of prison Ombudsmen and what distinguishes their work from the prison work of other Ombudsmen. Being on the scene alters the way in which complaints and inquiries are received and handled. Reception is changed in several ways. First, the threshold of effort required to lodge a complaint or make an inquiry is reduced by the face-to-face or telephone availability of the Ombudsman. Second, the reluctance of an inmate to complain is lessened by the protection against retaliation which is implicit in the Ombudsman's continued presence. Third, the complainant is more likely to express his grievance at an early stage when rectification is still possible.

Prison Ombudsmen take full advantage of their mobility within the walls. They have direct and immediate access to records, inmates, staff, and warden. They can approach problems at the operational level. This style facilitates the handling of simple requests for service, information or referral, and allows the Ombudsman to concentrate his efforts on more serious or difficult cases.

Three of the prison Ombudsmen in the United States — in Maryland, Michigan, and North Carolina — are lawyers, but the others and their deputies are not. Only one — Preston Barton in Kansas — is a professional criminologist. The first Canadian Correctional Investigator was a woman. Despite the variety of their backgrounds and despite the structural kaleidoscope of their offices, the workings of the correctional Ombudsman offices have been remarkably similar. By definition, they differ from the traditional general purpose offices in singling out the complaints of prisoners for special attention. This attention is compensatory: it helps to put the inmate on a footing comparable to that of an ordinary citizen in his dealings with government.

Inmate, guard, administrator, warden, commissioner, legislator, governor: there is substantial support for the Ombudsman among all of these, but it seems to grow on the way up. Both popularity and success can be illuminated by contemplating the following different but interrelated ways of viewing an Ombudsman office:

> It is the interposition of the third-party principle into the resolution of grievances, so that no man is the judge of his own case. In the prison context, with a nudge from the courts, Ombudsmen have for the first time made officials accountable to an external arbiter.
>
> It provides a speedy and inexpensive way of limiting administrative discretion which heretofore has been largely uncontrolled.[48] Ombudsmen make a significant contribution to the development of fair standards and fair procedures within prisons. The creation of an Ombudsman or Ombudsman-like office has been concurrent with the formal upgrading of internal grievance procedures in Kansas, Maryland, Michigan, North Carolina, and Wisconsin.
>
> It is a vehicle for crisis intervention. As already noted, Ombudsmen can be helpful in preventing or controlling prison violence.
>
> It is a sensitive feed-back relay which is triggered by complaints and inquiries to identify salient information and communicate it to appropriate supervisory and policy-making officials.
>
> Finally, the Ombudsman symbolizes the pursuit of "justice as fairness" by using reason and moral persuasion rather than force. It is both civilized — and civilizing!

Notes

*The author is grateful for a Fellowship for Independent Study and Research from the National Endowment for the Humanities, which facilitated this study.

1. "We Refuse to be Responsible for the People We Imprison," address to the National Conference of Christians and Jews, Philadelphia, November 1972, reprinted in *Thoughts on Prison Reform* by the American Bar Association Commission on Correctional Facilities and Services (1975), p. 20.
2. See Stanley Anderson, "Ombudsmen and Prisons in Scandinavia," *66 Nordisk*

Tidsskrift for Kriminalvidenskab (1978), pp. 211-46. (Single copies will be sent free upon request to the author at the Department of Political Science, University of California, Santa Barbara 93106.)

3. See Timothy L. Fitzharris, *The Desirability of a Correctional Ombudsman* (University of California, Berkeley: Institute of Governmental Studies, 1973). See also Brian Taugher, "The Penal Ombudsman: A Step Toward Penal Reform," 3 *Pacific Law Journal* (1972), pp. 166-89.
4. See Russell G. Oswald, *Attica: My Story* (Doubleday, 1972), p. 119. See also Tom Wicker, *A Time to Die* (New York: Quadrangle, 1975), pp. 176, 308.
5. See Stanley Anderson, *Ombudsman Papers: American Experience and Proposals* (University of California, Berkeley: Institute of Governmental Studies, 1969), pp. 29-32.
6. See David Fogel, "Overseeing Fairness: The Ombudsman," in "*. . . We Are the Living Proof . . .*": *The Justice Model for Corrections* (Cincinnati, Ohio: Anderson, 1975), pp. 230-36. At p. 235, Fogel notes: "An Ombudsman is still another stratum of the multi-tier conflict resolution system we are constructing in this chapter."
7. The "slave of the state" doctrine was articulated in Ruffin v. Commonwealth, 62 Va. (21 Gratt) 790, 796 (1871).
8. Coffin v. Reichard, 143 F.2d 443, 445 (6th Cir. 1944), *cert. denied,* 335 U.S. 887 (1945).
9. Walter Gellhorn, *When Americans Complain: Governmental Grievance Procedures* (Cambridge, Mass.: Harvard University Press, 1966), p. 148.
10. Gellhorn, *When Americans Complain,* p. 150.
11. But see Manfred von Nordheim and Richard W. Taylor, "Prisoners' Right to Petition West German Legislatures for Redress of Grievances," 4 *Political Science Discussion Papers* (Kent State University, Summer 1972), pp. 51-60.
12. Total civil filings in the United States District Courts were slightly more than doubled during the 17 years from 1960 to 1976, inclusive. During the same period, prisoner petitions (both civil rights and habeas corpus petitions are included among civil filings) increased nine-fold, from 2,177 to 19,809 (4,780 from federal prisoners and 15,029 from state prisoners). From 1975 to 1976, the increase of prisoner petitions was only 2.6%, and these petitions declined as a percentage of all civil filings from 18% to 15.2%. See *1976 Annual Report of the Director,* Administrative Office of the U. S. Courts, pp. 93-96.

    Habeas corpus petitions in the Superior Courts of the State of California trebled during the ten years from 1966 to 1976, from approximately 3,000 to 9,000. From 1975 to 1976, they increased only 1.5%. See Judicial Council of California, *1977 Annual Report of the Administrative Office of the California Courts,* p. 198.
13. Banning v. Looney, 213 F.2d 771 (10th Cir.), *cert. denied,* 348 U.S. 859 (1954).
14. U. S. Const., Eighth Amendment. See Holt v. Sarver, 309 F. Supp. 362 (E. D. Ark. 1970). (Arkansas penitentiaries must either close or improve sanitation and medical conditions and eliminate overcrowding, segregation, and the use of inmates as guards.)
15. U. S. Const., Fifth and Fourteenth Amendments. See Morrissey v. Brewer, 408 U. S. 471, 33 L.Ed. 2d 484, 92 S. Ct. 2593 (1972) (upon revocation of parole, the individual must be given some opportunity to be heard) and Wolff v. McDonnell, 418 U. S. 539, 41 L.Ed. 2d 935, 94 S. Ct. 2963 (1974) (in prison disciplinary hearings, the accused must be given written notice of charges, an opportunity to call witnesses, and written findings of fact). But see Baxter v. Palmigiano, 425 U. S. 308, 47 L.Ed. 2d 810, 96 S. Ct. 1551 (1976) (in prison

disciplinary hearings, the accused need not be assigned counsel or given the right of confrontation, and adverse inferences may be drawn from his silence).

16. The Administrative Office of the California Courts comments upon the growth and decline of habeas corpus petitions in the State Courts of Appeal as follows: "The beginning of the upward trend coincided with the United States Supreme Court decision in *Morrissey* v. *Brewer* . . . , and would appear to be attributable to . . . that decision. The current decrease suggests that the effects of that decision have been assimilated." See *1977 Annual Report,* p. 186 (footnote omitted).
17. 42 U. S. C. Section 1983. See Monroe v. Pape, 365 U. S. 167, 5 L.Ed. 2d 492, 81 S. Ct. 473 (1961) and Burrell v. McCray, 516 F.2d 357 (4th Cir.), *cert. denied,* 426 U. S. 471 (1976). See also "Comment: Exhaustion of State Administrative Remedies in Section 1983 Cases," 41 *University of Chicago Law Review* (1974), pp. 537-56, and "Comment: 42 U.S.C. Section 1983 Prisoner Petitions – Exhaustion of State Administrative Remedies," 28 *Arkansas Law Review* (1975), pp. 479-90.
18. In addition to permitting access to "jailhouse lawyers" (Johnson v. Avery, 393 U. S. 483, 21 L.Ed. 2d 718, 89 S. Ct. 747 [1969]), prison authorities must provide law libraries or the assistance of lawyers or law students (Bounds v. Smith, 430 U. S. 817, 52 L.Ed. 2d 72, 97 S. Ct. 1491 [1977]). See generally Bruce R. Jacob and K. M. Sharma, "Justice After Trial: Prisoners' Need for Legal Services in the Criminal-Correctional Process," 18 *Kansas Law Review* (1970), pp. 493-628.
19. See John H. Wood, Jr., "Federal Prisoner Petitions," 7 *St. Mary's Law Journal* (1975), p. 501.
20. *1975 Report to the Governor of Iowa and the Sixty-Sixth General Assembly, Second Session, by the Iowa Citizens' Aide,* pp. 5-6.
21. Complaint No. 62A/100/05, *Ombudsman Quarterly Report: Second Quarter, Third Year* (July 1, 1976; mimeo), p. 8.
22. Holt v. Sarver, 309 F. Supp. 362 (E.D. Ark. 1970); *aff'd* 442 F.2d 304 (9th Cir. 1971).
23. M. Kay Harris and Dudley P. Spiller, Jr., *After Decision: Implementation of Judicial Decrees in Correctional Settings* (Washington, D. C.: Resource Center on Correctional Law and Legal Services; mimeo, November 1976), p. 20.
24. Arkansas has not taken advantage of this opportunity. In a letter to me dated January 5, 1977, Assistant Attorney General Robert A. Newcomb says: "In light of the fact that the Supreme Court has failed to rule that exhaustion of state remedies is a necessary prerequisite to the filing of a 42 U.S.C. Section 1983 suit, this office has decided not to seek legislation implementing an inmate grievance procedure . . . similar to the one existing in Maryland and North Carolina." This bears out the observation in "Comment: Exhaustion," 41 *University of Chicago Law Review* (1974), at p. 556, that a modified requirement of exhaustion "would act as an incentive for state agencies to provide complete interim relief during the state administrative process, so as to assure an opportunity to correct their own errors."
25. David Fogel, *"We Are the Living Proof . . .": The Justice Model for Corrections* (Cincinnati, Ohio: Anderson, 1975), p. 232. See *A Proposal to Establish an Experimental Ombudsman For the Minnesota Department of Corrections* (Minneapolis: University of Minnesota, November 15, 1971; mimeo), 51 pp.
26. The Gellhorn statute may be found in Stanley Anderson, ed., *Ombudsmen for American Government?* (Englewood Cliffs, N.J.: Prentice-Hall for the American Assembly, 1968), pp. 159-73.
27. *A Report on the First Six Months of Operation of the Ombudsman for the*

Minnesota Department of Corrections (January 1973), p. 7.

28. *Ombudsman for Corrections*: *1972-73 Annual Report,* p. 3. But see n. 32 (below).
29. Definitions of these categories are supplied in the *1973-74 Annual Report,* pp. 4-5, and in the *1974-75 Annual Report,* p. 4. A case summary from each category is provided in the *1974-75 Annual Report,* pp. 6-10, and in the *1975-76 Annual Report,* pp. 11-19. Otherwise, the Ombudsman does not supply case notes in his annual reports.
30. Dennis Goldenson, *An Evaluation of the Minnesota Corrections Ombudsman Program* (July 23, 1973; typescript, 33 pp.).
31. Gerald Strathman, *Minnesota Ombudsman for Corrections*: *An Evaluation Report* (November 1974; mimeo, 55 pp.), p. 2.
32. Staff did not feel that the Ombudsman was "fulfilling his responsibility concerning staff grievances." See *An Evaluation Report,* p. 2. In 1974-75, the Ombudsman received 24 complaints from staff members. Here, the Ombudsman is more insistent that he not become involved until "all other channels have been utilized," particularly "union and civil service assistance." See *1974-75 Annual Report,* p. 3.
33. *An Evaluation Report,* p. 3. (Emphasis in original.)
34. *An Evaluation Report,* p. 2. The 56 recommendations are listed at pp. 47-50. The Ombudsman made 43 recommendations in 1975-76. At the end of the year, two of these were pending and twelve had been rejected. The remaining 29 were accepted, one only partially. See *1975-76 Annual Report,* pp. 28-30.
35. *1975-76 Annual Report,* p. 29. See also the Ombudsman for Corrections' *Presentation on Prisoners' Rights, Grievance and Disciplinary Procedures at Stillwater State Prison* (April 5, 1973; mimeo, 11 pp., plus appendices).
36. See the *Ombudsman's Investigation Report of the August 5, 1973, Incident at the State Reformatory for Men at St. Cloud* (November 1, 1973; typescript, 27 pp.).
37. See the *Ombudsman's Investigation Report of the Deaths of John Love and Thomas Durham* (December 12, 1973; typescript, 14 pp.) and *Investigation of the Deaths of Rick Fultz and James Martin* (May 1, 1974; typescript, 21 pp.).
38. Quoted by Bryce Nelson, "Prisoners' Ombudsman a Sympathetic Listener," *Los Angeles Times,* October 1, 1972, p. A-13.
39. Quoted by Michael W. Fedo, "Prison Ombudsman: The Minnesota Experience," 128 *America* (May 5, 1973), p. 410.
40. Quoted by Edgar May, "Prison Ombudsmen in America: They Listen to Both Sides," 1 *Corrections Magazine* (January/February, 1975), p. 48.
41. May, "Prison Ombudsmen in America," p. 47.
42. *Prison Life and Human Worth* (Minneapolis: University of Minnesota Press, 1974), p. 153.
43. Howard Lesnick, "Grievance Procedures in Federal Prisons: Practices and Proposals," 123 *University of Pennsylvania Law Review* (1974), p. 29.
44. See Executive Order No. 14 (February 3, 1972), which is appended to the Minnesota Ombudsman for Corrections' annual reports, *supra,* notes 28-29.
45. See generally Ronald Goldfarb, *Jails*: *The Ultimate Ghetto* (Anchor Press/Doubleday, 1975).
46. See *1974 Annual Report of the New York City Board of Correction,* p. iii: "During 1974, the Board received and acted upon over 390 inmate requests and complaints and resolved countless problems varying greatly in complexity." See also Steve Gettinger, "The Board of Corrections: Prison Watchdog Agency," 2 *Corrections Magazine* (June 1976), pp. 36-37.

47. See John E. Moore, "Ombudsmen and the Ghetto," 1 *Connecticut Law Review* (1968), p. 248.
48. See generally Kenneth Culp Davis, *Discretionary Justice* (Baton Rouge, La.: Louisiana State University Press, 1969). See also James A. Jablonski, "Controlling Discretionary Power in Prison Organizations: A Review of the Model Act," *Washington University Law Quarterly* (1973), pp. 563-606.

12. Offender Rights Litigation

Alvin J. Bronstein

Crime, repression, and injustice have always characterized the human condition, and perhaps inevitably so. America, however, was founded on an act of faith that a free and just society was possible. In that rare moment of hope in the eighteenth century, when the Founding Fathers somehow matched idealism of aspiration with realism about human nature, the Declaration of Independence and Bill of Rights enshrined certain notions of rights and liberties which still determine our rhetoric and at least some of our reality.

The prison system, as we now know it, did not then exist. As David Rothman demonstrated in *The Discovery of the Asylum*,[1] prisons were instituted in a Jacksonian hope that human improvement was possible if a criminal's unfortunate upbringing could be overcome in an antiseptic and healthy setting, a hope given urgency by the fear that unless deviant activity was controlled, the very openness of American society would cause its demise. The purposes of prison were thus benevolent, though born of fear.

As we know, however, benevolence does not imply respect. And without respect, human rights are meaningless, especially where fear and insecurity are present. And this is the heart of the matter. It is the conflict between these motivations and interests which is central to the development of the legal rights of offenders. In the main, prisoners' rights issues revolve around the question: Does the Constitution follow a person into prison? The answer given by most cases today seems to be "yes, to a great extent." This is in marked and comforting contrast to the two versions of a "no" answer that were consistently given until just a few years ago. In 1871, a Virginia judge wrote quite explicitly that prisoners have no more rights than slaves.[2] That idea was a bit too raw for most judges, at least as expressed, and so the theory and verbalisms shifted: conditions inside prisons were off-limits to judicial scrutiny. A refusal to "interfere with internal prison administration" became the basis for a persistent and virtually uniform refusal to enforce barely any constitutional rights for prisoners. The result, of course, was the same, regardless of the right-remedy verbalisms: prisoners were left to the not-so-tender mercies of their keepers.

With such a background, it is hardly surprising that abuses developed right from the beginning, and abuses of the cruelest sort: physical brutality, gross medical neglect, the silence rules, racial discrimination, kangaroo courts for disciplinary matters, incredible tortures such as the

Tucker telephone (a device used at the Tucker Reformatory in Arkansas where telephone wires were attached to the prisoners' genitals and an electric current generated through) hot boxes and dark cells (segregation cells with a solid door and no light), chain gangs, bread and water diets and worse, economic exploitation by the convict lease system and otherwise, rigid censorship of mail and reading matter, narrowly restricted visitation rights, along with mindless and brutally hard work. The list is lengthy and as varied as the depth of human cruelty, about which Auschwitz and Attica have taught us so much. All of this was compounded by prison sentences longer than anywhere in the western world, and by virtual invisibility, except for guided tours and the aftermaths of periodic riots.

These abuses have obviously resulted from more than the courts' "hands off" attitude. At least two separate factors are involved, the second of which has become increasingly important in the last few years: the inherent nature of a prison and the increasing proportion of black and Latin prisoners.

The American prison involves confinement in a closed setting for punitive purposes. Regardless of whether there are walls, prisoners are confined to a very small geographic area. They are generally very poor in material goods, if not before entry into prison then certainly while there; they are deprived of heterosexual relationships, of family, and of companions and social activities of their choice; they are generally denied meaningful work. Except for political prisoners (whose existence is an unacknowledged fact in America), their social status is generally about the lowest in society.

Additionally, prisoners are subjected to many "status degradation ceremonies," from haircutting to being known solely by a number. These humiliations reinforce their own sense of being losers, society's rejects. The deprivations and degradations, which are often seen by the prisoner as unjust and excessive, pervade every aspect of the prisoner's life. Of particular importance, as the English sociologist F. E. Emery put it, is that.

> There is constant awareness [by the prisoners] that the deprivations and degradations are being imposed by men with whom they are in close daily contact. It is this sense of personally inflicted punishment that gives the prison the character of "strife" and creates its pervading atmosphere of hatred.[3]

The administration is of course aware of this "strife" and tension. It also knows that its personnel are heavily outnumbered by the inmates, that the inmates do not acknowledge that either the guards or the administration have the right to inflict such hardships on the prisoners, and that the interplay between guards and inmates is thus ambiguous, hostile, and often dangerous.

The result is that the administrators' predominant and explicit concern is for security, keeping the lid on. As the American Correctional Association bluntly puts it: "The fundamental responsibility of prison management is the secure custody and control of prisoners."[4] To most prison administrators, as to most bureaucrats, that means keeping matters as close to a fixed and quiet routine as possible. Anything that smacks of spontaneity, of getting "out of line," of acting up, of independence, is to be squelched, quickly and emphatically. Groupings and associations are discouraged; both planted and spontaneous informers are everywhere. Control is even extended to the prisoners' very thoughts. For example, prison administrators have punished inmates for the contents of private diaries even though they were not circulated, for "bad attitudes," for sympathizing with prison strikes, and the like. The ideal, it seems, is a true totalitarian system.

Of crucial importance in this connection has been the invisibility of these institutions. Prisons are usually far away, physically and emotionally, from major population centers. Both as cause and effect of this invisibility, the community ordinarily has as little interest in the people it sends to prison as most of us have in our garbage — we want it disposed of safely, quickly, and without much mess, but we don't particularly care how.

Such total control obviously is not easily achieved, for human beings can rarely be controlled so neatly by mere force. Resistance, both violent and peaceful, inevitably flares up, in turn producing more controls. The prison administration is thus often in the position of trying to shut an over-stuffed suitcase — it's very hard to do, you have to press down very hard and persistently, and sometimes the suitcase will break.

This kind of pressure is not really relieved by claims for some kind of rehabilitational ideal. Partly this is because it is an axiom of penology that custody always dominates treatment. Equally important, we do not really know how to change behavior, especially in a prison setting, and even if we did, we have neither the clinicians nor other resources to try. We do not even make a serious effort at providing literacy and job skills — elemental necessities for a decent life. Instead, we put men and women to work at largely useless tasks for demeaning wages. And society makes it almost impossible for them to get jobs when they get out by imposing a long list of job disqualifications.

All of these traditional elements in prison life, apart from anything else, have always made most prisons into live volcanoes, frequently on the verge of eruption. They have made prison existence the closest thing in America to a true police state.

Today, however, this unstable situation is compounded by the racial and ethnic frictions that agitate the entire community. Although this factor has also been noted before, a few observations may be useful, first about the prison and the black community, and secondly, about the black-white confrontation in prison.

For many of us — and not just those professionally involved — prison represents one of those basic facts of life that make it a metaphor for other events and institutions. But for most whites, the prison remains a strange and unfamiliar phenomenon, at the periphery of their lives. Relatively few whites go to prison or jail, even with all the drug law enforcement. For black and Latin people, however, the prison is more than a metaphor — it is a pervasive element of life in the ghetto.

Prison is central to the black experience because it is the culmination of so many other repressive and discriminatory forces in society. The process begins with the white cop on the beat shaking down and cursing out the black kid. It continues through segregated and spirit-blighting schools, through the juvenile court, through meaningless and dead-end jobs, demeaning welfare policies, the adult court, the probation officer, and so on. In all of these, except for a few big cities, the administrators are white and the subjects black or Latin.

For this reason, today's prisons are inevitably being affected and indeed shaken by the upheavals in our society at large, as we try to move, convulsively and as yet disappointingly, toward equality and justice. Watts, Detroit, Newark, and other urban riots are as relevant to understanding prisons today as are the studies by Sykes, Clemmer, and Cressey which examine the sociological aspects of prisons, the inmate subculture, and how these forces doom prisons to failure.[5] It is no coincidence that many of the classics of Black literature, such as those by Malcolm X, Eldridge Cleaver, Bobby Seale, George Jackson, and others, are prison memoirs, in whole or in part.

Moreover, the strains in prison are much greater than in the outside world, for many reasons. In a very real sense, the prison is like the outside world, squeezed into a very small space. The total and largely self-contained society that is prison contains all the evils of that outside world, only much more concentrated. All the things that blacks and Latins are protesting against outside exist in prison in a relatively pure form.

For this reason, militancy is especially great in prison, not because of a few agitators, but because the repression — whether justified or not — is harsh and undiluted. Because prison is one of the most severe sanctions in our society, the subjects of that sanction include the most alienated and most aggressive members of society. And since the sense of injustice is obviously most developed where the penalties are the greatest, the resentment and bitterness at real and imagined injustices are obviously very deep and pervasive. There is enough real unfairness throughout our criminal justice and correctional systems so that there is little need to resort to the imagined variety. Prison is thus a radicalizing experience, with many subjects who are ready for such an experience.

The prisoners' rights movement grew directly out of the civil rights and civil liberties movements when lawyers and civil rights-civil liberties organizations turned more and more to the courts to challenge what were essentially legal barriers to equality and liberty. Many of the leading prisoners' rights lawyers are veterans of the civil rights legal movement and they were complemented by a small but increasing number of sympathetic judges.

Much of this work originally left the prisons unaffected. The "hands-off" attitude of most courts and the special problems of federal interference in state prison systems together with the enormous tasks confronting a relatively small number of lawyers with meagre resources precluded a meaningful assault on prison abuses at that time. Two events were significant in changing this: the Attica Rebellion and the Supreme Court's 1961 decision in *Monroe* v. *Pape*,[6] which resurrected the Civil Rights Act of 1871. The latter enabled lawyers to seek damages and injunctions in federal courts against state abuses of an individual's rights.[7] After ten years of federal court activity dealing with state civil rights deprivations, connections began to be made between racial segregation and the American criminal justice system. It was seen as no accident that blacks and Latins so disproportionately filled our prisons. When Attica exploded in September of 1971, it created an unmatched awareness of prisons and their nature. It was no longer true that prisons and prisoners were "out of sight, out of mind." The prisoners' rights movement began in earnest.

The judicial attitude has changed drastically from the *de facto* rightlessness that was almost universally accepted for prisoners little more than a decade ago. Courts today are now willing to intervene somewhat in prison administration. While judicial definition of the rights of prisoners in America is a continuing process, an overview of the current law in some of the important areas is a barometer of the victories the prisoners' rights movement has achieved, and how much further it needs to travel.

Due Process

The Supreme Court has recently issued opinions in a number of cases which spell out the kind of due process rights that prisoners are entitled to at disciplinary hearings. The first case which addressed this issue was *Wolff* v. *McDonnell*.[8] In *Wolff*, the Court said that although a prisoner's rights are diminished by virtue of incarceration, "there is no iron curtain drawn between the Constitution and the prisons of this country." The Court ruled that before a prisoner could be seriously penalized for a disciplinary violation — the serious penalties in this case being the taking away of good time credits and/or solitary confinement — the state must provide certain minimum procedures. Prisoners are entitled to at least 24-hour written notice of the charges against them. They have the right to call witnesses and present documentary evidence in their defense when doing so would not be unduly hazardous to institutional safety or correctional goals. The prisoner also has the right to an impartial hearing body to consider the proceeding, and the right to a written statement by the hearing body as to the evidence relied upon and the reasons for whatever disciplinary action is taken.

The Court also said in *Wolff* that while it was not required, it would be useful for prison officials to state their reasons for refusing to call a witness. While the Court held that the prisoner had no right to cross-examine witnesses at a disciplinary hearing, it ruled that prison officials could in their discretion permit this. Finally, the Court said that there was no right to counsel in a disciplinary hearing. It should be noted, however, that even though the Supreme Court did say that a prisoner was entitled to the minimum procedures outlined above, this was substantially less than had been ordered by many lower state and federal courts.

In two cases that followed *Wolff*, the Court addressed some due process issues which were left open by the earlier decision. In a case from Rhode Island,[9] the Supreme Court reversed a favorable lower court decision and ruled that even in a situation where a prisoner faced possible new criminal charges for the same offense which he was being given a disciplinary hearing for, he was not entitled to have either retained or appointed counsel at the disciplinary hearing; he was not entitled to cross-examine witnesses at the disciplinary proceedings, and that if he chose to remain silent at the disciplinary hearing — rather than give incriminating evidence which might be used against him later on in the criminal charges — prison officials could draw an adverse inference from that silence. In the second case,[10] the Supreme Court reversed a favorable lower court decision dealing with California prisoners, ruling that a prisoner was not entitled to the procedures outlined in the *Wolff* case when he was faced with the loss of various privileges rather than the more serious penalties of the loss of good time or solitary confinement.[11]

Finally, the Supreme Court did leave the situation open for possible improvement in the future by stating that their conclusion was "not graven in stone. As the nature of the prison disciplinary process changes in future years, circumstances may then exist which will require further consideration and reflection of this Court." The Court felt that at this time they had properly balanced the interests of the prisoners and the needs of the institution.

The Supreme Court also has recently addressed the due process issue in connection with classification and transfer. In a case involving Massachusetts prisoners,[12] the Court reversed a favorable lower court decision and held that prison officials had absolute discretion to reclassify and transfer prisoners to a more secure institution without any procedural protections. The Court refused to hold that any change in the conditions of confinement having a substantial adverse impact on the prisoner involved is sufficient to invoke the protections of the due process clause. The Court distinguished its earlier decision in *Wolff* v. *McDonnell* by saying that in the earlier case the state itself and not the Constitution had provided a statutory right to good time and had specified that it was to be forfeited only for serious misbehavior.

In a second case from New York,[13] the Court reaffirmed what it said in the Massachusetts case about transfer, but this decision contained some language which suggests that a prisoner could not be punished by a transfer for engaging in otherwise constitutionally protected activity. In this case there was a claim that the prisoner involved was transferred because he had been circulating a petition in the prison and thus was engaging in First Amendment activity. The Supreme Court remanded the case to the Court of Appeals for further proceedings on that issue.[14]

Cruel and Unusual Punishment

Prisoners have an absolute right to be free from cruel and unusual punishment under the Eighth Amendment. Nevertheless, while it is an easy matter to state the basic right, it is extremely difficult for prisoners to persuade the courts to act when faced with anything less than barbaric prison conditions.

Historically, the Eighth Amendment's ban on cruel and unusual punishment was aimed at preventing a recurrence of torture and barbarous punishments common in England and colonial America, such as disemboweling and decapitation. During the nineteenth century, this provision was thought to be virtually obsolete as these punishments were no longer imposed. In 1910, however, the Supreme Court gave added force to the Eighth Amendment, holding that the Amendment's protections were not tied to a particular theory or point in time.[15]

The Eighth Amendment rests upon fundamental considerations of human decency: it has been held to contain a "basic prohibition against inhuman treatment" and its basic underlying concept "is nothing less than the dignity of man." The amendment was designed to assure that the state's punishing power be exercised within the limits of civilized standards, and it "must draw its meaning from the evolving standards of decency that mark the progress of a maturing society."[16] An 1892 Supreme Court decision, *Logan* v. *U.S.*, provides the touchstone for the Amendments application to conditions in prisons. It held that the government is ". . . bound to protect against lawless violence all persons in their service or custody in the course of the administration of justice."[17]

At present there appear to be three principal tests that are applied under the Eighth Amendment: whether the punishment shocks the general conscience of a civilized society; whether the punishment is unnecessarily cruel; and whether the punishment goes beyond legitimate penal aims.

Under these rather vague guidelines, various courts have found that the cumulative impact of substandard conditions constituted a system of cruel and unusual punishment, as have certain specific practices or conditions. Among the specific practices which have been held to violate the Eighth Amendment are overcrowding, inadequate medical treatment, physical abuse by guards, solitary confinement in strip cells or for excessive periods of time, lack of outdoor exercise or recreation, inadequate diet, and almost all forms of corporal punishment.

More recently a federal district court in Alabama added a new element in Eighth Amendment law in holding that Alabama's entire prison system was in violation of the constitutional ban against cruel and unusual punishment. The district court in Alabama said in *Pugh* v. *Locke*[18] that "the evidence in these cases . . . establishes that prison conditions are so debilitating that they necessarily deprive inmates of any opportunity to rehabilitate themselves or even maintain skills already possessed." Such a statement is the first clear recognition that prisons can make those confined within their walls worse off than when they arrived.

Since the groundbreaking decision in Alabama in 1976, a number of other courts have followed Judge Frank M. Johnson, Jr.'s lead and have found that prisoners were actually debilitated by the conditions of their confinement, and that such confinement constituted cruel and unusual punishment. Of particular importance are two decisions, one by a federal court and the other by a state court, holding that the entire state prison systems in Rhode Island and Tennessee were unconstitutional.[19]

Even more recently, the Supreme Court appeared to ratify the Eighth Amendment approach taken by the courts in the Alabama case and similar prison cases. In upholding a lower court decision that confinement for more than thirty days in Arkansas's segregation cells constituted cruel and unusual punishment,[20] three principles were approved by the court. First, in deciding whether the conditions of confinement in a prison violate the Eighth Amendment, a court should consider the totality of conditions of confinement. Second, a remedial order in a "totality of conditions" suit should address each factor which contributed to the overall violation or which in the court's determination may be necessary to remedy the overall violation, whether or not that item represents an independent constitutional right. Finally, in appropriate cases, a court may enunciate specific minimum standards, compliance with which is necessary to remedy the total constitutional violation.

On other than Eighth Amendment grounds, one court has barred the denial of visits to men in a segregation unit because they refused to shave.[21] The Seventh Circuit, on Eighth Amendment grounds, barred the use of tranquilizing drugs to punish juveniles.[22] The court did say that authorities could use the drugs in an ongoing therapeutic program, however.

Censorship, Free Communication and Access to the Courts

Although there has been much judicial attention paid to the First Amendment rights of prisoners, this is still a developing area of the law. The greatest degree of protection thus far afforded to prisoners' correspondence has been with courts, counsel, and government officials. Most prison systems now permit, in principle if not always in practice, uncensored communications to those correspondents.

While it is clear that an institution may not refuse to mail court-directed letters, whether and under what circumstances they can open and read them is not as clear. In *Wolff* v. *McDonnell*,[23] the Supreme Court considered a related question: Whether letters determined to be from attorneys may be opened by prison officials in the presence of the prisoner or whether such mail must be delivered unopened as long as there is no evidence of contraband. While the issue is clearly stated, the Court never really resolved it, concluding instead:

> We think, that [the prison officials,] by acceding to a rule whereby the inmate is present when mail from attorneys is inspected, have done all, and perhaps even more than the Constitution requires.[24]

Whether an inmate *must* be present is not decided. The Court did note, however, that prison officials could require that an attorney desiring to correspond with a client first identify himself and the client and that all letters be marked as having come from a lawyer.

After *Wolff* it is still unclear to what extent prison officials may open and read mail between inmate and lawyer. The lower federal courts are split. In *Sostre* v. *McGinnis*,[25] the Second Circuit Court of Appeals ruled that a prison may not delete, withhold, or refuse to mail communications to courts — even when the communications are irrelevant to the prisoner's case or are even false and malicious — unless it is determined that the prisoner is "abusing" his rights by communicating about "restricted matters." However, to aid prison officials in determining such "abuses," the court has allowed prison officials in its jurisdiction the full right to open and read *all* outgoing and incoming correspondence. Other courts have disagreed, holding that prison authorities may not as a general practice read attorney-client mail.

Aside from legal correspondence, prisoners still may not write whatever they please to whomever they please, although it is clear that prison authorities no longer have total power to limit prisoners' correspondence. At the very least, prison officials must provide a means by which mail may be sent and received by inmates, and the officials may not require inmates to sign an authorization allowing examination of their mail in order to make use of the mails. However, a prison still may maintain an approved list of correspondents for each prisoner as long as the list is supported by the government's interests in order, security, or rehabilitation. In certain very limited categories, prison authorities may stop all correspondence with given individuals. For example, a Virginia court has said that correspondence between prisoners in different institutions in the same prison system may be prohibited.[26] On the other hand, the same court held that a rule prohibiting correspondence between inmates and former inmates was unconstitutional.

Despite repeated challenges in the courts, the practice of opening and reading correspondence continues unabated. However, in *Procunier* v. *Martinez*,[27] the Supreme Court did establish certain limitations on the right of prison authorities to *censor* mail. Inmate mail may be censored only if the letter jeopardizes security, order, or rehabilitation, and the regulations may only be as broad as is necessary to meet those goals. However, officials may not censor mail simply to eliminate unflattering opinions, factually inaccurate statements, or inflammatory racial, political, or religious views.

In *Procunier*, the Court also noted minimum procedures which must be followed before a letter may be censored. A prisoner must be notified that a letter written to him or her was rejected and must be given an opportunity to protest that decision. Further, any complaints must be referred to a prison official other than the person who originally disapproved the letter.

In two related opinions the Supreme Court has considered access to the media through the use of interviews. Unfortunately, the opinions retreated from the point reached by some of the more progressive lower federal courts. In *Pell* v. *Procunier*,[28] the Court considered the constitutionality of regulations which prohibited face-to-face interviews between press representatives and the individual inmates whom they specifically name and request to interview. The Court held that as long as the regulation was applied neutrally, without regard to the content of the expression, it was valid, since there were alternative avenues of communication open to inmates who wanted to reach the press, particularly the mails. Turning to the question of whether a prohibition of face-to-face interviews violated the rights of the press, the Court noted that it was sufficient that the press personnel be allowed to talk to anyone they encountered while touring the institution. Also, the result of stopping face-to-face interviews left the press in the same position as the general public. The Court concluded that as long as the press had access to sources of information available to the general public, the right to freedom of the press was not abridged by this limitation.

Similarly, in *Saxbe* v. *Washington Post Company*,[29] the Court considered the constitutionality of a prohibition of all press interviews with designated prisoners. The Court again noted that there were other means to get information and that, with regard to interviews, the press was receiving the same treatment given the general public.

Pell and *Saxbe* make it clear that as long as there are alternative means of communication, interviews with members of the press may be barred.[30] As a result, an inmate's right to communicate by mail with the media is made even more important than it was. In related developments since those decisions, a number of states and the Federal Bureau of Prisons now permit media access to individual prisoners.

Despite some advances in recent years, prison officials continue to exercise a heavy hand of censorship on the kinds of books, magazines, and other reading materials that prisoners may possess and read. In some states, prisons maintain a list of approved publications for inmates, while in others the decision as to what books and magazines are legitimate is made on an ad hoc basis. Typically, controversial political, religious, or socially significant literature and documents are censored and only reading matter of the most innocuous nature permitted.

Cases challenging these overly restrictive policies have succeeded only where the courts have agreed to employ the judicial test of "clear and present danger" to determine whether prison discipline or security will be undermined by allowing inmates to read and possess the material in question. The "clear and present danger" test, which governs official attempts to limit First Amendment activity in the free world, places the burden on the prison officials to demonstrate a compelling state interest centering around prison security or prison discipline *prior* to any censorship. Under this standard, much of what has traditionally been censored has now been cleared by some courts.

In an early case,[31] a federal court ordered that New York state prisoners have the right to receive *Fortune News*, the newsletter of the Fortune Society, an organization of former inmates which publishes articles and information on prison alternatives, ex-convict's rehabilitation, and other related activities. The court found that the mere assertions that the newsletter did not accurately reflect conditions in the prisons failed to show a compelling reason why it should be banned. In similar decisions, a New York federal district court permitted Black Panthers to receive the Panther newspaper and a Nebraska court allowed copies of *Muhammed Speaks* into the prisons.[32]

What the prison officials are allowed to do may vary depending upon the type of detention involved. A Delaware court has held that if the prisoner is in solitary confinement non-legal reading material may be prohibited altogether.[33] On the other hand, a federal district court in California has held that pre-trial detainees should be allowed to receive any reading material that may lawfully be delivered by the postal service.[34]

With respect to the writings of prisoners, the same rules which apply to censorship of inmate mail apply to censorship of articles. Material written by prisoners may not be stopped unless it is likely to interfere with a legitimate governmental interest in security, order, or rehabilitation. For example, a Vermont court held that prohibition of an inmate newspaper may not be based on disagreement with its editorial comments.[35]

A Rhode Island court has held that an interview with one's own attorney is a right, subject to restrictions on the time, place, and manner of the interview.[36] An attorney-client interview may be restricted only under the most extraordinary conditions. A Pennsylvania court has held, for example, that where a prisoner's actions in segregation constituted a danger even to his counsel, the prison administrators had a duty to prohibit counsel from seeing his client until the situation changed.[37] In *Procunier* v. *Martinez,*[38] the right of an attorney to interview his or her client has recently been extended to law students and legal paraprofessionals working for an attorney.

Finally, the Supreme Court recently reaffirmed some earlier decisions which had held that prisoners must be afforded some access to legal materials and that prisoners could not be punished for providing legal assistance to other prisoners. In *Bounds* v. *Smith,*[39] the Court ruled that access by prisoners to the courts was a fundamental constitutional right and that state officials had an affirmative obligation to insure that access by providing adequate law libraries or some alternative involving a legal assistance program.

Religious and Racial Discrimination

Under the First Amendment all persons are guaranteed the right to the free exercise of their religious beliefs. Recognizing that this right is "preferred," that is, of particular significance under the Constitution, the courts have held that freedom of religion does not terminate at the prison door.[40]

Although most of the litigation has concerned minority religious groups such as the Black Muslims, restrictions exist even on the more widely practiced religions. In the most recent cases, the courts have required prison administrators to show a compelling and substantial justification for any restrictions on the practice and exercise of religion in the prisons. Where security, safety, or prison discipline may be disrupted by religious exercises, the courts have upheld limitations. In the only case involving religious rights to reach the Supreme Court, *Cruz* v. *Beto*,[41] it was held that a Buddhist prisoner must be afforded "a reasonable opportunity of pursuing his faith comparable to the opportunity afforded fellow prisoners who adhere to conventional religious precepts."

Generally, the courts have upheld the right of prisoners to practice their religion, to wear religious symbols such as skullcaps, to have reasonable access to special diets because of religious belief, and to receive religious reading material.[42]

Following a decision by the Supreme Court invalidating various forms and practices of racial discrimination,[43] the courts have been consistent in condemning racial segregation and discrimination in prisons. They have rejected the arguments of prison officials that integration would lead to racial conflict and the breakdown of order — although in special situations where violence is imminent they have allowed temporary separation of the races — and have allowed blacks equal rights to reading material and religious exercises.

Political Rights

The essential political rights secured by the First Amendment — speech, association, assembly, and belief — have been given precious little breathing space in prisons. The very nature of imprisonment traditionally has been held to require severe limitations on the right to assemble and associate with others. Moreover, speech has been restricted whenever prison officials claim that it endangers prison security or discipline. And beliefs, though not as susceptible to manipulation or destruction by prison authorities, nevertheless have been effectively controlled by various forms of punishment — segregation, harassment, denial of parole, and so forth — which are often imposed on the prisoner who makes known his unpopular political beliefs.[44]

The regulation and restriction of political activities are not matters that are usually covered by written rules. Each particular assertion by a prisoner of his political right has been dealt with on an ad hoc basis, with individual decisions varying greatly not only from prison to prison, but from prisoner to prisoner within a single institution.

The law is unclear. Several courts have held that First Amendment rights follow a person into prison and may be restricted only where their exercise creates a clear and present danger to the orderly administration of the institution. Unfortunately, however, the courts have generally subordinated First Amendment rights to the prison's determination that the speech or political activity threatened prison discipline or security. Despite occasional flourishes of constitutional rhetoric stressing the importance of First Amendment rights for prisoners, the "hands-off" policy still has a secure grip in this area.

In one important case in this area a federal court ruled that prisoners who were attempting to collect and solicit funds for the Attica Brothers Defense Committee could not be prevented in a discriminatory manner from soliciting funds and making direct contributions to the support of those prisoners who were indicted as a result of the 1971 Attica rebellion.[45] More recently, a federal court ruled that prisoners in Rhode Island could not be prevented from using funds in an inmate welfare fund to pay for distributing a political leaflet.[46]

A number of courts have ruled that prisoners could not be punished for expressing radical beliefs, and in this context at least one court has held that political discussions in an administrative segregation unit was protected First Amendment activity, subject only to time (not "after lights out") and manner (no incitement or threats of incitement to disturbance) restrictions.[47]

The issue of whether prisoners have a right to associate with one another and to form political organizations has only recently been raised. In *National Prisoners Reform Association* v. *Sharkey*,[48] prison officials refused to allow members of the NPRA — an interracial group made up of both prisoners and persons from the outside — to enter the prison in order to meet, although the group had met on prior occasions inside the prison and without incident. The court enjoined the prison officials' denial of permission to enter, reasoning that other established prison organizations met together as well as with outside persons and that the only distinction in the NPRA was its interracial character.

However, the idea that prisoners could engage in organized union activities was recently given harsh treatment by a majority of the Supreme Court. In *Jones* v. *North Carolina Prisoners Labor Union*,[49] the Court overruled a favorable decision and held that a state regulation that prohibited prisoners from soliciting others to join a union and barred union meetings and bulk mailings concerning the union from outside sources did not violate the First Amendment. The decision, giving great deference to the asserted interests of the prison officials, stated that the fact of confinement and the needs of the penal institution impose limitations on constitutional rights, including those derived from the First Amendment and particularly associational rights within prison walls.

The Court, in a giant step backward, refused to apply the normal First Amendment balancing-of-interests test to prisoners. They held that the state need only show a rational basis for interfering with the First Amendment rights of prisoners rather than the traditional compelling state interest. Furthermore, recent attempts by prisoners to form unions and to obtain certification as collective bargaining agents have met with little success.[50]

Privacy and Personal Appearance

Most prison officials insist that the right to privacy ceases to exist on entry into the penal institution. Prisoners' mail is censored, and in many prisons their visits with family, friends, and even attorneys are monitored by prison officials. Most courts, however, have not addressed this issue seriously and the important right of personal privacy must continue to be advocated.

Although the courts have moved lethargically in this area, they have ruled that searches of body cavities must be carried out with some minimal protections and without the purpose of humiliating, degrading, or harassing the prisoner.[51] The 1973 National Advisory Commission on Criminal Justice Standards and Goals Report on Corrections provides that any regulations on this subject should include avoiding undue or unnecessary force, embarrassment or indignity to the prisoner, and respect for a prisoner's rights and property. Recently, one court disapproved of a strip search (removal of clothing) which involved a former prisoner seeking to visit a co-defendant in a pre-trial facility to discuss new charges.[52] The court held that at least "real suspicion is necessary before such a search can be required."

The familiar scene of prisoners dressed identically in gray garb, short haircuts, with no mustaches or beards, is changing although at a fairly slow pace. The changes may have more to do with changing styles and tastes in the free society than with anything else. The changes themselves are relatively insignificant given their purpose. For instance, in New York, although prisoners no longer wear gray uniforms, they are now required to wear forest green work clothes.

In some places mustaches are permitted but may only be grown on the upper lip and cannot extend below the corners of the mouth. In general, regulations requiring a uniform appearance exist in almost all prisons. The regulations, although supported by prison officials as necessary health and safety measures, in reality deprive the prisoner of his sense of identity and presence, and enforce regimentation in the prison.

It should be noted that the denial of "afros" has been upheld against an equal protection claim.[53] Also, where "afros" were permitted by regulation, the denial of long hair was upheld against an equal protection argument. However, the First Amendment religious liberty argument has been successful with respect to personal appearance. The Eighth Circuit has established the right of a Native American prisoner to refuse a haircut on the grounds of his religious principles.[54]

Medical Care, Rehabilitation, and Physical Security of Prisoners

Lack of adequate medical, dental, and psychiatric care is the rule in all penal institutions.[55] The primary cause of this situation is the lack of competent medical personnel to treat the tens of thousands of men and women who pass through the correctional system each year. In many prisons, only the most serious ailments are treated and often these are the subject of haphazard and mediocre care; minor ailments are often ignored for lack of a doctor or nurse, or for more callous reasons — a guard may refuse to allow a prisoner to attend sick call.

The Supreme Court has recently held that a state must provide treatment for a prisoner's serious medical needs.[56] While the prisoner is not, according to the courts, the ultimate judge of what medical treatment is necessary or proper, where he can demonstrate obvious neglect, deliberate indifference, or intentional mistreatment, a remedy will be afforded. Similarly, prison officials may not overrule a doctor's medical judgment concerning a prisoner's treatment.

Under these guidelines courts have found that constitutional rights were denied in a variety of situations; these include the failure of prison medical authorities to treat a prisoner for previously diagnosed cancer; the refusal of a warden to permit a prisoner to receive medication prescribed by prison doctors; the interference of prison authorities and doctors in the convalescence of a prisoner operated upon by surgeons; and segregating a prisoner with another known to have tuberculosis.[57]

Prisoners have won several lawsuits in recent years in which federal judges have held that prison care in particular state prison systems is totally inadequate and unconstitutional. Relief was afforded in these cases by the granting of broad injunctive remedies requiring prison officials to submit and effectuate detailed plans for comprehensive health services.[58]

The issue of whether prisoners can be the subject of medical experimentation has recently received attention. In the absence of stringent safeguards, the answer is clearly no. *Kaimowitz* v. *Department of Mental Hygiene*[59] dealt with an involuntarily detained mental patient upon whom the mental health authorities wished to perform psychosurgery. The court ruled that such a patient could not provide the informed consent required to perform such an operation. There have been several other similar cases in the prison context as well.

With respect to the so-called non-therapeutic experimentation on prisoners, the issues involved have just begun to reach the courts. Non-therapeutic experimentation refers to studies conducted to obtain information and not to treat any particular individual. Several governmental and other organizations have recognized the problems with such experimentation in the inherently coercive setting of a prison.[60] Recently, a large number of states and the Federal Bureau of Prisons have banned the use of prisoners for non-therapeutic medical experiments.

One of the central vices of prison life is the enforced idleness that prisoners must endure. Few prisons provide meaningful work, educational or vocational training opportunities. Cases, including those in the Supreme Court involving commitments to mental hospitals, juvenile institutions, and other agencies have suggested that officials have a constitutional obligation to provide adequate treatment and/or rehabilitation programs for the inmates of those institutions.[61] It has been successfully argued, building on these cases, that while a prison may not be required to provide educational and vocational programs, it is forbidden to allow conditions which make rehabilitation difficult to achieve. Thus, the court ruled in *Pugh*[62] that a prison system could not constitutionally debilitate a person or render him less able to successfully re-enter society.

It is clear that a prisoner has a right to be protected against violence or sexual assault.[63] Several recent court decisions have recognized the rape problem in prisons. Claims by prisoners that prison authorities have not provided adequate protection have been upheld and in the context of escape prosecutions, courts have sustained proof of prior sexual assaults as a valid defense.[64]

Parole and Probation

Parole, among other things, serves as an alternative to continued imprisonment. Prisoners are selected for release and, theoretically, are provided with controls, assistance, and guidance to help them serve the remainder of their sentence in the free world. Parole is the predominant method of release for prisoners today, and "the parole system has long been recognized as the single most inequitable, potentially capricious, and uniquely arbitrary corner of the criminal justice map."[65]

The question of whether the due process clause applies to the processing of applications for parole was resolved in *Greenholtz* v. *Inmates of the Nebraska Penal and Correctional Complex*.[66] The answer is that the issue is essentially determined by reference to state law.

The Court's holding in that case was well-stated by the Sixth Circuit Court of Appeals in *Wagner v. Gilligan.*[67] There the Court stated:

> In Greenholtz, the Supreme Court rejected the claim of prison inmates that a protected liberty interest is created automatically whenever a state provides for a possibility of parole. However, under the Nebraska statute, the Nebraska Board of Parole was required to release eligible inmates unless any one of four designated reasons to defer release could be found. The Court held that the expectancy of release provided by the Nebraska statute "is entitled to some measure of constitutional protection." The Court emphasized that "this statute has unique structure and language and thus whether any other state statute provides a protectible entitlement must be decided on a case-by-case basis."[68]

As for the Nebraska inmates in question, the Supreme Court held that, "The Nebraska procedure affords an opportunity to be heard, and when parole is denied it informs the inmate in what respects he falls short of qualifying for parole; this affords the process that is due under these circumstances."[69]

As for Ohio inmates, however, the Court of Appeals ruled that the corresponding Ohio statute, O.R.C. § 2967.03, is purely discretionary and, therefore, does not create a protected statutory entitlement.[70]

The Visible Institution

In considering the development of prisoners' rights in recent court decisions, it is important to be aware that there is a great distinction between decisions of the Supreme Court and those of lower courts. The Supreme Court has dealt primarily with narrow procedural issues, while a number of lower courts have recently begun to look at the substantive and systemic issues in prisons or prison systems, examining the totality of conditions in those systems, and then issuing decisions which attempt to remedy the broad and total constitutional defects in those systems.

In the decision dealing with the entire state prison system in Alabama,[71] Chief United States District Judge Frank M. Johnson, Jr. found constitutional infirmities in the lack of any rational classification system; the warehousing of aged and infirm prisoners; the lack of adequate protection for prisoners and the resulting incidence of violence; the state's interference with any meaningful visitation; the total absence of meaningful vocational, educational or other programs, and the resulting overwhelming idleness; the inherent problems in large, rural, isolated institutions that warehouse prisoners primarily in dormitories; the tremendous overcrowding in the institutions; the serious public health hazards caused by the physical and sanitary conditions of the institutions; the total absence of adequate medical and mental health care for prisoners; and the lack of adequate staff resources in terms of numbers, competence, and racial background.

Judge Johnson found that the totality of those conditions necessarily and inevitably debilitated prisoners in those institutions — physically and psychologically — making them less able to successfully re-enter society, and that this constituted a gross violation of the cruel and unusual punishment clause as well as a violation of the due process clause of the Constitution.

The court then ordered the state of Alabama to comply with various "minimum constitutional standards." Among other things, it required the state to reduce its prison population to the designed capacity of each institution (a reduction of 42%); to provide each prisoner with a minimum sixty square feet of living space; to provide each prisoner with a meaningful job and the opportunity to participate in recreational, educational, and vocational training and pre-release transition programs; to provide each prisoner with certain minimum personal articles, such as linens, toilet articles, hot and cold water, reading and writing materials; to provide necessary medical and mental health care according to certain published standards; to provide minimum staff in various specific locations at all times to prevent violence; and to provide certain minimum food, public health, correspondence, visitation, and other physical standards. In addition, the court set forth a timetable for bringing each of the major institutions into compliance with the standards; a plan for the hiring of appropriately trained and educated staff whose racial and cultural background is more similar to prisoners; and a plan for the reclassification of all Alabama prisoners to identify those for whom transfer to community-based facilities would be appropriate and ordered the state to establish those facilities.

Finally, the Alabama court said that inadequate funding or claimed lack of resources is no answer to the existence of unconstitutional conditions and warned that failure to comply with the minimum standards would necessitate the closing of those "several prison facilities herein found to be unfit for human confinement."

As previously noted, a number of other federal courts and one state court have looked at similar conditions in state prisons, and have provided the kind of sweeping relief designed to remedy systemic unconstitutionality. These decisions will hopefully set the standard for future development of the law in this area.

Even those rights, however, which are now guaranteed by the courts are often illusory for many prisoners. Implementation and enforcement of these rights rest primarily in the hands of prison officials who often continue to fight for the status quo. Litigation is costly and time-consuming and there are few lawyers serving prisoners in this area. Most prison systems are so diseased and bankrupt that their achievements represent only the smallest and earliest steps of a very long journey.

Just as in any other movement for social change, litigation can only be the beginning of, or catalyst for, lasting reform. The issues involved in the prisoners' rights movement are essentially political and ultimately must be addressed by the legislative branch of government. There is a glimmer of hope in many state legislatures and in the Congress. Faced with enormously increasing costs of constructing new prisons and the growing realization that most of our prisons do nothing for most prisoners except debilitate them — and thereby frustrate the interests of society — legislative bodies are taking a hard look at reforming sentencing practices and the utilization of a range of sanctions as alternatives to imprisonment. For the many men and women who will still be confined in prisons, there is an important contemporary movement to develop minimum standards for the treatment of prisoners.[72]

Notes

1. Little, Brown (1971).
2. *Ruffin* v. *Commonwealth,* 62 Va. (21 Gratt) 790 (1871).
3. Oxford University Press (1970).
4. *Manual of Correctional Standards,* 3rd ed. (1966), p. 366.
5. Sykes, Gresham M., *Crime and Society,* Random House (1967); Clemmer, Donald, *The Prison Community,* Holt, Rinehart and Winston (1940); and Cressey, Donald R., *Crime and Criminal Justice,* Quadrangle Press (1971).
6. 365 U. S. 167, 5 L.Ed. 2d 492, 81 S.Ct. 473 (1961).
7. Municipalities and other local government units are now included among those "persons" to whom the Civil Rights Act, 42 U.S.C. §1983, applies. In *Monell* v. *Dept. of Soc. Ser. of the City of New York,* 436 U.S. 658, 56 L.Ed. 2d 611, 98 S.Ct. 2018 (1978), the Supreme Court overruled that part of *Monroe* which immunized governmental units and held that the Tenth Amendment was not a bar to suing governmental units directly when a constitutional deprivation arises from a governmental practice or custom.
8. 418 U.S. 539, 41 L.Ed. 2d 935, 94 S.Ct. 2963 (1974).
9. *Baxter* v. *Palmigiano,* 425 U.S. 308, 47 L.Ed. 2d 810, 96 S.Ct. 1551 (1976).
10. *Enomoto* v. *Clutchette,* 425 U.S. 308, 47 L.Ed. 2d 810, 96 S.Ct. 1551 (1976).
11. However, in a recent unexplained decision, the Supreme Court affirmed a lower court decision requiring *Wolff* due process safeguards for an intra-prison transfer to administrative segregation. *Enomoto* v. *Wright,* (U.S. District Court, N.D. Cal. 9/30/76) (unreported decision), summary at 46 U.S.L.W. 3325 (11/15/77), *aff'd per curiam,* 429 U.S. 912 (1978).
12. *Meachum* v. *Fano,* 427 U.S. 215, 49 L.Ed. 2d 451, 96 S.Ct. 2532 (1976).
13. *Montanye* v. *Haymes,* 427 U.S. 236, 49 L.Ed. 2d 466, 96 S.Ct. 2543 (1976).
14. In a very significant opinion, the Court of Appeals on remand held that a prisoner who was punitively transferred either for petitioning for redress of grievances or for providing legal assistance to other prisoners, both constitutionally protected

activities, does have standing to challenge his transfer. *Haymes* v. *Montanye,* 547 F.2d 188 (2nd Cir. 1976).

15. *Weems* v. *United States,* 217 U.S. 349, 54 L.Ed. 793, 30 S.Ct. 544 (1910).
16. *Trop* v. *Dulles,* 356 U.S. 86, 2 L.Ed. 2d 630, 78 S.Ct. 590 (1958).
17. 144 U.S. 263, 36 L.Ed. 429, 12 S.Ct. 617 (1892).
18. *Pugh* v. *Locke,* 406 F.Supp. 318 (M.D.Ala. 1976), *aff'd in substance, sub nom, Newman* v. *Alabama,* 559 F.2d 283 (5th Cir. 1977), *cert. den. in relevant part, sub nom, Alabama* v. *Pugh,* 438 U.S. 781, 57 L.Ed. 2d 1114, 98 S.Ct. 3057 (1978).
19. *Palmigiano* v. *Garrahy,* 443 F.Supp. 956 (D.R.I. 1977); *Trigg* v. *Blanton,* No. A-6047, Memorandum Opinion (Chancery Court, Davidson County, Tennessee 8/23/78).
20. *Hutto* v. *Finney,* 437 U.S. 678, 57 L.Ed. 2d 522, 98 S.Ct. 2565 (1978).
21. *Agron* v. *Montanye,* 392 F.Supp. 454 (W.D.N.Y. 1975).
22. *Nelson* v. *Heyne,* 491 F.2d. 352 (7th Cir. 1974).
23. 418 U.S. 539, 41 L.Ed. 2d 935, 94 S.Ct. 2963 (1974).
24. *Id.* at 577.
25. 442 F.2d 178 (2nd Cir. 1971).
26. *Laurence* v. *Davis,* 401 F.Supp. 1203 (W.D.Va. 1975).
27. 416 U.S. 396, 40 L.Ed. 2d 224, 94 S.Ct. 1800 (1974).
28. 417 U.S. 817, 41 L.Ed. 2d 495, 94 S.Ct. 2800 (1974).
29. 417 U.S. 843, 41 L.Ed. 2d 514, 94 S.Ct. 2811 (1974).
30. The Supreme Court recently reaffirmed the limitations on press access to prisons in *Houchins* v. *KQED, Inc.,* 438 U.S. 1, 57 S.Ct. 553, 98 S.Ct. 2588 (1978).
31. *Fortune Society* v. *McGinnis,* 319 F.Supp. 901 (S.D.N.Y. 1970).
32. *Shakur* v. *McGrath,* 69 Civ. 4493 (S.D.N.Y. 12/31/69).
33. *Johnson* v. *Anderson,* 370 F.Supp. 1373 (D.Del. 1974).
34. *Dillard* v. *Pitchess,* 399 F.Supp. 1225 (C.D. Cal. 1975).
35. *The Luparar* v. *Stoneman,* 382 F.Supp. 495 (D.Vt. 1974).
36. *Souza* v. *Travisono,* 368 F.Supp. 959 (D.R.I. 1973), *aff'd in part,* 498 F.2d 1120 (1st Cir. 1974).
37. *Mims* v. *Shapp,* 399 F.Supp. 818 (W.D.Pa. 1975).
38. 416 U.S. 396, 40 L.Ed. 2d 224, 94 S.Ct. 1800 (1974).
39. 430 U.S. 817, 52 L.Ed. 72, 97 S.Ct. 1491 (1977).
40. See for example, *Barnett* v. *Rodgers,* 410 F.2d 995 (D.C.Cir. 1969); *Brown* v. *Peyton,* 437 F.2d 1228 (4th Cir. 1971).
41. 405 U.S. 319, 31 L.Ed. 2d 263, 92 S.Ct. 1079 (1972).
42. *Kahane* v. *Carlson,* 527 F.2d 492 (2nd Cir. 1975); *Barnett* v. *Rodgers, supra,* n.40.
43. *Washington* v. *Lee,* 390 U.S. 333, 19 L.Ed. 2d 1212, 88 S.Ct. 988 (1968).
44. See for example, *Sostre* v. *McGinnis, supra,* n.25.
45. *Butler* v. *Preiser,* 380 F.Supp. 612 (S.D.N.Y. 1974).
46. *O'Connell* v. *Southworth,* 422 F.Supp. 182 (D.R.I. 1976).
47. *Sostre* v. *McGinnis, supra,* n.25.
48. 347 F.Supp. 1234 (D.R.I. 1972).
49. 433 U.S. 119, 53 L.Ed. 2d 629, 97 S.Ct. 2532 (1977).
50. See for example, *Matter of Prisoners Labor Union* v. *Helsby,* 354 NYS 2d 694 (1974).
51. *Wolfish* v. *Levi,* 573 F.2d 118 (1978); *Sostre* v. *Preiser,* 519 F.2d 763 (2nd Cir. 1975).
52. *Black* v. *Amico,* 387 F.Supp. 88 (W.D.N.Y. 1974).
53. *Martinez* v. *Mancusi,* 433 F.2d 921 (2nd Cir. 1970).
54. *Teterud* v. *Burns,* 522 F.2d 357 (8th Cir. 1975).

55. See for example, *The Washington Post,* January 10, 1979, Editorial, "The Ordeal of Harry Tucker." The editorial, commenting on the $518,000 damage award to a Virginia State prisoner for injuries suffered as a result of inadequate medical care, noted the lack of medical care prevalent in jails and prisons throughout the country.
56. *Estelle* v. *Gamble,* 429 U.S. 97, 50 L.Ed. 2d 251, 97 S.Ct. 285 (1976).
57. *Runnels* v. *Rosendale,* 499 F.2d 733 (9th Cir. 1974); *Martinez* v. *Mancusi,* 443 F.2d 921 (2nd Cir. 1970); *Freeman* v. *Lockhart,* 503 F.2d 1016 (8th Cir. 1974).
58. Eg., *Newman* v. *Alabama,* 503 F.2d 1320 (5th Cir. 1974).
59. 2 *Pris. L. Rptr.* 433 (Cir.Ct. Wayne County, Michigan 1973).
60. The Federal Bureau of Prisons recently announced a ban on the use of prisoners for medical experiments in federal prisons and the Secretary of HEW recently promulgated regulations which essentially prohibit state institutions which receive federal funds from conducting experiments on prisoners. 43 Fed. Reg. 53652, 11/16/78.
61. See for example, *Morales* v. *Turman,* 383 F.Supp. 53 (E.D.Tex. 1974); *Wyatt* v. *Aderholt,* 503 F.2d 1305 (5th Cir. 1974).
62. 406 F.Supp. 318 (M.D.Ala. 1976).
63. Eg., *Woodhous* v. *Commonwealth of Virginia,* 487 F.2d 889 (4th Cir. 1973).
64. *People* v. *Harmon,* 232 N.W. 2d 187 (1975).
65. H.R. Rp. No. 94-184, 94th Cong., 1st Sess. at 3 (1975).
66. 442 U.S. 1, 60 L.Ed. 2d 668, 99 S.Ct. 2100 (1979).
67. 609 F.2d 866 (1979).
68. 609 F.2d at 867.
69. 442 U.S. at 16.
70. 609 F.2d at 867.
71. *Pugh* v. *Locke, supra.*
72. See for example, American Bar Association, *Tentative Draft of Standards Relating to the Legal Status of Prisoners,* 14 Amer. Crim. L. Rev. 1 (1977); American Correctional Association, *Manual of Standards for Adult Correctional Institutions* (1977); American Public Health Association, *Standards for Health Services in Correctional Institutions* (1976).

Index